# THE FOLKLORE OF SPAIN
# IN THE AMERICAN SOUTHWEST

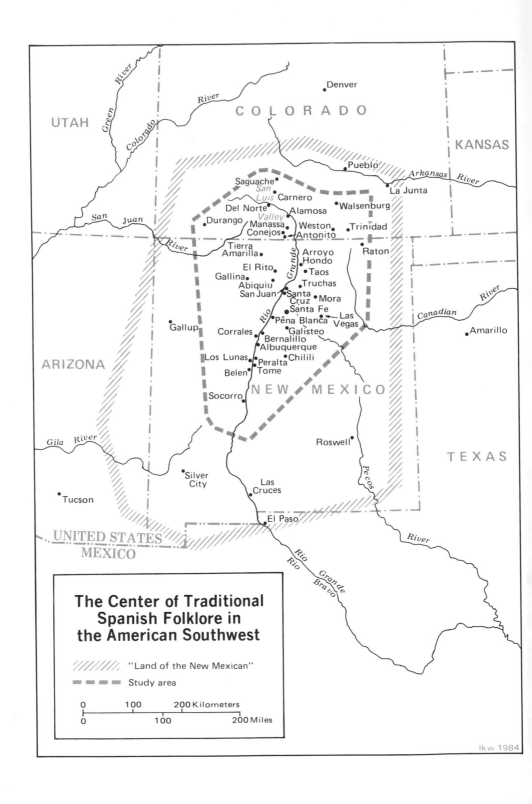

**The Center of Traditional Spanish Folklore in the American Southwest**

///// "Land of the New Mexican"

— — — Study area

| 0 | 100 | 200 Kilometers |
| 0 | 100 | 200 Miles |

Ikw 1984

# THE FOLKLORE OF SPAIN
# IN THE AMERICAN SOUTHWEST

## TRADITIONAL SPANISH FOLK LITERATURE
## IN NORTHERN NEW MEXICO
## AND SOUTHERN COLORADO

## BY AURELIO M. ESPINOSA
## EDITED BY J. MANUEL ESPINOSA

UNIVERSITY OF OKLAHOMA PRESS  :  NORMAN AND LONDON

BY AURELIO M. ESPINOSA
*Estudios sobre el español de Nuevo Méjico,* 2 vols. (Buenos Aires, 1930, 1946)
*Cuentos populares españoles,* 3 vols. (Madrid, 1946-1947)
*Romancero de Nuevo Méjico* (Madrid, 1953)

BY J. MANUEL ESPINOSA
*Spanish Folk Tales from New Mexico* (New York, 1937, 1977)
*First Expedition of Vargas into New Mexico, 1692* (trans.) (Albuquerque, 1940)
*Crusaders of the Rio Grande* (Chicago, 1942)

Library of Congress Cataloging-in-Publication Data
Espinosa, Aurelio M. (Aurelio Macedonio), 1880–1958.
  The folklore of Spain in the American Southwest.

  Bibliography: p.
  Includes index.
  1. Spanish Americans—Colorado—Folklore.   2. Spanish
Americans—New Mexico—Folklore.   3. Folk literature,
Spanish—Colorado—History and criticism.   4. Folk
literature, Spanish—New Mexico—History and criticism.
5. Espinosa, Aurelio M. (Aurelio Macedonio), 1880–
1958.   I. Espinosa, J. Manuel (José Manuel), 1909–
II. Title.
GR111.S65E87   1985      398'.09788      85-40473
ISBN 0-8061-1942-X (alk. paper)

95238

*To my parents*

*Aurelio M. Espinosa*

*and*

*Margarita García Espinosa*

—J. Manuel Espinosa

*Nuevo Méjico insolente,*
*entre los síbolos criado.*
*dime quién* ti *{ha} hecho letrado,*
*pa cantar entre la gente.*


*(Insolent New Mexico,*
*born among the buffaloes,*
*tell me who gave you the gift of letters*
*to enable you to sing among the people.)*
       —From the oral tradition of northern New Mexico

# Contents

# Illustrations

ix

# Preface

This book deals with the centuries-old traditional Spanish folk literature of the Spanish-speaking people of northern New Mexico and southern Colorado. It is also the story of the author, Aurelio M. Espinosa, New Mexico's pioneer folklorist, who during the first four decades of this century collected, studied, and documented in numerous scholarly publications here and abroad the folk literature of the region in all of its major aspects. The examples of folk literature presented and discussed in the following pages were collected by him directly from Spanish-speaking residents at all levels of society, mostly from the common people living in the quiet towns, villages, farms, and ranches that dotted the upper Rio Grande Valley between Socorro, New Mexico, and southern Colorado.

The traditional Spanish folk literature of this region, like that of other areas that have experienced cross-cultural influences over the centuries, has passed through subtle stages of evolution. Each successive generation has added new elements, sometimes mixing the old and the new and sometimes introducing new outside influences, but generally evolving under the influence of the local and regional environment. In no part of the American Southwest did Spanish culture take deeper root than in northern New Mexico and southern Colorado. New Mexico, first settled in 1598 by Spaniards from New Spain (Mexico), was for more than two centuries an isolated frontier outpost of the Spanish empire in America. It is the oldest Spanish-speaking community in the southwestern United States.

Aurelio M. Espinosa (1880–1958) was born in the region and lived there during the first thirty years of his life. He was the first folklore and linguistic scholar to study in depth and on a comparative basis the local Spanish dialect and the immensely rich body of Spanish folk literature that was popular among the Spanish-speaking people of northern New Mexico and southern Colorado. From 1902 to 1932 he engaged in fieldwork and research on the subject, working almost alone in this field. His scholarly publications laid the groundwork for scientific study of the Spanish folk literature of the region by those who followed in his footsteps.

It is fortunate that Espinosa studied and recorded in his publications the Spanish folk literature and language of the region in the early decades of this century, for in those years the continuity of the local Spanish folk scene was relatively undisturbed, and the oral tradition of the Spanish-speaking people, most of whose ancestors had lived in the region since the seventeenth and eighteenth centuries, was still a rich and largely untapped storehouse of Spanish folklore. Aurelio Espinosa saved from oblivion many examples of traditional folk literature that had been preserved among the Spanish-speakers of the Southwest, uncovering a unique regional expression of the folk literature of Spain in America. He demonstrated through his comparative studies that the Spanish folk literature of that region is linked to the common literary tradition of all Hispanic countries, as a part of the folk literature of the Western world, and that Spanish folklore was transmitted by Spain to her overseas possessions in the sixteenth, seventeenth, and eighteenth centuries.

In this book the major results of Aurelio M. Espinosa's research and writings on the Spanish folk literature of the region are brought together. Part One, written by me as my father's editor, presents a sketch of his life and work followed by a discussion of his fieldwork technique and research methodology. Part Two, written by Aurelio M. Espinosa, presents the highlights of all the major types of traditional Spanish folk literature found in the region, illustrated with extensive examples in Spanish and English translation. That part, the main body of the book, is based on an unpublished manuscript that he left among a portion of his papers preserved in my files. The manuscript was completed in the late 1930s. Its publication was postponed because of the author's more immediate interest in completing three other works in the same general field, which engaged most of his time for research and writing in the 1930s and 1940s. Those works were a revision of his earlier study of the Spanish dialect spoken in New Mexico (published in two volumes in 1930 and 1946), a comparative study of Spanish folktales (three volumes, 1946–47), and a collection of traditional Spanish ballads from northern New Mexico and southern Colorado (1953).

The only major change in the manuscript in Part Two is the omission of several chapters on related historical, linguistic, and religious trends. Two of those chapters, dealing with closely related fields in which Espinosa did pioneering research, have been edited slightly and included as appendices: "The Spanish Language of Northern New Mexico and Southern Colorado" (Appendix A), and "Spanish Tradition Among the Pueblo Indians" (Appendix B). The reader who is interested in an explanation of the words in

Spanish dialect that appear in the examples of folk literature presented in this study will find a comprehensive analysis in Appendix A.

I have included at the end of the volume a complete bibliography of Aurelio M. Espinosa's writings on Spanish and Spanish-American folklore and dialectology and a selective bibliography of other works relating to Hispanic and Hispanic American folk literature. In both the notes and the selective bibliography the references with publication dates before 1940 are Aurelio M. Espinosa's original ones; those with a later publication date have been added by the editor to bring up to the present this list of the most important works in the field. The two bibliographies should provide a fairly comprehensive introduction to the literature for readers who are interested in pursuing the subject in depth.

The most valuable library and archival collections that I consulted in preparing this study were Aurelio M. Espinosa's folklore library, which is in the private library of Aurelio M. Espinosa, Jr., at Stanford University; my own collection of Aurelio M. Espinosa's papers and publications; the History Library of the Museum of New Mexico, Santa Fe; the Library of the University of New Mexico; and the Library of Congress, Washington, D.C. In checking and updating the notes and bibliographical citations, I found the Library of Congress an invaluable aid; the opportunity to consult its unequaled holdings in Hispanic studies eased my task considerably.

In exploring the history and folklore of New Mexico, I made many visits to the region between 1931 and 1981. I also familiarized myself with most of the localities and byways of northern New Mexico and southern Colorado, "The Land of the New Mexican," where Aurelio M. Espinosa engaged in his folklore fieldwork. In the early 1930s I accompanied my father on several folklore expeditions throughout the area and also collected, under his direction, Spanish folklore material from the oral tradition of the region.

In editing this work, I am deeply indebted to my brother, Aurelio M. Espinosa, Jr., Professor Emeritus in the Spanish and Portuguese Department, Stanford Univeristy, Stanford, California, for his valuable comments and suggestions. To my wife, Betty, I am also especially grateful for her help and assistance.

*Glen Echo, Maryland*                                    J. MANUEL ESPINOSA

PART ONE

# Aurelio M. Espinosa: New Mexico's Pioneer Folklorist

by

J. Manuel Espinosa

# Espinosa's New Mexican Background
# and Professional Career

Aurelio Macedonio Espinosa was born on September 12, 1880, in El Carnero, Colorado, a small country town in the San Luis Valley of southern
Colorado about fifteen miles northeast of the town of Del Norte and approximately forty-five miles north of the present New Mexico–Colorado border.
His parents, Celso Espinosa and Rafaela Antonia Martínez, had homesteaded near El Carnero in 1878. There his father made his livelihood in
farming and in sheep and cattle raising, the occupation of most of the other
small landholders of the region. Nearby was the larger ranch owned by
Celso's father, José Julián Espinosa, who had moved to the locality from
northern New Mexico in 1870.

The Espinosa and Martínez families were descendants of Spanish ancestors who had come from Spain to the Viceroyalty of New Spain (Mexico),
had migrated from there to New Mexico in the sixteenth, seventeenth, and
eighteenth centuries, and thus were among the first settlers of northern
New Mexico. Later, in the middle of the nineteenth century, members of
the two families were among the first New Mexican settlers in southern
Colorado.

The Spanish settlements in what is now the northern half of the state of
New Mexico were established as defensive frontier outposts supporting
Spain's claim to a vast surrounding area. They were supposed to prevent
encroachments on the northern frontier of New Spain by rival colonial
powers and to bring Christianity to the large body of unconverted Indians
in the region. The Province of New Mexico, as it was named, was separated
from the centers of settlement in the Viceroyalty of New Spain to the south
by a barren stretch of approximately one thousand miles of hostile plains
and wilderness. Unlike the gradual merging of peoples and cultures on
other American frontiers, the establishment of the New Mexico colony was
an advance in a single leap into the distant north.

The first settlements dated from 1598, when Governor Juan de Oñate
led a colonizing expedition of 129 soldiers, their families, and a group of
Franciscan missionaries (a total of four hundred people or more) to San Juan

de los Caballeros, about twenty-five miles north of the present-day New Mexican capital of Santa Fe. San Juan became the first capital of the province that Oñate established. The colony's permanency was assured when it was organized as a royal province in 1609. A new capital was established at Santa Fe in 1610, with a government organized after the imperial Spanish colonial pattern. By 1680 the Spanish population totaled approximately twenty-eight hundred, about 90 percent of whom had been born in New Mexico. The Pueblo Indians of the region totaled about seventeen thousand. In the bloody Pueblo Indian Revolt of 1680 the entire Spanish colony was driven out, and some four hundred dead were left behind, including twenty-one of the thirty-three Franciscan missionaries. Most of the survivors settled in and around El Paso del Rio del Norte.

In 1692, Diego de Vargas, the appointed governor of the Province of New Mexico, led a preliminary expedition, with one hundred Spanish soldiers and one hundred Indian allies, to the rebellious region to determine the state of affairs there. He met no serious resistance, and in the following year he marched north from El Paso with about one thousand former residents plus recruits and Indian allies from the Viceroyalty of New Spain between El Paso and Zacatecas. On the second expedition he met bitter resistance, but after several bloody battles he reconquered and resettled New Mexico, and Santa Fe was restored as the capital of the province. Eighteen Franciscan missionaries accompanied the expedition, and before long the Pueblo Indian missions were restored and the work of Christianizing the Indians was resumed. The Pueblo Indian medicine men, who thought they had driven out Christianity and had restored their ancient religious authority, made their last stand by inciting a bloody revolt in 1696, when five missionaries and twenty-one Spanish settlers and soldiers were killed. With the quelling of that revolt, the region was permanently pacified. The villages and towns of the pre-1680 period were reestablished, and new ones were founded. The Spanish population of northern New Mexico was only about fifteen hundred in 1700, but by 1760 it had reached approximately seven thousand. In 1760 the largest cities in the north were Albuquerque, with a population of about eighteen hundred; Santa Cruz de la Cañada, with a population of approximately fifteen hundred; and Santa Fe, the capital, with about thirteen hundred.

The last half of the eighteenth century was a period of great colonizing activity in New Spain and in the frontier provinces on the north, modern-day California, Arizona, and Texas. Yet the migrations to New Mexico were scarce, and the increase in population was mainly a result of local natural growth. By the end of the eighteenth century the Spanish population of northern New Mexico, between Socorro and Taos, had reached about twenty thousand. The largest towns were Santa Cruz and Albuquerque, whose Spanish populations were approximately five thousand, and Santa Fe, with approximately three thousand residents. By that time the Spanish-speaking New Mexicans had outnumbered the Pueblo Indian population.

The Spanish civilization in New Mexico during the eighteenth century was not very different from that in the seventeenth. Northern New Mexico remained isolated from the rest of New Spain. The periodic trade caravans to and from the centers of New Spain provided the principal channels of communication with the outside world. The people lived the simple village and country life of the age. As in the previous century, their chief occupations were agriculture; raising stock, especially sheep, mules, and horses; and trading. There were the ordinary crafts in shops, where harnesses, saddles, shoes, bridles, kitchen utensils, primitive farm implements, wagons or carretas, and simple household articles were made for local consumption. There was weaving, and wearing apparel was tailored for local use. There were developments in religious painting and wooden statuary, jewelry making, fancy needlework and embroidery, and to some extent architecture. In these somewhat primitive arts and crafts the influence of Spain and New Spain generally prevailed, but new and independent patterns influenced by Indian designs often appeared. The material and artistic progress of Spain in the eighteenth century hardly reached New Mexico at all.

Aside from the usual labors in village, farm, and ranch, there were religious festivals, masses, marriages, baptisms, and military parades and exercises by the brave little band of soldiers that constituted the standing army of defense against hostile Indians. The people often assembled publicly and privately in dances, prayers, penitential processions, *velorios* for the dead, and burials. During marriage and baptismal festivities and also during the *prendorios*, or betrothal celebrations, there was feasting and drinking, singing of popular songs and ballads, and courting.

There were also more arduous and dangerous activities. The fifty soldiers garrisoned at Santa Fe and those assigned to outlying districts were often inadequate to protect the Spanish residents and their households against the attacks and depredations of Comanches, Apaches, Navajos, Utes, and other Indians. Bloody surprise attacks kept the villagers constantly in fear and on the alert. Frequently the colonists left their labors in the fields and joined the soldiers to defend the frontiers of settlement. The Pueblo Indians, whose Catholic missions were administered by the Franciscan friars, were sometimes friendly and helpful, but at other times they were indifferent or even hostile. The basic virtues of hard work, courage, and faith were developed among the Spanish residents. The struggle for existence was by no means easy.

Early in the nineteenth century the existence of the permanent Spanish settlements in New Mexico and the economic attraction of the Santa Fe trade hastened the westward surge of the Anglo-American frontier, which culminated in the occupation of New Mexico by the United States. When New Mexico passed into the hands of the United States after the war with Mexico between 1846 and 1848, the population had reached approximately 60,000 and still consisted largely of Spanish-speaking descendants of local families. Then railroads were built in northern New Mexico and southern Colorado beginning in the 1870s and 1880s, and it is estimated that 80 percent of the trackmen and crews of the railroad lines, totaling as many as 35,000, were recent arrivals from Mexico. Agriculture and mining attracted other immigrants from Mexico who were seeking to improve their economic status. Many settled west and north of the older Spanish-speaking villages and settlements of southern Colorado. By 1885 the Spanish-speaking population of New Mexico and southern Colorado had reached 100,000, and there was in addition an English-speaking population of 40,000. After the 1880s the influx of population from the United States increased rapidly. By 1915 the Spanish-speaking population of New Mexico numbered approximately 175,000, about 50 percent of the total population. There were in addition 50,000 Spanish speakers in southern Colorado. Approximately 80 percent of the rural population of northern New Mexico, between Socorro and the New Mexico–Colorado border, including the nineteenth-century Spanish-speaking settlements in southern Colorado, still consisted of families of early New Mexican Spanish origin.

On the basis of family records and tradition, Aurelio Espinosa traced his lineage to Captain Marcelo Espinosa, who accompanied the conqueror and founder of New Mexico, Governor Juan de Oñate, in 1598. Captain Marcelo Espinosa was the son of Antonio de Espinosa, a resident of Madrid, Spain. Captain Espinosa, it is claimed, returned to the part of New Spain south of El Paso after the conquest of New Mexico and settled in the vicinity of Cerro Gordo, which lay about midway between El Paso and Zacatecas in the area from which Governor Vargas recruited settlers for his colonizing expedition to New Mexico in 1693. In the early eighteenth century, soon after the reconquest of New Mexico by Governor Vargas, one of the descendants of Captain Espinosa, Pedro Espinosa of Cerro Gordo, died while en route to New Mexico with a band of colonists, among whom was his fourteen-year-old son, Juan Antonio Espinosa, who had also been born in

Cerro Gordo. The lad arrived in northern New Mexico shortly thereafter, accompanied by several uncles. There, some years later, he married Teodora Quintana, and they had a son, also named Juan Antonio.[1]

Juan Antonio Espinosa's fourth son, by his second wife María Gertrudis Archuleta, was Antonio Espinosa, the father of José Julián Espinosa, Aurelio M. Espinosa's grandfather. Juan Antonio Espinosa had settled in what is now Rio Arriba County, in the vicinity of Santa Cruz de la Cañada, which lies in a fertile river valley about twenty-five miles north of Santa Fe. The *villa* (town) had been settled by a colony of Spanish families recruited in the area of Mexico City. It had formally been founded by Governor Vargas as La Villa Nueva de Santa Cruz de los Españoles Mejicanos in 1695. In contemporary documents the *villa* was often called La Villa Nueva de Santa Cruz de los Españoles; in common parlance it was known as La Villa Nueva. Later it was called simply Santa Cruz or La Cañada. The church records of Abiquiú, a village approximately twenty-five miles northwest of Santa Cruz, include an entry dated 1797 referring to a Juan Antonio Espinosa, apparently Aurelio M. Espinosa's great-great-grandfather.[2]

José Julián Espinosa, Aurelio M. Espinosa's grandfather, was born in El Rito, New Mexico, which was approximately fifteen miles north of Abiquiú and thirty miles west of Taos, on January 4, 1829. Like his father Antonio, José Julián was engaged at an early age in mercantile business and was the proprietor of a store and trading post at El Rito. He was active in community affairs and for a time served as subagent of the U.S. government for the Navajo Indians. In 1850 he married Rufina Montoya, daughter of Marcos Montoya, who was killed by Indians, and María Ignacia Martín. Rufina Montoya's brother, Captain Donaciano Montoya, was a noted Indian fighter who served in the Civil War and later was among those in charge of moving the Navajos to Bosque Redondo. Rufina Montoya's family was of Spanish lineage, having come to New Mexico from New Spain in the middle of the eighteenth century. Her mother, María Ignacia Martín, was related to Pedro Martín y Serrano, a lieutenant in the militia company of the district of Chama, who received a royal grant, known as the Piedra Lumbre grant, in the Chama Valley on February 12, 1766.[3]

On July 4, 1861, José Julián Espinosa enlisted in the Union Army at Fort Union, New Mexico, east of Santa Fe. On August 2 he was commissioned by Abraham Rencher, governor and commander in chief of the Territory of New Mexico, as captain of cavalry, Company D, First New Mexican Volunteers. He raised and outfitted the company at El Rito. At that time most of the Spanish-speaking New Mexican people were pro-Union because of their traditional enmity toward the Texans. Texans on

José Julián Espinosa (1829–1912), about 1870. *Files of J. Manuel Espinosa.*

various occasions had attempted to annex New Mexico to Texas under the guise of engaging in trading expeditions. Since the Confederacy invaded New Mexico from Texas with Texan volunteers, old hatreds prevailed.

Among other early duties in the Union Army, Espinosa escorted government wagon trains from Fort Union to Albuquerque. His company first served as mounted infantry and then as infantry. He participated in the battles of Valverde, near Fort Craig and Apache Cañon and Glorieta Pass, near Fort Union, the only important clashes between North and South in New Mexico during the Civil War. All were of strategic importance, since they eliminated the Confederate threat in New Mexico. Espinosa and his company marched south to assist the garrison at Fort Craig south of Socorro, New Mexico, late in January, 1862, arriving there on February 1. The Battle of Valverde took place on February 21, 1862, when the Confederate

Rufina Montoya Espinosa (1838–1900), about 1870. *Courtesy of Mrs. Avelina Vigil, Antonito, Colorado.*

troops attacked Fort Craig after marching north up to the Rio Grande, with the capture of Fort Union, the bulwark of the Union in the region, as their goal. Espinosa's company was a part of the Union Regiment commanded by Colonel Kit Carson, famous in the annals of the early American West as frontiersman, Indian agent, and soldier. The battle was won by the Confederate army, but Fort Craig itself refused to surrender. The Confederates then marched northward to attack Fort Union. Advancing to Albuquerque and Santa Fe, they engaged the Union forces at Apache Cañon and Glorieta Pass, west of the ruins of Pecos Pueblo. The Union forces won the day after being reinforced by a contingent of Colorado Volunteers from the Colorado mining area, including the so-called Pikes Peakers, against whom the "rough and fight-loving crowd" from Texas was no equal. Defeated, and with their supply depot ambushed and lost, the Confederates—"the Texans," in the

New Mexican view—withdrew to San Antonio. Thus the New Mexican chapter of the Civil War came to an end. After his discharge from the Union Army on May 31, 1862, José Julián Espinosa returned to El Rito, where he disposed of all his interests. He then moved to Taos, where he purchased a large tract of land with his brother Juan Antonio Espinosa and a Manuel Gómez. There they engaged in the cattle business and shortly afterwards erected a flour mill and a distillery.[4]

Aurelio M. Espinosa's maternal ancestors had also been part of the life and history of northern New Mexico from early Spanish colonial days. The first baptism in the records of San Felipe Church in old Albuquerque, dated 1706, was of Francisca García, whose godparents were Captain Juan González and his wife, María Manuela López. Captain Juan González was alcalde of Albuquerque in the early eighteenth century. Their daughter Petrona González married José Ignacio Martínez Serrano. José Manuel Martínez, one of their children, married Manuela Quintana. They were the parents of Julián Martínez, who married Catarina Ortiz. One of their children was another José Manuel Martínez, who married María Nicolasa Valdés. That couple were the parents of Rafaela Martínez, Aurelio M. Espinosa's mother. Thus, through his mother, Espinosa was a direct descendant of the original settlers of Albuquerque. Rafaela Martínez's paternal grandmother had come to New Mexico directly from Spain via New Spain in the latter part of the eighteenth century. In the beginning of the nineteenth century there were many members of this branch of the Martínez family in the Taos area and in the villages, farms, and ranches west and northwest to the Chama River valley.[5]

Espinosa's maternal great-grandfather José Manuel Martínez was the owner of farming and grazing lands near Abiquiú and one of Abiquiú's leading citizens. He was also the grantee of the well-known Tierra Amarilla land grant, which was made to Martínez and his eight sons and associates by the territorial deputation of New Mexico in Abiquiú on July 20, 1832, during the period of Mexican rule and confirmed by an act of the U.S. Congress on June 21, 1860. The grant was situated in Rio Arriba County on the banks of the Chama River. It was bounded on the east by a mountain range, on the west by the Laguna de los Caballos, on the north by the Navajo River, and on the south by the Nutrias River. Martínez did not live to occupy land on the grant, but between 1861 and 1865 there were 132 heads of families, or about six hundred people, living in villages in the area, where they built homes, tilled their fields, and tended sheep and cattle. In 1862, Francisco Martínez, one of José Manuel Martínez's sons, granted an allotment of land in the Tierra Amarilla grant to José Julián Espinosa, but the latter did not occupy the property. The settlers there were constantly harassed by Indian raids until the U.S. military camps gave them protection in the late 1860s.[6]

In 1870, José Julián Espinosa moved with his wife and family to El Carnero, Colorado, a picturesque site near Carnero Creek, a tributary of the Saguache River, below the foothills of the Saguache Mountains. There he engaged in farming and in the sheep and cattle business and held a number of county offices, such as road supervisor, deputy assessor, and justice of the peace. He was an intimate friend of Ouray, chief of the Utes, and Ouray's wife Chepita, who frequently stopped at the Espinosa home. He was also a close friend of Father J. B. Pitaval, the parish priest, and of other Catholic clergy in the area. Julián Espinosa enjoyed reading history and recounting stories to his children about their ancestors. Among the books in his library was a copy of William Hickling Prescott's *History of the Conquest of Mexico*. He died in Del Norte, Colorado, on July 12, 1912, at the home of his daughter, Luisa Espinosa, with whom he had spent his last years. He was buried at El Carnero, from the old church for which he had donated land and which he had helped build.[7] The church records of El Carnero for October 2, 1882, state that a burial plot for the Espinosa family was being provided to "Señor J. Julián Espinosa, the only person who will not pay anything for such a burial plot, since the said Señor J. J. Espinosa has donated ten acres of land and a house as property of the church.[8] Although El Carnero has disappeared from the map, the old cemetery is still there— an isolated acre of weather-beaten and broken crosses and gravestones surrounded by miles of open fields. Julián Espinosa's wife, Rufina Montoya, is also buried there.

When the Espinosas settled in El Carnero, there were already a score of small towns and villages in the San Luis Valley, extending about one hundred miles to the north, west, and east of the New Mexico–Colorado border and south into northern New Mexico. The oldest settlements had been founded between 1851 and 1860 by New Mexican families from Taos and Questa, along with others from the Abiquiú and El Rito area. The first settlements were San Luis (1851), San Pedro (1852), San Acacio (1853), and Conejos (1854). The first settlers were harassed by the Utes and Apaches, who considered the San Luis Valley their own domain, and some returned to their former homes in New Mexico, but new settlers continued to move into the area.

Some other Espinosa relatives had already established themselves in the region in those early years. Juan de la Cruz Espinosa is listed among the fifty New Mexican families who founded Conejos in 1854. The fifty families

came from Llanito, Nuestra Señora de Guadalupe de la Cueva, Ojo Ca-
liente, and Sevilleta, which were all small settlements east and northeast of
El Rito. They transplanted the names of those villages to some of the new
settlements in southern Colorado. Two brothers, José Adan and Antonio
Espinosa, settled on the San Juan River across from Rosa, Colorado, in the
1880s. They were sons of Francisco Espinosa, a brother of José Julián
Espinosa. José Adan Espinosa was deputy sheriff of the Rosa justice-of-the-
peace court and was known as the bane of rustlers. Apparently few of the
settlers homesteaded; they simply squatted on the land.[9]

The total Spanish-speaking population of southern Colorado was not
more than about three thousand in 1880. They lived in small towns and on
ranches, and their main occupation was farming and sheep and cattle
raising. It was an isolated, rugged frontier existence. In the winter the
people lived shut in in their adobe houses, while in the summer they were
widely scattered, working on their farms and their irrigation ditches and
tending to their sheep and cattle. Their way of life was not much different
from that of the ranchers and farmers between Albuquerque and Taos in
northern New Mexico. The New Mexican Spanish settlers had been beck-
oned by the fertile land of the beautiful San Luis Valley, which is surrounded
by some of Colorado's more lofty mountain ranges, including on the east the
Sangre de Cristo Range and on the southwest the rugged San Juan Mountains. Both ranges extend south into New Mexico on either side of the Rio
Grande Valley.

The permanence of the New Mexican settlements in the San Luis Valley
can be attributed largely to the military protection that the United States
afforded them in 1852 when it established Fort Massachusetts, which was
moved six miles south to a new location and renamed Fort Garland in 1858.
The fort was designed to keep in check the hostile Utes, who had long
claimed the San Luis Valley as a favorite hunting ground, and thus to
safeguard the newly acquired Spanish-speaking settlements there. After the
Ute war of 1879, most of the Utes removed from the valley in the
mid-1880s, and the main obstacle to settlement in southern Colorado
disappeared.

Celso Espinosa, Aurelio Espinosa's father, was born on March 28, 1856,
in El Rito, New Mexico, where his father, José Julián Espinosa, had been
born and where his grandfather Antonio had eventually settled. He was the
second of fourteen children and was fourteen years old when his family
moved to the San Luis Valley. On January 14, 1878, he married Rafaela
Antonia Martínez. Celso Espinosa homesteaded at El Carnero, as noted
earlier, where he engaged in farming and sheep raising. During the years

A nineteenth-century New Mexican home at El Rito, 1951. *Courtesy of Vicenta Espinosa, Santa Fe.*

between 1880 to 1895 the family lived at El Carnero or nearby, at Los Mogotes, at Los Valdeses, at Kennah Creek, and at White Water, where Aurelio, the future folklorist and linguist, attended the public schools. Celso Espinosa was a teacher in the public schools, and the first school that Aurelio attended was his father's school, where the children were taught to read and write in both Spanish and English. Of Celso and Rafaela's eight sons and six daughters, the older children were born in southern Colorado and the younger ones in northern New Mexico. The children grew up in relatively comfortable surroundings, considering the rugged frontier character of life in the region.[10]

As a boy Aurelio spent the summers in the southern Colorado mountains north and west of the San Luis Valley with his uncle Don Ramón Martínez, who grazed his sheep and cattle on the mountain slope west of El Carnero. There Aurelio came to know the shepherds' life and listened with interest as they passed the time recounting traditional tales, ballads, verses, proverbs, and other bits of traditional Spanish folk literature. Besides helping the men who looked after Don Ramón's sheep and cattle, Aurelio often went on full-day outings with his uncle, fishing and hunting deer.

The trips over the mountains and streams were made on foot and on horseback.[11]

To give their children the opportunity for better schooling, Aurelio's parents moved to Del Norte, the county seat of Rio Grande County. Celso Espinosa was determined to obtain the best education possible for his children. In the fall of 1895, Aurelio entered Del Norte High School, from which he graduated in June, 1898. That fall the family left their home in Del Norte and moved to Boulder to help support Aurelio and his older brother, who had enrolled at the University of Colorado. Aurelio graduated from the university in June, 1902, with the degree of bachelor of philosophy. His chief studies were Romance languages, Latin, and philosophy. During his last year at the university he was a teaching assistant in French and Spanish.[12]

In 1905, Espinosa married María Margarita García of Santa Fe, who was also a descendant of old Spanish families of the Santa Fe area. Family records show that one of her ancestors was Lieutenant General Roque Madrid, who was one of Governor Vargas's chief officers in the reconquest of New Mexico and later the *alcalde mayor* of Santa Cruz. The marriage took place at the Church of the Immaculate Conception in Albuquerque.[13]

Thus, when Espinosa began in the first years of this century to collect traditional New Mexican Spanish folklore and to study the Spanish language as spoken in the region, he was very much a part of the locale through his many family relationships throughout the upper Rio Grande Valley.

In September, 1902, Aurelio M. Espinosa began his professional career as professor of modern languages at the University of New Mexico in Albuquerque. In 1904 he received the degree of master of arts from the University of Colorado for work done in absentia and in summer residence. During his first years of teaching at the University of New Mexico, he became seriously interested in the language and folklore of northern New Mexico and southern Colorado and in the more general fields of Spanish dialectology and literature. He served as professor of modern languages at the University of New Mexico until 1910.[14]

During the regular academic years 1907–1908 and 1908–1909 and during the summer sessions, Espinosa, on leave of absence from his post at the University of New Mexico, was a graduate student at the University of Chicago. He also was a teaching fellow in Spanish there during the summer sessions of 1907, 1908, and 1909 and during the regular academic year 1908–1909. In September, 1909, he received the degree of doctor of philosophy, cum laude, majoring in Romance languages and literatures and minoring in Indo-European comparative philology. His doctoral dissertation, "Studies in New-Mexican Spanish," was published in three parts between 1909 and 1914 in the *Revue de Dialectologie Romane*. This study on Spanish-American dialectology attracted the attention of scholars in the United States and abroad, and as a result Professor John Ernst Matske of Stanford University offered Espinosa a post at Stanford University as assistant professor of Romanic languages. Espinosa began his teaching career at Stanford in September, 1910, and Stanford became his base of operations thenceforward for his folklore field trips and research.[15]

At Stanford, Espinosa became professor of Romanic languages in 1921 and was chairman of the department from 1932 until his retirement in 1947. He was largely responsible for drawing outstanding language students to Stanford and attaining eminence for the university's Spanish department in both undergraduate and graduate work. When he had arrived at Stanford in 1910, only undergraduate Spanish was taught there. He organized a graduate studies program and subsequently directed the writing of fifty master's theses and twelve doctoral dissertations, one-third of them on his favorite subjects, folklore and dialectology. The graduate students he trained later distinguished themselves in the fields of Spanish literature, folklore, and linguistics. One of his students was Juan B. Rael, a leading authority on Hispanic-American folk literature. His courses at Stanford ranged from undergraduate courses in the Spanish language to such subjects as modern Spanish literature, Old Spanish, the folklore of Spain, and Spanish ballads.[16]

Espinosa pursued his folklore studies with unflagging enthusiasm for nearly half a century. His working regimen was rigorous, including as it did his teaching and administrative duties, his direction of graduate studies, the publication of textbooks, and other educational responsibilities at Stanford. Yet his folklore fieldwork and research continued unabated, and his scholarly publications mounted in volume. Surrounded by his notes, bibliographical files, and books, he often studied late into the night and on into the early hours of the morning, organizing and classifying his materials and transferring them directly to typewritten copy. Espinosa had a remarkable memory and carried an immense amount of information in his head. In his classes, lectures, and seminars he often quoted passages from Spanish prose and poetry, sometimes at considerable length, to illustrate and analyze the literary subjects under discussion.

Still he found time for recreation, playing tennis, and fishing (which was his favorite sport), attending football games and social events connected with his teaching and administrative responsibilities, and spending time with his family. As his children grew up, he prepared them for their first years in school by compiling graded booklets by hand to instruct them in learning the alphabet, words, and elementary sentence structure in English and Spanish. He liked to entertain his family at the dinner table by reciting verses in Spanish, Old Spanish, Latin, and other Romance languages, and Sanskrit or by telling humorous stories and anecdotes that were usually related to or gleaned from folklore.

Espinosa was one of the early leaders in the United States in promoting the teaching of Spanish language and literature. During the first three decades of this century he pioneered in the preparation and publication of textbooks. He published twenty-two such textbooks, including grammar, conversation, and composition books; histories of Spanish literature; a book on Spanish pronunciation; and editions of the works of modern Spanish dramatists for collateral reading. His textbooks were widely used for many years in American colleges and universities. In recognition of his experience in the preparation of textbooks, Espinosa was made the general editor of the Stanford Spanish Series, and from 1936 until his retirement from Stanford in 1947 he was the general editor of Spanish textbooks for the Oxford University Press. He was one of the founders of the American Association of Teachers of Spanish in 1917 and was the editor of the association's official organ, *Hispania*, during the first nine years of its existence from 1917 to 1926. He served as president of the association in 1928. He published a number of articles on teaching methods in *Hispania*. Between 1925 and 1930 he carried out experiments to measure the linguistic abilities of students of Spanish at Stanford, and as a result, with the collaboration of a colleague at Stanford Professor Truman Kelly, an expert on aptitude tests, he devised the Stanford Spanish Tests, which were used for the placement of Spanish-language students at the class levels ascertained by the tests.

During those years Espinosa actively promoted the organization and collaboration of scholars in the fields of folklore and dialectology. In 1909 he was one of the organizers and founders of the Société Internationale de Dialectologie Romane, which had its headquarters in Brussels. In several articles Espinosa urged his colleagues in the Southwest to collect traditional Spanish folk literature from the region before the folklore disappeared.[17] He was associate editor of the *Journal of American Folklore* for many years, beginning in 1914, and was president of the American Folklore Society in 1924 and 1925. He was one of the organizers and founders of the Linguistic Society of America and was an associate editor of its official organ, *Language*, from 1925 to 1931. In 1929 he was president of the Pacific Coast branch of the American Philological Association. He was consulting editor of the *New Mexico Quarterly* from 1930 to 1936 and served as associate editor

of *Western Folklore* from 1947 to 1953. In 1931 the New Mexico Folklore Society was established with his encouragement. In 1946 the society began publication of the *New Mexico Folklore Record*.[18]

Espinosa's most significant contributions to scholarship and letters were in the fields of dialectology and folk literature. As stated above, he laid the groundwork for the study of Spanish-American dialectology and the folklore of the American Southwest on a scientific basis for future researchers in those fields.[19] He pursued these studies as a tireless scholar and prolific writer from the first decade of this century until his health failed him in the 1950s. His publications on folklore and dialectology between 1907 and 1955 included over one hundred books, monographs, and articles, of which approximately 60 percent date from before the 1930s, when he was working in those fields almost alone.[20]

In dialectology Espinosa's pioneer work was his dissertation, "Studies in New-Mexican Spanish." Part one of that work covers phonology; part two, morphology; and part three, the English elements. Part one was published as a book by the University of Chicago Press and reprinted by the University of New Mexico in 1909.[21] In the "Studies," Espinosa showed that the Spanish spoken by residents of northern New Mexico and southern Colorado, who were isolated for over two centuries from the direct influence of the urban centers of Spanish America, developed from the language of Spain's Golden Age during the sixteenth and seventeenth centuries, with local dialect traits that are also found in Spain, as well as other parts of Spanish America. In addition, Espinosa identified the peninsular origins of the first Spanish settlers in New Mexico: they were principally from Castile, Andalucía, and Estremadura, although there were representatives from northern Spain as well. The sources of New Mexican Spanish are to be found in the Castilian speech of the sixteenth century; to a lesser extent in the dialects of Andalucía, Asturias, Santander, and León; and in a few cases in Galician and other western Hispano-Portuguese dialects. To those sources must be added the influences on the language resulting from later developments over the years. Espinosa's "Studies," were a major contribution to dialect studies and became a model for other studies of Spanish dialectology.

Important new studies in Hispanic dialectology and phonetics during the three decades following the publication of Espinosa's "Studies" led to updating of parts one and two.[22] In 1930 and 1946 parts one and two of the "Studies" were translated into Spanish under Espinosa's direction by Amado Alonso and Angel Rosenblat with extensive additional comparative notes and separate essays by them. This revised edition was published by the Institute of Philology of the University of Buenos Aires in two volumes. In his introduction to part one, the Spanish scholar Amado Alonso states, "The work of Espinosa presents systematically the richest study we have on dialect forms; no other Spanish dialect, either before or after him, has been so minutely catalogued in its phonetic and morphological variants." Alonso adds, "One need only leaf through the leading subsequent works on Spanish philology to certify the great leap forward that his 'Studies' gave to the field of Spanish dialectology." Sixteen years later, in 1946, in publishing the Spanish edition of part two, Alonso added: "Today, sixteen years later . . . the Spanish dialect of New Mexico, thanks to Professor Espinosa, continues to be the most minutely studied regional variety of Spanish." This edition of Espinosa's "Studies" represents to this day the basic work on New Mexican Spanish dialectology.

Part three of the "Studies," on the English elements, examines in detail the influences on the Spanish language of the region resulting from contact with English speakers. Since the occupation of the region by the United States in the 1840s, the Spanish speakers' vocabulary had incorporated hundreds of words of English origin, with many English words completely Hispanicized. Espinosa's article on speech mixture in New Mexico, published in 1917, opened yet another uninvestigated area in the dialectology of the region: the speech elements and vocabulary used by Spanish-speaking mining and railroad workers in the late nineteenth and early twentieth centuries.[23] His studies were the basic source of information on this subject in H. L. Mencken's monumental work *The American Language*. Mencken referred to Espinosa as "the greatest living authority on American Spanish."[24] Among the sources of Espinosa's dialect and linguistic studies was his vast knowledge of folk literature in the New Mexico area.

The branches of traditional Spanish folk literature found in northern New Mexico and southern Colorado that Espinosa chose for special study were ballads and other poetic compositions; folktales and anecdotes; proverbs; sayings; riddles; prayers; children's games and nursery rhymes; folk drama; myths, legends, and superstitions; and the Spanish influence on the folklore of the Pueblo Indians. He collected material from the older settlements in the upper Rio Grande Valley between Socorro, which is approximately seventy-five miles south of Albuquerque, and the San Luis Valley in southern Colorado. That was the geographic area where the local Spanish folklore tradition was most vigorously alive in the Southwest, and it remains so today.

Espinosa's published collections and comparative studies contributed to

Aurelio M. Espinosa about 1930. *Files of J. Manuel Espinosa.*

our knowledge of the Spanish folk literature not only of northern New Mexico and southern Colorado but also of California, Arizona, Texas, Mexico, other parts of Spanish America, and even of Spain.[25]

One of the most remarkable features of the centuries-old traditional Spanish folk poetry found in the oral tradition of northern New Mexico and southern Colorado is the fidelity of its preservation in its distinctive forms. Espinosa was the first to collect and study those forms, and especially significant as a contribution to Hispanic literature are his studies of the traditional Spanish ballads he found in the region. Those ballads furnish us with one of the most interesting and archaic collections from oral tradition anywhere in the Spanish-speaking world. Many of them are versions of old Spanish ballads brought to the New World by the first Spanish settlers in the sixteenth century. Espinosa's first collection from the region, published in 1915, included 27 versions of ten traditional ballads of sixteenth- and seventeenth-century origin. In 1931 he collected 47 additional versions of fifteen different traditional ballads in northern New Mexico and 9 versions of four different religious ballads from the oral tradition of the Pueblo Indians, all of which he published the following year. By 1941 he had collected over 100 versions of twenty different old Spanish ballads in northern New Mexico and southern Colorado.[26] The subject matter of those ballads falls into general groups of verses that express happy and hopeful love; verses that express unhappy and rejected love; philosophical and proverbial themes; riddles; religious themes; and humorous and burlesque verses. Espinosa's revised ballad collection published in Spain in 1953 contains 248 versions and a few fragments of ninety Spanish ballads from New Mexico. Of the ninety he identified twenty-seven as *romances tradicionales*. The musical scores for twenty-eight were included.

New Mexicans refer to the Spanish ballads as *corridos*, as they are called in some other parts of the Spanish-speaking world. New Mexicans also give the name *corridos* to other balladlike compositions, some of which made their way into the region directly from Mexico in the late eighteenth and nineteenth centuries. Espinosa collected and included in his earliest publications a number of these popular poetic compositions, which are also called *cuandos* or *inditas*. Their themes are sometimes similar to those of the *romances tradicionales*, but they also deal with local political topics, historical episodes, notorious events, and the like.

Another interesting type of folk poetry found in New Mexico is the *décima*, a long, complicated riddle preserved in oral tradition in hendecasyllabic or octosyllabic meter and in five strophic groups, the first of four verses and the remaining four of ten each. The *décima* is found in the oral tradition of all Spanish-speaking countries and deals with almost any subject. Some *décimas* are quite old, although most of them date from the eighteenth century or later. It is remarkable that these long and complicated riddles in verse have been handed down and preserved virtually unchanged in oral folk tradition over several centuries. Of twenty-four *décimas* collected by Espinosa and published in 1915, four have been traced back to the seventeenth century.

The most popular verse form in the oral tradition of the Spanish South-west is the Spanish *copla*, known in the region as the *verso*, an octosyllabic quatrain that expresses in its four short verses a complete idea. In New Mexico thousands of these bits of the philosophy of the people have been preserved in oral tradition. *Echar versos*—to compose, sing, or recite the popular *versos*—was during the eighteenth and nineteenth centuries a popular pastime at almost any social gathering in New Mexico, and the *cantadores*, or popular poets and singers, were held in high esteem among the people. Although a very large and important part of the repertoire of the New Mexican *cantador* has always consisted of traditional material that can be traced back to sixteenth- and seventeenth-century Spain, the greater part is of more recent origin. *Versos* are a clearly exuberant form, and new ones seem to have appeared almost every day. The melodies are numerous, and all have modern changes. Before 1909, Espinosa had collected about five hundred *versos* in northern New Mexico and southern Colorado. He published some of them in his "Studies" in 1909 and another collection of fifty-four in 1935. In 1930 he published a collection of eighty *coplas*, *corridos*, and *versos* gathered from the oral tradition of California, some of which had been introduced into California from Mexico in the late eigh-teenth century and others in the nineteenth century. Some fifteen hundred *coplas populares* or *versos* collected by him in northern New Mexico and southern Colorado remain unpublished.

The Spanish folktales that have been preserved in northern New Mexico and southern Colorado are as interesting as the various forms of folk poetry. They are for the most part of European origin, having been transmitted through the rich heritage of Spain, which for many centuries was unique as a crossroads for the folktales of the Phoenicians, Greeks, Romans, Arabs, Jews, and Germanic peoples who had lived there. From Spain traditional folktales were transmitted in oral tradition to all parts of Spanish America beginning in the early sixteenth century. They abound in New Mexico, many in perfect versions, others with a mixture of different folktale ele-ments, and some with locally added details.

Espinosa was the first to collect traditional Spanish folktales from the Southwest, and indeed from any part of the former Spanish borderlands of the present United States. He first published a collection of eighteen short folktales from the oral tradition of New Mexico and Colorado in his "Stud-ies" in 1909, and a larger number, most of which he had collected between 1908 and 1910, were published in 1911 and 1914. In all he published eighty-five folktales and anecdotes, the majority of which were old tradi-tional tales. In addition he established the guidelines for later collections made by his students and others. In 1940 he published twelve Spanish folktales from California, which he had collected earlier in localities along the old Camino Real between San Francisco and Santa Barbara. All but one were similar to versions going back to the sixteenth and seventeenth centuries that he had collected previously in New Mexico and Spain. Several of his students, most beginning in the 1930s and others in the 1940s and later, expanded considerably the number of traditional Spanish folktales collected from northern New Mexico and southern Colorado. To date, over a thousand versions have been collected, of which hundreds have been published. Espinosa identified over 80 percent of them as types found in Spain.

To facilitate the comparative study of the folktales in the oral tradition of Spain and those of New Mexico and other parts of Hispanic America, Espinosa made a field trip to Spain in 1920 under the auspices of the American Folklore Society. In the years 1923 to 1926 he published 280 versions of Spanish folktales that he had collected in Spain. A revised edition of the collection, with extensive comparative notes, was published in Spain in three volumes from 1946 to 1947. That monumental work is his most significant single contribution to Hispanic folk literature.

One of Espinosa's most interesting folktale studies, to which he devoted many years of research, was tracing the origins and transmission of the "Tar Baby" story, widely known in the United States since the publication of a version of it by Joel Chandler Harris in 1880 among his *Uncle Remus* stories, which were taken from the Negro folklore of the Old South. As a result of Harris's book, and since it was discovered that the story was popular among Negroes of Africa as well as those of North America, it was believed that the story had originated in Africa. Espinosa found 152 versions of the folktale from widely scattered parts of the world. He traced the origins of the "Tar Baby" story to India, where he found a version in the literature of ancient India before the Christian era. He concluded that the folktale had been transmitted from there to Europe and Africa over the years and from Europe and Africa to America, principally through Spain in the early years of discovery and colonization. The story is found in the folklore of the Spanish-speaking people of New Mexico and among the Pueblo Indians.

The traditional Spanish folktales, like the ballads, throw considerable light on the popular mind of the New Mexican people over the last three centuries: their concepts of morality and ethics; human virtues and failings; sorrows, joys, and humor; political, religious, and social views; and history.

New Mexico is also particularly rich in traditional Spanish proverbs and riddles, some of which are in assonance or rhyme and represent archaic materials. Espinosa published the first collection of Spanish proverbs from the oral tradition of New Mexico, 632 in number, in 1913, and the second collection, 165 riddles, from the same region in 1915. In 1918 he published a collection of 50 Spanish riddles from the region between San Jose and Santa Barbara, California. Of the proverbs, about 70 percent are found, with insignificant differences, in the sixteenth-century literature of Spain as part of the general Spanish proverb tradition so skillfully used by Cervantes through the mouth of Sancho Panza. The riddles, although not as numerous as the proverbs, are just as important for folklore studies. They are frequently more archaic, some dating from the thirteenth to the sixteenth centuries. Similar versions of the riddles have been published from the oral tradition of Spain and other parts of the Spanish-speaking world. Most of the traditional children's games, nursery rhymes, and children's rhymes and songs have a similar history. A collection was published by Espinosa in 1916 and augmented in subsequent publications.

The Spanish missionaries brought with them to all parts of Spanish America in the sixteenth and seventeenth centuries genuine religious folk plays, as distinct from the learned dramas presented in the theaters of Spain and in the large capitals of Spanish America. The folk dramas were introduced principally for religious instruction. The presentation of some of these plays is still a part of the religious tradition of New Mexico and other parts of the Spanish-speaking world. Espinosa collected several versions of such plays in the first decade of this century, but they remain unpublished.

Another type of folk dramatization brought from Spain is the colorful spectacle called *Moros y cristianos*, a traditional mock battle between Moors and Christians, usually ending with the latter rescuing a cross or a statue of the Blessed Virgin. It was popular for several centuries in all parts of the Spanish-speaking world, and it was first performed in 1598 in New Mexico, where manuscripts for the performance still exist. Espinosa found a partial manuscript; others have since been documented. He also found abundant evidence that this popular dramatic performance was presented on special occasions in various localities in New Mexico until the beginning of this century and that for a number of years the Pueblo Indians included modified versions of the mock battle in some of their celebrations.

An interesting part of the folk theater of New Mexico, as in other parts of Spanish America, was the Spanish folk play of American origin depicting local historical events or episodes. Two plays of this type are known: *Los Comanches*, a late eighteenth-century play, and *Los Tejanos*, composed not long after 1841. Both of these plays are written in the traditional octosyllabic verse. *Los Comanches* depicts a bloody battle with the Comanche

Indians in northern New Mexico. This play, containing 515 lines, was presented in various localities in northern New Mexico until recent years. Espinosa published a version of it in 1907. *Los Tejanos* deals with an expedition into New Mexico by Texans in 1841 and their defeat and capture by New Mexicans. We have no knowledge of any recent presentation of this play, and only one manuscript, discovered by Espinosa in Chimayó in 1931 and published by him in 1943 and 1944, is known. *Los Tejanos* contains 492 lines.

Espinosa also explored the influence of Spanish folklore among the Pueblo Indians of New Mexico and northeastern Arizona. His first study on this subject was published in 1916 and followed by nine more studies published between 1918 and 1952. They deal with speech mixture; survival from early days of the word *Castilla*, meaning Castilian or Spaniard, in various Indianized forms; influences on prayers and hymns; features of Indian dances and ceremonies performed on Catholic religious feast days, including those of the patron saints of the Pueblos designated in early days by the Spanish missionaries; influences assimilated in prayers for rain, in vows and petitions, and even in masked dances; influences on Pueblo Indian folktales and nursery rhymes; and Spanish religious ballads found in the oral tradition of the Pueblo Indians. Franz Boas wrote: "The investigations of Prof. Aurelio M. Espinosa, Dr. Elsie Clews Parsons and my own have shown clearly that a great amount of American Indian material can be traced directly to Spanish sources. . . . There is no doubt that Romance sources have added a great deal to the lore of America and that in some cases even stylistic characteristics of Romance story-telling may be traced in native tales." [27]

Herbert E. Bolton wrote in 1929 in his essay "The Significance of the Borderlands": "Among the most priceless treasures of any country are its historical records and its folklore. . . . Not the least important part of our heritage has been the Hispanic appeal to the imagination. The Spanish occupation has furnished theme and color for myriad writers, great and small. Lomax and Dobie, Lummis and Willa Cather, Bret Harte and Espinosa have shown that these inter-American bounds have a Spain-tinged folklore as rich as that of the Scottish border embalmed by Sir Walter Scott." [28]

During his long professional career, Espinosa received many honors in recognition of his contributions to Hispanic scholarship and letters. In addition to the offices he held in professional organizations, the numerous honors and distinctions he received included corresponding membership in the Sociedad Mejicana de Geografía y Estadística (1912); corresponding membership in the Sociedad Chilena de Historia y Geografía (1914); corresponding membership in the Royal Spanish Academy of the Language (1921); knighthood conferred by King Alfonso XIII of Spain, with the title Knight Commander of the Royal Order of Isabella the Catholic (1922); and corresponding membership in the Hispanic Society of America (1925). He was awarded an honorary degree of doctor of letters by the University of San Francisco College for Women in 1934, and that same year he received an honorary doctor of laws degree from the University of New Mexico, with the citation "Pioneer and leader in the study of the Spanish literary heritage of New Mexico . . . famed son of the Spanish Southwest." Later he received two of Spain's highest civilian awards: the title of Commander of the Order of Alfonso el Sabio and membership in the Instituto de Cultura Hispánica.

On the occasion of his death on September 4, 1958, the Department of Spanish and Portuguese of Stanford University drew up a memorial resolution which refers to some of his personal qualities as a scholar and teacher: "The hundreds of young men and women who studied under Professor Espinosa, many of whom hold important positions in the academic world, will long remember him for his scholarship, his lively and interesting lectures, and his sympathetic understanding of students and their problems. They could always count on his friendly advice. His many colleagues and friends, both within and without the University, will miss his lively friendship and sage counsel."

A decade after his death Espinosa was elected by the New Mexico Folklore Society as the first person to be placed on its New Mexico Folklore Roll of Honor. His name is thus inscribed on a bronze plaque permanently placed near the entrance to one of the main reading rooms in the University of New Mexico Library.

# Major Stages in the Development of Espinosa's Folklore Studies

Between 1902 and 1915, Aurelio M. Espinosa pursued his chosen field of research assiduously, traveling extensively throughout northern New Mexico and southern Colorado to study in depth the phonology and morphology of the Spanish dialect spoken in the region and to collect, firsthand, extensive materials representing the major types of folk literature that existed there.

Espinosa's graduate studies at the University of Chicago in Romance philology, modern and classical languages, and comparative literature sharpened his knowledge in those fields and prepared him in modern scientific research methodology. The faculty of the University of Chicago, one of the leading graduate schools in the United States at that time, included nationally and internationally recognized scholars in many fields of research. The director of Espinosa's doctoral studies and of his doctoral dissertation was Dr. Karl Pietsch, a distinguished German scholar in the fields of Romance philology and literature, who had received his Ph.D. at the University of Halle, Germany. Pietsch typified the German scholars who contributed much to the development of graduate research in North American universities at the turn of the century, pursuing the scientific methods for which the German universities came to be widely known in the late nineteenth century.

By 1910, Espinosa had made preliminary comparative studies of his New Mexican collections of folk literature and had become convinced, through his study of Hispanic and European publications on the literary and popular origins of folk literature, that the folk literature retained in the memory of the Spanish-speaking people of northern New Mexico and southern Colorado was derived from the popular Spanish folk literature transmitted to America by the early settlers during the fifteenth, sixteenth, and seventeenth centuries. His later studies, using the growing bibliography of significant collections and comparative studies on western European folk literature between 1910 and 1930, fortified and confirmed his initial conclusions in this regard.

Espinosa's first study of the folk literature of nothern New Mexico and southern Colorado, published in 1907, contains the text, with notes on dialect peculiarities and versification, of the play *Los Comanches*, a hand-written manuscript of which he had found in northern New Mexico.[1] Folk drama was only one of the aspects of Spanish folk literature in the region that captured Espinosa's attention during those years. In 1910 he prepared an essay, published the following year, in which he listed the following folklore materials which he had been gathering in northern New Mexico and southern Colorado since 1902. In 1911 at the annual meeting of the Philological Association of the Pacific Coast he presented a short paper that contained a revised listing classified as follows: (1) traditional ballads; (2) modern ballads; (3) vulgar ballads; (4) *décimas*; (5) *inditas, cuandos*, series of *quintillas*; (6) riddles and riddle questions, (7) proverbs (*refranes* or *dichos*); (8) games and diversions of adults; (9) children's games and nursery rhymes; (10) legends, superstitions, and remedies; (11) satirical ballads against the Americans and against the Church; (12) folktales; (13) songs; (14) *coplas*; (15) astronomy; (16) cooking; (17) "Los trovos del viejo Vilmas"; (18) idioms and comparisons; (19) the English language in New Mexican folklore; (20) New Mexican names for the fauna and flora of New Mexico; (21) prayers and incantations; (22) *pastorelas* or nativity plays; (23) *Los Comanches*, a heroic-dramatic poem; (24) dramatic versions of (a) The Apparition of Our Lady of Guadalupe, (b) The Massacre of the Innocents and the Flight of the Child Jesus into Egypt, and (c) The Childhood of Christ.[2]

In 1910, Espinosa wrote, "I am at present especially interested in the literary and purely linguistic side of Spanish folk-lore."[3] He indicated that he was attempting to carry out this work in a scientific manner and that therefore some of the material would remain unpublished for some time. He noted that "the comparative method of studying folk-lore, which is at the same time historical, seems to be the only method by which to obtain good results. To pursue this method to advantage in all branches of the study is a long, laborious task."[4] Espinosa added that he was plowing new ground and that his materials were all original. He lamented the fact that he was compelled to publish bare facts, with little comparative method, since nothing of importance had been published on the subject up to that time, and expressed the view that the abundant materials that he had already found in northern New Mexico and southern Colorado "seem to furnish ample proof that vast treasures of folk-lore are to be found in Texas, California, and Arizona, not to speak of Mexican folk-lore studies, which to my knowledge, no one has ever touched upon."[5] He added, "The folk-lore study of Spanish-America is a field that is unlimited." In South America important pioneer folklore research was then being done largely through the personal efforts of several specialists, including Rodolfo Lenz, Ramón A. Laval, and Julio Vicuña Cifuentes, all of Chile.

Great interest in the traditional Spanish ballad was created in Spanish America in 1906 when Ramón Menéndez Pidal, who had succeeded Marcelino Menéndez y Pelayo as Spain's leading modern ballad scholar and had embarked on a lifelong study of traditional ballads throughout the Spanish-speaking world, published an important article that made known the existence of such ballads from the oral tradition of Spanish America. On a visit to a number of Spanish-American countries in 1905, Menéndez Pidal had learned from Vicuña Cifuentes and Laval that they had collected traditional Spanish ballads in Chile before 1905. Other South American folklorists as well had already collected traditional Spanish ballads. Some of them, such as Vicuña Cifuentes in Chile and Robert Lehmann-Nitsche in Argentina, provided Menéndez Pidal with ballads which were included in his publication. None of the ballads had been published up to that time.

In 1909, on a visit to the United States, Menéndez Pidal met Espinosa, who informed the Spanish scholar that he had been collecting traditional Spanish ballads in northern New Mexico and southern Colorado since 1902. During the next few years other Spanish ballad collections from America were published, adding considerably to the material published by Menéndez Pidal. The first major collections published were those of Vicuña Cifuentes in 1912 and Espinosa in 1915. Others published ballad collections from Chile, Cuba, Santo Domingo, and Mexico. Espinosa and several of the others indicated that they were publishing their findings as contributions to Menéndez Pidal's extensive ongoing ballad project.[6]

Espinosa began publishing his findings within the limitations of the Hispanic-American folklore studies then available in the hope that they would make a useful contribution to comparative Hispanic folklore. Between the years 1907 and 1916 he published thirteen articles and monographs containing materials, with comparative literary and linguistic comment and notes, in the following categories: secular folk drama; myths, superstitions and beliefs; folktales; proverbs; popular comparisons; "Los trovos del viejo Vilmas"; short folktales and anecdotes; miscellaneous materials; riddles; children's games; nursery rhymes and children's songs; and ballads. The articles were published between 1910 and 1916. In addition, he edited, with comparative notes, "Folk-Tales of the Tepecanos," an extensive collection of folktales from Mexico collected by J. Alden Mason and published in 1914. That same year he also published "Comparative Notes on New Mexican and Mexican Spanish Folk-Tales," the first comparative study on this subject. During this same period, his "Studies in New-Mexican Spanish" was published, and three other articles on aspects of the subject were published in European and American publications.

In carrying out these pioneering studies, Espinosa placed upon himself rigorous literary and linguistic requirements. He considered a thorough knowledge of the Spanish dialect spoken in the region, that is, of the language of the orally transmitted folk literature found there, to be a primary prerequisite. To verify the literary origins and characteristics of his findings, he considered that it was essential to have the greatest possible knowledge of Spanish literature and history from the earliest examples of its literary and folk tradition. Since much of Spanish folk literature is in verse, he mastered the study of Spanish versification in its various forms throughout the history of Spanish literature.

Espinosa attached great importance to the widest possible knowledge of modern and classical languages, which enabled him to consult directly the known sources for the comparative study of his findings. He also followed the latest research in the social sciences to gain insights from comparative studies in history, anthropology, and social psychology that related to folklore. In those fields important studies had appeared in the late eighteenth and early nineteenth centuries and were published more extensively in the last half of the nineteenth and in the twentieth century.

Last, but not least, Espinosa based his comparative study of the folk literature of northern New Mexico and southern Colorado on materials that he himself collected in the region. None of his published collections and studies of the folklore of the region included materials collected by others; in fact, he was working virtually alone in the field. Only in a few cases were his materials supplemented by those of others, relatives and friends whom he inspired to send him materials of the type that he was gathering.

By background, temperament, physical stamina, intellectual capacity, and professional training Espinosa was uniquely prepared to implement the rigorous standards and principles that he set for himself in pursuing his folklore fieldwork and comparative research. As a native New Mexican of Spanish-speaking background, he was fluent from childhood in the Spanish language as it was spoken in northern New Mexico and southern Colorado. As professor of modern languages at the University of New Mexico from 1902 to 1910, he perfected his knowledge of French, Italian, Portuguese, German, Latin, and Greek. During those years he read assiduously the works on Spanish literature and history that were available to him. His knowledge of languages and comparative literature was expanded through his graduate studies in Romance versification, Old Spanish, classical literature, and comparative Indo-European philology at the University of Chicago. There his language studies included Sanskrit, Hebrew, German, Latin, and Greek.

The library and archival resources first available to him were limited to those of the University of Colorado, the University of New Mexico, and the New Mexico Historical Society. While in Chicago, he was able to consult the richer materials in the University of Chicago Library and the Newberry Library. At Stanford University, the university library and the University of California Library in Berkeley were readily at hand. In the years that followed, he visited the Library of Congress and other leading libraries in the United States as well as the Biblioteca Nacional, the Biblioteca de la Real Academia de la Lengua, and other public and private libraries in Spain.

In pursuing his study of folk literature, Espinosa corresponded extensively with colleagues in the United States, Spain, Germany, France, England, Belgium, other countries of Europe, and Spanish America. He had met Ramón Menéndez Pidal in Chicago in 1909, and they became lifelong friends and correspondents on the subjects of Spanish philology and literature. He had a close correspondence with Lenz, Vicuña Cifuentes, and Laval, the pioneer folklorists in Chile, and with José María Chacón y Calvo, Fernando Ortiz, and Carolina Poncet in Cuba. He became a close friend of anthropologists Franz Boas and Elsie Clews Parsons and historian Herbert E. Bolton in the United States, and with them he carried out extensive correspondence on scholarly matters. The list expanded in subsequent years. Boas, as an officer of the American Folklore Society, which had been founded in 1888, was instrumental in the promotion of Hispanic folklore studies for publication in the *Journal of American Folk-Lore* beginning in 1910, and some of Espinosa's studies began to appear in the journal at that time.

Espinosa often repeated his early theory, stated in his first publications, that most of the folk material found in the oral tradition of New Mexico and Colorado had its origins in Spain, with little change after being transmitted to the region in the sixteenth and seventeenth centuries via New Spain (Mexico). In 1914 he wrote, "After I began publishing my New Mexican Spanish folk-lore material, some four years ago, I made the somewhat sweeping assertion that in my opinion most of the material was traditional, that is, Spanish. Further study has strengthened this opinion more and more. The traditional material—whether it be ballads, nursery rhymes, proverbs, riddles, folk-tales, or what not—may have sometimes undergone some modifications and amplifications, but it has survived; and not only has it survived, but it has remained practically untouched by foreign influences."[7] This view was amply confirmed as his collections of traditional folk literature increased in volume and as he compared them with published materials on the folk literature of Spain, Spanish America, and other countries of Europe.

A recent folklorist, in referring to the origins of Spanish folk tradition in New Mexico and Colorado, has stated, with regard to the folktales: "In their outlook on these folktales, members of the Espinosa group have been steadfastly Spanish. There is a constant identification of New Mexico with Spain in the comparison and analysis of the tales and even in the wording of the titles of their published collections. The identification extends also to the narrators themselves and one could almost gain the impression that the New Mexican colonists proceeded directly from Spain to their new home in America without stopping in Mexico." The writer then goes on to say that there are local factors that serve to explain this, namely, that the older generation of New Mexicans "preferred" to be designated as "Spanish," especially in Espinosa's day.[8] These comments represent a misreading of the facts. The Espinosa studies in question were on the traditional folk literature and language found by him in northern New Mexico and southern Colorado, the sources of which are to be found in fifteenth-, sixteenth-, and seventeenth-century Spain and were transmitted to the region from Spain via New Spain (Mexico) beginning in the sixteenth and seventeenth centuries. In speaking of "Spanish" folklore in New Mexico, Espinosa is not referring to local psychological or "preference" factors relating to the Spanish-speaking settlers of New Mexico. He is referring to the origins of the Spanish language and folk literature in the region. He has demonstrated through his extensive comparative studies that approximately 90 percent of the traditional Spanish folk literature of the region can be traced to the folk literature of Spain.

As Espinosa has shown, a major reason why nearly all the Spanish folklore material found in northern New Mexico is of Spanish origin is that for nearly three centuries, beginning in 1598, Spanish-speaking settlers in the region were isolated from direct personal contact with the outside world. Thus the Spanish dialect as spoken in northern New Mexico and southern Colorado has continued to preserve characteristics of fifteenth- and sixteenth-century Spanish. The language and the folk literature of the region, including its versification and other literary characteristics, have their origins in Spain.

Needless to say, in many parts of Spanish America certain linguistic traits of popular speech have been preserved because of the rural conditions of the areas. Some of the dialectal peculiarities have been modified over the years by later developments in the various Spanish-American countries under the pressure of differences in the linguistic environment; that is, the degree to which urban norms and characteristics were, or were not, present has been, no doubt, one of the most important factors. The special abundance and frequency of local dialectal developments, as found in New Mexico and Colorado, is in complete harmony with the historical-cultural explanation of Spanish dialect phenomena, since life in New Mexico developed in isolation during the colonial period and even after the annexation of the region by the United States. In other words, the Spanish-speaking inhabitants of the region, in their local speech and folk tradition, were not influenced by urban standards that might have modified the rural character of their linguistic and cultural environment. They had never lived in direct contact with the large cities of Hispanic America, which would have radiated to them the standard language and the changes of a superior cultural environment. Their language, their cultural heritage, and their traditional folklore remained closer to those of fifteenth- and sixteenth- and seventeenth-century Spain.

During the years from 1916 to 1930, Aurelio M. Espinosa's folklore research focused more and more on the comparative study of the materials that he collected in folk literature, with special reference to their origins. In Europe, especially in Finland and Germany, some important comparative studies of the folktale were published during this period. In Spain, studies of the folktale were still neglected, but important ballad studies were being carried out by Ramón Menéndez Pidal and his collaborators. Modern comparative studies of the Spanish ballad had begun in nineteenth-century Spain and Germany. In the comparative study of folktales, the nineteenth-century pioneers were German, beginning with the Grimm brothers. The subject of folklore methodology is discussed in a later chapter, but it is important to mention here that Espinosa kept abreast of these works, thus acquiring a broader framework for his comparative studies. Under his direction four large collections of Spanish folktales, gathered from the oral tradition in America, were published. They were those collected by J. Manuel Espinosa in northern New Mexico, by J. Alden Mason in Puerto Rico, by Howard Wheeler in Mexico, and by Herminio Portell Vilá in Cuba. A large collection of Spanish folktales, described below, was the result of Espinosa's expedition to Spain in 1920. Meanwhile, he was in correspondence with an expanding number of colleagues in the United States, Hispanic America, Spain, Germany, France, Italy, Portugal, Finland, and other European countries, who were engaged in folklore studies.

Between 1916 and 1930, Espinosa published fifty articles and four volumes on folklore and dialectology. Of the articles, six were on New Mexican Spanish folklore, three on New Mexican dialectology, two on Spanish folk literature and dialectology of California, nine on Puerto Rican folk literature, seventeen on Spanish folk literature, and two on the general subjects of the science of folklore and the transmission of folk literature. One volume on Mexican folklore and the unannotated text of the folktales that he had gathered in 1920 from the oral tradition of Spain, in three volumes, complete the list of his publications between 1916 and 1930.

Between 1930 and 1955, Espinosa published nine books and forty-four articles on Spanish folklore, philology, and dialectology. Of the books, two volumes represent the revision of parts one and two of his "Studies in New-Mexican Spanish." One volume is an extensive collection of New Mexican Spanish ballads; three volumes represent his comparative study of Spanish folktales; a separate volume contains a selection of his Spanish folktales; and of the three remaining books, one deals with Spanish balladry and the others contain selections from the folk literature of New Mexico and California prepared as textbooks for use in Spanish-language classes. Of the articles published during this period, fourteen were on New Mexican Spanish folk literature; seven dealt with Spanish influences on the Pueblo Indians of New Mexico; one was a collection of Pueblo Indian folktales; three were comparative studies of folk literature from California; two were on New Mexican Spanish dialectology; one was on Spanish philology; one was on Cuban folk literature; thirteen were on Spanish folk literature, including folklore methodology; one was on general European folk literature; one was a comparative study of Spanish and Spanish American folktales; and four were in the general field of Hispanic folk literature.

Approximately two-thirds of Espinosa's studies between 1930 and 1955 were concerned with traditional Spanish ballads and folktales in Spain and America. His most exhaustive research activity from 1920 to 1945 was on the Spanish folktale, culminating in his three-volume work entitled *Cuentos populares españoles, recogidos de la tradición oral de España*. In connection with this research, Espinosa made his exhaustive study of the origins of the "Tar Baby" story, on which he published ten articles and a sixty-four-page essay in volume two of his *Cuentos*, which still represents the most definitive comparative study of this ancient folktale. He planned to publish a more detailed study of the "Tar Baby" folktale at a later date in a separate volume, but it did not materialize.

Espinosa's study of the Spanish folktale represents his major work in the field of folk literature. In the two volumes of comparative notes he discusses the history of each of the several hundred Spanish folktales studied and traces each one back to its oldest known origins in the literature of Europe and Asia. He classifies the fundamental elements of the many versions of each folktale to identify the basic motifs and to establish their distinctive and true types. In some cases he has attempted to identify their archetypes or most primitive origins. Thus his extensive comparative notes are a significant contribution to the comparative study of European folk literature. Earlier folktale studies had neglected, and many of them had omitted, the contributions of Spanish folk literature. Espinosa filled this large void and demonstrated that the Hispanic contribution is as important as that of any other part of Europe. In addition, his comparative notes on the folktales of Spain further document and confirm the conclusions that he had reached in his first comparative studies many years earlier—namely, that the various types of Spanish folk literature found in the oral tradition of the Spanish-speaking world beyond Spain, including northern New Mexico and southern Colorado, have their basic origins in Spain and were first transmitted overseas from Spain in the sixteenth and seventeenth centuries. By the same token, the traditional Spanish folktales of northern New Mexico and southern Colorado are linked to the folk literature of western Europe and to that of more ancient civilizations, transmitted through many diverse channels over the centuries.

# Espinosa's Folklore Fieldwork

The three principal Spanish-speaking regions where Aurelio M. Espinosa collected traditional Spanish folk literature were northern New Mexico and southern Colorado, the former Spanish California coastal area between San Francisco and Santa Barbara, and Spain. His folklore fieldwork in New Mexico and southern Colorado was carried out extensively and continuously between 1902 and 1911, frequently between 1912 and 1932, and on occasional short visits to the region in the 1930s, 1940s, and early 1950s. His collections in California were made between 1911 and 1919. His expedition to Spain covered a period of four and one-half months in the fall and winter of 1920.

Espinosa's background was especially to his advantage in carrying out his fieldwork in northern New Mexico and southern Colorado. He was born and reared in the region, was of local lineage, and was fluent in Spanish. He had a thorough knowledge of the Spanish dialect spoken by the older residents of the region. In addition, his extensive study of Spanish literature and his folklore research in Spain and other parts of Spanish America enabled him to acquaint his informants readily with what he was looking for and to jog their memories and thereby expand his findings in many unexpected ways.

In collecting folklore materials, Espinosa personally wrote down by hand the material as it was recited to him by the narrator, recording carefully the linguistic peculiarities of pronunciation, vocabulary, grammar, and phrasing. Occasionally he copied down the language of the narrator in phonetic script, and he later published the texts, as recited to him, both in Spanish orthography and in phonetic script. Since much of the folk literature transmitted in oral tradition is in verse, he believed that the collector of traditional Spanish folk literature should have a thorough knowledge of Spanish versification, as he himself did. He wrote: "The New Mexican ballads are on the whole versions that have undergone little change since the 16th century. The old assonances and the octosyllabic verse help us to detect the changes and to observe here and there a necessary line. But, on the whole, they present no special problem for the linguist." He added that a close analysis of the language of some of the versions of traditional ballads collected by others indicated clearly that they had been brought to America by recent Spanish immigrants or were expanded, modern versions. In his publications he strove to reflect accurately in his texts the language that his informants had used in narration and in verse. Thus his published texts are contributions to the study of both Spanish folk literature and Spanish-American dialectology.

When Espinosa began his folklore studies in the first decade of this century, the Spanish-speaking population of northern New Mexico totaled approximately 175,000, and that of southern Colorado, 50,000. His fieldwork in the region was carried out within an area that included about 150,000 Spanish-speaking people. Of these he estimated that approximately 80,000 did not speak the English language at all, though some understood a few words in English.

Throughout his published collections he describes the types of people from whom he collected folklore. In northern New Mexico and southern Colorado they represented a cross-section of the Spanish-speaking population: farmers and ranchers and their families; farm and ranch laborers; shepherds; household servants, both adults and children of all ages; and villagers of all social levels. A large number of these informants were not at all familiar with the English language, especially in the remote country districts. In the two largest centers and their environs, Albuquerque and Santa Fe, the informants were farmers, shop clerks and other workers, artisans, porters, laundry women, shopkeepers, school children, and beggars. In addition, Espinosa notes as the sources of some of his findings his own grandfather, his parents, relatives, and local friends and acquaintances. All were Spanish-surnamed residents of long standing.

In his published texts of folk literature from New Mexico and Colorado, Espinosa did not systematically give the name and age of each informant for every item collected, but he usually indicated the locality where it had been recorded. In publishing his first folktale collection in 1911, for example, he wrote: "All these folk-tales were collected during the years 1908, 1909, and 1910, directly from the mouths of the people. I heard and took down personally every folk-tale in my collection with the exception of Nos. 5, 6, 7, and 10 of those here published, and of four more (not here included), which were heard and taken down by my father in Albuquerque." A similar kind of authentication, along with linguistic and comparative notes, is found in all of Espinosa's published collections. It is clear that his primary interest was to collect and classify folklore materials as contributions to

Two New Mexican cronies in the countryside near Albuquerque, 1902. *Photograph by D. T. Duckwall, Jr., Albuquerque, courtesy of the Photograph Collection, Library of Congress.*

literature and dialectology, for comparative literary and linguistic study. The only types of folk literature for which he carefully indicates the name and age of each informant, as well as the locality in which each item was collected, are the ballad and the *décima*.

The other types of folk literature, however, such as folktales, proverbs, riddles, children's rhymes, anecdotes, sayings, prayers, and various types of short verses and poetic compositions, he found in such great abundance that he generally did not consider it essential to include details regarding the narrators. Concerning the folktales that he collected, he wrote that there were many more awaiting the patient and determined collector. In regard to proverbs and riddles, he noted, "A complete or fairly complete collection of the New Mexican Spanish proverb would be easy to compile among the Spanish pupils in the schools. . . . The same might be done with the riddles." In publishing a sampling of 632 proverbs, he added: "All the proverbs in my collection were gathered in Albuquerque and Santa Fe from less than a half dozen persons. I believe that with care and patience one could gather several thousand in New Mexico." Concerning the hundreds of short verses, called *versos* or *coplas*, he wrote: "The creative age of the *coplas* has not been ended. They are still being created, and in all probability always will be as long as Spanish is spoken in New Mexico. . . . They are recited or sung on festive occasions, at baptisms, wedding festivities, dances, and other merry-making occasions." On publishing a selection of 54 *versos* from New Mexico, he noted that before 1931 he had collected 1,250 versions.

With regard to the traditional Spanish ballads from northern New Mexico and southern Colorado that he published in 1915, on the other hand, he wrote, "Traditional Spanish ballads are no longer widely known, and it was necessary to question hundreds of persons to be able to find the few versions that I obtained. . . . Everything that sounded to me like a traditional ballad I noted down, as I visited the villages and ranches of New Mexico." His grandfather told him that when he was a child the recitation and singing of ballads, traditional and modern, were considered as a popular pastime by all and were sung almost everywhere by masters, servants, farm laborers, shepherds and beggars. The popularity of traditional Spanish ballads seems to have declined rapidly in the late nineteenth century. Such ballads were sung to him by only seven persons and he committed the melodies (called *tonadas*) to memory. Espinosa wrote: "These singers told me that they sang the ballads simply for their own pleasure and to entertain others, just as they sang any other song, accompanied by a guitar, *musiquita de boca* (harmonica), or with no accompaniment at all. In earlier days they sang the ballads to the accompaniment of a guitar, at home or at family reunions, but in the country and in the mountains the poor farm worker or shepherd sang them to the accompaniment of a very simple instrument they called *vigüela* (which also means guitar in New Mexico), made with a stick of wood, slightly curved, with a single string of sheep gut, played like a *birimbao*."

In 1911, after four years of intensive study of the Spanish dialect spoken in the region, combined with the collecting of folk literature from oral tradition, during which period he had interviewed hundreds of New Mexicans, Espinosa published an account of the status of his research up to that time. In that account he singled out twenty-one people who had provided him with folklore materials and stated that "many more" could have been mentioned. Those listed from New Mexico included four from Albuquerque, two from Santa Fe, and one each from Ranchos de Atrisco, Taos, Abiquiú, Peña Blanca, Nutrias, Los Griegos, Barelas, Bernardo, Puerto de Luna, Tierra Amarilla, and Sabinal. Colorado produced one from Conejos, one from Del Norte, and two from Trinidad.[1]

The twenty-seven versions of ten traditional ballads, twenty-five versions of modern popular ballads, and twenty-two *décimas* which he col-

A housewife baking in her outside oven, northern New Mexico, 1902. *Photograph by D. T. Duckwall, Jr., courtesy of the Photograph Collection, Library of Congress.*

lected between 1902 and 1915 and published in the latter year are accompanied in each case by the name and age of the narrator and the locality where the material was obtained. The narrators were from Albuquerque (12), Belén, Gallegos, Juan Tafoya, Peña Blanca (3), Pajarito, Puerto de Luna (3), Nutritas, Ranchos de Albuquerque, Santa Fe (2), Socorro (5), Los Padillas, Bernardo, Antón Chico, Vallecitos, Carrumpa (2), and Taos, New Mexico, and from Del Norte (2), Trinidad, Conejos, and Weston in Colorado.[2]

In his collection of 248 ballads and ballad fragments obtained from Spanish-speaking residents of northern New Mexico and southern Colorado and published in 1953, Espinosa indicated, in each case, the name and age of the informant and the place where the ballad was collected. He transcribed each item in the Spanish dialect in which it was recited or sung to him, using modern Spanish orthography.[3] The ballads were recited to him by 130 individuals, 88 males and 42 females, ranging in age from fifteen to ninety-two, with most of them in the thirty-to-eighty age group. The ballads were collected in the following sixty-one localities: Abiquiú, Alameda, Albuquerque, Alcalde, Belén, Bernalillo, Canjilón, Cañón de Jémez, Cañón de Taos, Carrizoso, Central, Cerro, Chacón, Chimayó, Cochití, Cuba, Española, Galisteo, Gallegos, Guchupange, Isleta Pueblo,

Juan Tafoya, La Joya, Las Lagunitas, Las Vegas, Leyba, Los Brazos, Los Candelarias, Los Lunas, Los Padillas, Magdalena, Nutrias, Pajarito, Pecos, Peña Blanca, Peralta, Polvadera, Pueblito, Puerto de Luna, Rio Mimbres (Faywood), Ranchitos de Taos, Ratón, Sabinal, San Juan, San Juan Pueblo, Santa Clara Pueblo, Santa Cruz, Santa Fe, Scholle, Socorro, Taos, Tomé, and Truchas in New Mexico, and Alamosa, Antonito, Conejos, Del Norte, Manassa, Pondo, Rocky Ford, and Trinidad in Colorado.

In the introduction to his 1953 collection of ballads, Espinosa cautioned that during the preceding thirty-five years New Mexico had attracted people from many parts of the world, among them Spanish-speaking people from Mexico, Central America, and even Spain. He stated: "From these Hispanic people of New Mexico I have not collected ballads, but it is possible that some of the New Mexicans who recited them to me may have learned some versions from them."[4]

The same people who recited ballads to Espinosa were also sources of other types of folklore materials; thus, a large part of his other findings was collected in the same localities listed. A number of other localities, however, are mentioned throughout his works as places where he collected folklore materials.[5]

As we have seen, early in his studies Espinosa had arrived at the conclusion that nearly all the Spanish folklore that he had collected had been transmitted originally from Spain. But published materials from Spain and Spanish America on the folktale were as yet few in number. From Spain, fewer than one hundred folktales from oral tradition had been published. Meanwhile, between 1910 and 1920, several important collections of folktales from Mexico, Puerto Rico, and the Pueblo Indians of New Mexico had been published. For serious comparative studies, a more extensive collection of folktales from Spain was very much needed. Thus, thanks to the interest of Franz Boas and the generosity of Elsie Clews Parsons, Espinosa made a folklore expedition to Spain in 1920 under the sponsorship of the American Folklore Society.

Espinosa arrived in Madrid early in July, 1920, and proceeded immediately to nearby San Rafael to consult with Ramón Menéndez Pidal in making plans for his itinerary. Menéndez Pidal not only gave Espinosa valuable advice, but also provided him with a carefully prepared folklore map of Spain which served him as a constant guide and companion. Espinosa also received useful suggestions from other friends at the Centro de Estudios Históricos in Madrid.

The American began his folklore expedition in Santander in northern Spain, where Miguel Artigas, director of the Biblioteca Menéndez y Pelayo,

Villagers passing the time of day, northern New Mexico, 1902. *Photograph by D. T. Duckwall, Jr., courtesy of the Photograph Collection, Library of Congress.*

assisted him in making local contacts. He collected his first folktales in Santander at the Casa de los Pobres, where many of the aged from all the municipalities of the province were gathered. The old people of both sexes told him many folktales from their localities. He took down about a dozen folktales. He also visited other villages neighboring Santander: Cabuérniga, Santillana, Torrelavega, and smaller ones.

Artigas advised that after his preliminary activity in Santander, Espinosa should visit the nearby mountain village of Tudanca, which was in an isolated region rich in folklore, and he made advance arrangements with his friend José María de Cossío, a landholder there, to introduce Espinosa to the villagers of the region. Accordingly, Espinosa went to Tudanca, following the mountain trails by horseback and on foot. In Tudanca and nearby Santotís, "going from house to house," often accompanied by Cossío, he collected many folktales and several ballads from the villagers. In collecting folktales and ballads among the poorer people, Espinosa offered a small sum of money, but it was never requested and rarely accepted.

After spending three days in Tudanca and Santotís, Espinosa returned to Santander, and from there he set out for the south en route to Burgos, in Castile. His friends in Santander had recommended that he spend a few days in Reinosa, at the southern edge of the province of Santander, where they were sure he would hear many folktales and ballads. In that pictur-

Mountain scene with a local woman in the foreground near Santander, Spain, in the 1930s. *Courtesy of the Ministry of Transportation, Tourism, and Communications, Madrid, Spain.*

esque town, high in the Sierra de Reinosa, he spent six days collecting folktales and ballads. One traditional ballad was sung to him by a twelve-year-old girl, Angelita Negro. From Reinosa he visited nearby Fontibre, a small village of about twenty humble abodes and fifty inhabitants near the source of the Ebro River, where he collected more folktales and some traditional *coplas* and anecdotes.

In Burgos, Espinosa remained several days, also visiting the neighboring villages of Villatorre, Plazuela de Muñó, Urbel del Castillo, and Villahoz, Salas de los Infantes, and Santo Domingo de Silos and small villages to the east such as Contreras, Covarrubias, Ontoria, Cubillos, Cuevas, Mambrillas, Hortigüela, and Barbadillo del Mercado. This was the first Castilian territory he visited, and he found ballads and folktales in abundance. This region was the locale of the famous "Leyenda de los infantes de Lara," the site of the neighboring pueblos of Lara, Campo Lara, San Millán de Lara, and the Castle of Lara. He spent three days in Salas de los Infantes, where he collected a number of ballads and folktales. From Salas he traveled by foot to the villages of Castrovido and Hacinas, where he collected several folktales and traditions relating to the well-known legend. He spent a day and a night in Barbadillo, after visiting Salas, where with the help of the village schoolmaster, Don León Abad, he collected more folktales and ballads. He then walked from Barbadillo to Santo Domingo de Silos via Contreras, a distance of seven or eight kilometers, following narrow trails through small villages for which the classic and archaic *tartanas*, or horse-drawn two-wheeled carriages, served as transportation from place to place. Here and there along the way he saw groups of villagers at work threshing wheat with their ancient wooden implements drawn by horses or oxen as in the days of Scipio Africanus. Others were winnowing the wheat with pitchforks and other primitive instruments.

Espinosa arrived at Contreras on a hot afternoon, at the very moment when a group of village farmers were about to begin their lunch, or brief afternoon rest, and several of them approached him with curiosity. Espinosa told them what he was looking for, to draw them out, and little by little his listeners responded. After three hours he left with two versions of traditional ballads and a folktale relating to the Infantes de Lara. The folktale was recited by a friendly woman, Doña Juana Martín, sixty-eight years of age, who had never traveled outside of Contreras, where she was born. It was a somewhat short, but beautiful version of a traditional folktale which dealt with some of the details of the famous legend, the prodigious birth of the seven *infantes*, the vengeance of Doña Lambra, and her death and that of Ruy Velázquez at the hands of Mudarra. It was an important find for the study of the ballad, for it contains some verses from an ancient ballad hitherto unknown in modern tradition. The two verses in question refer to Doña Lambra's abusive words to the mother of the *infantes* on their prodigious birth:

"Doña Urraca, doña Urraca, bien te puedes alabar,
que has parido siete infantes como puerca en muladar."

That evening Espinosa proceeded on foot to the Monastery of Santo Domingo de Silos. There he spent the night with the good fathers and the next day collecting folklore materials on the quiet streets.

From Burgos, Espinosa traveled to Valladolid, where he remained five days, collecting versions of the same types of folktales that he had gathered in the provinces of Santander and Burgos: picaresque tales, animal tales, tales of enchantment, accumulative tales, and so on. In the first week of September he left Valladolid for Soria, to the east of Burgos, the most easterly region of Castilian territory.

Soria was the first place he visited where the wealth of folklore material taxed his endurance. In ten days he collected about thirty of what he considered to be the most interesting folktales of his collection: some entirely new animal tales, accumulative tales, picaresque tales, and a few "Cinderella"-type tales. He collected what he referred to as his best "Juan Oso" story in the village of Blacos in the province of Soria. He also gathered traditional material in the nearby villages of Garrey, near Numancia, and in the ancient town of Calatañazor. Leaving Calatañazor, he made a long and tiresome journey to León, where he remained three days, collecting folktales both there and in the neighboring village of Villecha. Then he went on to Astorga and Porqueros, to the west, where he collected more folktales.

His next visit was to Zamora, which he found equal to Soria in abundance of folklore material. In the *barrio* of San Vicente, outside the walls of the city, he collected a dozen of the most interesting folktales in his collection. He found so much material in the city and its immediate environs that he did not have time to visit many of the nearby villages. He discovered there, as Menéndez Pidal verified in collecting ballads, that in some regions of Spain, where some modern tales and ballads are known along with the old, the local country people never confused the old traditional material with newly learned material. The woman who narrated to him some of his best versions of the "Niña sin brazos" tale also narrated modern versions of the same story, which, she said, were not old but had been learned from others. The really old versions, Espinosa writes, "were told with an easiness and charm of expression absolutely beyond the powers of any modern compiler of stories."

Toward the end of September, Espinosa left Zamora for Segovia, via Salamanca and Medina del Campo. He remained five days in Segovia and in the nearby villages of Valseca and Fuente Pelayo, where material was plentiful, although not as abundant as in Soria and Zamora. From there he went to Ávila, in the extreme south of Old Castile, where he found himself in a region as prolific in folklore as Soria and Zamora. There he found a version of the "Tar Baby" story.

After a short visit to Madrid, in October he left for Cuenca, in the eastern part of New Castile, where he remained a week. Here again he found folktales and ballads in abundance. From Cuenca he visited Metilla and Utiel, in the province of Valencia, and from there he proceeded to Granada, making his longer journeys by train and automobile.

In Granada, Espinosa's first visit was to the famous Alhambra. On leaving the Alhambra, he approached the guide on the subject of popular

Village neighbors, Avila, Spain, in the 1930s. *Courtesy of the Ministry of Transportation, Tourism, and Communications, Madrid, Spain.*

Village woman, Segovia, Spain, in the 1930s. *Courtesy of the Ministry of Transportation, Tourism, and Communications, Madrid, Spain.*

Young farmer plowing, southern Spain, 1930s. *Courtesy of the Ministry of Transportation, Tourism, and Communications, Madrid, Spain.*

folktales, and the latter replied, "Yes, I know an old gypsy who can tell you popular tales all day and all night." The next day the guide took Espinosa to the gypsy *barrio* of El Albaicín, the old Moorish quarter of Granada, opposite the Alhambra. The gypsy woman knew only two folktales worth collecting, but once in the *barrio gitano*, Espinosa easily found many more. He later visited other parts of the city of Granada. There he came in contact for the first time with Andalusian Spanish, and he wrote, "Since in all localities I took down the folktales as they were recited, the work went a little slowly at first." He also visited the nearby town of Santa Fe, and he left Granada with a sizeable collection of folktales of all kinds.

The next stop was Sevilla, where he remained ten days, collecting folktales there and at Triana, Santiponce, and Utrera. Folktales were plentiful everywhere. In some villages he often had a waiting list of people who were anxious to tell him a tale. From there he went to Córdoba, where he remained six days and collected many folktales and ballads. Most of the folktales from Córdoba, including interesting new versions, were collected in the *barrio* called El Campo de la Verdad across the Guadalquivir River from the city.

On November 20, Espinosa left Córdoba for Ciudad Real, where he remained three days. He wrote, "Ciudad Real and the country about have never been investigated in the folk-lore line." He found the region as prolific, and apparently as archaic, in its folk literature as any region in Spain. The folktales he found there, as in Soria and Zamora, were among the most interesting in his collection. At the end of November he visited Toledo, the last stop on his folklore expedition to Spain. In Toledo he walked about the ancient streets of the city "collecting folktales in its patios that actually seem to slumber in past ages." He copied down by hand all the folktales, ballads, and riddles he could find, among them one of his best "Pedro de Urdemalas" stories (prototypical of the New Mexican "Mano fashico" tales) and another story which he had heard mentioned before but had never taken down in full. A collection of some fourteen folktales from Toledo, Madridejos, and Villaluenga was the result of six days spent in Toledo. Having completed his mission, Espinosa returned to Madrid to prepare for his return to the United States. There he collected three more folktales, recited by the servants of his friend Tomás Navarro Tomás. On December 9, 1920, he left Cádiz by ship for New York, from which he returned to California.[6]

As in the case of his collections in the Spanish Southwest, Espinosa indicates that the folktales he collected in Spain were published to the best of his ability exactly as they were recited to him. He adds, "I personally copied down in my own handwriting all the stories in my collection, with the sole exception of the few I published [from Asturias] which were collected by Sr. [Eduardo] Martínez Torner [in 1912, and turned over to Espinosa by Menéndez Pidal] and which carry his name. Therefore these folktales will also be useful for linguistic studies, especially with regard to syntax and morphology."[7]

During the five months he spent collecting folklore throughout the peninsula, Espinosa visited most of the regions of Spain with the exception of Galicia, Aragón, Catalonia, and some of the regions of the Portuguese-Spanish border. He visited Santander, Palencia, Burgos, Valladolid, Soria, León, Zamora, Segovia, Ávila, Cuenca, Granada, Sevilla, Córdoba, Ciudad Real, Toledo, Madrid, and Zaragoza. He collected folktales in the cities, towns, and villages of all of these provinces and from people from five other provinces that he did not visit: Jaén, Málaga, Cáceres, Guadalajara, and Pontevedra. He collected a total of 302 folktales.[8] Of these, he published 280 in his *Cuentos populares españoles*. The specific locality in which each of the folktales was collected is indicated in each case.

Espinosa found that there was not a single region in Spain that he

Townsman passing the time of day in Toledo, Spain, in the 1930s. *Courtesy of the Ministry of Transportation, Tourism, and Communications, Madrid, Spain.*

visited where traditional folk literature could not be found in abundance. He lamented the fact that since the materials at hand were so abundant large collections of traditional folktales and legends had not already been made. His extensive collection made on his field trip to Spain provided a major resource for advancing the comparative study of Spanish folk literature.[9]

4

# Espinosa's Folklore Concepts and Research Methodology

Aurelio M. Espinosa approached the study of folklore primarily as a student of comparative folk literature. From that point of view he studied the literary, linguistic, historical, and geographical relationships of folk tradition. To describe his folklore concepts and his research methodology within the broad field of folklore, it is necessary to define precisely the branch of folklore on which he chose to focus his research.

In defining the world *folklore*, Espinosa stated that one must distinguish between folklore itself, that is to say, the materials of folklore, and the science of folklore. Folklore itself is popular knowledge. It is the accumulated store of what mankind has experienced, learned, and practiced across the ages as popular and traditional knowledge, as distinguished from technical, or so-called scientific, knowledge. Folklore consists of the beliefs, customs, superstitions, riddles, proverbs, songs, myths, legends, tales, ritualistic ceremonies, magic, witchcraft, and all other manifestations and practices of primitive and "ignorant people," the so-called "common people" in a civilized society. It has deep roots, and its traces do not disappear when peoples reach a high state of culture. Folklore may be said to be a true and direct expression of the mind of primitive man.

The science of folklore is that branch of human knowledge that collects, classifies, and studies in a scientific way the materials of popular knowledge, or folklore materials, in order to interpret the life and culture of peoples across the ages. Folklore crystallizes and perpetuates the forms of culture through which we can often explain the motifs, the spirit, the meaning of culture. The science of folklore therefore contributes greatly to the history and interpretation of human ideas. It is an important branch of human knowledge, an auxiliary science to anthropology, ethnology, history, psychology, sociology, religion, and literature.

Folklore as a science has followed two principal and different lines: (1) the study of popular beliefs and superstitions, including magic, primitive religion and ritual, folk festivals, and kindred traditions; and (2) the collection, classification, and study of folktales and other kinds of folk literature.

Each of these two important and fundamental fields of folkloristic investigation has practically become a distinct branch of science. The second of these fields, the branch of folklore that deals with the popular and traditional literature of primitive and modern peoples, is of capital importance for the study of the origins and development of European literature.[1] That second field of folklore investigation was the focus of Espinosa's research.

It is not necessary to discuss here all of the schools of folklore, or the various theories and interpretations of folklore materials developed over the years in the attempt to understand the origin, composition, transmission, and diffusion of folktales, some of which have been greatly modified and revised by modern folklorists since the turn of the century—for example, the mythological school, the Oriental school, and the anthropological school. The school of folklore that has inspired and influenced the concepts and research methodology of most modern students of folk literature is the Finnish school. Espinosa leaned more toward what he referred to as the neo-Oriental school. The Finnish and neo-Oriental schools of folklore are both modern developments of the Oriental school. They both consider India as the probable place of origin of a large number of the folktales and traditions that are found in Europe and in all countries of European acculturation, but they do not consider India as the only source of folktales or as the ultimate source.[2]

The Finnish school, under the leadership of Antti Aarne (1867–1925), Kaarle Krohn (1863–1935), and Walter Anderson (1885–1963), has as its chief aim the reconstruction of archetypes, or primitive, fundamental types of folktales. Espinosa wrote, "The work of the Finnish scholars is of the greatest importance because they have isolated the most stable and widely distributed elements or fundamental motifs of folktales in order to define the types and archetypes." Aarne and Krohn developed and advanced the historic-geographic method of investigation, and Anderson and others developed the method further.

The neo-Oriental school continues the work of the Oriental school along modern scientific lines and has much in common with the Finnish school. The leaders of this school are Americans and Europeans, including the German folklorist Johannes Bolte (1858–1937) and the American anthropologists Franz Boas (1858–1942) and Elsie Clews Parsons (1875–1941). Espinosa wrote: "The Neo-Orientalists study folklore in all of its branches, in relation to anthropology, history, psychology, and literature, and attempt to explain folklore as a social phenomenon, that is, as a functioning element of life and culture. They stress the relations between comparative folklore and comparative literature." In his study and classification of Spanish folktales, Espinosa borrowed the basic concepts and research methodology of both of these schools of folklore, but he was especially influenced by the latter.[3]

It should be noted at this point that, along with the folktale, the other type of Spanish folk literature that attracted Espinosa's greatest scholarly interest was the traditional ballad. These two types represent the major forms of traditional Spanish narrative folk literature. Traditional Spanish ballads represent *par excellence* the national popular narrative poetry of Spain. They have an importance and a literary history that surpass the ballad tradition of any other nation. The Spanish folktale, on the other hand, is a part of European literature in general. As indicated above, the traditional Spanish ballads that Espinosa collected from the oral tradition of New Mexico, Colorado, and California, and published with comparative notes, are the most extensive collections from those regions that have been made.

In his study of the Spanish ballad in Spain and Spanish America, Espinosa's principal literary influences were Spain's and the world's greatest modern authorities on the traditional Spanish ballad—Marcelino Menéndez y Pelayo, the leading literary scholar of Spain in the late nineteenth and early twentieth centuries, and his successor, Ramón Menéndez Pidal. Although Espinosa published important works on the traditional Spanish ballad, he deferred to his contemporary and close friend Menéndez Pidal as the authority on the subject. In fact, most of his Spanish ballad studies include an introductory statement indicating that they were modest contributions to the latter's research. The two hundred versions of Spanish ballads that he collected from oral tradition in Spain in 1920 were presented by him to Menéndez Pidal as a contribution to the latter's ballad research. Yet there was very little in the vast literary history and bibliography relating to the Spanish ballad with which he was not familiar. A good example of this is his study "Romances de Puerto Rico," published in 1918.[4] In that study Espinosa analyzes thirty-six Spanish ballads from the oral tradition of Puerto Rico, collected in 1914–15 by J. Alden Mason, many of them traditional Spanish ballads transmitted from Spain to America in the sixteenth and seventeenth centuries in the memories of early colonists and soldiers. He classifies and gives the literary history and historiography of each ballad and compares the common characteristics and variations of the same ballads as found in different regions in Spain from which the colonists came to America, and the different periods when they came, thus explaining in part the great discrepancies that are found in the modern versions found in America. Of Espinosa's dozen-odd publications on Spanish ballads in America that appeared during the years from 1915 to 1953, this one is singled out here as an interesting work of literary history. Others are more important as original contributions to folk literature or as carefully edited collections of texts.

Espinosa's comparative study of the Spanish folktale, his *Cuentos populares españoles*, was the center of his research activity and writing from 1930 to 1945. That study, which presents his general and specific folklore principles and theories and his folklore research methodology, has taken its place as the most important existing published study on the classification of the Spanish folktale. It is an essential guide for the comparative study of the Spanish folktale in relation to that of Spanish America and other Spanish-speaking regions of the world, and it is a significant contribution to the comparative study of the folktale tradition of Europe. The study of the folktale continues to attract great interest among folklore scholars throughout the world, but the classification of folktales still constitutes a problem widely discussed among folklorists that has not yet been definitively resolved.

Espinosa's folklore concepts and methodology, as noted earlier, follow those of the Finnish school of folklore investigation—the historic-geographic approach—modified by what he referred to as the neo-Oriental school. The historic-geographic method was developed during the late nineteenth century by Julius and Kaarle Krohn and effectively presented by the latter in his *Die folkloristiche Arbeitsmethode* (1926). It was Kaarle Krohn who first made systematic use of this method for the study of the folktale; it has also been applied to the study of the legend, the riddle, and the ballad. The basic assumption is that each tale has its own history and must be investigated independently. During most of the nineteenth century some folklore scholars attempted on theoretical grounds and without a thorough study of the tales themselves to answer the questions of the origin and meaning of folktales. Those who follow the historic-geographic method consider it essential that the investigator have available the largest possible number of versions of a given folktale before attempting to break it down into its basic elements—its motifs—and assigning it to an original tale-type. Also, general conclusions about the origin and migration of all tales, or of great groups of them, must await the accumulation of the most detailed treatment possible of many tale-types.

In the classification of folktales, the term *motif* is defined as any one of the parts or elements into which a folktale can be analyzed. In order to be a real part of a tradition, an element must have something about it that is more than commonplace and that will make people remember and repeat it. The term *tale-type* is used to designate narratives, no matter how complex or simple, capable of maintaining an independent existence in tradition. Some of the longer tale-types may contain dozens of motifs, and others, like certain anecdotes or animal stories, may consist of a single narrative motif, in which tale-type and motif are identical. It is usually possible to determine without great difficulty whether a particular narrative belongs or does not belong to a certain type, but there are often borderline cases in which there seems to be confusion between tale-types or in which a narrative has only a slight resemblance to a particular type. In brief, in the view of those who follow the historic-geographic method, the only way in which a tale-type can be formulated is to examine many variants of the type and then to study the striking resemblances and note the common characteristics. The investigator then brings together as many versions of the tale having similar characteristics as possible, and eventually he is able to make a satisfactory statement about the contents of the tale as an entity—that is, to determine its history, with a beginning in time and place, and the changes it has undergone in the course of its transmission. It is a problem of historical reconstruction.[5]

The neo-Oriental school, with which Espinosa identified himself, views the study of folktales in broader geographic perspective. Of course, the neo-Orientalists view them as tales, comparing them with those of all parts of the world, seeking their origin, and attempting to discover their true genealogy and evolution throughout the history of different peoples; at the same time, however, they examine to the greatest extent possible the ideas, customs, and culture of the primitive and modern peoples from whom folktales emanate. A traditional theme is studied in both written and oral literature, with full attention to the history of the known contacts of different peoples with one another. In this context, within the framework of the historic-geographic method, all of the versions of a tale that can be gathered are studied, their lineage is examined, and on the basis of the level of culture of the people from whom the tale was transmitted, its origin, history, and diffusion are established. Espinosa's studies demonstrated that in the classification of European folktales a more thorough study of Oriental sources was needed and that Spain, as the channel of transmission of many tales to other parts of Europe, was of greater importance than was generally assumed by students of European folklore.[6] He pointed out, however, that although it is an undeniable fact that an immense body of folktales and traditions were introduced to Europe from India, and in some cases it has been possible to confirm the Indian origin of a tradition, this is not definite proof that the legend does not go back to a previous era, and did not proceed from another people. He noted that some folktales and legends have been studied which precede Indian literature, and go back to Buddhist tradition, which greatly influenced the folk literature of India; but that even Buddhist tradition cannot be said to be the first source, since Buddha himself states that stories contained in his counsels were from earlier tradition. Espinosa wrote, "In short, one of the problems of the folklorist is to verify the most remote origin of a tradition; but surely even the earliest one discovered may not necessarily be the oldest form of the legend." [7]

In his *Cuentos*, Espinosa cites sources that show that Spain was the channel through which a rich body of Oriental tales and legends was transmitted to other countries of Europe. Some of the first important translations of ancient tales from the Orient were the works of Spaniards who wrote in Latin or Old Spanish in the twelfth century. In the thirteenth century an Arabic collection of animal stories, derived from a sixth-century Persian work containing some tales taken from ancient Indian sources, was translated into Spanish. Other collections of tales of Indian origin, which reached Spain via Arabic versions, were translated into Spanish in the thirteenth and fourteenth centuries. Aesop's *Fables* were translated into Spanish in the fifteenth century. In the sixteenth century Spanish translations of Boccaccio appeared, along with other collections of folktales and legends, but these were mostly of literary transmission and were separated more and more from the truly popular, oral tradition.

But literary sources, Espinosa emphasizes, were not the only means whereby traditional Oriental folktales and legends were transmitted to Spain and from there to other parts of Europe. Arabs and Jews lived for many centuries in Spain, and since they left a strong influence on Hispano-Christian culture, they undoubtedly left much of their folklore. He affirms that there is ample evidence that many of the folktales he collected from oral tradition in Spain in 1920 originated in India, transmitted directly by Arabs and Jews through many centuries of oral tradition in Spain. He ventures to say, for example, that since a papyrus preserved in Saint Petersburg that corresponds to Egypt's twelfth dynasty, or 3500 B.C., contains a story relating the travels of a shipwrecked mariner which is surprisingly similar to the *Odyssey* and to the *Sendebar* of India (which reached Spain through Arabic versions and was translated into Spanish in the thirteenth century), it would not be farfetched to suggest that a particular Spanish folktale, collected in Spain from modern oral tradition, might well have as its source an Iberian or Phoenician tale transmitted directly by oral tradition. The Phoenicians established colonies in Iberia in the eleventh century B.C. and in the following century founded Cádiz and Málaga, the latter becoming one of the most important commercial centers of the Mediterranean. Espinosa, generalizing on the course of history, adds, "Empires, languages, and civilizations disappear, but people, their customs, their ideas, their legends and their tales, persist, even though they may undergo important modifications from generation to generation."[8]

Espinosa concluded that the three most important problems presented in the study and classification of folktales were: (1) their origin: their earliest sources and their evolution, whether from a single or a multiple source, resulting from ethnic factors; (2) their reason for being: the causes of their origin and the ideas of the people concerned, resulting from their primitive or current history; and (3) their comparative study: the study of the transmission of tales and legends from people to people, their evolution in passing from one people to another, and the relation of these developments to literary themes.[9]

The first attempt at a classification of folktales was Antti Aarne's *Verzeichnis der Märchentypen*, published in 1910. In 1928, after Aarne's death, it was republished in English translation, with additions by Stith Thompson, as *Types of the Folktale*. In 1913 and 1932, Johannes Bolte and George Polívka published their epoch-making work *Anmerkungen zu den Kinder- und Hausmärchen der Brüder Grimm*, in five volumes, in which they classified the Grimm tales and their European variants, following in general the methods used by Aarne and Thompson. Bolte is described by folklorists as "the greatest of all students of the folktale in Germany, and perhaps of the world."[10] Bolte and Polívka added little, however, to the problem of the specific classification of the types. When Espinosa was preparing his two-volume study of Spanish folktales as part of his *Cuentos*, students of the folktale generally followed Aarne's catalog of so-called folktale types as their basic guide. In the 1930's, Thompson attacked the problem from a somewhat different angle. After many years of research in bringing together the apparently independent and fundamental elements or motifs of folktales, he published his five-volume *Motif-Index of Folk-Literature*. Espinosa stated in 1935, "This admirable and we hope almost complete catalog of what the author calls single motifs, is a great step forward in our classification problem. . . . On the whole, the word motif has in Thompson's index an exactness in meaning that the word type in Aarne-Thompson and in Bolte-Polívka does not have . . . , but its defects are obvious the moment we attempt to define a folktale motif, or single element."[11] Acknowledging that the above three works "will probably be the standard guides for the classification of the types for many years to come," he found them to be incomplete and unsatisfactory. The defects in their classification of folktales he attributed in general to limited geographic perspective and to the history of their formulation.

First of all, Espinosa pointed out that after the appearance of the first series of folktales by the Grimms in 1812, German scholars studied them with the belief that only the Germanic people possessed such popular narratives. [12] The so-called mythological school of folklore believed the Grimm tales to be the last remnants of Aryan mythology and maintained that the Germans were the only Europeans who knew them. This theory gave them an unwarranted importance, and even when by Espinosa's time it was known that folktales similar to many of those in the Grimm collections were to be found in all parts of Europe, scholars often compared them only to the Grimm variants. Some readers even believed that the Grimm folktales in translation had spread them through Europe. For this reason the Grimm variants have often been considered as the European types.

Espinosa pointed out that well-known investigators, such as Theodor Benfey in his epoch-making *Panchatantra*, Victor Chauvin in his *Bibliographie des ouvrages arabes*, Emmanuel Cosquin in his *Les Contes indiens et l'Occident*, and Bolte and Polívka in their *Anmerkungen*, speak of and refer to the Grimm variants as types, even though they cite numerous versions from all parts of Europe and the Orient. They set out to study the Grimm versions, and it is these versions that they analyze and develop into elements or motifs. Espinosa commented, "I do not pretend in any way to belittle the epoch-making *Anmerkungen* of Bolte-Polívka. In my own comparative study of Spanish folktales . . . I have made use daily of the bibliographies and notes of these scholars. My only objection is to the theory that the Grimm versions are types, and that they have often followed such a theory. Often they speak of the Germanic types, rather than the Grimm types, meaning by that the types found in Aarne-Thompson." [13]

Although the Aarne-Thompson catalog took into consideration the criticisms made of treating the Grimm versions as types, Espinosa stated that it was only necessary to make a random study of any fifty to one hundred or more European and Oriental versions of the so-called types, or groups of related types, found in the Aarne-Thompson catalog to see that it is a catalog of German types, or at best of Northern and Central European ones, and not of general types.

Despite such reservations, in his study of the Spanish folktale Espinosa's model was the monumental Bolte-Polívka study. [14] In 1934 he referred to Bolte-Polívka as "a model and guide for the detailed classification of the types of folktales of any region or country." He added, "Because many of the Grimm tales are versions of types that are quite well known in the general

European tradition, the work of Bolte and Polívka is overall the most important study that has been made to date on the classification of Occidental tales, on the basis of their actual constituent elements. The authors also cite and study literary versions from Asia and the Occident, but they do not attempt to establish theoretical primitive types or definitive ancient sources." [15]

Espinosa believed that the latter objective was an important one in folktale research, and he was deeply impressed by new and suggestive studies by some European folklorists of the Finnish school that appeared in the 1920s and 1930s which aimed to establish the fundamental types, the archetypes or primitive forms of tales. He wrote: "Walter Anderson, in his two works *Kaiser und Abt* and *Der Schwank von Alten Hildebrand*, has made studies of this type which are models of erudition and sound scholarship. . . . A definite classification of folk tales into their fundamental types can not be made until a large part of the supposed types have been studied in the manner done by Anderson on the two themes cited above." [16] Espinosa considered Kurt Ranke's *Die drei Brüder*, published in 1935, as another model of this kind of detailed comparative study of a single folktale type.

Anderson, in his *Kaiser und Abt*, studied 562 versions of a single folktale, the so-called tale of "The Three Questions of the King," and established over a dozen definite European types and four outstanding Oriental types. He was able to establish with a great degree of probability the geographical diffusion of the tale, and to identify one of the oldest versions as a primitive archetype, or *baustein*, which, although still tentative, could be properly called an archetype. Anderson used Kaarle Krohn's geographic method, by which the largest possible number of versions of a given theme are brought together, the elements or motifs of all are cataloged, and the types are established. In this process, no greater importance is given to old or literary versions than to modern versions. The independent elements or motifs are listed by letters of the alphabet and their variants as A1, A2, A3, B1, B2, B3, and so on. The types are established on the basis of the statistical superiority of identical or nearly identical versions, although other factors may often be considered.

This method was followed by Espinosa in his study of the "Tar Baby" story. He studied 318 versions of the tale, including twelve from Spain; and the twelve fundamental types of the story, with their variants, that he established for the different countries and regions seem to be quite definitive. He concluded that the oldest known version of the story is from India (*Jataka* 55) and that it traveled from there to Europe and Africa and then to America, principally by way of Spain. Not all folklorists have accepted his conclusions, but many have, including Kaarle Krohn.[17] Espinosa cautioned that it is not yet possible to ascertain the results and definitive value of these studies for the science of folklore, but he believed that there is no other scientific way to separate fundamental types from each other. It was his conviction that the definite classification of popular tales in their fundamental types will not be achieved until a large number of the supposed types have been studied in this manner.[18]

Espinosa affirmed that in general application it was an error to assume that any single version can establish a type. He stated, however, that this does not mean that any given individual version may not be a type, indicating that some versions are perfect examples of a type, others are imperfect examples, and others are mixed types. In short, in tradition anything can happen; a mixed type can become established in a locality as a new type and will then become a truly original type like any other definite type. It was his view that in attempting to establish the types of the folktale, the first task is the elimination of the extraneous elements or motifs, as these are the elements that tradition picks up, so to speak, as a given folktale is transmitted across the ages and that must be discarded to enable one to establish the primitive, fundamental types, from which one may venture to establish an archetype. He pointed out, for example, that in choosing a large group of supposed versions of a determined type, taken from the bibliographies already prepared by others, it sometimes happens that their study reveals that some correspond to entirely different types, and that others are literary versions that have no value for comparative studies.

Espinosa concluded that the motifs—the most elemental, and simple, as well as some dominant motifs or episodes—are found in tales that are very diverse in character, and that therefore the tale type must be determined not by the presence of this or that fundamental motif but by the presence of a group of fundamental motifs, especially combined to develop a determined plot that is adjusted to a definite plan in order, character, manner, and so on. He wrote that all this can be accomplished up to a certain point by studying all the known versions of a specific theme, but perhaps never in a definite or certain manner. As the ancient and modern tales often include myths, legends, and other traditions, mixed in and developed in a manner that is alien to the original tale as such, the problem of making a definitive classification, even in the case of a special group of similar or related tales, always presents great difficulties.[19]

In the comparative study of folktales, either to establish the fundamental types of modern oral tradition or to determine the archetypes or primitive forms, Espinosa agreed with Anderson that literary forms should not be disregarded when their form and style indicate that they do not come from traditional sources. He noted, "Anderson and his colleagues study them along with those from oral tradition, but do not give greater value to a literary version over one collected from oral tradition." [20] On this point, Espinosa stated: "The people do not confuse, as some believe, a popular and traditional tale or ballad with a version from a literary source or one popularized from such a source, no matter how similar they may be. The traditional folk tale collected today from oral tradition derives in most cases from very ancient sources, prior to the forms preserved in literature. It is a matter of the means of diffusion and transmission, and the versions found in modern oral tradition preserve, in general, the primitive popular forms with more fidelity than the literary ones." [21]

Espinosa's opinion on this point was also supported by Krohn, who wrote, "In very few cases do literary sources suffice. An ancient text presents a variant of real value, but it is only one of many that already circulated at that date in a determined region, while a larger number of modern oral versions from the same region provides us with the possibility of establishing a normal or typical version more faithful to the primitive form than the literary text." Krohn demonstrated that it already had been proven in various concrete cases that versions are found in oral tradition that are more similar, in some aspects, to the primitive form than the literary versions, noting that although Anderson in his *Kaiser und Abt* had presented a notable case of the importance of an ancient literary variant, with the help of this variant he was able to find also two modern oral versions more faithful to the original form. Thus, Krohn concluded, "If the literary versions are as necessary to establish the original form of a tale as those of oral tradition, the question as to whether or not the tale was first in written form has no practical value for the investigator." [22]

Espinosa concluded that in general there are in European tradition three classes or groups of folktales: (1) those that originated in the Orient, (2) those that are composed of motifs or elements that are Oriental but that have been rearranged to form the types known in the Occident, and (3) those almost entirely of Occidental elaboration.

Examples of the many folktales that originated in the Orient are the "Tar Baby" story, which, from the Indian version of the "Giant with the Matted Hair" of *Jataka* 55 to the modern Negro versions from our southern States, has remained practically unchanged in its fundamental elements or motifs; "The Tale of the Twelve Words of Truth"; "The Story of the Master-thief," of Herodotus; and "The Three Hunchbacks." In practically all of the tales that are composed of Oriental motifs or elements rearranged to form

Occidental types—such as "The Grateful Dead," "The Maid Without Hands," and the "Taming of the Shrew"—those motifs are combined anew and put in a new setting to conform with new ideas and customs in the Occidental world. Of entirely or almost entirely Occidental elaboration are such tales as the "Don Juan" legend, "Cinderella," "Snow White," and numerous doctrinal tales.[23]

By including the analysis of a great number of groups of related tales, Espinosa's comparative study of Spanish folktales enabled him to establish, with a great degree of accuracy, over one thousand different types of Spanish and European folktales. Of these, some five hundred were new in the sense that they did not appear in the Aarne-Thompson catalog.[24] This convinced him of the need, often repeated by him, for more studies of this kind for every group of related folktales before a more adequate catalog of the tale-type can be prepared. It should be noted here that Aarne and Thompson's *The Types of the Folktale* and Thompson's *Motif-Index* have been revised and updated, the former in 1961 and the latter in 1955–58, with the view of broadening their regional coverage and their value for comparative folktale study. In these revisions, Spanish folktale types and motifs receive a bit more attention; some of Espinosa's findings have been incorporated, and attempts have been made to accept some of the criticisms of others. Thompson consulted Espinosa in the preparation of the revised works and acknowledged his suggestions.

Espinosa's studies were a landmark in the investigation of the Spanish and Spanish-American, as well as the European, folktale. Stanley L. Robe has stated, "No comparable text has been published since the second edition of the *Cuentos populares espanoles* appeared in 1946–1947. The strongest feature of his methodology is that he draws his analysis from the tales themselves rather than assimilate a regional index into the framework of a larger classification device, as has often been the case in the preparation of [Aarne-Thompson's] *Types of the Folktale*." He adds, referring to Espinosa's lifelong New Mexican folklore studies: "Actually most of the scholarship based on versions collected in New Mexico is contained in the copious notes that fill the second and third volumes of Espinosa's *Cuentos populares espa-ñoles*. . . . He [Espinosa] has set the direction for later studies of the material, so that the more lengthy studies all bear the stamp of his procedures and interests."[25]

Since the publication of the *Cuentos*, collections of versions of Spanish folktales from Spain and Spanish America have increased in number, both before Espinosa's death in 1958 and notably since that time, although more from Spanish America than from Spain. But few new comparative studies of significance have appeared. Unfortunately for the general reader in this country, Espinosa's *Cuentos* has not been translated into English.[26] Its reading is a rewarding adventure in following the universal wanderings of folktales throughout history, carried from time immemorial in the long memory of the human mind.

In 1951, Espinosa published an interesting and challenging statistical comparison of Spanish and Spanish-American folktales.[27] Among other observations, he listed some of the many problems not yet definitely solved by folklorists in interpreting the origins, transmission, and elusive meaning of folktales. In his quest to ascertain which tales originated in the Old World and which in the New, and whether they originated among Spanish-speaking people, Indians, Negroes, or others, Espinosa states that we will be closer to an answer only when a much more determined effort is made by folklorists to assemble, and study carefully, a larger number of versions and variants of the tales in the Old World and the New.

In comparing Spanish and Spanish-American folktales, Espinosa defines Spanish-American folktales as follows: "In Spanish America, linguistic unity prevails in most regions, but there are some important exceptions. With respect to folktales, we use the term Spanish-American to denote folk tales collected from Spanish-speaking peoples in regions where the native languages are extinct or on the way to extinction. But we also call Spanish-American folk tales those collected from regions for the most part racially Indian, where the people or most of them speak Spanish, but have not absorbed completely what we might call European Spanish culture or even colonial Spanish culture."[28]

These two groups of Spanish-American folktales he defines more precisely as (1) those collected from Spanish-speaking people, racially Spanish or of mixed Spanish and Indian blood, in regions where the fundamental elements of Spanish culture are continued or have been completely absorbed, and where the language, religion, customs, and traditions of Spain are still dominant in spite of the many influences that may have penetrated from other sources; and (2) those collected from Spanish-speaking people also, but from regions predominantly Indian racially and where Spanish culture has not taken very deep root in spite of the widespread use of Spanish as the language of the community. Among the latter group, native Indian folktales narrated in Spanish are by no means rare, and Indian customs and ways of life prevail. Espinosa states that just how definitely indigenous some of the apparently non-Spanish elements found in many of the folktales of this region are is a complex problem not yet resolved by folklorists, since there are often confusing similarities in Spanish and Indian folkloristic elements.

In his statistical comparison of the Spanish-American folktales of the first group, Espinosa found that 80 to 90 percent of their subjects reflect peninsular Spanish types or their variants. Sometimes the types of variants have changed considerably, but at other times they are almost identical, even in the sequence of the elements involved. In this group he found that native Indian elements or those imported from Africa in certain Caribbean countries are not very significant. He notes, however, that his comparisons are based on the materials available from Spain in 1951, and that although abundant, they cannot be considered completely adequate for definitive comparative studies.

In summarizing the historical development of Spanish folk literature in the regions of Spanish America included in the first group, Espinosa indicated that the definite and permanent patterns—those that control the minds and the behavior of most Hispanic and Hispanized peoples—were probably established between the sixth and the sixteenth centuries, and that the history of Spanish folklore spanned much more than one thousand years. He stated that the folk tales that came from Spain to Spanish America four hundred, three hundred, two hundred years ago, or even more recently, came in well-established forms, to judge from the identical and almost identical types so frequently found in Spain and Spanish America. "At certain periods of their development and transmission," Espinosa wrote, "Spanish folk tales, perhaps all folk tales, seem to appear in definite fixed forms. In Spain and Spanish-America all folklore materials, traditional ballads, riddles, proverbs, nursery rhymes, etc., and apparently also folk tales, tend to remain in the once established forms. New inventions and new forms based on the traditional ones often appear, it is true, but the older forms do not disappear easily. And what is more, the people do not confuse the old and well-established types with the native inventions or foreign imported forms."[29] He added that a comparison of the relative vitality of Spanish and Spanish-American versions of folktales would be of great interest, but that to achieve it, the collection and study of a greater number of versions of each of the types that occur would be required.

With regard to the folktales in the second group—collected from people who speak Spanish in regions where the native Indian population predominates, where Spanish culture has not taken very deep roots and where native Indian folktales recited in Spanish are by no means rare—Espinosa's statistical comparisons indicate that Spanish types and variants appear in 50 to 55 percent of the versions studied—quite a different percentage from the 80 to 90 percent in the case of the first group. He concludes from those percentages that, although the materials available from the second group are not yet abundant, the native cultures of America are still a living and powerful factor, in spite of the assimilative power of a pervading Spanish and Spanish-American culture and the ever-changing modern patterns of culture. It was his view, however, that the Indians of all regions know more tales than they are willing to tell to the enthusiastic non-Indian collector.[30]

Espinosa concluded his study "Spanish and Spanish-American Folktales" with the statement, "Spanish-America, in general, although populated by peoples of different ethnic groups—even the population of Spain does not represent one ethnic group—, has developed and continues a civilization that is basically and fundamentally Spanish."[31] That essay represents his last important statement regarding some of his basic theories on the influence of Spanish folk literature in America.

# PART TWO

# Traditional Spanish Folk Literature in New Mexico and Colorado

by

Aurelio M. Espinosa

# Spanish Tradition in America

"They Speak the Argentine Language Here!" An American Folklorist in Spain. Pito Salces. The *Guitarristas* of Calatañazor. Customs, Beliefs, and Superstitions.

Folklore embraces all branches of popular knowledge that are in a great measure distinct from technical science. Therefore, we might define folklore as the direct expression of the psychology of mankind from its primitive origins to the present day, transmitted across the ages without the help of technical science. Those traditional elements or factors of civilization that are an important part of the spirit of peoples, that are transmitted from generation to generation, spontaneously, instinctively so to speak, without the aid of government—in fact, government itself is often tradition—are all important in cultural studies. In these elements of human behavior that constitute tradition, the character, the feelings, the manners and customs, the religious beliefs, the artistic powers, and, in short, the ideas of people are documented.

The science of folklore is that branch of human knowledge and investigation that collects, classifies, and studies with scientific method the materials of popular knowledge in their broadest sense in order to interpret as far as possible the life and the spirit of peoples across the ages.[1]

The persistence of Spanish tradition in a great part of America is so remarkable—in fact, so obvious—that those who live today in the midst of it often fail to realize its importance. This point is well illustrated by the following anecdote which was told to me on very good authority: In the year 1920 an Argentine training ship visited Spain. It first stopped at Cádiz. One of the sailors, on landing, heard the newsboys on the shore speaking Spanish and in great excitement shouted to his comrades: "¡Che! ¡Aquí hablan argentino!" ("Hey, there! They speak the Argentine language here!")

The scope of Spanish tradition in America is of such magnitude that the first attempts at portraying it can be very perplexing. When serious studies in New Mexican Spanish folklore and dialectology were begun in this country in the first decade of the present century, already sufficient comparative materials had been published in Spain and Spanish America to convince any serious investigator of the reality of Spanish tradition in New Mexico. As a result of comparative study, it is now a well-established fact that the folklore of New Mexico is for the most part of peninsular Spanish origin. The peninsular ballad tradition, for example, is so strong in New Mexico that not only Spanish-speaking New Mexicans but even a few Pueblo Indians of the Rio Grande Valley recite and sing old Spanish ballads today.

The extent and the vitality of Spanish tradition in New Mexico became clear to me after travel and study in Spain. In 1920 I made a folklore expedition to Spain, under the auspices of the American Folklore Society, for the purpose of collecting ballads, folktales, and other traditional materials. Everywhere, and very conspicuously in Old and New Castile, I met the same folktales, the same ballads, the same riddles and proverbs, the same language, of course, and even the same manners, customs, superstitions, and beliefs that I had previously found in New Mexico. Was this New Mexico or was it Spain? The answer is quite clear: it was the spirit of Spain, embodied in tradition and portrayed through the language and the religion of Castile. In the following paragraphs I will summarize a few of the most important personal experiences of my folklore expedition in Spain that amply illustrate the persistence of Spanish tradition in New Mexico.

I began my fieldwork in Santander with the help of Miguel Artigas, the noted Spanish literary critic, at that time the librarian of the Biblioteca Menéndez y Pelayo in Santander. On the first day of my visit, the poet López Argüello told me a folktale he had heard as a child from his mother, "La pega y sus peguitos" (The magpie and her young ones), practically the same story that I had heard from my mother in Colorado thirty years before and had published eight years before meeting Señor López Argüello. The story is of Oriental source and is found in the *Panchatantra*. The Spanish version found in New Mexico is quite similar to the version from Spain. There is nothing extraordinary about the similarity of the two Spanish versions in this case. My mother had heard it from her grandmother, and the grandmother had come directly from Spain to New Mexico in the last decade of the eighteenth century. Both versions are from northern Spain and only three generations apart. But we have other versions from New Mexico, the history of which we do not know, and they are very similar to the other two. Spanish tradition in New Mexico does not change much more, apparently, in five, six, or more generations than it does in three. My own Spanish version, directly transmitted to New Mexico by my mother's grandmother, which I published in 1912, is given below in English translation:

> Once there was a mother-pigeon that lived in the mountains where she had

a nest in an oak tree, with four young ones. One day a coyote came and said to her, "Friend pigeon, give me one of your little ones." "Indeed I will not," the pigeon replied. "If you don't give me one of them, I'll cut down the oak tree and eat them all," said the coyote. And forthwith the coyote began to strike the tree with his tail. The poor pigeon became frightened, threw down one of her little ones, and the coyote ate it. Shortly afterwards baldhead (the bittern) arrived, and when he saw the mother-pigeon weeping bitterly, he asked her, "Why are you weeping?" "How can I help weeping?" replied the pigeon. "The coyote came and ate one of my young ones." "And why did you give it to him?" asked baldhead. To this the pigeon replied, "Because he told me that if I didn't give it to him, he would cut down the oak tree with his tail and eat them all." "Very well," said baldhead, "but if he comes again, don't give him anything. And if he says that he will cut down the oak tree just tell him, 'It takes a sharp axe to cut an oak tree and not a coyote's tail, you fool!'" Baldhead then went away. Coyote appeared soon and said to the mother-pigeon, "Give me one of your little ones." "Indeed I will not," replied the pigeon. And coyote said again, "If you don't give it to me, I'll cut down the tree with my tail and eat them all." "It takes a sharp axe to cut down an oak tree and not a coyote's tail, you fool!" replied the pigeon. Coyote became very angry and went away, suspecting that baldhead was to blame for this. He found him drinking water at a spring, approached very slowly, and caught him. "You are the one who told the mother-pigeon not to give me another young one, and for that reason I am going to eat you," he mumbled. "Please don't do that, brother coyote," replied baldhead. "You must know that I am king of all the birds, and I'll take you to a place where you can eat them all. All you have to do is to go to that hill yonder and shout, 'I have just eaten bittern!'" Coyote consented to do as told. He went to the top of the hill and began to shout "I have just eaten bittern!" But he opened his mouth so wide that baldhead got away and shouted back, "You did no such thing!"

The version recited to me in Spain by Señor López Argüello is almost identical. The only difference is that in López Argüello's version the protagonists of the story are a fox and a family of magpies with their nest in a bush, whereas in the New Mexican versions the protagonists are a coyote and a family of pigeons with their nest in an oak tree.[2]

But many more suprises were still in store for me. At the famous Casona de Tudanca, the Casona de Tablanca of Pereda's novel *Peñas arriba*, I spent a few days with my distinguished friend José María Cossío. I went from Santander to Cabezón de la Sal by train, and from there to Cabuérniga by automobile. There I was to meet the mail carrier and go with him to Tudanca. When I reached Cabuérniga, I was met by a friend of Cossío, Señor Ormas, who invited me to lunch at his *casona*, or seignorial mansion. There I met his family and a brother of the famous lyric poet Núñez de

Arce. After lunch I left for Tudanca with the mail-carrier and another youth. We made the trip on horseback over difficult and dangerous mountain trails, and at times I was so afraid of the terrain that I dismounted and walked, leading my horse by the bridle. My companions laughed at my fears, but treated me with the utmost consideration because after all I was a friend of Cossío, the descendant of the lords of Tudanca. On the way my guides sang popular *coplas*, some of which were familiar to me, but I did not have time to stop and take them down. I was also very tired. "When will we arrive?" I asked continually. At last the promised land appeared. From the summit of a mountain they pointed out to me the valley of the Nansa River and the villages of Santotís, Cossío, and Tudanca.

As we approached the village of Santotís below the mountain, I observed a man standing by the road waiting for us. This was still a mile from Tudanca. With an air of great importance the man walked a few steps to meet me. Paying no attention to the *mozos*, whom he apparently considered his inferiors, he said to me: "¡Buenas tardes le dé Dios!" For the moment I did not know whether I was in Spain or New Mexico. This most Christian type of greeting, "May God give you a good afternoon!"—though rare in Spain today—is a very common type in Spanish New Mexico. It is an old traditional Spanish salutation. When I shook hands with him, he said: "Yo soy Pito Salces" (I am Pito Salces). He was a servant in the Casona; in fact, his ancestors had been servants of the Cossíos for generations. Pito Salces needs no introduction to students of Spanish literature. He was the famous Pito Salces of Pereda's novel *Peñas arriba*, the bear-hunter, the gallant youth who was in love with Tona. His real name was Eladio Gómez, but he called himself Pito Salces, the name with which Pereda made him immortal. But Pito Salces deserved to live forever. When I met him, he was eighty-four years old. He was still the mentally alert, loquacious, courageous, and haughty person depicted by Pereda.

Pito Salces was visibly moved when he heard me speak Spanish. With truly martial demeanor he dismissed my two road companions and took charge of me. He was now my official guide. He put my suitcase on the end of a stick and threw it over his shoulder and asked me to mount again, but I insisted upon walking. At the Casona we were received by Cossío and the village priest, Don Ventura. We entered and I was introduced to an aunt of Don José María, Doña Dolores, and to a sister, Doña Carlota.

On the following morning I was greeted by the Cossío family with the same formula used by Pito Salces: "Buenos días le dé Dios." I noticed that Pito Salces was treated almost as a member of the family, a survival of the old democratic spirit of Castile. Then, as I sat chatting with Don José

María, Pito Salces entered with wine and asked me: "¿Quiere su merced tomar la mañana?" (Do you wish to take a drink?). Again I wondered whether I was in Spain or New Mexico. People drink wine everywhere, of course, but to use exactly the same idiomatic expression, "tomar la mañana," is a survival of a tradition. After breakfast I went out to collect folktales. A young boy of about twelve years of age recited a short story, and I asked him his name. "Juanito Cabrero, para servir a Dios y a usted," he replied. Another survival and another surprise. In New Mexico we used to be told by our elders that the really polite and Christian child should always add "para servir a Dios y a usted" (at God's service and at your service) after giving one's name. Later I found this traditional Spanish formula in other parts of Spain.

One of the never to be forgotten experiences of my Spanish expedition was an evening spent at Calatañazor, the old Castilian-Saracen frontier village in the province of Soria. I left the city of Soria by automobile at noon and reached a point about a mile from Calatañazor at six. From there I walked to the village with two young *calatañazoranos*, down a steep declivity with no definite trail visible anywhere. Ruins of fortifications had to be traversed, and we were accompanied by sheep and goats being herded into the corrals for the night. By about eight we arrived at a *posada* (inn). It was a festival day, and in Spain, just as in New Mexico, a festival day means as a rule three or more festival days and nights. The village was full of people, the *posada* was crowded, and I had to sleep, or rather try to sleep, in a small room with a window that could not be opened. "It is better not to open the window anyway because you might catch cold." In any New Mexico village they tell you the same thing. There was so much to see and learn, however, that sleep was of no importance.

All that night and all next day and night there was dancing in the plaza. There was one dance, called *danza de corrillo*, that had a great resemblance to the old New Mexico *valse despacio*. Several couples, no definite number, held hands in a circle and walked around slowly in step with the music of the guitar, and at a regular repetition of the monotonous rhythm with quicker tempo the couples broke the circle and danced in pairs, either holding hands or separated. In the New Mexican *valse despacio* the circles are always of two couples and in the quick tempo repetition the couples dance holding hands in the usual manner.

The most conspicuous figures were the *guitarristas* (guitarists), who were at the same time *cantadores* (singers). These survivals of Spanish tradition were not those one sees in the woodcuts of old books, those we hear and read about. They were the actual *guitarristas* and *cantadores* in flesh and blood, executing their art, "doing their stuff." There is no difference between them and the New Mexican Spanish *guitarristas* and *cantadores*. There they were, the traditional popular musicians and singers of Spain, in the eastern frontiers of Old Castile, the spiritual brothers of the present-day New Mexican *músicos* and *cantadores*, of the Argentina gaucho *guitarrista* and *cantador* about whom we hear so much, and of other popular artists of their kind.

At one of the houses there were two *guitarristas*, and as *cantadores* they were in competition during the hour I visited the place. The *coplas* they sang were of the love and courtship types that one hears everywhere in the Spanish-speaking world today if one may judge from the published collections of popular *coplas*, or short four-, five-, or six-verse strophes, usually in octosyllabic meter. *Echar coplas* means "to sing popular verses or strophes." In New Mexico, however, the usual expression is *echar versos*. Among the many *coplas* that I heard were the following, of a religious character, both of which have almost identical versions in New Mexico:

Nadie diga en este mundo          Let no one say in this world,
"De esta agua no beberé."          "Of this water I'll not drink."
Por muy turbia que la vea          Although it may be muddy,
puede apretarle la sed.            one's thirst may become oppressive.

Esta noche soñé un sueño,          I had a dream last night,
el más feliz de mi vida;           the happiest of my life;
soñé que estaba durmiendo          I dreamed that I was sleeping
junto a la Virgen María.[3]        close by the Virgin Mary.

The similar New Mexican verses, the first of which was published by me in 1913, are the following:

Nadie diga en este mundo,          Let no one say in this world,
"De esta agua no beberé."          "Of this water I'll not drink."
Por revuelta que la vea            Although it may be muddy,
le puede apretar la sed.           one's thirst may become oppressive.

Antenoche tuve un sueño,           Night before last I had a dream,
el más feliz de mi vida;           the happiest of my life;
soñé que estaba sentado            I dreamed that I was seated
junto a la Virgen María.[4]        close by the Virgin Mary.

The numerous popular customs, superstitions, and beliefs that are found in New Mexico are for the most part of Spanish origin. The *luminarias*, little houses of sticks or bonfires that up to recent years used to be lighted in front of every New Mexican Spanish home on Christmas Eve, are well known in some parts of Spain. In Spain they are called by the same name. Even the modern lights, such as candles, lanterns, or electric lights, that are placed in balconies and windows on festival days in Spain are called *luminarias*. In Taos the *luminarias* are still a part of the religious ceremonies of Christmas in some homes. They are always nine in number, and they are lighted and kept burning every night for nine nights, from December 16 through December 24. A novena is held in honor of the Blessed Virgin, and the *luminarias* are lighted in the evening, after dinner, when the family begins to recite the rosary. Formerly the *luminarias* were placed sometimes on the roofs of houses. The Pueblo Indians of Taos, San Juan, and Isleta place lanterns or lighted candles on housetops on Christmas Eve today, probably a Spanish survival. Nowadays the *luminarias* are usually made by partly filling paper bags with sand and placing a lighted candle in the sand. The reason for the *luminarias*, New Mexicans say, is the duty of illuminating the way for the Magi Kings who are to come on Christmas Eve to adore the Child Jesus.

The betrothal ceremonies and festivities, called in New Mexico *prendorios*, and in Spain *toma de los dichos*, are essentially the same: the *pedir de la novia*, asking for the bride; the *dar la novia*, or consent of the parents sent through a near relative; the formal agreements before the parish priest; exchange of presents; and feasting and dancing. The baptismal celebrations are very much the same in New Mexico and in many of the villages of Spain. The *padrino* and *madrina* (godfather and godmother) take the *ahijado* (god-child-to-be) to church for the religious ceremony. As they leave the church, the children of the village wait outside to receive gifts of small coins. Both in Spain and New Mexico the *padrino* usually is most generous with his money. A *padrino* who doesn't give anything would disgrace the occasion. When the *madrina* returns the child to the mother, she usually says or sings, both in Spain and in New Mexico, "Here I return to you your child. He [or she] was a Moor [meaning pagan] when I took him with me, and now he [or she] is a Christian." Feasting and dancing follow. The *padrinos* and the parents of the *ahijado* are now *compadres*; that is, they are spiritually related, just like near relatives, and they must live in peace and bear one another's burdens. The *ahijado* is another son to the *padrinos*.

There exist also in New Mexico and Spain the *compadres* by consent (*compadres de mano*, or *compadres* by hand, in Spain, but in New Mexico simply *compadres*) as a result of the ceremony of promise and consent called *valerse a los compadres*, "to agree to become compadres." The contracting parties, men and women, boys and girls, shake hands, and that is all. In New Mexico children very often take the *compadre* pledge, which usually consists of holding each other by the little finger of the right hand, swinging the arm from right to left and repeating the following formulae:

| | |
|---|---|
| Canastita de flores | Little flower basket, |
| no te derrames, | do not overflow, |
| que en esta vida y en la otra | for in this life and in the next |
| somos compadres. | we are *compadres*. |
| | |
| Carretita y carretón, | Little cart, big cart, |
| los que se valen al compadre | those who agree to become |
| y a la comadre y se desvalen | *compadre* and *comadre* and repent |
| se les rompe el corazón.[5] | die of a broken heart. |

In both Spain and New Mexico the belief prevails that *compadres* by consent and agreement are just as much *compadres* as those of the religious ceremony.

Examples of New Mexican Spanish beliefs, customs, and superstitions of Spanish source can be given by the hundred. The proof of their peninsular Spanish provenience is the fact that they are pan-Hispanic; that is to say, they are found not only in Spain and New Mexico, but in most other Spanish-speaking countries as well. Some of them are pan-European, and Spain was only the medium that transmitted them to Spanish America.

The beliefs, customs, and superstitions relative to San Antonio (Saint Anthony) and his miracles are legion, and so far as can be ascertained, exactly the same ones appear in Spain and New Mexico and in other regions of Spanish America. Some of these are found also in many countries of Christian Europe. San Antonio is the saint who finds all lost articles and even lost children, grants all sorts of petitions, and is the special patron of lovers who are in good faith. He accomplishes all these things continually, and woe to those who doubt his powers. Both in Spain and in New Mexico we find that the devoted followers of San Antonio can not have their petitions denied, for if they are, San Antonio himself will suffer. His image is then hung face down in a well, often the head may even be submerged in the water, and there San Antonio remains, punished, until he grants what is asked of him. If San Antonio can not find a *novio* or *novia*, the case is hopeless, absolutely hopeless. "Look here, baldhead, if you don't find my children for me, something is going to happen to you!" a New Mexican Spanish mother once said to San Antonio when her children were lost. San Antonio, of course, found the lost children.[6]

The superstitions relative to St. John's Eve (la Noche de San Juan), the twenty-third of June, are especially interesting. They are similar in most Spanish-speaking countries and are, therefore, survivals. Whoever wishes to know what the future will bring to him (or her) will empty an egg into a glass of water and put it under the bed on St. John's Eve. The next morning the form that the egg assumes will tell everything: if the form of a ship appears, a sea voyage is foretold; if a person appears, it means marriage during the year; if a skeleton or coffin appears, death will come during the year, etc. This superstition is found in New Mexico, Chile, Castile, Galicia, Andalucía, and Portugal. If a young woman looks into a well or fountain on St. John's Eve, she will see not only her reflection in the water, but also that of her future husband. This superstition is found in New Mexico, in Chile, and in Andalucía. If on St. John's Eve, exactly at twelve o'clock, a young woman throws a bucket of water on the street from her window or door, the first young man to step on the wet ground will marry the girl, or else one who has the same name. This superstition is found in New Mexico and in Andalucía. There are many more.[7]

The superstition of the evil eye, that is, of an eye supposed to be capable of inflicting harm or illness, is a pan-European survival. In New Mexico the superstition is fundamentally the same as in Spain, but there are some differences in the remedies applied. In Spain the illness is called *mal de ojo*, and in New Mexico *mal de ojo* or simply *ojo*; in Spain the verb, "to cast the evil eye upon," is *aojar*, whereas in New Mexico the form *ojar*, derived from *aojar*, or the expression *hacer ojo* is used. In New Mexico, as well as in Spain and southern Europe generally, the condition necessary for the evil is beauty, real or apparent, and not only persons but also animals and even plants and objects may be victims of the evil eye. The evil eye may not be caused intentionally or consciously in New Mexico, Chile, and Spain. The admiration, momentary attraction, or affection that one may have for a person, especially a child, may cause the dire results. To avert the evil, one should always say to a child one admires, "*¡Dios te guarde!*" (May God protect you!), or make the sign of the cross. Women, especially old and sickly women, very ugly and unclean women, or women witches are especially dangerous evil-eyers. In Spain witches and all gypsies are especially feared as evil-eyers. The intentional evil-eyers of Italian tradition are apparently unknown in Spain and Spanish America.

In the case of the evil eye, important changes have apparently taken place in New Mexico tradition, especially with respect to the remedies applied. These may be because of Pueblo Indian influence, for the superstition of the evil eye in one form or another seems to be universal.

In general Spanish tradition, according to evidence from Chile, New Mexico, and some parts of Spain, the illness caused by the evil eye begins with vomiting, high fever, and general weakness. The eyes of the victim, especially, have a ghastly and demoniacal aspect. The usual remedies are prayers, especially the Credos, and often herbs that vary according to the locality. The attendant superstitions which involve Friday are also pan-Hispanic. In Andalucía, Galicia, and Chile, the belief prevails that the fever and general evil effects of the malady are at their height on Fridays and that no evil-eyed person can suffer the illness more than three Fridays. On the third Friday, the patient dies or recovers. In New Mexico it is generally believed that the crisis is reached on the first Friday. After that day the patient either recovers or dies.

Among the remedies for the evil eye that are apparently exclusive to New Mexicans are the following: when the first signs of the evil eye appear, or even before they appear, if it is suspected that a child has been evil-eyed, the suspected evil-eyer takes water in her mouth and spits it into the child's mouth and on its face, or gives the child the water to drink with her mouth. She then holds the child close to her, well wrapped to produce a sweat. The child is then put to bed. A variant of the above superstition is to collect the sweepings from the four corners of the room and boil them in water; the evil-eyer takes this water in her mouth and spits it into the child's mouth. Another remedy is to put the child to bed and to place under the head of the bed a glass of water into which the white of an egg has been emptied. If the next day an eye appears formed on the egg white, the evil eye has disappeared and the child will recover.[8] The other general Spanish remedies mentioned above, such as making the sign of the cross over the child, reciting the Credos, and the like, are also applied.

Although the very essence and spirit of popular traditions militate for harmony, unity, and permanence—in short, mental homogeneity—in time changes do take place. Human memory weakens, new environments appear, and necessity and imagination play their parts. One must consider also changes resulting from the influence of new cultural contacts. In New Mexico, for example, the Mexican Indian, the New Mexican Indian, and the Anglo-American cultural contacts have all introduced changes. These changes have not been significant in the more artistic aspects of tradition, such as ballads, short popular songs, riddles, proverbs, nursery rhymes, and the like. We have already seen how the *cantadores* of Calatañazor sang traditional popular *coplas* that are still sung practically unchanged in New Mexico. But in customs, superstitions, and beliefs, changes are much more common. Old Spanish customs are preserved in New Mexico today only in the isolated villages where the majority of the folk are still Spanish-speaking. At Christmastime, for example, the *nacimientos*, or cribs, are now rare, and the Christmas tree is popular everywhere. Even in Spain the Christmas tree, of Germanic tradition, is now popular.

# Traditional Spanish Ballads

The Old Spanish Ballads. The Historical, Frontier, Carolingian, and Novelesque Ballads. Traditional Spanish Ballads in New Mexico. Novelesque Ballads. *Gerineldo*. The Lovelorn Maiden. Religious Ballads. Burlesque Ballads.

A Spanish *romance* or ballad may be defined as a brief narrative poem, of an episodic character, with concise, spirited, and dramatic dialogue and composed in long sixteen-syllable assonanced verses. There are ballads of so many types, however, that a precise, comprehensive definition of the genre as a whole is well-nigh impossible. One may classify the *romances* according to their origin, their artistic form, or their traditional character. Most of the really popular ballads of the *Romancero*, or Spanish balladry, over a thousand in number, are traditional; that is, they have gone through a long period—two hundred years or more—of collective elaboration.

The following classification may serve to give some idea of the wonderfully rich body of Spanish *romances* that have been so much admired and utilized by the creative spirits of many races and peoples since their first appearance in the ballad collections—*Cancioneros de romances* or *Romanceros*—in the sixteenth century:

1. The old historical ballads that sing the praises of the Castilian heroes in their struggles to reconquer Spain from the Arabs and to achieve political and religious unity.
2. The frontier ballads that relate the history and legends of the conquest of Granada.
3. The Carolingian ballads that develop in Spain the most popular themes of the history and legend of Charlemagne and the twelve peers of France.
4. The novelesque or chivalric ballads that develop lyric themes of the general folklore of Europe.
5. The religious ballads that give expression to the religious devotions and feelings of the Spanish people of the sixteenth and seventeenth centuries.
6. The erudite ballads, ballads that show evidence of individualistic, learned elaboration of traditional themes in the sixteenth century.

7. The artistic ballads, those of purely learned sources, composed by known poets.

8. The burlesque ballads, those in which insignificant persons or even beasts or insects play the parts of heroes.

9. The more recent popular ballads, composed by individual poets, or the product of collective elaboration, often also traditional and dating from the eighteenth century.

10. The modern local ballads, which are not traditional.

Of the above groups or classes, those that in their best examples are generally considered as the flower of Spanish balladry are the old historical ballads, the frontier ballads, the Carolingian ballads, and the novelesque ballads. Let us first consider briefly the old historical ballads, the oldest and finest examples of the *Romancero*. These are the ones that have been most widely admired; several of them have become the common possession of creative writers of many countries. Their origin and development are most interesting. They are ultimately derived from old epic poems composed in the eleventh, twelfth, and thirteenth centuries, when the Spanish people were achieving their first definitive triumphs over the Arabic invaders. They represent the intense national and religious feeling of the Castilians in their long struggle to reconquer Spain and achieve national and religious unity. These epic poems deal with the deeds of kings, national heroes, and other great leaders of Castile during the first centuries of a national consciousness. They are aristocratic, seignorial, and for the most part historical. They were composed for an aristocratic public and sung or recited in the palaces of kings and noblemen or in the midst of the Castilian hosts that marched to the battlefields. Although it appears that about a dozen long epic poems of this character were composed in Castile in the eleventh and twelfth centuries, only two have come down to us in anything like their original form, the *Cantar de mio Cid*, or *Poem of the Cid*, and the *Crónica Rimada*, or *Rhymed Chronicle of the Cid*. Fragments of others have been discovered by modern investigators, especially Marcelino Menéndez y Pelayo and Ramón Menéndez Pidal, in the prose chronicles of the thirteenth and fourteenth centuries. The chronicles often followed the old epic poems very closely, and in prosifying them they retained here and there passages from the poems, including verses or series of verses with the usual meter and assonance.

These old, aristocratic epics did not disappear, however, after they were prosified in the chronicles. In the thirteenth and fourteenth centuries they became the poetry of all classes, both aristocratic and plebeian. During those centuries the bitterest struggles between the Christians and the

Moslems took place. The intensity of the struggle created a new and powerful nationalism, and the old Castilian counts Fernán González and Garcí-Fernández; the Castilian kings Fernando el Grande, Sancho II, and Alfonso VI; and the invincible Castilian hero, the Cid, all sung in the old epics, were no longer merely Castilian heroes of a bygone age. In the thirteenth and fourteenth centuries the old epic poems that sang their deeds became the common property of all Spaniards and thus became popular and democratic. The old epics continued, then, not only in prosified form in the chronicles, but also in a new, popularized and democratized form in the imperfect manuscript copies of the army captains and street jongleurs.

But the ordinary memory of man could not and would not preserve the epic poems in their entirety; the result was that the nobleman, the soldier, and the man in the street each retained in his memory certain episodes of the epics: those that pleased his fancy; those that had a universal, human appeal; and those that flattered his national vanity. These episodes of the old epics, preserved in the oral tradition of the people, popularized, changed, and developed by successive generations, finally came to be appreciated as popular, traditional poetry and were collected from oral tradition in the *Romanceros* or ballad collections of the sixteenth century. These isolated parts of the old epics are precisely the oldest and the best historical Spanish ballads. Their form and spirit, and even their meter, are similar to those of the epic poems from which they are derived. Generally speaking, they differ from them only in length.

Once the genre had been developed, toward the end of the fourteenth century, ballads began to be composed independently, and some ballads may have developed not only independently, but also concurrently with those derived from the old epics. In fact, the ballads of all the other classes, such as the frontier, Carolingian, and novelesque ballads, are of independent source. These were originally composed by individual poets and probably were never or seldom communal in origin. However, both the old historical ballads derived from the epic poems and those of independent origin and development, when once taken over by the people and made popular, underwent changes. After a certain period of collective elaboration, if they continued to be preserved in oral tradition, they may be said to have become traditional and anonymous.

An example of one of the best of the old Spanish historical ballads is given below in the English translation of John Gibson Lockhart, whose *Ancient Spanish Ballads*, published in London in 1823, is now a classic among English-speaking peoples. The ballad relates the episode of the old epic in which the young Cid goes to Burgos, the capital of Castile, with his father, Diego Laínez, to do homage to the king, but refuses to kiss the king's hand:

> Now rides Diego Laínez, to kiss the good king's hand;
> three hundred men of gentry go with him from his land,
> among them young Rodrigo, the proud knight of Bivar.
> The rest on mules are mounted, he on his horse of war.
> They ride in glittering gowns of soye, he harnessed like a lord;
> there is no gold about the boy, but the crosslet of his sword;
> the rest have gloves of perfume, he gauntlets strong of mail;
> they broidered cap and flaunting plume, he crest untaught to quail.
> All talking with each other thus along their way they passed,
> but now they've come to Burgos, and met the king at last.
> When they came near his nobles, a whisper through them ran,
> "He rides amidst the gentry that slew the Count Lozan."
> With very haughty gesture Rodrido reined his horse;
> right scornfully he shouted when he heard them so discourse,
> "If any of his kinsmen or vassals dare appear,
> the man to give them answer, on horse or foot, is here."
> "The devil ask the question!" thus muttered all the band.
> With that they all alighted to kiss the good king's hand;
> all but the proud Rodrigo; he on his saddle staid.
> Then turned to him his father (you may hear the words he said),
> "Now light, my son, I pray thee, and kiss the good king's hand;
> he is our lord, Rodrigo; we hold of him our land."
> But when Rodrigo heard him he looked in sulky sort.
> I wot the words he answered they were both cold and short,
> "Had any other said it his pains had well been paid,
> but thou, sir, art my father; thy word must be obeyed."
> With this he sprung down lightly, before the king to kneel,
> but as the knee was bending, out leapt his blade of steel.
> The king drew back in terror when he saw the sword was bare.
> "Stand back, stand back, Rodrigo, in the devil's name beware.
> Your looks bespeak a creature of father Adam's mould,
> but in your wild behaviour you're like some lion bold."
> When Rodrigo heard him say so, he leapt into his seat,
> and thence he made his answer, with visage nothing sweet.
> "I'd think it little honor to kiss a kingly palm,
> and if my father's kissed it, thereof ashamed I am."
> When he these words had uttered, he turned him from the gate;
> his true three hundred gentles behind him followed straight.
> If with good gowns they came that day, with better arms they went;
> and if their mules behind did stay, with horses they're content.[1]

Next in importance to the old historical ballads are those of the four-teenth and fifteenth centuries that are called the frontier ballads. These ballads have to do with the conquest of Granada, the final triumph of Christian Spain in its seven-century struggle against the Mohammedans, and with the realization of national unity. They came into existence in the midst of the battles they describe. They possess the realism and the spir-ited dialogue of the old historical ballads and like them are the quintes-sence of Spanish character. The frontier ballads are the last manifestation of the creative epoch of the Spanish ballad. They differ from the old historical ballads in that they represent individually greater unity and completeness of narrative. Rather than a fragment or an episode from an epic poem, each one is complete in itself. History is mixed with legend, as in the older ballads, but on the whole their historical character has not been obscured so much by legend.

The subject matter of some of the best of the frontier ballads may be briefly outlined: the lamentations of the Moors when news is received at Granada of the capture of Alhama and Antequera; the heroic deeds of the young Bishop of Jaén, Don Gonzalo, who marches to battle with his Castilian army and, when he alone remains, attacks his enemies single-handed and fights with utmost valor but is finally captured and taken as a prisoner to the dungeons of the Alhambra; the romantic and memorable departure of the king of Granada, Boabdil, to attack the Castilian hosts, accompanied by the flower of the Moorish nobility, all armed with silver helmets and swords the hilts of which are of shining gold, the Moorish mothers, wives, and lovers weeping but applauding and urging them to defend the kingdom; the daring deeds of the Moorish knight Tarfe, who fights his way to the very gates of the camp of the Catholic kings and insults the Castilians by riding about with a portrait of the Virgin Mary tied to the tail of his horse; and the valiant deeds of the Castilian knight Garcilaso de la Vega, who secretly leaves the Christian camp, challenges the Moor, and, when derided on account of his youth, opens the duel and slays Tarfe, removes the protrait of the Virgin from the Moor's horse, and kisses it with great reverence; the daring sally of the Castilian hosts under the leadership of Don Alonso de Aguilar to attack a powerful Moorish army near Granada, their crushing defeat, and the gallant stand of Don Alonso, who is finally killed by the Moors; and on and on.

The Carolingian ballads treat of subjects that belong to the cycle of Carolingian chivalry. Although the subject matter is foreign to Spain, the Carolingian ballads became truly popular and traditional. They relate the historical and legendary exploits of Roland, Renaud de Montauban, the Marquis of Mantua, and some of the other twelve peers of France and other marvelous adventures vaguely related to the Carolingian cycle. These ballads bring to the *Romancero* more sentimentality, more of the love themes—often very passionate love—more of the supernatural and fantastic elements, and more elegance in the form of composition. The themes of a few may be mentioned: the story of the Marquis of Mantua, who finds the dead body of his nephew Baldwin in a forest and takes the extraordinary and solemn oath of never shaving his beard, eating at a table with a tablecloth, or sleeping on a bed, and so on, until he obtains vengeance; the story of Count Irlos, who has gone to a distant war and is famous also for his long beard of fifteen years, who dreams that his wife is unfaithful to him; the figure of the passionate Melisenda, who is held captive by the Moor Almanzor and through a window of her prison speaks amorous phrases to another royal captive, who happens to be her husband, Gaiferos; the story of the Infanta, the daughter of Charlemagne, who makes ardent love to Gerineldo, the king's page; the sad story of Doña Alda, the bride of Roland, who awakens from the prophetic dream that reveals to her his tragic death.

The novelesque ballads, a rather general group which includes *romances* of many different types, deal with the more general themes of the folklore of Europe, both classical and medieval; they also are very old, perhaps as old as some of the historical ballads derived from the epics. They have as subject matter the universal human themes of love, fidelity, honor, valor, vengeance, and ideal justice. They are chivalric and romantic, and the lyric element is often predominant. In other respects they are similar to the old historical ballads: they are dramatic, have concise and forceful dialogue, and are of a truly traditional character. The contents of a few examples may be given here. One of the most popular narrates the romantic story of the ideal knight and lover, who is loved by all the ladies who lay eyes on him, even to the point of giving their lives for him. There are several tragic ballads of this type: *Gerineldo*, classed also as a Carolingian ballad, Virgil, Tristan, and Lancelot of world fame. Other novelesque ballads treat of the faithless wife who is surprised by her husband and her subsequent death, an Oriental theme; the wedding that was to be or the finding of the long-lost husband, a common theme in European folktales; the story of the persecuted woman, wife or daughter, also a common theme in folktales; and other common folk themes: the romantic story of the warrior-woman, the daughter of a prince, who, disguised as a knight, goes to war in the king's service for seven years and in the end marries the king's son; the knight who returns from war and speaks to his wife, who does not recognize him; the charming lyric themes of the prisoner's lamentations; the sad wanderings of the turtledove that has been left "a widow and in grief"; the classic complaint and commiseration for the one who disdains love's charms; and the Lorelei theme, found in the ballad of Count Arnaldos.

The real greatness of the *romancero* is to be found in the fact that it inspired and gave origin to one of the great dramatic literatures of the world. Many of the dramatic productions of Lope de Vega, Guillén de Castro, and others are inspired directly in the historical ballads, preserved for the most part in the oral tradition of the sixteenth century. Even the legend of Don Juan is found in an old Spanish ballad from which Tirso de Molina may have taken it to give it the definite artistic form that the world admires.

The ballads of Spain are also of unique importance in European literary history: they have not only influenced and given inspiration, subject matter, and even literary form to important literary genres and developed a great national drama, but they have also been a source of inspiration for dramatic compositions in other countries. The Spanish ballads long ago traversed the national frontiers to be translated into other languages, to be incorporated into poetic legends, and to be dramatized by the lovers of the beautiful in many lands. Some of them—a few of the Cid ballads and some of the Carolingian and novelesque ballads, for example—are now the common property of universal literature. If Cervantes was right when he said in the prologue to his immortal *Don Quijote* that all works of art are to be judged by "that ancient legislator called the public," the world-wide popularity of the Spanish ballads, greater by far than that of any other ballads known to us, would indicate their superior artistic merit.[2]

A large number of the old Spanish ballads, especially of the novelesque type, are still recited and sung wherever Spanish is spoken: in Spain, in all parts of Spanish America, in New Mexico and California, and among the Spanish-speaking Jews in Africa, in the Balkans, and in the Orient. As noted earlier, even the Pueblo Indians of New Mexico who speak Spanish recite and sing old Spanish ballads today.[3]

Turning to the old Spanish ballads still preserved in the oral tradition of Spanish New Mexico, in 1893, Charles F. Lummis, who knew much about New Mexico, stated that he doubted that many Spanish ballads were to be found there; as examples of what he had been able to find he cited a fragmentary version of one ballad and a modern, lyrical, balladlike composition. He was probably not acquainted with the rich balladry of Spain, and his New Mexican informers gave him only what he asked for.[4] Twelve years later, when serious investigations were begun in the field of New Mexican Spanish folklore, it was discovered that in New Mexico the Spanish ballad tradition was not only alive but also vigorous. Twenty-seven versions of ten different traditional Spanish ballads recorded in the six-teenth and seventeenth centuries were published by me in 1915.[5] Since that time the number of traditional Spanish ballads found in the oral tradition of New Mexico has been increased to over one hundred versions of twenty-seven ballads, or nearly three times the number that appeared in the first important publication on the subject.[6] This large number of traditional Spanish ballads of the sixteenth and seventeenth centuries gives New Mex-ico a distinguished place in the history of the *Romancero*. Other traditional ballads, those of the eighteenth century, of which New Mexico has also some versions, will be discussed in a later chapter.

Of the various important classes of Spanish ballads recorded in the sixteenth and seventeenth centuries—the historical, frontier, Carolingian, novelesque, erudite, and artistic ballads—only the novelesque are pre-served in great numbers in modern oral tradition. In Spain and among the Spanish Jews, examples of historical ballads have not been found. One Cid ballad has been found in Chile. This same ballad was known in New Mexico in almost identical form, if we may judge from the following opening lines recited by Don Juan Ortiz of Santa Fe: "Victorioso vuelve el Cid—de las guerras de Valencia."[7] According to Sr. Ortiz, the ballad was known to others in Santa Fe, but as yet it has not been found. In any case, after finding the above line we can truly say that El Cid Campeador, the protagonist of Castilian hegemony, has not been completely forgotten in Spanish New Mexico. His exploits at Valencia took place in the closing years of the eleventh century. At the beginning of the twentieth century, nine centuries later, his exploits were still remembered in one of the most distant corners of the Hispanic world, Santa Fe, New Mexico.

But the Cid also lives in quaint old expressions in New Mexico, such as "¡Éste sí es el Cid Campeador!," meaning "This boy is certainly unruly (or brave)!" Even a feminine form is used: "¡Ésta sí es la Cid Campeadora!" The phrase "No se ganó Zamora en una hora," or "Zamora wasn't won in an hour," widely used in New Mexico, is an echo of the siege of Zamora by the Cid and Sancho II in the year 1072.

With the exception of the above cited line from a Cid ballad, and the *Gerineldo* ballad cited below that may be classified as either Carolingian or novelesque, nearly all the Spanish traditional ballads that are to be found today in New Mexico are of the novelesque class. Love, honor, fidelity, infidelity, war, legends that have their origin in Arabic traditions, and deep religious emotion and feelings are their themes. The New Mexican ballads are, on the whole, versions that have undergone little change since the sixteenth century. The old assonances and the octosyllabic verse help us to detect the changes and to observe here and there a missing line. But, on the whole, they present no special problems for the linguist. They interest chiefly the student of comparative literature, the creative artists, and all lovers of the beautiful.

In the following pages of this chapter I shall discuss briefly a few of the outstanding examples of traditional Spanish ballads found in New Mexico. Several of the novelesque, religious, and burlesque ballads will be given in the original Spanish and in English translation.

## Novelesque Ballads

1. *Delgadina se paseaba—por una sala cuadrada.* This is the European theme of the incestuous father, the old classic tale of Apollonius of Tyre and of numerous medieval stories of the persecuted child, found also in modern folklore tradition. The New Mexican versions are long and complete, although not a single one of the several versions has the traditional peninsular beginning.[8] In Spain the versions of this ballad are so numerous that collectors do not take them down any more.

2. *Gerineldo, Gerineldo—mi camarero aguerrido.* This ballad tells the fantastic legend of the love of a supposed daughter of Charlemagne, Emma, and Eginhard, the emperor's chamberlain. The New Mexican versions are especially noteworthy because New Mexico seems to be the only region in Spanish America where this ballad has been found in complete versions. The New Mexican versions are not only complete but also very well preserved.[9] Menéndez Pidal has studied over 160 versions in a study of the origins of the ballad and has pronounced the New Mexican versions among the best and most archaic now extant. There are two sixteenth-century versions of this ballad.

3. *Una niña en un balcón—le dice a un pastor: Espera.* This is the tale of the maiden who makes love to a shepherd and is rejected by him; later, when he returns to apologize for his rudeness in rejecting the love of so beautiful a maiden, he himself is rejected because now that he is willing, she is not. This is the ballad of which Lummis cited a few lines. A modern peninsular version published by Menéndez Pidal as an example of one of the finest from modern tradition[10] is in no way superior to some of the New Mexican versions.[11]

4. *Francisquita, Francisquita,—la del cuerpo muy sutil.* 5. *Andándome yo paseando—por las orillas del mar.* These two ballads have infidelity as their

theme. One is in assonance -*í*, the other in assonance -*ó*. The first one has some basis in history. [12]

6. *En una playa arenosa—una blanca sombra vi.* The theme of the dead wife who appears to the husband who is wandering in search of her is briefly but very artistically developed in this lyrical ballad. The ballad is not common in modern tradition. [13] In a modernized form, *¿Dónde vas, Alfonso Doce—dónde vas, triste de ti?*, applied to Alfonso XII looking for his dead wife, Queen Mercedes, the versions are more numerous.

7. *Catalina, Catalina,—paño blanco de lino es.* This is a beautiful and charming tale of fidelity in love, the search for the lost husband, and the happy reunion of the husband and wife. The first Spanish version was published in 1605. The New Mexican versions are very faithful to the old form, although the opening lines have been forgotten. [14]

8. *Chiquita, si me muriere,—no me entierres en sagrado.* This is the universal lyric theme of the lover who dies of love and does not wish to be buried in sacred ground, but rather in the open fields, where the cattle and sheep may trample upon his grave and the shepherds may sing of his cruel fate. It represents a small spark of the Spanish Renaissance that finds expression in the spirit of the *Romancero*. [15]

The best New Mexican example of a traditional Spanish novelesque ballad is the ballad of *Gerineldo*. Given below is a long and complete version in the traditional sixteen-syllable assonanced verses:

> —Gerineldo, Gerineldo,—mi camarero aguerrido,
> ¡quién te pescara esta noche—tres horas en mi servicio!
> —¿Tres horas, dice, señora?—¡Ojalá que fueran cinco!
> Si porque soy vuestro criado—quiere usted burlar conmigo.
> —No quiero burlar de ti;—*de deveras* te lo digo.
> —¿Para qué horas de la noche—iré yo a lo prometido?
> —Entre las ocho y las nueve—cuando el rey esté dormido.
>     A las ocho de la noche—Gerineldo va al castillo;
> halla la puerta entreabierta,—da un fervoroso suspiro.
> —¿Ese atrevido, quién es,—que ha venido a mi castillo?
> —Señora, soy Gerineldo—que vengo a lo prometido.
>     Ya lo agarra de la mano—y se van para el castillo;
> ya se acuesta Gerineldo—con calenturas y fríos;
> se acuestan boca con boca—como mujer y marido.
>     Cosa de la media noche—el rey pidió sus vestidos;
> se los lleva un criado dél;—de Gerineldo es amigo.
> —¿Dónde está mi Gerineldo,—mi camarero aguerrido?
> —Señor, se metió en la cama—con calenturas y fríos.
> Se sienta el rey en la cama,—y se pone sus vestidos;

toma su espada en la mano—y se va para el castillo;
los halla boca con boca—como mujer y marido.
—Si mato a mi Gerineldo,—que yo lo crié desde niño,
si mato a mi hija, la infanta,—queda mi reino perdido;
les pondré en medio la espada,—que sepan que son sentidos.
    Ya se levanta la dama,—muy triste y desconsolada.
—Levántate, Gerineldo,—mi camarero aguerrido;
la espada del rey mi padre—entre los dos ha dormido.
Se levanta Gerineldo—muy triste y despavorido.
—¡Valía más haberme muerto!—¡Valía más no haber nacido!
—No lo digas, Gerineldo,—mi camarero aguerrido,
que yo le diré a mi padre—que te estimo por marido.
    —¿Dónde estabas, Gerineldo,—mi camarero aguerrido?
—Señor, jugando a las damas;—ni he ganado ni he perdido.
—Mucho disimulo es ése,—Gerineldo, a lo que he visto.
—Señor, yo seré la carne,—vuestra merced el cuchillo;
corte de donde quisiere,—de mí no sea dolido.
—Levántate, Gerineldo, mi camarero aguerrido,
que dice mi hija, la infanta,—que hoy te estima por marido.
Se levanta Gerineldo—pegando saltos y brincos.
Se fue pronto pal castillo,    como otra vez había ido.
Y *ai* se tomaron las manos—como mujer y marido.[16]

"Gerineldo, Gerineldo, my valiant chamberlain,
would that I could have your services for three full hours tonight!"
"Three hours you say, my lady? I wish that they might be five!
But because I am your servant you are making sport of me."
"I'm not making sport of you; I mean all that I have said."
"At what time, then, of the night can I come to visit you?"
"Come by between eight and nine, when the king is fast asleep."
    To the castle Gerineldo went as soon as it was eight;
the door he found slightly open and he gave a fervent sigh.
"Who can be that daring person who thus comes into my castle?"
"I'm Gerineldo, my lady; pray remember what you promised."
    Now she takes him by the hand and leads him into the castle.
When Gerineldo retires, he feels now cold, now with fever.
They go to sleep mouth to mouth truly as husband and wife.
    When it was about midnight, the king called for his day clothes;
one of his servants helped him; he was Gerineldo's friend.
"Now, where is my Gerineldo, my valiant chamberlain?"
"He has retired, Your Majesty; he feels now cold, now with fever."
The king sits up in his bed and then puts on his apparel;
he took his sword in his hand and to the castle he went;
he found the two mouth to mouth truly like husband and wife.

I cannot kill Gerineldo; he's been like a son to me;
The princess I cannot kill for my kingdom would be lost;
I'll put this sword between them, so that they will know I came."
  Next morning the princess got up; sad and distressed she became.
"Get up, Gerineldo," said she, "my valiant chamberlain,
for my father's sword lies sleeping here between the two of us."
Gerineldo got up quickly; he looked sad and sorely frightened.
"Would that I had died!" he said, "that I had never been born!"
"Do not say that, Gerineldo, my valiant chamberlain,
for I mean to tell my father that you I desire to wed."
  "Where were you, Gerineldo, my valiant chamberlain?"
"I was playing checkers, Sir; I have neither won nor lost."
"What hypocrisy, Gerineldo, after all that I have seen!"
"Sir, I now will be the flesh, and Your Majesty the knife;
cut then wherever you wish, and feel no mercy for me."
"Arise, my dear Gerineldo, my valiant chamberlain,
for the princess says she wishes to be considered your wife."
Gerineldo arose at once, leaping and dancing with joy.
He went forthwith to the castle just as he had gone before.
And there the two pledged their troth and became husband and wife.

## The Lovelorn Maiden

The novelesque ballad which follows relates the tale of the lovelorn maiden
who is rejected by a shepherd but in the end finds revenge when the
shepherd returns seeking her love. As stated above, it is in no way inferior
to the modern peninsular Spanish version published by Ramón Menéndez
Pidal. The primitive Spanish version dates from the sixteenth or seventeenth century.

Una niña en un balcón—le dice a un pastor:—Espera,
que aquí te habla una zagala—que de amores desespera.
—No me hables de esa manera,—le responde el grande vil,
—mi ganado está en la sierra,—con él me voy a dormir.
—Te doy una pila de oro—y tres cañas de marfil,
tan solo porque te quedes—esta noche aquí a dormir.
—No quiero tu pila de oro—ni tus cañas de marfil;
mi ganado está en la sierra,—con él me voy a dormir.
—Mira qué lindos cabellos,—y llevarás que contar;
el sol se enamora de ellos—cuando me siento a peinar.
Mira que pulido pie—para un zapato dorado.
Mira que soy niña tierna, y que estoy a tu mandado.
—No me hables de esa manera,—le responde el grande vil,
—mi ganado está en la sierra,—con el me voy a dormir.

—Te doy las mulas y el hato,—el catre y el almirez,
tan sólo porque te quedes—esta noche y otras tres.
—No quiero mulas ni hato,—ni el catre ni el almirez;
mi ganado está en la sierra,—con él me voy otra vez.
—Mira, pastor aturdido,—no me quieres entender;
me dejas con mi vergüenza—cuando te empiezo a querer;
a la vuelta de tu viaje—no vas a saber qué hacer.
    —Zagala, dueña de mi alma,—zagala, vuelvo a venir.
Zagala, cuando me *hablates*—tus palabras no entendí.
Perdóname, gran señora,—si en algo yo te ofendí.
—Cuando quise, no *quisites*,—y ahora que quieres, no quiero;
pues llora tu soledad,—que yo la lloré primero.
—Te doy todo mi caudal—con todo lo que yo habito,
tan solo porque me dejas—hablar contigo un ratito.
—Cuando quise, no *quisites*,—y ahora que quieres, no quiero;
pues llora tu soledad,—que yo la lloré primero.
—Mira, zagalita hermosa,—dueña de mi corazón,
perdóname esta faltita,—que tu siervo es el amor.
—Cuando quise, no *quisites*,—y ahora que quieres, no quiero;
pues llora tu soledad,—que yo la lloré primero.
    —Haré de cuenta que tuve,—una sortijita de oro,
y que se cayó en el mar,—y así la perdí del todo.[17]

(Instead of *el grande vil*, other New Mexican versions have *el villano vil*, the
usual reading in the peninsular versions. The dialectic forms *hablates,
quisites*, represent *hablaste, quisiste*.)

A young girl on a balcony—says to a shepherd: "Please wait,
for here a shepherdess calls—and she is desperate for love."
"Do not speak to me that way,"—the boorish rustic responds,
"my flock grazes in the mountain,—with it I'm going to sleep.
I'll give you a pile of gold—and three reeds of ivory
if only you'll deign to stay—and sleep in my room tonight."
"I don't want your pile of gold—nor your reeds of ivory
my flock grazes in the mountain,—with it I'm going to sleep."
    "Just look, what beautiful hair—and you'll have a tale to tell;
the sun falls in love with it—whenever I'm combing it.
Look what a delicate foot—proper for a golden shoe.
See what a tender child am I,—and that I'm at your command."
"Do not speak to me like that,"—the boorish rustic responds,
"my flock is in the mountain,—with it I'm going to sleep."
"I'll give you the mules and ranch,—the bedstead and the brass mortar,
if only you'll stay with me—this night and another three."
"I don't want your mules nor ranch—nor the bed nor the brass mortar;

my flock grazes in the mountain—to it I'm returning now."
"Look here, you bewildered shepherd,—you don't want to understand;
You leave me with my dishonor—just when I'm starting to like you;
Wnen you return from your trip,—you will not know what to do."
"Shepherdess, love of my soul,—shepherdess, I'm back again.
Shepherdess, when you spoke to me—your words I misunderstood.
Please forgive me, noble lady,—if I have offended you."
"When it was my wish, you would not,—and now that you wish, I do not;
so weep in your solitude now,—as I wept in mine before."
"I promise you all my riches—and all wherein I now dwell,
if only you will permit me—to talk with you a short while."
"When it was my wish, you would not,—and now that you wish, I do not;
so weep in your solitude now,—as I wept in mine before."
"Look, my beautiful shepherdess,—dearest owner of my heart,
forgive me this trivial fault,—for love is your faithful servant."
"When it was my wish, you would not,—and now that you wish, I do not;
so weep in your solitude now,—as I wept in mine before."
"I shall imagine I had—a ring of gold for your hand,
but it fell into the sea—and thus I lost it forever."

A Chilean version of the ballad published by Julio Vicuña Cifuentes is almost identical with the New Mexican version.[18] Chile and New Mexico are too far apart, however, even to consider the question of possible influences. Both versions seem quite archaic and correspond faithfully to the sixteenth- or seventeenth-century original.

## Religious Ballads

1. *Por el rastro de la sangre—que Jesucristo derrama*. This is a ballad on the Passion of Christ that depicts in beautiful, sonorous, and impressive verses the grief of the Virgin Mary as she follows the way of the Cross to Calvary.[19] The Virgin Mary following the way of the cross is a favorite theme in Spanish tradition. In Spain and Spanish America some of the most beautiful *romances de la Pasión*, or Passion ballads, develop this theme. One of the most popular, *Por el rastro de la sangre*, narrates briefly the story of the Virgin following the traces of the blood shed by the Savior as he carries the cross to Mount Calvary and meeting with St. John, who tells her that Christ has been crucified. The peninsular and Spanish American versions are similar, although some have the assonance *á-a* throughout, while others have *á-o*. The New Mexican version given below is from Taos. It is in *á-a* assonance in the first nine verses, in *á-o* in the next three, in *á-a* again in verses 13–18, in *ó* in the next two, and in *ó-o* in the last two.

2. *Un angel triste lloraba—de ver la cuenta que dio.* 3. *A orillas de un ojo de agua—estaba un ángel llorando.* This is the theme of the angel found by the Virgin Mary weeping because a soul that had been committed to its care had been condemned. She intercedes with her Divine Son and He permits her to take the condemned soul out from the fires of hell because its owner had once (or several times) recited the rosary in her honor. The two most common versions begin with the different opening verses, as cited above, but the rest of the ballad is practically identical in all the versions. [20]

4. *Al pie de este santo altar—la Virgen está llorando.* This beautiful ballad describes in verses of deep feeling the lamentations of the Virgin at the foot of the Cross. The version given below is one of the finest traditional Spanish ballads dealing with the lamentations of the Virgin found in the Spanish-speaking world, whether in learned or popular literature. In its present form, the ballad is in assonanced quatrains throughout and contains a few narrative lines, not included here, which appear as stage directions for the delivery of the lamentations. [21]

5. *En el Monte de Santa Lucía—estaba la Virgen María.* In this ballad the Virgin tells the Christ Child of a dream she has had—a brief account of the Crucifixion that is to come. The first version of the ballad found in New Mexico was recited by a Santa Clara Indian woman; it was collected by Miss Barbara Freire Marreco in 1913. We now possess several New Mexican Spanish versions. [22]

6. *Cuando San José y la Virgen—se volvieron ya del templo.* 7. *La Virgen buscaba al Niño—por las calles y las plazas.* These are two beautiful ballads on the biblical story of the lost Christ Child.

8. *En el monte murió Cristo—Dios y hombre verdadero.* This is a traditional Spanish religious ballad on the Passion [23] that has been changed in part into a prayer. It is a very short one, but also one that certainly comes from a sixteenth- or seventeenth-century Spanish original. It is included in one of the Santa Cruz Penitente manuscripts. It has one assonance throughout.

Of the religious ballads described, versions of number 1, 2, 4, and 8 are given below.

> Por el rastro de la sangre—que Jesucristo *redama*
> camina la Virgen pura—en una fresca mañana.
> Como era tan de mañana—la hora que caminaba,
> las campanas de Belén—solas se tocan el alba.
> La *incontró* San Juan Bautista,—y de esta manera le habla:
> —¿No me has visto por aquí—al hijo de mis entrañas?
> —Por aquí pasó, Señora,—antes que el gallo cantara;
> cinco mil azotes lleva—en sus sagradas espaldas.

Una cruz lleva en sus hombros—de madera muy pesada;
padeciendo por nosotros,—a Jesús atormentaban;
Una corona de espinas—con que ha de ser coronado;
tres clavos lleva en sus manos—con que ha de ser enclavado.
Soga a la garganta lleva—que más de cien *ñudos* daba;
cada estirón que le daban—mi Jesús se arrodillaba.

Luego que oyó esto la Virgen—cayó en tierra desmayada.
San Juan, como buen sobrino,—luego acude a levantarla.
—Levántese, tía mía,—que no es tiempo de tardanza,
que en aquel Monte Calvario—se suena una ronca caja.
Se suena una ronca caja—y un destemplado tambor;
póngase luto la Virgen,—que es muerto Nuestro Señor.

Verónica trae un manto—con que le limpiaba el rostro,
con un letrero que dice:—"Cristo murió por nosotros." [24]

Following the way of the Cross by the blood that Christ had shed
the Virgin, one cool morning, walked sadly on, ahead.
So early it was in the morning when she traveled on her way,
that Bethlehem's bells alone rang out the dawning of the day.
She met Saint John the Baptist, and asked him with doleful voice,
"Have you seen my beloved Son, the source of all my joys?"
"Yes, lady, I have seen Him, He passed on this very road;
it was long before cock crow, with His Cross, a weighty load.
On His bleeding back five thousand stripes of lashes cruel He bore;
for our sins my tortured Jesus has suffered anguish sore.
A crown of thorns He carried, His crown of ignomy;
three nails also He carried to nail Him on a cross for me.
About His neck was a heavy rope with a hundred knots, and these
at every jerk and pull caused Jesus to stumble to His knees."

When the Holy Virgin heard this, fainting she sank to the ground;
Saint John, good nephew, revived her, as was heard a distant sound.
"Rise up, rise up, my Lady, for there is no time to wait;
already the tocsin on Calvary is sounding your Son's sad fate.
Oh, Virgin, don your mourning, for Christ, Our Lord, is dead."
These words, when the tocsin sounded, Saint John in compassion said.

Veronica brought a cloth to wipe the Savior's face;
"Christ died for us!" reads the legend, in letters we plainly trace.

Un ángel triste lloraba—de ver la cuenta que dio.
El alma que tenía a su cargo—el Malo se la llevó.

Image of the Sorrowful Mother, Santa Cruz Church,
Santa Cruz, New Mexico, 1931. *Photograph by J. Manuel
Espinosa.*

La Virgen le dice al ángel:—No llores, niño varón,
que yo le rogaré a Cristo—que esta alma tenga perdón.
La Virgen le dice a Cristo:—Hijo de mi corazón,
por la leche que *mamastes*—esta alma tenga perdón.
Cristo le dice a la Virgen:—Madre de mi corazón,
¿para qué quieres esta alma—si tanto nos ofendió?
La Virgen le dice a Cristo:—Hijo de mi corazón,
pastoreando sus ovejas—mi rosario me rezó.
Cristo le dice a la Virgen:—Madre de mi corazón,
si tanto quieres esta alma—sacala de fuego ardor.
La Virgen como piadosa—a este riesgo se metió.
Con su santo escapulario—a su devoto sacó.

El Demonio enfurecido—a los cielos se subió:
—Señor, el alma que me *distes*—tu madre me la quitó.
—Quítate de aquí, maligno,—quítate de aquí, traidor,
que lo que mi madre hiciere—por bien hecho lo doy yo. [25]

An Angel was sadly weeping—because he'd failed in his charge.
The soul given to his care—the Evil One had carried off.
The Virgin says to the angel: "Do not weep, my little one,
for I propose to ask Christ—that this soul may be forgiven."
The Virgin then says to Christ: "Dearest Son, love of my heart,
because of the milk I fed you—let this poor soul be forgiven."
Christ responds thus to the Virgin: "Dearest Mother of my heart,
why do you defend this soul—which so often offended us?"
The Virgin replies to Christ: "Dearest Son, love of my heart,
while watching over his sheep—my rosary he would pray."
Christ then says to the Virgin, "Dearest Mother of my heart,
if you love this soul so much,—snatch it from the burning fires."
The Virgin always merciful—took this risk upon herself.
With her holy scapular—her devoted one she freed.
The devil, surprised and furious—up to the heavens he rushed:
"Lord, the soul You had given me—your mother stole it from me."
"Begone from here, accursed one—you traitor, begone from here.
For whatever my mother does—I consider to be well done."

Al pie de este santo altar—la Virgen está llorando
por Jesús, su Hijo Divino,—y su Pasión contemplando.
En su santísimo llanto—aclama y dice:—¡Ay, Jesús!
¿Que haré sola en este monte?—¿Quién te baja de la cruz?
¡Ya murió el poder divino!—Así empieza a lamentar:
—En este amargo Calvario—no hay quien te venga a bajar.

Hincada al pie de la cruz—alza los ojos, lo ve:
—¡Ay, mi Dios y mi Jesús!—¿En qué te amortajaré?
¡Ay, Jesús de mis entrañas!—¡Ay, mi Jesús! ¡Ay de mí!
También me falta un sepulcro—en que sepultarte a ti.

José Nicomedes llega—al Calvario de Jesús,
donde está su dulce Madre—y lo bajan de la cruz.
—¡Ay Jesús! ¡Ay, qué dolor!—Te bajan hecho pedazos.
Llega hasta mi corazón—y te recibo en mis brazos.
Tres clavos te remacharon—en pies y manos, Señor.
Estos mismos traspasaron,—Hijo Mío, mi corazón.
Ya llegó la hora divina,—Redentor de cielo y tierra;
que te bajen de la cruz,—que mis brazos ya te esperan.
¡Ay, Jesús, con que dolor!—¡válgame Dios qué pesar!
¡te han de quitar de mis brazos—para llevarte a enterrar!
Ya lo llevan al sepulcro;—dice la Virgen:—¿Qué haré?
¿Con qué corazón lo siento?—¿Con qué ojos lo lloraré?
Ya mi corazón no puede—sufrir tan grande pesar.
Mis ojos son unas fuentes—más que las aguas del mar.
—¡Adiós, Hijo de mi vida!—¡Adiós, divino Santuario!
¡Adiós, Jesús Nazareno!—¡Adiós, mi triste Calvario!

Por este camino amargo—donde el Señor padeció,
caminó esta triste madre,—y a su Calvario volvió.
Llega a su Calvario y dice,—se queja, lamenta y llora:
—¡Adiós, Jesús Nazareno,—hasta vernos en la gloria![26]

At the sacred feet of her dying Son the Virgin Mother is weeping,
in all His cruel anguish a close communion keeping.
All lonely in her sorrow, through holy tears exclaiming,
"My Son, my God, my only one, there is not one remaining
to take you down! God's power is dead; 'twas crucified with You.
Alone upon this bitter mount, My Son, what shall I do?"
Embracing then His holy feet, raising her streaming eyes,
"I have no winding sheet for You, no sepulchre," she cries.
"Nowhere to place Thy Sacred Form, no bands nor linen fine.
Oh pity me, my only one, Beloved Son divine!"

Then Joseph and Nicodemus arrive on Calvary
where stands the Sweetest Mother, exclaiming, "Woe is me!"
They take the Sacred Body down from the cruel cross,
the while His mournful Mother bewails her bitter loss.
"Oh Jesus, my Son, my only one, what pain burns in my heart

as my loving arms receive You, wounded in every part!
Three nails transpierced your hands and feet. These very nails, my Son,
have pierced the fibers of my heart, my Lord, my God, my only one!
My arms await the dire moment, Redeemer of heaven and earth!
When from the cruel cross is lowered Your Body of infinite worth.
But Oh, what cruel sorrow! My Jesus, with what pain
they take you away for your burial, snatch you from my arms again!"
Tenderly they bear the Body to its final resting place.
Oh, who shall depict the anguish of that loving last embrace!
"With what heart shall I mourn Him, and with what eyes shall I weep?"
She cried. "My heart is broken with suffering so deep.
My eyes are like two fountains far greater than the sea.
Farewell, my Son, my very life!—Farewell, my Calvary!"

Along the bitter, bitter road the suffering Lord had trod,
grief-stricken, the Virgin returned, bewailing her Son and God.
"Jesus of Nazareth, fare thee well!" she said midst sighs and tears.
"A long farewell until we meet where Your lasting glory appears!"


En el Monte murió Cristo,—Dios y hombre verdadero,
no murió por sus pecados,—murió por pecados nuestros.
En una cruz fue clavado—con duros clavos de hierro.
¡Oh dulce Padre de mi alma!—¡Oh dulcísimo Cordero!
Yo soy este pecador que—tan ofendido te tengo,
que ni la tierra que piso,—Padre mío, no merezco.

Todos los dias me acuerdo—del Divino Sacramento,
y de la Hostia Consagrada—que se consagró en tu pecho.
Señor Mío Jesucristo,—este ejercicio te ofrezco;
creo me lo recibirás—con mucho agradecimiento.[27]


Christ died on Calvary, True God and True Man;
He died not for His sins, He died for the sins of Men.
On a cross He was nailed with cruel iron nails.
"Oh sweet and loving Father! Oh most sweet Lamb!
I am the sinner indeed who has so much offended you,
that I do not deserve the earth on which I tread.

Every day I am mindful of the Most Blessed Sacrament,
of the Consecrated Host, consecrated in Your Heart.
Oh my Lord Jesus Christ, I offer you this penance;
I trust that you will accept it with much gratitude and love."

## Burlesque Ballads

1. *Estaba Señor Don Gato—en silla de oro sentado.* 2. *Estaba el Gatito Prieto—en su silleta sentado.* Mr. Cat is seated on a chair, elegantly dressed. News comes to him that a bride has been found for him. In his anxiety to see her, Mr. Cat jumps and gets hurt. He dies and the mice celebrate the event. The ballad is very old. Spanish and Portuguese versions have been found that date from the sixteenth century. [28]

3. *El piojo y la liendre—se quieren casar.* This ballad develops the burlesque theme of the prospective wedding of two lice. All the animals are willing to help, contributing music and food, but when a mouse appears as *padrino* or best man, the cat arrives, eats the *padrino*, and spoils everything. There are Spanish and Spanish American versions. [29]

4. *Ora que estamos solitos—les contaré una mentira.* A narrative of impossible happenings, a very common theme in Spanish burlesque ballads and other poems. In the New Mexican version a crow flies with a wagon on its back, a swallow flies along with a spruce tree, a frog takes a walk all dressed up, a cricket is seen in a tavern drinking wine, and so on. [30]

An example of a traditional Spanish burlesque ballad from New Mexico is given below; it is a version of number 1, above, from Santa Cruz:

> Estaba el gatito prieto—en su silleta sentado,
> con su media de pelillo—y zapato alpargatado.
> Le han llegado las noticias—que había de ser casado
> con una gata morita,—hija del gato bragado.
> El gato de la alegría—se cayó de arriba abajo;
> se ha quebrado la cabeza—y la mitad del espinazo.
> —Tráiganle quien le confiese—al gatito enamorado.
> —Confieso a mi confesor—que he sido un gato malvado.
> Y si de ésta no me escapo—no me entierren en sagrado;
> entiérrenme en un arroyo,—donde me pise el ganado,
> que digan los gachupines,—"Aquí murió el malhadado;
> no murió de tabardillo,—ni de dolor de costado,
> murió de un dolor de amores—que le dio desesperado."
> Los ratones que lo saben—se visten de colorado,
> a lo español y francés,—lo que le luce al soldado. [31]

The little tiny black cat—was seated upon his chair,
with his finest stockings on—and his fiber sandals too.
The information has reached him—that his marriage had been arranged
to a little dark-skinned kitten—daughter of the strutting cat.
So great was the cat's delight—that he had a grievous fall;

his head was completely smashed—and half of his back was broken.
"Bring someone, please, to confess him—the poor little cat in love."
"I confess to you, my Confessor, that I have been a bad cat.
If I don't come out of this—don't bury me in sacred ground;
Bury me in an arroyo—where cattle may tramp upon me,
Let the *gachupines* say: 'Here died the ill-fated one;
He did not die of sunstroke—nor of a pain in his side,
He died from the pangs of love—which he could no longer bear.'"
The mice on learning the news—in their great joy dress in red,
in the Spanish and French manner—in the style befitting soldiers.

It should be noted here that the theme of despair in love, expressed in the verses beginning with "Y si de ésta no me escapo" and ending with "que le dio desesperado," is the subject matter of an entirely different ballad, number 8 of our novelesque group. This fusion of two ballads is not an unusual phenomenon in folklore; in fact, it is one of the important factors in the development of tradition.

If the real worth of Spanish ballads as lasting works of art is to be found in the human appeal manifested in their worldwide popularity and diffusion, a few gems having become the common patrimony of western European literature, it is no less true that their genuinely popular and traditional character is also attested by their longevity. Hegel, in his *Aesthetics*, called the traditional balladry of Spain "a necklace of pearls."[32] As the traditional ballads cited in the preceding pages clearly demonstrate, the contributions of Spanish New Mexico to this widely admired genre are of the greatest significance.

# Hymns, Prayers, and Other Religious Verses

Popular Themes: Christ of the Passion, Prayers and Hymns (*Alabados*) of the
Penitentes, the Child Jesus, the Holy Family, the Virgin Mary, the Matins;
the Bachelor's Prayer. Special Invocations.

The history of the Catholic Church in Spanish America is the continuation
of its history in Spain. Catholicism was transported to America in exactly
the same form, with all its doctrines, ceremonies, pomp, and traditions.
The Franciscan missionaries who labored in New Mexico for nearly two and
one-half centuries established there the same institutions that they had in
Spain to keep alive the fires of the faith among the colonizers and their
descendants and to Christianize the Indians.

There are popular prayers, ballads, hymns, dramatic representations,
legends, and beliefs which keep alive in the hearts and in the memories of
the people practically all the scenes of the birth, life, sufferings, and death
of Christ, special devotion to the Virgin Mary, and prayers to favorite saints.
While many of these ceremonies and practices are inspired directly in the
liturgical ceremonies of the Church, many others are of popular origin and
have a history as old as the Church itself.

## Christ of the Passion

The Christ of the Passion has been ever present in the tradition of Catholic
Spain. In New Mexican tradition He has been the special object of adoration and reverence from the days of the *conquistadores* to the present time.
When entering New Mexico, the first *conquistador* and colonizer, Juan de
Oñate, not only whipped himself in the company of his soldiers in reverence to Christ Crucified on Holy Thursday of the year 1598, but also
everywhere and on many occasions erected large wooden crosses before
which he prayed for victory that he might succeed in Christianizing the
Indians. The complete gospel narrative of the Passion and Death of Christ is
commemorated in various forms of Spanish traditions: prayers, hymns,
ballads, dramatic compositions, and iconography, a related popular artistic
expression of religious sentiment. In New Mexican tradition all these manifestations of Spanish religious tradition are to be found in popular form.

Christian communities in early times gave dramatic forms to some of the scenes of the Passion as they were depicted in the gospels, at first perhaps as ceremonies accessory to the liturgy of the mass during Lent. In the Middle Ages religious worship was always very real, very dramatic. The mass, with its dramatic action and dialogue between the officiating priest and his assistants, the choir, and the people who participated, was in reality drama of the highest form. The elaborations of the liturgy called *tropes* were soon developed, and these may be considered the beginnings of the Passion plays of Christian tradition. The people then developed independent scenes, among them the scene of the Descent from the Cross, and began the truly popular religious drama, often separated from the official ecclesiastical ceremonies.

The so-called Easter plays of mediaeval Catholic tradition were a development of the earlier *tropes*, with the addition of the characters of Pilate, Judas, the Roman soldiers, Mary Magdalen, and so on. From these were developed the Passion plays of the fourteenth and fifteenth centuries. In the fifteenth century the Church authorities took a great interest in the Passion plays, but in the sixteenth century they generally left them to the people. The plays had become too long and complicated, with legendary elements added, and were often a source of mirth and amusement in some respects rather than of sorrow and devotion. From that time on, the Passion play was relegated to the people.

In Spain, however, the scenes of the Passion were not altogether relegated to the people, being continued, in a way, by the *autos sacramentales* produced in the streets of Madrid on carriages, each of which, as it passed along, represented a scene from a secular play in honor of the Eucharist or some scene from the Passion. Moreover, popular religious drama had a greater development in Spain than in any other European country. Nowhere in Europe are the scenes of the Passion and Death of Christ popularized for public devotion as in some cities of Spain: Barcelona, Seville, Toledo, Valencia. The religious orders and confraternities that have represented in one form or another some of the outstanding scenes of the Passion are legion. Holy Week in Seville has produced since the sixteenth century practically every scene that can be dramatized.

The Passion was a popular theme for dramatization in all parts of the Spanish world. Among the scenes of the Passion that have been popularly dramatized in New Mexico there is the popular dramatic representation called *La primera persecución de Jesús* (The first persecution of Jesus). I know of two manuscript versions from Taos. The older and better version is very short and represents the visit of the three Magi Kings to the Child Jesus at

This carved wooden sculpture of Saint Francis in Santa Cruz Church, 1931, is believed to have been brought to New Mexico from Spain, by way of New Spain, in the last decade of the seventeenth century. The Franciscans directed the church administration and were the only clergy in colonial New Mexico until the late eighteenth century. *Photograph by J. Manuel Espinosa.*

Images of Jesus of Nazareth (Jesús Nazareno), the Sorrowful Mother, and Christ in the Sepulcher by a New Mexican religious artist of the late eighteenth century. Side altar, Santa Cruz Church, 1931. These religious images are carried in local Holy Week processions. *Photograph by J. Manuel Espinosa*.

Bethlehem, the Herodian persecution and massacres, and the flight to Egypt. This popular composition, which is still produced in Taos, is not properly speaking a Passion play; it is more fully described in another chapter.

Scenes from the Passion are apparently no longer performed today in New Mexico, although it seems that they were often staged up to the end of the nineteenth century. No texts of any of them have been found, but certain fragments of ballads and other verse narratives that have been preserved may have been parts of such plays. According to authentic information, a Passion play was part of the Church ceremony of Holy Week, following the mass on Good Friday, although some of the preparatory scenes were performed on previous days; Roman soldiers with helmets, the Centurion, and the Cyrenian appeared in them in costume. The play began with the adoration of Christ on the Cross, represented by a large image of Christ crucified on a huge cross. Longinus then appeared with his lance, often on horseback. It is said that at Tomé, Longinus actually entered the Church on a horse to pierce the side of the Savior. All this was accompanied by weeping and by the singing of sacred hymns, perhaps some of those, cited below, now found only in the ritual manuscripts of the Penitentes. Next, the lamentations of the Virgin took place. The lamentations are preserved in one of the most beautiful traditional Spanish ballads now found in New Mexico. The Descent from the Cross followed, and the lamentations continued. The image of Christ was taken down from the cross and delivered into the arms of the Virgin Mary. Finally, there took place the *Santo entierro*, or the burial. This consisted of placing the body of *nuestro padre* Jesús in the sepulchre, a large wooden box, to be venerated in the Church. I myself have witnessed some of the above scenes. None, to my knowledge, are performed today, except in the ceremonies of the Passion that are included in the practices of the Penitentes. The Ecce Homo, or Jesús Nazareno, of which there are still in New Mexico some very realistic iconographic examples, may have appeared also immediately before the scene of the Crucifixion.

Although these traditional scenes of the Passion were performed by the people, the Church officials approved them and took part in them. The scene of the Descent from the Cross, with the lamentations of the Virgin, was especially popular, and at Taos, Santa Fe, and other places it lasted longer than the other scenes, with ecclesiastical sanction and direction. The lamentations of the Virgin are found in several popular versions.

### Prayers and Hymns (*Alabados*) of Penitentes

The *hermanos penitentes*, or Penitent Brothers of the society now called La Sociedad de Nuestro Padre Jesús Nazareno, represent an interesting New Mexican Spanish religious survival. Just when this Catholic religious society of New Mexican flagellants was given its present name we do not know. Up to the turn of the century its members were usually called Los Hermanos Penitentes de Nuestro Padre San Francisco. (The Penitent Brothers of Our Father Saint Francis), and there is much evidence to indicate that the society was a popular development of the Third Order of Saint Francis.[1] The members of this lay religious brotherhood are generally referred to as Penitentes. The Passion of Christ is the central theme of the religious ritual and ceremonies of the Penitentes.

A study of the ritual, with its traditional Spanish prayers, ballads, hymns, and Passion narratives, together with the practices now in vogue, reveal at once the Spanish origin of the society and of practically all its ritual and ceremonies. The same or similar practices were common in mediaeval Europe. In modern Spain most of the ceremonies, including self-flagellation as penance for sin, are still to be found. The religious processions of various parish religious groups during Holy Week, with the carrying of heavy crosses, for example, are still commonplace in Madrid, Toledo, Seville, Valencia, and other cities in Spain. Similar examples can be given from some of the countries of present-day Hispanic America.

The New Mexican Spanish *penitentes* have practiced flagellation since the earliest years of the conquest, attested to by the fact that they did so when Oñate entered New Mexico in 1598, it was described by Father Benavides in the 1630's,[2] and religious societies have practiced it to our knowledge until recent years not only in New Mexico (the Penitentes), but also in Mexico, Spain, Italy, and other countries. At Santa Fe, members of the Third Order of Saint Francis, or *terciarios*, who flagellated themselves especially during Holy Week ceremonies, had their Franciscan chaplain and maintained a chapel which in the seventeenth and eighteenth centuries adjoined the Church of San Miguel. Its concession was annulled in 1826.

In the nineteenth century the Penitentes were numerous in northern New Mexico. After the American occupation, they were frequently in conflict with the ecclesiastical authorities, but the society seems to have flourished most when the opposition of the Church was the strongest. New Mexican ecclesiastical authorities of that era sometimes spoke rather harshly about the organization. Very often the conflict between the Penitentes and the Church seems to have been precipitated by overzealous ecclesiastics who attempted to stamp out too abruptly old customs such as these.[3]

The members of the Penitente brotherhood are Catholic men who gather during Lent to perform certain religious rites, consisting of prayers and hymns about the Passion and Death of Christ, and who, in addition, practice flagellation during Holy Week and on other special occasions, such as the night of a vigil held for a deceased member. The march to Calvary from the *morada*, or chapel, on Good Friday is the special occasion for flagellation, and up to the end of the nineteenth century it was the usual custom to simulate a crucifixion: a Penitente was tied to a cross, which was raised for the period of the Agony on the Cross or for such time as the Penitente could endure. The Lenten and other devotions of the organization are not of New Mexican origin but are traditional Spanish prayers, hymns, and Passion ballads—the work, no doubt, of Franciscan missionaries of the seventeenth and eighteenth centuries or versions of Spanish originals printed in Spain in the sixteenth and seventeenth centuries.

The organization of the New Mexican Penitentes is very simple. The local *morada* has an *hermano mayor*, chief brother, as its supreme director,

A New Mexican Penitente (member of the New Mexican Catholic lay brotherhood called La Sociedad de Nuestro Padre Jesús Nazareno) standing beside wooden crosses used in Penitente religious ceremonies. Penitente *morada* (chapel and meeting place), Arroyo Hondo, New Mexico, in the 1940s. *Photograph by Juan B. Rael, courtesy of the Division of Community Life, Smithsonian Institution.*

who holds office for four or five years together with as many as eleven other officers: the *pitero cantador*, or leader in singing; the *curandero*, or doctor who looks after the wounds of the members during their religious exercises; and others. The officers are usually selected from those who have finished their flagellation period of four or five years and are not obliged by the rules to whip themselves any more. Until recent years, the various *moradas* of northern New Mexico, some thirty in number, sometimes sent representatives to a general assembly that met usually at Santa Cruz to discuss matters of interst to the society, but there is no well-defined central organization. The local *morada*, with its officers, is an independent unit. It alone decided whether or not to send delegates to the general assemblies at Santa Cruz. Some Penitentes speak of the Santa Cruz chapel as the *morada madre*, or mother chapel, which seems to indicate that the general meetings held there may have been a continuation of meetings that were formerly the regular assemblies of a general and more highly organized society that since the days of Governor Vargas in the last years of the seventeenth century had its center at Santa Cruz. The division of the society into *moradas* of independent rule and organization was probably the result of the ecclesiastical opposition in the first half of the nineteenth century.

The entire ritual and actual ceremonies and practices of the New Mexican Penitentes are a commemoration of the Passion and Death of Christ. Although now continued chiefly by the lower classes in the old Spanish-speaking rural areas, the institution is not of popular origin. The Spanish tradition itself has a mediaeval Catholic origin, monastic in its beginnings. Even in the modern imperfect and garbled versions of the prayers, hymns, and religious ballads that are found in the hand-written *cuadernos*, or hymn books, of the New Mexican Penitentes, recopied and handed down from one generation to another, the learned sources are clearly observable. The existence of this mediaeval Spanish institution, a society of Christian flagellants, with their traditional Spanish ritual in prayers, hymns, ballads, and Passion narratives, is one of the most extraordinary features of Spanish tradition in New Mexico.

Of the various traditional Spanish prayers and Passion ballads that are found in the ritual and prayer manuscripts of the present-day New Mexican Penitentes, none appears to be a modern composition. All are versions of traditional Spanish seventeenth- and eighteenth-century compositions. The ballads *Por el rastro de la sangre, Un ángel triste lloraba*, and some of the traditional forms of the prayer *Bendito y alabado* certainly go back to the sixteenth and seventeenth centuries. The religious ballads preserved by the Penitentes are among the gems of the contribution of northern New Mexico and southern Colorado to Spanish balladry, the *romances tradicionales*.

One of the longest and best of the Passion narratives in verse—one that is chanted or sung at the *morada* on Holy Thursday—consists of 144 octosyllabic quatrains, or 576 verses. It narrates the complete story of the Crucifixion. The first 52 and the last 24 verses of this version are the following:

| | |
|---|---|
| Con mansedumbre y ternura | With meekness and deep affection |
| y señas de fino amor | and signs of the most pure love, |
| les previno a sus discípulos | the Lord for his twelve disciples |
| la última cena el Señor. | provided the Last Supper. |
| Y con mucha caridad, | And with the greatest charity, |
| que en los mortales no ves, | the charity we never see, |
| después de haber cenado | after the supper was over |
| les lava humilde los pies. | He humbly washed their feet. |
| Luego consagró su sangre | He then consecrated His blood, |
| y con cariñoso afán | and with affectionate zeal |
| se les dio muy escogido | He gave Himself to them |

New Mexican Penitente holding a handmade flute used in Penitente religious ceremonies. Penitente *morada*, Arroyo Hondo, New Mexico, 1940s. *Photograph by Juan B. Rael, courtesy of the Division of Community Life, Smithsonian Institution.*

en accidente de pan.
Por este medio dispuso
aquel nuevo testamento,
sacrificándose así
para desterrar el viejo,
pues en este sacrificio
era sangre de animales,
y en el nuevo la de Cristo
para redimir mortales.
Y para mayor firmeza
de lo que en él ordenó
les hizo beber su sangre
en el cáliz que les dio.
También quiso que durara
el sacramento en su Iglesia,
y para ello potestades
a sus discípulos deja.
Estos las comunicaron,
del modo que ha de durar,
a sus hijos sacerdotes
hasta que vuelva a juzgar.
Y al mismo tiempo les manda
que al hacer el sacrificio
se acordasen del Señor
por tan grande beneficio.
Concluida que fue la cena
dio gracias al Padre Eterno,
y con tal echó a nosotros
el más saludable ejemplo.
Despidióse de su madre
con gran ternura y dolor;
el de la madre fue grande,
pero el del Hijo mayor.
Después de esta despedida
con sus discípulos fue
desde la ciudad al huerto,
donde había orado otra vez.
En la cena antes les dijo
que habían de experimentar
que aquella misma noche
todos lo habían de dejar.

. . . . . . . . . . . . . . . . . . . . . . .

Ya resucita Jesús,
ya el tercer día ha sacado
de allá del seno de Abrán
los justos depositados.
Consigo al cielo los sube,

in the accident of bread.
In this way He established
the New Testament and Faith,
thus sacrificing Himself
to do away with the Old;
for in the Old they offered
as a sacrifice animals' blood,
while in the New it is Christ's blood
that was shed for the sins of men.
And to confirm their faith
in all the things he commanded,
He gave them in the chalice
His precious blood to drink.
This Sacrament He wished
should abide in His living church,
and for that purpose He gave
to His disciples His powers.
These have then transmitted them
and their powers are thus continued
in all the priests who follow them
until He comes to judge.
He also commanded them
that when offering the sacrifice
they should do it in remembrance
of Him Who did such good.
And when the supper was finished
He gave thanks to the Father,
giving us thus an example
of what we too must do.
He took leave of His Mother
with deep affection and sorrow;
great was the Mother's sorrow,
but greater was that of the Son.
After this sad parting
with His disciples He went
from the city to the garden,
where He had prayed before.
He had told them during the supper
that it would come to pass
that on that very night
all of them would abandon Him.

. . . . . . . . . . . . . . . . . . . . . . . . . . . .

On the third day Jesus has risen,
and has already delivered
from the bosom of Abraham those
just souls that were waiting there.
He took them with Him to heaven,

que se mantuvo cerrado
hasta que sirvió de llave
la sangre que ha derramado.
Con la cual el nuevo Adán
recuperó aquella tierra
que primero había perdido
*causa* una serpiente fiera.
Reconozcamos despúes
a Nuestro Jesús Amado;
nuestros yerros son la causa
que le ponen nuevos clavos.
Acabemos con su muerte
nuestras culpas, sus agravios,
y no le ofendamos más,
que seremos muy ingratos.
*Intercédenos*, María,
se borren nuestros errores,
ya que vuestro Hijo os dejó
por madre de pecadores.

the heaven that was ever closed
until it was opened at last
by the blood that Christ has shed.
In this manner the New Adam
recovered all that paradise
that in ages past he had lost
through the serpent's evil advice.
Les us praise forever and ever
the name of Our Loving Jesus;
our sins alone are to blame
for the nails that pierced his flesh.
He died for us; let us end
our life of sin and His grief
and let us offend Him no more,
for we would be most ungrateful.
Intercede for us, Virgin Mary,
that our sins may be forgiven,
for Your Son has deemed to name you
as the mother of all sinners.

As a sample of part of the ritual of the Penitentes, the complete ceremony, with the password and prayers performed on the arrival of each Penitente at the *morada* after the door has been closed, as found in the Santa Cruz manuscripts, is given below. Most of the language of the ceremony is in ocotosyllabic verse.

—Dios toca en esta misión
las puertas de su clemencia.
—Penitencia, penitencia,
que quieres tu salvación.
—San Pedro me abra las puertas,
bañado entre clara luz;
soy esclavo de María;
traigo el sello de Jesús.
Pregunto a esta cofradía,
¿Quién a esta casa da luz?
—Jesús.
—¿Quién la llena de alegría?
—María.
—¿Quién la conserva en la fe?
—José.
—Luego bien claro se ve
que siempre habrá contrición
teniendo en el corazón
a Jesús, María y José.
Para entrar a esta misión

"In this mission God unbolts
the gates of His boundless mercy."
"Penance we preach, penance,
for you wish your salvation."
"May Saint Peter open the gates,
for me with brilliant light;
I am the slave of Mary;
I have the seal of Jesus.
I ask this confraternity,
"Who gives light to this house?"
"Jesus."
"Who fills it with joy?"
"Mary."
"Who keeps it in the faith?"
"Joseph."
"It is perfectly clear, then,
that all those will be saved
who hold in their hearts
Jesus, Mary, and Joseph.
In order to enter this mission

| | |
|---|---|
| el pie derecho pondré, | I will put first my right foot, |
| y alabo a los dulces nombres | and will praise the sweet names |
| de Jesús, María y José. | of Jesus, Mary, and Joseph." |

The door is opened and the penitent enters, stepping in first with his right foot. He then kneels and on his knees he advances toward the Cross on the altar. In the long prayer that the penitent recites while venerating the Cross, he is often accompanied by all those present. Sometimes the prayer is omitted. After the veneration of the Cross, the penitent recites the following prayer in verse, performing the various acts indicated in the words:

| | |
|---|---|
| —Señor Mío Jesucristo, | My Lord, Jesus Christ, |
| yo soy este pecador | I come, a grievous sinner, |
| que vengo a hacer mi ejercicio | to perform my exercises |
| y cumplir mi devoción. | and accomplish my devotions. |
| Besaré este santo velo | I will kiss this holy veil |
| para que mi alma suba al cielo; | so that my soul may be saved; |
| besaré esta santa mesa, | I will kiss this holy altar |
| que es lo que mi alma confiesa; | for it confirms my faith; |
| besaré esta santa cuerda | I will kiss this holy cord |
| para que mi alma no se pierda. | that my soul may not be lost. |

All those present then pray:

"—Adorámoste, Nuestro Señor Jesucristo y bendecímoste que por tu Santa Cruz redimiste al mundo y a mí pecador también."

"We adore Thee and we bless Thee, Our Lord Jesus Christ, because through Thy Cross Thou hast redeemed the world and also me, a sinner."

The Penitente then withdraws from the altar backwards, always facing the Cross and on his knees. He then kisses the feet of the *hermano mayor* and asks pardon of all those he may have offended, and the others answer him:

"—Perdónenme, hermanos míos, si en algo los he ofendido y escandalizado.
—Que le perdone Dios, que de nosotros ya está perdonado."

"Pardon me, brothers, if in any way I have offended you and scandalized you."
"May God pardon you, because we have already pardoned you."

In most of the *moradas* the above ceremony apparently takes place only at the beginning of the Lenten ceremonies, when the Penitentes first gather at the *morada* for their regular Lenten exercises. Each Penitente enters individually until all have been received.

## The Child Jesus

In New Mexico, as in all Spanish-speaking countries, the veneration for the Child Jesus is deeply rooted in popular tradition. Prayers to the Child Jesus are taught to New Mexican children by their parents and relatives as soon as they learn to speak. Among the most beautiful nursery rhymes known by children we find the following:

| | |
|---|---|
| Dijo el gallo: | Said the cock, |
| —¡Cocorocó! | "Kokoroko! |
| ¡Cristo nació! | Christ is born!" |
| | |
| Dijo la cabra: | Said the goat |
| —¡Me, me! | "Ma, Ma! |
| ¿Donde? ¿Donde? | Where? Where?" |
| | |
| Dijo la oveja: | Said the sheep, |
| —¡Be, be! | "Ba, ba! |
| ¡En Belén! | In Bethlehem!" |
| | |
| Dijo la mula: | Said the mule, |
| —¡Vamos a ver! | "Let us go and see!" |
| | |
| Dijo el buey: | Said the ox, |
| —¡No es menester! | "It is not necessary!" |

This New Mexican Spanish Christmas rhyme is traditional. There are similar versions from Argentina and Chile and from several parts of Spain.[4] The verses are pan-European and are a survival from mediaeval Latin rhymes. In such a well-known book as *Songs of the Nativity* by William Henry Husk we find the following mediaeval Latin version: "The cock croweth, *Christus natus est* [Christ is born]; the raven asketh, *Quando?* [When?]; the cow replieth, *Hac nocte* [This night]; the ox crieth out, *Ubi? Ubi?* [Where? Where?]; the sheep bleateth out, *Bethlehem*."[5]

The Child Jesus born of the Virgin Mary in the stable at Bethlehem and adored by the Magi Kings and by the shepherds is the special object of adoration, love, and pity. No more beautiful lyric poetry has ever been written than some of the verses composed by Lope de Vega for his *Los pastores de Belén* (The shepherds of Bethlehem). The following verses are sung by the Virgin Mary and the shepherds when the Divine Child trembles and weeps from the cold:

| | |
|---|---|
| No lloréis, mis ojos; | Do not weep, my love; |
| Niño Dios, callad, | Child God, do not weep, |
| que si llora el cielo, | for if heaven weeps, |
| ¿quién podrá cantar? | who will ever sing? |

| | |
|---|---|
| Vuestra madre hermosa, | Your beautiful mother, |
| que cantando está, | who is now singing, |
| llorará también, | will weep also, |
| si ve que lloráis. | if she sees you weeping. |
| | |
| Los ángeles bellos | The angels on high |
| cantan, que les dais | are singing, for you give |
| a los cielos gloria | joy to heaven and |
| y a la tierra paz. | peace to earth. |
| | |
| De aquestas montañas | From these mountains |
| descendiendo van | the shepherds are coming |
| pastores cantando | singing joyously |
| por daros solaz. | to bring you comfort. |
| | |
| Niño de mis ojos, | Dear Child, my love, |
| ea, no haya más, | come, weep no more, |
| que si el cielo llora, | for if heaven weeps, |
| ¿quién podrá cantar?[6] | who will ever sing? |

There are many prayers, ballads, legends, and dramatic representations that continue the general Spanish cult of the Divine Child, and some are traditional and very old. The popular verses that may be compared to those of Lope de Vega, although not so beautiful, are numerous. Among the most popular are the following, found as separate verses to the Child Jesus or as part of the dramatic compositions called *Los pastores*, discussed in another chapter. In *Los pastores* they are usually put in the mouths of the shepherds.

| | |
|---|---|
| Duérmete, Niño chiquito, | Go to sleep, little Child, |
| duérmete, amado mío; | go to sleep, my love; |
| mis pecados fueron causa | it is on account of my sins |
| que estés temblando de frío. | that you suffer from the cold. |
| | |
| Duérmete, Niño chiquito, | Go to sleep, little Child, |
| duérmete, mi Redentor; | go to sleep, my Redeemer; |
| duérmete tierno querido | go to sleep, my dear one, |
| hasta unirme con mi Dios. | until I meet my God. |
| | |
| Alarrú, Niño chiquito, | Lullaby, little Child, |
| alarrú, mi vida mía; | lullaby, my life; |
| duérmete, Niño chiquito, | go to sleep, little Child, |
| que la noche está muy fría. | for the night is very cold. |
| | |
| ¡Quién pudiera, Niño lindo, | Would, beautiful Child, |
| lograr en esta ocasión | that on this occasion |
| que te sirvieran de cuna | a cradle could be made for you |
| telas de mi corazón! | from the tissues of my heart! |

The novenas to the Holy Child (el Santo Niño), especially to the Santo

Niño de Atocha, are very popular in New Mexico. The expression "¡Santo Niño de Atocha!" to express surprise or sorrow, asking the help of the Divine Child to avert disaster or suffering, is heard in New Mexico today. There is a popular prayer in verse to the Santo Niño de Atocha that has many variants, the differences being chiefly in their length. The version given below, which is one of the shorter ones, in its Spanish form consists of nine octosyllabic quatrains, each quatrain with the second and fourth verses in assonance:

| | |
|---|---|
| ¡Adiós, Niñito de Atocha, | Hail, Child of Jesus of Atocha, |
| mi dulzura y mi placer! | my sweetness and my joy! |
| Hermosura de la gloria, | Heavenly beauty, |
| ¿cuándo te volveré a ver? | when will I see you again? |
| | |
| Manuelito de mi vida | Manuelito, my life, |
| líbrame de Lucifer. | save me from Lucifer's wiles. |
| Hermosura de la gloria, | Heavenly beauty, |
| ¿cuándo te volveré a ver? | when will I see you again? |
| | |
| Jardín lleno de delicias, | Garden of all delight, |
| y matizado clavel, | multiple-hued carnation, |
| delicia de los arcangeles, | joy of archangels, |
| ¿cuándo te volveré a ver? | when will I see you again? |
| | |
| Lucerito de mi vida, | Morning star of my life, |
| de la más linda mujer, | born of the loveliest of women, |
| encanto de las virtudes, | joy of heavenly virtues, |
| ¿cuándo te volveré a ver? | when will I see you again? |
| | |
| Naciste, divino Niño. | You were born, divine Child, |
| en la ciudad de Belén. | in the city of Bethlehem. |
| Gloria de (de)nominaciones, | Glory of denominations, |
| ¿cuándo te volveré a ver? | when will I see you again? |
| | |
| Cielo estrellado, divino, | Starry heaven, divine, |
| y todo mi menester, | the end of my desires, |
| gloria de los principados, | glory of principalities, |
| ¿cuándo te volveré a ver? | when will I see you again? |
| | |
| Por tus santísimos padres | Through your divine origin |
| y por tu divino ser, | and your divine essence |
| gloria de los mismos tronos, | glory of thrones, I ask, |
| ¿cuándo te volveré a ver? | when will I see you again? |
| | |
| Por el natal que tomaste | Through your divine birth |
| de una peregrina Ester, | from an Esther full of grace, |
| gloria de los querubines, | I ask, glory of Cherubim, |
| ¿cuándo te volveré a ver? | when will I see you again? |

| | |
|---|---|
| Por el suspenso y afán | By the suspense and agony |
| de mi señor San José, | suffered by St. Joseph, I ask, |
| gloria de los serafines, | glory of the seraphim, |
| ¡cuándo te volveré a ver? | when will I see you again? |

The lost Christ Child found with the high priests in the temple is sung in New Mexico in traditional Spanish ballads, usually incorporated in the texts of the popular dramatic composition *El Niño Perdido* (The lost Child). A version from Taos, modernized into strophic form in two different meters and with changes in assonance, is the following:

La Virgen buscaba al Niño—por las calles y las plazas,
y a todos los que veía—por su Hijo preguntaba.
—Decid si habéis visto—al sol de los soles,
al que nos alumbra—con sus resplandores.
Dénos, Señora, las señas,—por si acaso lo encontramos.
—Es blanco como la nieve,—y como la aura encarnado.
Tiene unos cabellos—como el sol dorado;
sus labios y boca—son flores del año.
—Por aquí pasó ese Niño,—según las señas que dais
Al templo se encaminó,—id allá y lo hallaréis.
—Dios os pague, hijos,—esa buena nueva.
Ya encontrará alivio,—el alma en su pena.
Partió el Alma Divina,—al templo se encaminó.
Entre todos los doctores,—al Sol de Justicia halló.[7]

The Virgin sought the Child through streets and squares,
and asked all those she met if they had seen her Child,
"Tell me if you have seen the sun of all the suns,
that one who gives us of his divine light."
"Describe him, dear Lady; we may meet him perchance."
"He is as white as snow, and as fair as the dawn.
The locks of his forehead are of a golden hue;
his lips and his mouth are the flowers of the season."
"That child passed by here, to judge from that description.
Go to the temple, lady, and you will find him there."
"The Lord reward you, children, for the good news.
My grieved heart will now find more comfort and peace."
The Blessed Mother to the temple directed her steps.
Among the doctors the sun of all justice she found.

## The Holy Family

The Holy Family is a special object of veneration in New Mexico as well as

The eighteenth-century Catholic church in Santa Cruz, New Mexico, 1931.
*Photograph by J. Manuel Espinosa.*

in all Spanish countries. In New Mexican Spanish tradition, popular dramatic compositions, numerous prayers, hymns, nursery rhymes, and a few ballads attest the great popularity of the veneration for the Holy Family. The first prayer that New Mexican Spanish children learned from their mother's lips is the following one, no doubt traditional. It is known by all. As noted earlier, the Penitentes of New Mexico have a version of it in their ritual, and some of its verses are found in other New Mexican prayers.

—¡Bendito y alabado sea el
   Santísimo Sacramento del altar!
—¡Ave, María Purísima!
—¿Quién en esta casa da luz?
—Jesús.
—¿Quién la llena de alegría?
—María.
—¿Quién la conserva en la fe?
—José.
—Pues bien claro se ve
que siempre habrá contrición,
teniendo en el corazón.
a Jesús, María y José.

Blessed and praised be the
   Most Holy Sacrament of the altar!
Hail, Most Pure Mary!
"Who gives light to this home?"
"Jesus."
"Who fills it with joy?"
"Mary."
"Who keeps it in the faith?"
"Joseph."
   "It is perfectly clear, then
that all those will be saved
who hold in their hearts
Jesus, Mary, and Joseph."

¡Salgan los espíritus malignos
y entre la suma bondad,
y se estampe en mi alma
la Santísima Trinidad!
   Purísima Concepción,
Madre del Verbo Divino,
échame tu bendición
y guíanos por buen camino,
que yo la recibo en el nombre
del Padre y del Hijo
y del Espíritu Santo, Amén.

May all evil spirits depart
and may true virtue enter
and may the Most Holy Trinity
take possession of my soul!
   Most Immaculate Conception,
Mother of the Divine Word,
give me your blessing
and show us the right way,
for I now receive it in the name
of the Father, and of the Son,
and of the Holy Ghost, Amen.

There are shorter versions, but none omits the beautiful verses beginning with "¿Quién en esta casa de luz?" and ending with "a Jesús, María y José," which are mumbled even by infants just learning to speak. In religious processions, such as first-communion processions, children used to sing the complete version given above. These verses are the oldest form of the prayer and are traditional. They probably came from Spain in some form in the seventeenth century. In the *Noche buena, autos al nacimiento del Hijo de Dios*, a seventeenth-century Spanish work by Gómez Tejada de los Reyes, we find in one of the *villancicos*, or Christmas carols, the following version of the above lines, one very close to the New Mexican prayer and probably one of the oldest versions:

—Zagal, ¿dónde está mi bien?
—En María, Jesús y José.
—¿Adónde está mi alegría?
—En Jesús, José y María.
—¿Adónde toda la luz?
—En María, José y Jesús.[8]

"Youth, where is my greatest treasure?"
"In Mary, Jesus, and Joseph."
"Where is my joy?"
"In Jesus, Joseph, and Mary."
"Where is all my light?"
"In Mary, Joseph and Jesus."

In a Chilean version of the widely known Spanish traditional children's prayer that begins with the words "Con Dios me acuesto, con Dios me levanto," (I retire with God, and I rise with God) we find the following version of the verses in question:

—¿Quién es mi luz
—Jesús.
—¿Quién es mi guía?
—María.
—¿Quién corona la fe?
—José.
   Con vosotros viviré
lleno de paz y alegría,
y me serviréis de guía
Jesús, María y José,

"Who is my light?"
"Jesus."
"Who is my guide?"
"Mary."
"Who sustains the faith?"
"Joseph."
   With you I will live
in peace and in happiness,
and you will guide me,
Jesus, Mary and Joseph,

y el Santo de mi nombre,               and also the saint
Amén.[9]                                 whose name I bear, Amen.

From the numerous popular hymns dedicated to the Holy Family it is
not easy to select a typical example. Comparison of many of them with
similar compositions from Spain and Spanish America reveals, as usual,
that some are traditional and very old. Many changes have taken place,
however; here and there new verses appear and sometimes entirely new
strophes have been added. In New Mexican tradition the most popular
hymns in honor of the Holy Family are called alabanzas de Jesús, María y
José (praises to Jesus, Mary, and Joseph). All are in the well-known traditional Spanish octosyllabic meter, the meter of the Spanish ballads and, in
fact, the most popular meter of Spanish poetry generally. The longest hymn
of this series contains twenty-eight octosyllabic rhymed quatrains, or 112
verses. Many of these quatrains appear in shorter versions, so the essential
differences between the various versions are to be found in the number of
quatrains they contain. Below, with translation, are six quatrains from the
long version cited above; it appears in a Penitente ritual and hymn manuscript from Peña Blanca:

Daremos gracias con fe                   With faith and great hope
y crecidas esperanzas,                   we will give thanks,
cantando las alabanzas                   by singing the praises
de Jesús, María y José.                  of Jesus, Mary, and Joseph.
   Canten dulces serafines,                 Let sweet seraphim sing,
que yo les ayudaré,                      for I will help them,
a cantarles los maitines                 to sing the matins
a Jesús, María y José.                   to Jesus, Mary, and Joseph.
   Los tres reyes del oriente,              The three kings from the East,
por grande dicha se ve,                  what a great joy it is!
que adoran en el portal                  have come to adore
a Jesús, María y José.                   Jesus, Mary, and Joseph.
   Esta Sagrada Familia                     This Holy Family
de Dios escogida fue.                    was chosen by God.
Ya saben sus santos nombres              Their names you know:
de Jesús, María y José.                  Jesus, Mary, and Joseph.
   En el trance de la muerte,               At the hour of my death,
cuando agonizando esté,                  when I am in my last agony,
me asistan los santos nombres            may the holy names assist me
de Jesús, María y José.                  of Jesus, Mary, and Joseph.
   —¡Misericordia, Señor,                   "Mercy, my Lord, One God,
Dios Uno, Trino!— diré,                  Triune God!" I will say,
poniendo de intercesores                 begging for the intercession
a Jesús, María y José.                   of Jesus, Mary, and Joseph.

## The Virgin Mary

The cult of the Virgin Mary in New Mexico is universal. Traditional Spanish ballads preserved in New Mexican tradition in which the Virgin Mary plays the chief role have already been cited in chapter 6, above. They are found like many others in the manuscripts of the Penitentes. Not only ballads but also poetic compositions of other types, prayers, invocations, folktales, anecdotes, and miracles about the Virgin Mary abound in New Mexican tradition.

In the *coplas populares*, called simply *versos* in New Mexico, la Virgen de los Dolores, the traditional Spanish Virgin of Sorrows, is the most popular. Of the following two *coplas*, which are very popular in New Mexico, the first one is found in identical form in Spain, and the second one is apparently not only traditional, but also very old, for its syntax—the use of the subjunctive for the imperative in affirmative commands or requests in the second person singular—is that of fourteenth- and fifteenth-century Spanish.

La Virgen de los Dolores
quiere mucho a los Manueles,
porque se llama su hijo
Manolito de los Reyes.

Our Lady of Sorrows
loves all those called Manuel,
because her son's name is
Manolito of the Kings.

Madre mía de los Dolores,
Tú has de ser mi intercesora.
En la hora de mi muerte
Tú me defiendas, Señora.

Dear Mother of Sorrows,
intercede for me.
In the hour of my death,
Blessed Lady, assist me.

The May devotions to the Blessed Virgin are universally observed in New Mexico. Up to within recent years, it was the custom in every home to adorn with flowers of the field and garden a specially constructed altar in honor of the Virgin. Every night, prayers, including the rosary, were recited by all the members of the family, and hymns were sung. The hymns to the Virgin usually sung during the month of May included the well-known "Dulcísima Virgen del cielo delicia" (Most sweet Virgin, joy of Heaven") and "Venid y vamos todos con flores a María" (Come, let us all offer flowers to Mary), both of which are traditional Spanish hymns to the Virgin found in devotional books of Spain and Spanish America.

But the recitation of the rosary was not limited to the month of May. The devotion of the rosary was widespread in all Spanish Catholic families of New Mexico until the end of the nineteenth century. It is only in recent years that the devotion has decreased. The rosary, prayers, and other devotions were usually recited every night of the year, and hymns and ballads

The annual procession in 1933 from the Catholic Cathedral, Santa Fe, to El Rosario Chapel, outside the city, carries the wooden figure of La Conquistadora (Our Lady of the Conquest; Our Lady of the Rosary). The statue, about three feet high, is believed to have been brought to New Mexico in 1598 by the first Spanish governor, Juan de Oñate. Withdrawn in 1680, it was returned to Santa Fe by Governor Diego de Vargas in 1693. *Photograph by J. Manuel Espinosa.*

appropriate for the feast celebrated or for the season of the year were sung. The special rosaries for the sick and for the dead have always been popular. In saying the rosary for the dying and for the dead, traditional prayers, ejaculations, and verses accompany the *ofrecimientos* or special offerings of each of the mysteries of the rosary.

These *ofrecimientos* are numerous and varied, and most of them are traditional. In the rosary for the dying or for those recently deceased, and for whom a *velorio*, an evening of prayers and hymns for the dead, in this case, is being held, one of the most common forms of the verse offering at each mystery is the following:

| | |
|---|---|
| Los ángeles en el cielo | The angels in heaven |
| alaban con alegría, | sing joyous praises, |
| y los hombres en la tierra | and men on earth |
| responden:—¡Ave, María! | reply, "Hail, Mary!" |

When the rosary is recited for the souls in purgatory, the above formula is also used, but a more common one is the following, a traditional Spanish one to be sure, and òne not altogether of popular origin, for there are two Latin verses in the original text:

| | |
|---|---|
| Por las ánimas benditas | For the blessed souls |
| que en el purgatorio están | who are in purgatory |
| ofrezco este misterio. | I offer this mystery. |
| Lux perpetua luceat eas. | May perpetual light shine upon them. |
| ¡Requiescant in pace, Amén! | May they rest in peace, Amen! |

A very extraordinary Spanish religious survival still found in New Mexico, although not generally, is the custom of singing matins in bed at the first signs of dawn. These matins are called *oraciones* or *alabanzas del alba* (dawn prayers or praises). The grandfather or eldest person in the family begins the singing, and the other members from their beds, wherever they may be, respond and join in the singing. According to available sources of information, the same custom exists in the country villages of Spain, Chile, and other regions of Spanish America. One of the best versions from New Mexico is the following:

| | |
|---|---|
| Cantemos el alba; | Let us sing the matins; |
| ya viene el día. | daylight is coming. |
| Daremos gracias. | We will give thanks, |
| ¡Ave, María! | Hail, Mary! |
| Ángel de mi guarda, | My Guardian Angel, |
| noble compañía, | most noble company, |
| vélame de noche | watch over me at night, |
| y guárdame de día. | and protect me during the day. |
| Ya nació María | Mary was born |
| para el consuelo | for the comfort |
| de pecadores, | of sinners, |
| y luz del cielo. | and to be the light of heaven. |
| Tan bella grandeza | Such magnificence |
| no quiso ver | Lucifer, |
| la sierpe fiera | the venomous serpent, |
| de Lucifer. | did not wish to see. |
| María Divina, | Mary Immaculate, |
| con ser tan pura, | although most pure, |
| fué celebrada | was indeed famous |
| por su hermosura. | for her beauty. |
| Éstas sí son flores; | These indeed are flowers; |
| éstas sí que son. | indeed they are. |
| Gracias a María; | We thank Mary; |
| gracias al Señor. | We thank the Lord. |
| En suma pobreza | In the greatest poverty |
| ya parió María, | Mary gave birth |
| al Verbo Encarnado, | to the Word Incarnate, |
| Nuestro amparo y guía. | our refuge and guide. |

La Conquistadora in one of the many dresses in her wardrobe in 1933. The statue is kept on a side altar in the Catholic Cathedral, Santa Fe. *Photograph by J. Manuel Espinosa.*

| | |
|---|---|
| Que todos los santos | May all the saints |
| del cielo nos valgan. | in heaven protect us. |
| ¡Oh, Jesús Divino, | Oh, Divine Jesus, |
| guía nuestras almas! | guide our souls! |
|    La mula se espanta |    The mule is frightened |
| con el resplandor, | at such radiance, |
| y el buey con el vaho | and the ox with his breath |
| calienta al Señor. | gives warmth to the Lord. |
|    ¡Viva Jesús! |    Hail, Jesus! |
| ¡Viva María! | Hail, Virgin Mary! |
| Cantemos todos | Let us all sing |
| en este día. | on this day. |
|    Bendito seas, |    Blessed be you, |
| sol refulgente. | shining sun. |
| Bendito seas, | Blessed be you, |
| sol del oriente. | sun from the East. |
|    Bendita sea |    Blessed be |
| tu claridad. | your light. |
| Bendito sea | Blessed be the one |
| quien nos la da. | Who sends it to us. |
|    Quien el alba canta |    Those who sing the matins |
| muy de mañana | early in the morning |
| las indulgencias | obtain the indulgences |
| del cielo gana.[10] | granted by God. |

Of traditional Spanish prayers and hymns in New Mexico, there seems to be no end. A large number of hymns, not all of them traditional or really popular, were collected and published by Father Rallière in 1877 in his book *Cánticos espirituales*. Another abundant collection of traditional prayers, including the various versions of "El bendito," "El sudario a las ánimas del purgatorio" (the prayer for the souls in Purgatory), traditional versions of the Act of Contrition, the numerous and diverse prayers to the saints, exorcisms, and the like, could be compiled without great difficulty.

### The Bachelor's Prayer

Turning to a lighter vein of religious tradition, one finds many examples of the survival of a special prayer, a humorous one, but one which is very common in all Spanish countries: *la oración del soltero* or *de la soltera*, the prayer of the bachelor or maiden who is looking for a wife or husband. The traditional and popular versions from Spain, Chile, and New Mexico that have been published are very similar. One of the best from New Mexico, which has taken on some modern dress, is the following *oración del soltero*:

Despúes de tantos quebrantos
yo me quiero desposar,
y pido a todos los santos
que me quieran ayudar.
   Siendo mis pesares tantos
ya me arriesgo al matrimonio,
y pido a todos los santos
que me libren del demonio.
   Santa Sinforosa,
si yo he de encontrar esposa,
que sea mujer de casa,
cumplida, limpia y virtuosa.
   Santa Gertrudis,
que esté llena de virtudes.
Para guardar tal tesoro,
espero que tú le ayudes.
   Santa Elena,
que sea una mujer buena,
que cumpla con sus deberes,
y que no me tenga en pena.
   Santa Tomasa,
que cuide bien de su casa,
y no quiera averiguar
cuanto se mueve en la plaza.
   Santa Juliana,
que no se esté en la ventana,
mirando a los que pasan
y oyendo palabra vana.
   Santa Miquela,
que no sea de las que velan,
que deben a todos los santos,
y a cada uno su vela.
   Santa Inés,
si sabe hablar inglés,
que sepa decir, "No,"
y cuando debe, decir "Yes."
   Santa Delfina,
que no sea espadachina,
que no sea curandera,
astróloga ni adivina.
   Santa Dorotea,
ni muy linda ni muy fea;
pero no sirva de pena
si el mundo se ríe de ella.
   Santa Margarita,
si por ventura es bonita,

After a long string of troubles
I wish to get married,
and I beg all the saints
to come to my assistance.
   My troubles are now so great
that I am brave enough to marry,
and I beg all the saints
to protect me from evil.
   Saint Sinforosa,
if I really find a wife,
may she be a good housekeeper,
dutiful, neat and virtuous.
   Saint Gertrude,
may she be of fine character.
To keep such a treasure,
I hope you will help her.
   Saint Helen,
may she be a good woman,
may she perform all her duties,
and may she bring me no grief.
   Saint Thomasa,
may she take good care of her home,
and may she never worry
about what happens in the plaza.
   Saint Juliana,
may she not stay at the window,
looking at the passers-by
and listening to vain words.
   Saint Miquela,
may she not be one of those
who are always praying to the saints,
offering each a candle.
   Saint Agnes,
if she knows English
let her know when to say, "No,"
and when to say, "Yes."
   Saint Delfina,
I hope she won't be quarrelsome;
may she not be a medicaster,
an astrologer, or soothsayer.
   Saint Dorothy,
neither very beautiful nor very ugly;
but she must not worry me
if everybody laughs at her.
   Saint Margaret,
if perchance she is beautiful,

que sepa prenderse bien,
y ser limpia y exquisita.
   Santa Catalina,
que sepa bien la cocina,
y no quiera pasar los días
en la calle o en la esquina.
   Santa Ana,
que no quiera andar galana,
paseando de casa en casa
bailando la varsuviana.
   Santa Isabel,
que nunca me sea cruel;
que a la tarde y a la mañana
me dé sopitas de miel.
   Santa Rosa,
que no sea muy mugrosa;
que *amás* de bailar *tustepe*
sepa hacer alguna cosa.
   Santa Sofía,
que se esté en casa de día,
y que no le sea costumbre
darme la comida fría.
   Santa Enriqueta,
que no me salga coqueta
y quiera pasar los días
paseando en la bicicleta.
   Santa Damiana,
que no sea tan cristiana,
que abandone sus quehaceres
a la primera campana.
   Santa Rosario,
que cuide bien de mi diario,
y no quiera gastar tanto
cual si fuera millionario.
   Santa Beatriz,
que ella me haga muy feliz;
y que sea mi escogida
una de las de San Luis.[11]

I hope she will know how to dress,
and be neat and dainty.
   Saint Catherine,
I hope she will be a good cook,
and not wish to spend her time
in the streets or on the corners.
   Saint Anne,
may she not overdress,
and go from house to house
dancing the varsouvienne.
   Saint Elizabeth,
may she always be good to me;
whether it be late or early
may she always give me fine food.
   Saint Rose,
may she not be too unkempt;
and besides dancing the two-step
may she also know how to work.
   Saint Sophie,
may she stay at home during the day,
and may she never have the habit
of giving me cold food.
   Saint Henrietta,
I hope she will not be a flirt
and want to spend all day
riding around on her bicycle.
   Saint Damiana,
may she not be so religious
that she will give up her work
the moment the first bell rings.
   Saint Rosario,
may she be careful with my money,
and not wish to spend freely
as if I were a millionaire.
   Saint Beatrice,
may she make me very happy;
and may my chosen one be
one of the most virtuous.

## Special Invocations

The traditional Spanish formula used in exorcising is rare in New Mexico. The prayers and brief invocations to the saints who are believed to be the special patrons of certain phenomena, however, are almost as common as in Spain. A few of the shorter ones, all traditional and in verse, are the following:

| | |
|---|---|
| Señora Santa Ana, | Dear Saint Anne, |
| Señor San Joaquín, | Dear Saint Joachim, |
| arrullá este niño, | lull this baby, please, |
| se quiere dormir. | he wishes to go to sleep. |
| | |
| San Lorenzo, | Saint Lawrence, |
| barbas de oro, | you of the golden beard, |
| ruega a Dios | pray to our Lord |
| que llueva a chorros. | that it may rain abundantly. |
| | |
| San Isidro, | Saint Isidore, |
| labrador, | tiller of the soil, |
| ruega a Dios | pray to our Lord |
| que salga el sol. | that the sun will come out. |
| | |
| Santa Bárbara bendita, | Blessed Saint Barbara, |
| que en el cielo estás escrita | your name is written in heaven |
| con papel y agua bendita, | on holy paper with holy water, |
| Santa Bárbara doncella, | Saint Barbara Virgin, |
| líbranos del rayo | guard us ever against |
| y de la centella. | thunderbolt and lightning. |

The following invocation is recited on setting a hen:

| | |
|---|---|
| Padre mío, | Dear Father, |
| San Amador, | Saint Amador, |
| todas pollitas, | may one be a rooster, |
| y un cantador. | and the rest pullets. |

# Modern Local Ballads (*Corridos*)

Balladlike Narratives in Strophic Form. The Narrative Poets. Don Norberto Abeyta. Religious Narratives in Octosyllabic Strophes.

In addition to the various traditional Spanish novelesque, religious, and burlesque ballads preserved in New Mexican oral tradition that have been discussed in an earlier chapter, many more recent popular ballads are found in New Mexico. Reflecting closely their Spanish prototypes, they furnish additional evidence of the vigor and persistence of Spanish tradition in New Mexico. Of modern local ballads—that is to say, ballads in octosyllabic meter and in assonance, the traditional Spanish ballad form, but composed in New Mexico—examples are numerous. In fact, they are still being created. Political campaigns, untimely or violent deaths, and notorious crimes furnish the themes for most of them. Some of the versions of this class of ballads that one hears in New Mexico are of Mexican origin, such as the famous ballad of Macario Romero, which came from Mexico in the last years of the nineteenth century. Although most of these ballads lack the spirit of the traditional ballads and have little interest for comparative literature, they represent, nonetheless, an important aspect of popular local folk narrative.

In the following pages, examples are given of modern New Mexican Spanish popular ballads that reflect traditional Spanish ballad themes and also of modern ballads on local themes composed in New Mexico. The former, although traditional, do not belong to the older Spanish ballad tradition of the sixteenth and seventeenth centuries. Most of them date from the eighteenth century, and their Spanish prototypes are often documented in Agustín Durán's *Romancero*.[1] Examples of this type of popular New Mexican ballads are:

1. *A la Virgen del Rosario—le suplico me dé aliento*. This is a long and well-preserved ballad of 114 regular sixteen-syllable verses. It relates the tragic death of two lovers at the hands of an outraged husband. Durán gives a similar peninsular Spanish version.[2]

2. *En la ciudad de Sevilla—dos caballeros paseaban*. This is the tale of the even more tragic death of a young woman, her brother, and one of her

admirers at the hands of a jealous lover. There are similar versions from Asturias and Castile.

3. *Mató un alcalde en su tierra—y por una buena causa*. A young woman elopes with her lover after a fierce struggle in which her father and others are killed. The elopers are pursued, and the young woman becomes separated from her lover; in the end the lovers are reunited. A similar version is published by Durán.[3]

4. *Estaba don Pedro un día—paseándose por su casa*. This ballad narrates a tale of bloody vengeance, not unlike the story of the death of Count Lozano at the hands of the young Cid in the old Spanish ballads, but apparently it is not related to that tradition.[4]

5. *Atención, señores míos,—Membruno se va a casar*. This is a traditional Spanish ballad of the eighteenth century, inspired in the French ballad of Malborough, *Malborough se en va en guerre*. Versions similar to the New Mexican have been published from Spain, Portugal, and Chile.[5]

6. *Por este plan de barranca,—sin saber como ni cuando*. This ballad is a late elaboration, not earlier than the eighteenth century, of an old traditional theme, the same theme as that of numbers 4 and 5 of the traditional novelesque ballads listed in chapter 6, above: infidelity in love and death of the guilty ones. The version is in strophic form, with different assonance or rhyme for each quatrain. This form of the old ballad is found also in Mexico.

7. *Abajo de una barranca—me dio sueño y me dormí*. This ballad is also an elaboration of an old theme, the lover who seeks his loved one and relates his affliction to a bird. No traditional Spanish ballad has been found that develops the same story as this New Mexican version, but it is certainly an old theme. It is also related to the ballad of the wife who seeks her lost husband, number 7 of the previously listed novelesque ballads. It is classified here as a more recent ballad because, as in the case of number 6, discussed previously, it is in strophic form, an almost certain indication of its late elaboration. On account of the beautiful lyric character of this late elaboration of an old ballad and also because the other more recent popular ballads are quite long, it is the only example of this class that we will cite in full. The version is apparently incomplete.

Abajo de una barranca—me dio sueño y me dormí.
Cuando ya hube despertado—un cuervo *vide* venir.
Eran tantas las acciones—que aquel cuervo me mostraba,
que estuve de preguntarle—qué era lo que allí buscaba.

—Vine a ver por qué te quejas—de esta vida dolorida;
vine a ver si tus trabajos—se remedian con mi vida.
—No quiero tu vida, cuervo,—ni por mí te den la muerte;
lo que quiero es a mi esposa,—que de ella vivo ausente.
—Yo no conozco a tu esposa,—ni la podré conocer;
dame una seña, siquiera,—que yo te la he de ir a traer.[6]

Far down in a deep ravine—sleep overcame me one day;
and as soon as I awoke,—I observed a crow approach.
The motions were so insistent—which that crow was making me,
that I finally inquired—what it was that it desired.
"I have come to ask you why—you bewail your sad life so;
and to see if through my death—your sorrows can be relieved."
"I do not desire, dear crow,—that you give your life for me;
all I seek is my dear wife,—whose absence causes my grief."
"Your dear wife I do not know,—nor can I recognize her;
give me a token, at least,—and I'll go and bring her to you."

The modern balladlike compositions that have been composed in New
Mexico are legion. There are probably hundreds and hundreds of them on
political, religious, and commonplace themes of a purely local character.
They are never called *romances* in New Mexico, however, for not even the
real *romances tradicionales* receive that name. The name for *romance* or ballad
in New Mexico is *corrido*, which is the name generally given both in Spain
and in Spanish America to the more recent ballads. In New Mexico,
however, many modern ballads and balladlike compositions are also called
*cuandos*, probably from the very common occurrence of the word *cuando*,
"when," at the beginning of the composition. Most of the *cuandos* or *corridos*
are composed in the usual ballad form of sixteen-syllable verses, but, as a
rule, they are in strophic form, in quatrains, or have very frequent changes
in assonance. Many of these ballads and balladlike compositions are by
well-known popular poets, while others are by writers who are not well
known. They appear in printed broadsides and in the newspapers, especially on the occasion of religious festivals, often with the author's name.
Some of these compositions can scarcely be called ballads, since they are
intentionally written in quatrains and have little or no dialogue.

The following is an example of a modern local ballad in the traditional
Spanish ballad meter and with the rapid movement and realism of the
traditional ballad, although in imperfect strophic form. Widely known in
the early decades of this century, it exemplifies the sentiments and feelings
of a disgruntled New Mexican who in a few concise verses gives voice to his
indignation in the year 1909 over a new immigration of English-speaking

Americans from Oklahoma into New Mexico.[7] The English translation is given in prose.

Año novecientos nueve,—pero con mucho cuidado,
voy a componer un cuando—en nombre de este condado.
Voy a cantar este cuando,—Nuevo Méjico mentado,
para que sepan los *güeros*—el nombre de este condado.
Guadalupe es, el firmado—por la nación mejicana,
madre de todo lo creado,—virgen, reina soberana.
Voy a cantar estos versos,—ya comenzaré el primero;
señores den atención—al punto que me refiero.
Voy a hablar del extranjero,—y lo que digo es verdad.
Quieren tenernos de esclavos,—pero eso no les valdrá.
Señores, pongan cuidado—a la raza americana;
vienen a poseer la tierra,—la que les vendió Santa Anna.
Cuando entraron de Oklahoma,—sin saber el castellano,
entraron como los burros,—a su paso americano.
Vienen dándole al cristiano,—y haciéndole al mundo guerra;
vienen a echarnos del *país*—y a echarnos de nuestra tierra.
A todo el mundo abarcaron,—y se hacen del bien ajeno.
Ora les pregunto yo—a los que están sin terreno,
los voy a reconvenir,—como un hombre jornalero.
Se han quedado como burros,—*nomás* mascándose el freno.
Se acabaron las haciendas—y los ganados menores;
ya no hay *onde* trabajar,—u ocuparnos de pastores.
¿Qué les parece, señores,—lo que vino a suceder?
No hay más que labrar la tierra—*pa* podernos mantener.
Es nación muy ilustrada—y afanosa en saber;
trabajan con mucho esmero,—y todos quieren tener.
Su creencia es en el dinero,—en la vaca y el caballo,
y ponen todo su haber—en la gallina y el gallo.
Son nación agricultora,—que siembra toda semilla;
por ser comidas de casa—siembran melón y sandía.
También siembran calabazas,—raíces y de todas yerbas;
y comen de todas carnes,—peces, ranas y culebras.
Hábiles son en saber,—y de grande entendimiento;
son cirujanos, doctores,—y hombres de grande talento.
¿Qué les parece, señores,—lo ilustrado que son,
que hacen carritos de *fierro*—que caminan por vapor?
El que compuso este cuando—no es poeta consumado;
es un pobre jornalero—que vive de su salario.
Mi nombre no les diré, ni les diré en todo el año.
Soy un pobre pastorcito—que apacienta su rebaño.[8]

In the year nineteen hundred and nine, with very great care, I am going to compose a popular ballad for the honor of this country. I am going to sing this ballad, Oh famous New Mexico!, so that the fair haired ones [Anglo-Americans] will know the name of this country. It is Guadalupe country, the name adopted by the Mexican nation, the name of the mother of all creation, the Virgin, the sovereign queen. I am going to sing these verses now, beginning with the first one. Pay attention, gentlemen, to what I am going to say. I am going to speak about the foreigners and all I say is true. They wish to have us as their slaves, but they will not succeed. Now listen, gentlemen, to what I am going to tell you about the American people. They have come to take possession of the land that Santa Anna sold to them. When they came from Oklahoma, without knowing a word of Spanish, they came in like donkeys, at the American pace. They have come to molest everybody and to fight against all. They have come to expel us from the country and to take our lands. They have already taken possession of everything and robbed everybody. And now I am going to put the case before you and even scold you, those of you that have lost your land, as a plain workingman. You are now like donkeys, and all you can do is to chew your bridles [complain and grieve, but to no avail]. You have no more haciendas, you have no more sheep. We have no place where we can work or herd sheep. What do you think of all this, gentlemen? All we can do now is to till the land to be able to live. The Americans are very learned and are always seeking knowledge; they work hard and all wish to be rich. They believe in money, cows, horses, and poultry. They are an agricultural people and sow all kinds of seeds, melons, squash, roots, and herbs. They eat all sorts of meats, fish, frogs, and snakes. They learn quickly and are a people of great understanding; they are surgeons, doctors, and men of great talent. Just think how learned they must be when they make iron wagons that run by steam. The one who composed this ballad is not a consummate poet; he is a poor laborer who lives from his wages. I will not tell my name, not for a whole year. I am just a poor shepherd who tends his flock.

Poetic compositions of a narrative character written in octosyllabic meter and in strophes of a varying number of verses have been composed, no doubt, by learned and popular poets throughout the three centuries of New Mexican history. Their strophic forms are quatrains, quintains or *quintillas*, sixains, and octaves. The most common strophe is the quatrain, and next in popularity are the quintains and sixains. Of a somewhat learned character, although most of them are traditional, are the *décimas* or narrative poems that begin with a quatrain and continue with a series of ten-verse strophes, also in octosyllabic meter. These will be discussed briefly in chapter 9.

The majority of these poetic narratives are extraordinarily long. One, composed of thirty-eight octosyllabic sixains, by the popular poet Juan Ángel, on the judicial execution of a certain woman named Paulita in 1861, was published by me in 1915.[9] Among the most prolific of the popular poets of New Mexico was Don Norberto M. Abeyta, of Sabinal. One of his interesting manuscripts contains eleven compositions, long and short, in quatrains and sixains, called *cuandos* or *corridos*. The longest is a political narrative written in 1893 in praise of the Democratic party after Antonio Joseph had for eight successive years been elected territorial delegate to Congress over his Republican opponents. It consists of fifty-two octosyllabic sixains, or a total of 318 verses, and while it praises Antonio Joseph and the Democratic party in general, there are digressions of a religious nature, thrusts at Martin Luther, arguments in favor of the teaching of Spanish in the schools of New Mexico, and other matters of a purely local character. In stanza 10, for example, Don Norberto complains because Spanish-speaking children are taught by teachers who do not know Spanish—which he calls *el castellano*, as many New Mexicans still do—and who use texts printed in New York that cannot be understood; in stanza 13 he expresses a well-known truth, namely, that in order to learn a foreign language one first has to know well one's own language:

| | |
|---|---|
| *Ora* hablaré por los maestros<br>que aquí nos quieren poner.<br>Sin saber el castellano<br>quieren enseñar inglés.<br>Los libros de Nueva York<br>ya nos hablan al revés. | Now I'll speak about the teachers<br>that they wish to bring us here.<br>Although they don't know any Spanish<br>they think they can teach us English.<br>They bring us books from New York<br>that we can not understand. |
|   Ninguno puede estudiar,<br>antes de saber la propia,<br>*otra* idioma que le den,<br>aunque le echen una tropa.<br>Pues nos van a motejar;<br>—Quizás esta gente es loca. |   No person can ever learn,<br>until he knows his own well<br>a foreign language in school,<br>even if obliged by law.<br>They will scoff at us and say,<br>"Perhaps these people are crazy." |

Don Norberto, however, is but one of many popular and prolific New Mexican poets. Manuscripts of popular composers of religious poetry in praise of the Virgin Mary or the saints, and on religious events and festivals of significance, are especially numerous.

Two examples of New Mexican Spanish narrative poems, both in octosyllabic quatrains, are given below. The first one, taken from the manuscripts of Don Norberto, is a petitionary poem to Saint Gonzaga of Abaranda, asking him to intercede with the Virgin Mary that the war between the United States and Spain may soon end. It was written at the beginning of the Spanish American War of 1898 and is a fairly good example of the popular poet's art.

San Gonzaga de Abaranda,
aparecido en el mar,
concédeme mi salud;
luego te voy a bailar.
    San Gonzaga de Abaranda
tu ves mis necesidades,
pide a la Virgen María,
que está llena de piedades.
    Ahora en tu mes florido,
en el que todos te claman,
pídele, santo glorioso,
por América y España.
    Por esos pobres soldados,
que están en guerra peleando;
pídele, santo glorioso,
que la paz vaya triunfando.
    Ellos están respetando

el juramento prestado,
y exponen todos su vida
por su patria, descarriados.
    Dicen que la golondrina
de un *volido* pasa el mar.
En las Islas Filipinas
comenzaron a pelear.
    San Gonzaga, yo te pido,
pero de buen corazón,
pide a la Virgen María
por todita la nación.
    Mira que su intercesión
es oída con mucho anhelo;
esto lo dijo el Señor,
y ella es la puerta del cielo.
    Pídele a esa Virgen Pura;
por ella todo se alcanza;
su hijo le dio ese poder,
pon el dedo en la balanza.
    Pídele, aunque seas porfiado,
que se calmen estas guerras,
pues yo estoy esperanzado
que las penas no prefieran.
    Ella es la puerta del cielo,
su Divino Hijo lo dijo;
yo te prometo bailar,

Saint Gonzaga of Abaranda,
you who appeared on the sea,
grant me health, I ask of you,
and soon I will dance for you.
    Saint Gonzaga of Abaranda,
you are aware of my needs,
call upon the Virgin Mary,
who is a storehouse of mercy.
    In this your flowery month,
when all of us seek your aid,
pray to her, glorious saint,
for America and Spain.
    Pray for those unhappy soldiers
who are now engaged in war;
pray to her, glorious saint,
that peace may begin to triumph.
    They are showing themselves
faithful
to their oaths of loyalty,
and all are risking their lives,
though misguided, for their countries.
    We often hear that the swallow
crosses the sea in one flight.
'Twas in the Philippine Islands
that soldiers began to fight.
    Saint Gonzaga, I beg you,
from the bottom of my heart,
to pray to the Virgin Mary
for the welfare of our country.
    You know that her intercession
is always of special weight;
Our Lord Himself has said it,
and she is the gate of heaven.
    Pray then to the Virgin Mary;
she can help us in all things;
for her Son gave her that power;
place your finger on the scales.
    Keep beseeching, without ceasing,
that this fighting may be ended,
for I'm hopeful of the fact
that they don't prefer these troubles.
    She is the gateway of heaven,
Her Divine Son is a witness;
as for me a dance I promise,

y con mucho regocijo.
En fin, ya voy a acabar,
San Gonzaga, yo lo digo,
ponte pronto a suplicar
que venga la paz contigo.
Santo, vuelve a suplicar,
aunque te llamen porfiado.
¿No ves que con estas guerras
queda el mundo desolado?
Oye a esos pobres soldados,
que ausentes de sus familias.
exhalan tristes latidos
en las Islas Filipinas.
Si la paz viene contigo,
no se te vaya a olvidar,
que con corazón contrito
tu indita voy a bailar.

performed with the greatest joy.
Now I am going to close,
Saint Gonzaga, but I repeat,
start your supplications soon,
that you may bring peace with you.
Dear Saint, persist in your prayers,
even though they call your obstinate.
Do you not see that the war
will leave the world disconsolate?
Do hear those poor helpless soldiers,
who far away from their loved ones,
breathe their last in agony
in the Philippine Islands.
And if you bring peace to us,
don't fail to remember this,
that with a most contrite heart
your *indita* I will dance.

An *indita* is a popular New Mexican Spanish dance, executed in the manner of a *jota* or jig, accompanied by songs. Some of the songs show a notable influence of Pueblo Indian music and subject matter.

## Religious Narratives

Another popular poetic composition that I shall cite is a religious poem, or *alabado*. It is a long poetic narrative, taken from a Penitente manuscript, of certain scenes from the Passion. In the original Spanish it consists of forty-one octosyllabic quatrains, or 164 verses. There are many like it in the Penitente manuscripts in various types of octosyllabic strophes. Similar compositions are found in all Spanish-speaking countries. The version given below is an excellent example of this type and is beyond question traditional. We cannot call these narrative poems in ocotosyllabic quatrains *romances* in the proper sense of the word, but they are often as beautiful as the traditional ballads.

Ven, pecador y verás
a Jesús Sacramentado
padeciendo por el hombre,
tan cruelmente azotado.
En el huerto estaba Cristo,
de sus doce acompañado,
y les dice en tierna voz:
—Hoy voy a ser entregado.
Con humilde devoción

Come, sinner, and you will see
Our Eucharistic Jesus,
suffering pain for mankind,
and scourged in a most cruel way.
Christ had gone into the Garden,
His twelve apostles with Him,
and gently he said to them,
"Today I'm to be betrayed."
And then·with humble devotion,

tomó su divino cuerpo,
y les dio a beber su sangre,
que es el Nuevo Testamento.
    Les dice a sus escogidos
Cristo, Nuestro Redentor:
—Velar y llorar conmigo,
que no nos tiente el traidor.
    Ya ven venir al traidor,
quien a Jesús va a entregar.
Al encuentro salió Cristo
y les dice: —¿A quién buscáis?
    Ellos con voz obligada:
A Jesús—le respondieron;
pues venían a buscar
a Jesús el Nazareno.
    Jesús les dice: —Yo soy—
y les vuelve a preguntar.
Ellos cayeron en tierra,
sin poderse levantar.
    Segunda vez les pregunta,
con un amor verdadero;
—¿A quién buscáis, inhumanos,
que vienen con atropello?
    Ellos dicen: —A Jesús—
y a tierra vuelven a caer.
Sólo de ver al Criador
no pudieron avanzar.
    Jesús dice a los judíos:
—¡Oh, desdichadas criaturas,
a Cristo van a entregar
para afirmar la escritura!
    ¡Qué corazón, oh, cristianos!
Aquel beso de traición
entregó a los fariseos
a este Divino Señor.
    Llegan estos inhumanos
para poderlo prender.
Le escupen su rostro bello,
y comenzó a padecer.
    Dos falsos calumniadores
una terrible voz dieron,
que podía destruir el templo
y fabricarlo en tres días.
    No respondiendo Jesús
ni tan sólo una palabra,
los calumniadores falsos
mas calumnias levantaron.

He gave them His Divine Body,
and gave them His Blood to drink,
which is the New Testament.
    To His Apostles He said,
Christ, Our Reedemer and Ruler,
"Watch and weep a while with me,
lest we fall into temptation."
    Now they see the traitor coming,
who is to betray the Lord.
Christ at once went out to meet them
and he asked, "Whom do you seek?"
    They were obliged to respond,
"We seek Jesus of Nazareth,"
because indeed they were seeking
Jesus Christ, the Nazarene.
    Jesus replies, "I am He,"
and again He asks the question.
They all fell then to the ground,
and were unable to rise.
    And again Jesus asks them,
with a sweet and loving voice,
"Oh, cruel ones, whom do you seek,
since you come with such tumult?"
    "We seek Jesus," they reply,
falling to the ground again.
At merely seeing Our Lord
they were unable to move.
    Jesus then says to the Jews,
"Most unfortunate of men,
you're about to betray Christ
to confirm the Holy Scriptures."
    Oh, Christians, what a cruel heart!
That treacherous kiss of Judas
betrayed to the Pharisees
our Most Divine Lord and God.
    These cruel accusers drew near
to make Christ their prisoner.
They spat on His Divine Face,
and His sufferings began.
    Two false and wicked accusers
cried out the terrible words,
that He could destroy the temple
and rebuild it in three days.
    Jesus, Our Lord, did not answer,
not a single word He said;
the malicious slanderers
made many more false reports.

Image of Jesus of Nazareth, Santa Cruz Church, 1931. *Photograph by J. Manuel Espinosa.*

El pontífice decía:
—En nombre de Dios Divino,
¿eres tú el Hijo de Dios,
Cristo, Rey de los judíos?
    Jesús dice a los judíos:
—Yo soy el Dios verdadero,
y verán mi majestad
sobre las nubes del cielo.
    Con una voz muy ufana
levantaron a mi amado
el que había maldecido,
el que había blasfemado.
    ¡Pequé, mi Jesús, pequé!
¡Pésame el haber negado!
Tres veces a Cristo niegan
antes de cantar el gallo.
    Después de tantos martirios
que le dio aquel pueblo ingrato,
por las calles le pasearon
a la casa de Pilatos.
    Ya la sentencia está dada
por un falso emperador.
Presidente allí Pilatos
dijo: —¡Muera el malhechor!
    Judas que lo había vendido,
viendo a Jesús sentenciado,
arrepentido volvió
el dinero que ha ganado.
    —¡Es pecado contra el cielo!
gritaba desesperado.
—Vendí la sangre inocente
del Señor Sacramentado.
    Sólo de ver las afrentas
que Jesucristo sufrió,
el que lo había vendido
desesperado se *horcó*.
    Con risa *facinorosa*
mofaron a mi Jesús.
Decían los fariseos:
—¡Muera, muera un una cruz!
    Una corona *de entrañas* [*sic*],
con tan terribles espinas,
pusieron en su cabeza
y en esas sienes divinas.
    Una cruel soga le echaron
y comenzó a padecer;

The High Priest then asked of Jesus,
"In the name of God I ask,
are You the true Son of God,
the Christ, the King of the Jews?"
    Jesus replied to the Jews,
"Indeed I am the True God;
My majesty you will see
far above the clouds in heaven."
    With boastful, boisterous clamor
they falsely accused my Lord
that grave falsehoods were His words,
that His replies were blasphemous.
    Oh, my Jesus, I have sinned!
I repent having denied you!
Jesus was denied three times
before they heard the cock crow.
    After so many cruel torments,
from the ungrateful populace,
He was carried through the streets
to the house where Pilate dwelt.
    The sentence had been pronounced
by a faithless emperor.
As judge, Pilate has declared,
"Let the evildoer die!"
    Judas, he who had betrayed Him,
when he heard the sentence given,
repenting his act gave back
the money he had received.
    "It is a sin against heaven!"
in utter despair he cried,
"I sold the innocent Blood
of Our Eucharistic Lord."
    After witnessing the insults
that Jesus was forced to suffer,
the one who had betrayed Him
hanged himself in his despair.
    With laughter and mean sarcasm
they scoffed at our Divine Lord.
The Pharisees kept on shouting,
"Come, let Him be crucified!"
    A crown of cactus they made,
with sharp and terrible thorns,
and this they placed on His Head,
thus piercing His Divine Temples.
    They tied Him with a cruel rope
and His sufferings began;

y le limpió el sudor
una piadosa mujer.
    Un dolor tan penetrante
que sintió su corazón,
de ver morir a Jesús
en su Sagrada Pasión.
    Lo conducen al Calvario,
descalzo y con un madero;
tres veces ha caído en tierra;
lo levanta el Cirineo.
    Así pagó el homicida
tan mal al que así murió,
que cuando llegó al Calvario
el aliento le faltó.
    ¡Adiós, adiós, Jesús mío,
adiós, Rey de cielo y tierra,
que moriste por el hombre
en una cruz verdadera!
    Ya vienen los fariseos
a darle hiel y vinagre;
y entonces el Redentor
aclamó a su Eterno Padre.
    El sol ya se ha oscurecido
y no alumbra su luz;
el mundo se ha conmovido
viendo morir a Jesús.
    Se rompió el velo en tres partes;
las piedras se dividieron;
y la luna y las estrellas
ya todas se conmovieron.
    Tiembla tres veces la tierra

de ver a Jesús pendiente.
De verlo en aquella cruz
¿qué hombre no se arrepiente?
    Llega María Magdalena,
dando clamores al cielo,
y le dice a Jesucristo:
—¿Hasta cuándo Dios eterno?
    Dos varones lo bajaron,

lo entregaron a María.
Con tierno llanto le dice:
—¡Ay, Jesús del alma mía!
    Lo agarra en sus dulces brazos
bañada de compasión;

the sweat of His Divine Face
was wiped by a pious woman.
    What a penetrating pain
she felt deep within her heart,
upon seeing Jesus dying
suffering His Sacred Passion.
    They took Him to Mount Calvary
barefooted, carrying His Cross;
three times He fell to the ground;
the Cyrenian gave Him aid.
    The homicide so rewarded
the one who died for the world,
that when He reached Calvary
He fainted from exhaustion.
    Farewell, farewell, my Jesus,
Farewell, King of heaven and earth,
You died on a cross for mankind
for mankind, on a True Cross!
    There they come, the Pharisees,
to give Him gall and vinegar;
and then Our Divine Redeemer
called on His Heavenly Father.
    The sun has been lost in darkness
for it gave its light no more;
the earth itself shook and trembled
on witnessing Jesus' death.
    The veil of the temple ripped;
and the stones were rent asunder;
the moon and stars in the heavens
failed to follow their true course.
    Three times the earth shook and
        trembled
when Jesus hung on the Cross.
Seeing Him there on that Cross
who would not amend his life?
    Mary Magdalen arrived
lamenting with bitter tears,
and she said to Our Lord, Jesus,
"How long, my Lord, till we meet?"
    Two men lowered Him from the
        Cross,
and delivered Him to Mary.
Weeping softly she addressed Him:
"My Jesus, my Heart, My Love!"
    Then she takes Him in her arms
weeping with tender compassion;

su dulce cuerpo lo abraza,
traspasada de dolor.

    Fue enterrado en un sepulcro,
el cual José le donó.
Asimismo la mortaja
de su mano se la dio.

    Después de tantos martirios
al sepulcro fue María,
pero hallandolo tapado
en el mismo Dios confía.

    *Abajó* un ángel del cielo
y las piedras removió,
y diciéndole a María:
—¡Ya Cristo resucitó!

    Con un amor verdadero
ya lo han visto con su madre,
y glorioso subió al cielo
a la diestra de Dios Padre. [10]

lovingly she embraces Him,
transfixed with sorrow and grief.

    He was buried in a tomb
that was provided by Joseph.
And the shroud to clothe His Body
this also Joseph supplied.

    After so much suffering
Mary visited the tomb,
but finding it closed and sealed
she put all her trust in God.

    An angel came down from heaven
and straightway rolled back the stones,
and thereupon said to Mary,
"Christ is not here; He is risen."

    Showing His true Divine Love
He appeared then to His mother,
and ascended into Heaven
to the right of God the Father.

# The Spanish *Coplas Populares*

New Mexican *Coplas* or *Versos*. Traditional *Coplas*. Happy and Unhappy Love. Philosophy, Religion, and Humor. Pride and Love for Castile. The Music of the *Coplas* and Ballads. The *Décima* in Spain and Spanish America.

The Spanish *copla* has been mentioned many times in previous chapters. The term denotes any short poetic composition of a popular character in one single strophe or stanza, as a rule in octosyllabic meter, although shorter meters are also used. Since the sixteenth century the most common strophic form is the *cuarteta*, an octosyllabic quatrain with verses two and four in assonance or rhyme. This octosyllabic quatrain is the modern Spanish *copla par excellence*, the most popular type of *copla* wherever Spanish is spoken. Next in popularity and importance in Spanish tradition are the sixain, an octosyllabic strophe of six verses, and the *seguidilla*, a quatrain of two heptasyllabic verses which alternate with two pentasyllabic verses.

The popular *coplas* constitute one of the outstanding manifestations of the soul of Spain. They reflect the philosophy of the common people expressed in lyric form—their feelings and sentiments, their joys and sorrows. Hundreds of *coplas* have come down from the sixteenth and seventeenth centuries with little or no change and thus have become traditional, just as in the case of the ballads, proverbs, and riddles that express certain fixed ideas and traits of Spanish character. Being a lyric manifestation, new *coplas*, some based on the older ones and others of a more independent origin, have been composed continuously. Popular poets compose them at will. As an Andalusian *seguidilla* states:

| | |
|---|---|
| Del polvo de la tierra | From the dust of the ground |
| saco yo coplas. | I get my *coplas*. |
| No bien se acaba una, | As soon as I finish one, |
| ya tengo otra. | I compose another. |

In New Mexican Spanish tradition the two most common types of *coplas*, or *versos*, as New Mexicans call them, are the quatrains and the sixains, both in the traditional octosyllabic meter and with varying assonance or rhyme arrangements. A few are found in other metrical forms, such as the following popular and well-known *copla*, which consists of a pentasyllabic quatrain:

139

| Ojitos negros, | Black eyes, |
|---|---|
| firme color, | a sign of constancy, |
| mucho te quiere | my heart is deeply |
| mi corazón. | in love with you. |

The octosyllabic quatrain, however, is by far the most common type, not only in New Mexico but in all other parts of the Spanish-speaking world as well. The great popularity of the octosyllabic quatrain type of *copla* in New Mexico is another eloquent example of the persistence of Spanish tradition in this corner of the Spanish world. Of over twelve hundred *versos* or *coplas* that have been collected from New Mexican oral tradition, about 75 percent are octosyllabic quatrains, the rest being for the most part octosyllabic sixains.

Already in the sixteenth century the Spanish poet and prosodist Juan Rufo described the *copla* as "cuatro versos de un romance," or four ballad half-lines. As a matter of fact, metrically considered, the octosyllabic quatrain that we call a *copla* is the equivalent of two complete ballad verses. In the remarks made below on the music of the New Mexican Spanish traditional ballads, attention is called to the fact that musically considered, the quatrain *copla* is the equivalent of four ballad half-verses or two ballad verses. The musical variations are only four, one for each octosyllabic verse of the *copla*, that is, one for each half-verse (an octosyllabic hemistich) of each two ballad verses. In the ballads, the variations are repeated every two verses. The octosyllabic quatrain type of *copla*, then, has in New Mexico exactly the same metrical form, and the same type and number of musical variations, as the ballad.

In addition to the *coplas* that have come down from the sixteenth and seventeenth centuries, one may also consider as traditional those that are found today in identical or practically identical form in widely separated parts of the Spanish-speaking world. The reason why some of the *coplas* have been preserved unchanged across the centuries is to be found in the universality of the ideas that they express. Once put in simple form, these universal motives of human life remain fixed, like the proverbs, riddles, and idiomatic expressions of language. In fact, many of the traditional quatrain *coplas* are of a sententious or proverbial character. Some of these have been found in identical or almost identical form in every Spanish country where *coplas* have been collected.

The New Mexican Spanish *versos*, then, represent popular lyric poetry, and, as Cervantes says, "por el hilo se sacará el ovillo" (from the thread we can judge the quality of the skein). The examples cited below may be classified under six general groups or classes:

1. *Coplas* that express happy and hopeful love.
2. *Coplas* that express unhappy and rejected love.
3. Philosophic and proverbial *coplas*.
4. Religious *coplas*.
5. Humorous and burlesque *coplas*.
6. *Coplas* that express pride and love for Castile.

## Happy and Hopeful Love

[1]Antenoche a media noche
*vide* luz en tu ventana.
Era la luz de tus ojos,
lucero de la mañana.

Night before last, at midnight,
I saw a light in your window.
It was the light of your eyes,
my dear love, my morning star.

[2] Antenoche fui a tu casa,
tres golpes le di al *candao*.
No estás buena para amores,
tienes el sueño *pesao*.

At your house, night before last,
three times I knocked at your door.
You do not make a good lover,
much too soundly do you sleep.

[3] De las estrellas del cielo
he de bajar una o dos,
para hacerte una corona
como la del Niño Dios.

Of the stars that grace the heavens
I must bring down one or two,
to fashion for you a crown
like the one of the Child Jesus.

[4] De la manzana mordí,
del vino bebí una gota;
del besito que te di
dulce me quedó la boca.

I took a bite from the apple,
and I drank a drop of wine;
and from the kiss I gave you
my mouth has now become sweet.

[5] Dicen que no nos queremos
porque no nos ven bailar.
A tu corazón y al mío
les debían de preguntar.

They say we are not in love,
because they don't see us dance.
To your heart and to my heart
the question ought to be asked.

[6] Dices que me quieres tanto,
no me subas tan arriba,
que las hojas en el árbol
no duran toda la vida.
*Nomás* un véano duran,
hasta que el aire las tira.

If you love me as you say,
you should not praise me so much,
for the leaves that grace a tree
really can not last forever.
Just one summer do they last,
until they are blown away.

[7] El clavel que tú me *dites*
el día de la Ascensión,
no fué clavel sino clavo,
que clavó mi corazón.

That carnation you gave me
on the feast of the Ascension,
was actually an arrow
that transfixed my very heart.

[8] El día ue tú *nacites*
nacieron todas las flores;
y en la pila del bautismo
cantaron los ruiseñores.

The day on which you were born
all the flowers yielded blossoms;
and on your baptismal font
nightingales began to sing.

[9] Eres chiquita y bonita,
y así como eres te quiero;
parece que eres hechita
por las manos de un platero.

You are beautiful and little,
and I love you as you are;
it seems that you have been fashioned
by the hands of a silversmith.

[10] Eres linda entre las lindas,
linda sin comparación;
lindos tu padre y tu madre,
linda tu generación.

You are fair among the fair,
beautiful beyond compare;
handsome your father and mother,
and beautiful your lineage.

[11] Pájaro que vuelas alto
y en el pico llevas flores,
llévale este papelito
al dueño de mis amores.

Listen, bird, flying so high,
carrying flowers in your bill,
please transport this little note
to the mistress of my heart.

[12] Dicen que lo negro es triste,
yo digo que no es verdad;
tú tienes los ojos negros
y eres mi felicidad.

They say that black denotes sadness,
I say that it is not true;
for you have black eyes,
and my happiness is you.

[13] ¡Qué dichosa carta escrita!
¡Quién fuera dentro de ti,
para darle mil abrazos
al ángel que te ha de abrir!

Oh, what a fortunate letter!
Would that I were inside you
to give a thousand embraces
to the angel that opens you!

[14] Voy a escribir una carta
acordándome de ti;
dale un besito a mi nombre
y haz de cuenta que yo fui.

I am going to write a letter
thinking of you at the time;
please kiss my name when you read it
and imagine it is I.

## Unhappy and Rejected Love

[15] Cada vez que cae la tarde,
me dan ganas de llorar;
este corazón cobarde
no lo puedo consolar.

Every day when evening comes,
I feel a desire to weep;
to this poor heart of mine
I can never give relief.

[16] Cantando la chara estaba
porque penas no tenía.
Si esa dicha fuera mía,
otro gallo me cantara.

The lark was singing its song
because it had no afflictions.
If that good fortune were mine,
another would be my song.

[17] Hasta la cama en que
duermo
se compadece de mí,
de las vueltas que me doy
acordándome de ti.

Even the bed I sleep on

takes pity on me,
because of my constant turning
thinking about you.

[18] Levántate de mañana
y verás mi patio regado
con lágrimas de mis ojos;
toda la noche he llorado.

Get up early in the morning
and you'll see my patio wet
from the tears that I have shed;
I have wept all through night.

[19] ¡Malhaya la ropa negra,
y el sastre que la cortó!
Mi negrita tiene luto
sin haberme muerto yo.

Cursed be the clothes of mourning!
Cursed be the tailor too!
My dear love is dressed in mourning
although I have not yet died.

[20] ¡Qué malas entrañas tienes,
al decir que te amo poco,
sabiendo, morena ingrata,

que tu amor me tiene loco!

Oh how cruel you are, indeed,
when you say I love you little,
when you know, my ungrateful
brunette,
that I'm just crazy about you.

[21] Si porque te quiero quieres
que yo la muerte reciba,
hágase tu voluntad;
muera yo porque otra viva.

If just because I love you
you now wish for me to die,
be it so, and may I die
that another one may live.

[22] Toma esta llavita de oro
y abre mi pecho y verás,
lo que te estimo y te quiero
y el mal pago que me das.

Take this little golden key,
open my heart and you'll see
how much I prize and love you
and how cruel you are to me.

[23] Tres meses hay que te vi,
tres meses que estoy sufriendo.
Mientras no me des el sí
siempre estaré padeciendo.

Three months ago I saw you,
I've been suffering three months.
As long as you refuse me
I will continue to suffer.

[24] Ya la luna tiene cuernos,
y el lucero la acompaña.
¡Ay, qué triste queda un hombre
cuando una *güera* lo engaña!

The moon is now at last quarter,
and the morning star appears.
Oh, how sad a man becomes
when a fair-haired girl deceives him!

## Philosophic and Proverbial *Coplas*

[25] Cuando un pobre se
emborracha
y un rico en su compañía,
la del pobre es borrachera,
la del rico es alegría.

When a poor man drinks too much

in a rich man's company,
the poor man is called a drunkard,
the rich man a jolly fellow.

[26] Cuatro palomitas blancas,
sentadas en un romero,
una a la otra se decían:
"No hay amor como el primero".

Behold four little white doves
perched on a rosemary bush,
they were saying to each other,
"There's no love like the first love."

[27] El amor y el interés
se fueron al campo un día;
pudo más el interés
que el amor que le tenía.

Love and selfishness decided
to go one day to the country;
selfishness was more powerful
than the love he had for her.

[28] El que enamora y no da
no puede cobrar un celo;
antes debe agradecer
que lo quieran pelo a pelo.

The lover who gives no gifts
can not at all become jealous;
he ought to be very thankful
to be loved just as he is.

[29] En esta vida emprestada
es de la ciencia la llave
el que sabe que no sabe
y el que no sabe nada.

In this borrowed life of ours
he is beyond doubt the wisest
who is sure that he knows nothing
or who knows nothing at all.

[30] Hay palos que son dichosos
y hay palos que no lo son;
de los unos hacen leña
y de los otros carbón.

Some pieces of wood are lucky,
and others are not so lucky;
out of some firewood is made,
and out of others charcoal.

[31] Ninguno cante victoria
aunque en el estribo esté,
que algunos en el estribo
se suelen quedar a pie.

Let no one boast of victory
because success seems at hand;
some with a foot in the stirrup
have had to walk in the end.

[32] Si Dios me diera dinero
como arenas tiene el mar,
gastaría como un loco,
todos los días un real.

If God were to give me money
as much as the sands of the sea,
I would spend it like a mad man,
every single day a nickel.

[33] Si yo tuviera un peral
te mandaría una pera;
porque el que de amor espera
de amor va a desesperar.

If I possessed a pear tree
I would send a pear to you;
because he who trusts in love
will despair of love at last.

[34] Tengo una cadena de oro
y una *llavita* de plata.
El amor que bien se *añuda*
con trabajo se desata.

I have a little gold chain
and a little silver key.
When the bonds of love are true,
the bonds can never be broken.

[35] Un pato se echó a nadar
y otro voló diciendo;
—Hay muchos que sin pensar
pagan las que están debiendo.

A duck started out to swim,
and another flew off saying,
"Many, without knowing it,
suffer for the wrongs they've done."

A northern New Mexican family with their adobe home in the background, 1902. *Photograph by D. T. Duckwall, Jr., courtesy of the Photograph Collection, Library of Congress.*

## Religious *Coplas*

Since a number of religious compositions have been cited in previous chapters, only four religious *coplas* are included in this section. The subject of the first is Saint Anthony, one of the most popular saints in Spanish tradition. The other three are *coplas de Navidad*, or Christmas *coplas*, of the type sung by the shepherds in the popular play *Los pastores*; these are in the form of hexasyllabic sixains—quatrains with the last two verses repeated.

[36] ¿Qué quieren con San Antonio,
que tanto se acuerdan de él?
San Antonio está en la gloria.
¡Quién estuviera con él!

What do you wish from Saint Anthony,
you who call on him so often?
Saint Anthony is in heaven.
Would that I were there with him!

[37] Voy para el portal
con gusto infinito,
a llevarle al Niño
este corderito;
a llevarle al Niño
este corderito.

I go to the manger
with infinite joy,
to take to the Child
this nice little lamb;
to take to the Child
this nice little lamb.

[38] Voy para el portal
con gusto y anhelo,
a llevarle al Niño
este caramelo;
a llevarle al Niño
este caramelo.

I go to the manger
with joy and desire,
to take to the Child
a piece of my candy;
to take to the Child
a piece of my candy.

[39] Voy para el portal
con mucha alegría,
a ver a Jesús,
a José y María;
a ver a Jesús,
a José y María.

I go to the manger
with very great joy,
so I may see Jesus,
and Joseph and Mary;
so I may see Jesus,
and Joseph and Mary.

## Humorous and Burlesque *Coplas*

[40] Antenoche fui a tu casa
tres ocasiones por verte,
y me dijo tu hermanita,
—Ya ese gallo no divierte.

Night before last I attempted
three different times to see you,
and your little sister told me,
"That rooster isn't amusing."

[41] Asómate a esa ventana,
mira lo que están vendiendo:
los calzones de tu amante,
hechos un vivo remiendo.

Come and look out of your window,
and you'll see what they are selling:
the trousers worn by your lover,
covered with all kinds of patches.

[42] En la ciudad de no sé *ónde*
adoran no sé qué santo;
le rezaban no sé qué,
u le ofrecían no sé cuánto.

In the town I know not where
they worship some saint or other;
I know not what they prayed to him,
or how much they offered him.

[43] Estos muchachitos de *ora*,
cabecitas de algodón,
no le dan provecho al mundo,
ni al diablo, ni a la nación.

These young striplings of today,
with their little cotton heads,
are of no use to this world,
to the devil, or our country.

[44] Estrellita reluciente,
que alumbras el callejón.
A las bonitas un beso,
a las feas un guantón.

Beautiful, resplendent star,
that lights up this narrow lane.
Kisses for the pretty girls,
for the ugly ones just slaps.

[45] La que se casa con viejo
ha de tener dos trabajos:
el sobarle las rodillas,
y estirarle los zancajos.

The girl who marries an old man
will have two principal tasks:
to rub his knees on occasion,
and to straighten up his socks.

[46] La vecina de aquí enfrente
compró un gato muy barato,
y le dijo a su marido:
—Mira, hijito, tu retrato.

My neighbor across the street
very cheaply bought a cat,
and then she said to her husband,
"Behold your picture, my dear."

[47] No te vistas, gavilán,  
ni te pongas mi corona,  
porque te vas a quedar  
como el que chifló en las loma.

Be careful, you hawk, you thief,  
and do not put on my crown;  
you'll be like the one who whistled  
alone on top of a hill.

[48] Un tonto me pidió un beso,  
y no se lo quise dar,  
porque los besos de tonto  
saben a huevos sin sal.

A fool wanted to kiss me  
and I, of course, turned him down,  
because the kisses of fools  
taste just like unsalted eggs.

[49] ¡Válgame Dios de los  
cielos!  
¿cómo quieren que yo cante,  
con la barriga vacía  
y el pellejito tirante?

Goodness gracious, my friends,  

how can I continue singing,  
when I have an empty stomach  
and my poor skin is stretched taut.

## Pride and Love for Castile

Pride and love for Castile sometimes appear in New Mexican tradition—a sign that the former motherland has not been entirely forgotten. A rose in New Mexico is usually called *rosa de Castilla*, Castile rose. The beauty of a lover's locks of hair is frequently compared to a beautiful rose from Castile.

[50] De los chinos de tu frente  
me darás una semilla,  
para sembrar en oriente  
una rosa de Castilla.

From your lovely curly locks  
I hope you'll give me a sample,  
that I may plant in the East  
a beautiful Castile rose.

The lover herself may be compared in the lyrical *coplas* to a Castile rose that has just come to bloom.

[51] Rosa de Castilla en rama,  
acabada de reventar,  
¡como a mi vida te quiero,  
y no te puedo olvidar!

My love, a Castilian rose  
that has just begun to bloom,  
I love you with all my heart,  
and I can never forget you.

Pride in the former motherland is even more eloquently expressed in the following six-verse *copla* from Taos:

[52] Si porque me ves con *teguas*  
me desprecias, vida mía,  
el domingo me verás  
con zapatos de *chalía*,  
pisando la misma tierra  
que pisan los de Castilla.

If because I wear moccasins  
you esteem me less, my love,  
on Sunday you will see me  
wearing slippers of mohair,  
and stepping on the same ground  
as that those from Castile tread.

The fifty-two *coplas populares* given above illustrate sufficiently the wide range of human experience and ideas that the *coplas* express.[1] They are also evidence of the fact that Spanish folk poetry is still in its creative period, for in spite of the fact that many of the *coplas* which have been cited are traditional, many others are original in substance, if not in form. Of the fifty-two *coplas* cited, two (numbers 22 and 26) are similar to published peninsular Spanish versions, while seventeen, or 31 percent of the total, have either identical or almost identical forms in Castile, Aragon, Andalucía, and Argentina. These seventeen are traditional beyond a doubt and have come down in Spanish tradition in America in the same way as the traditional ballads, prayers, folktales, and other forms of folk literature. A few examples of the peninsular Spanish and Argentine versions are given below to illustrate their similarity.

New Mexican Spanish *copla* 2 has the following form in Andalucía:

| | |
|---|---|
| Anoche estuve en tu puerta, | I went to your home last night, |
| tres golpes le di al candado; | three times I knocked at your door; |
| para tener amor, niña, | to be a really good lover, |
| tienes el sueño pesado.[2] | you sleep too soundly, my love. |

New Mexican Spanish *copla* 5 has the following form in Aragon:

| | |
|---|---|
| Piensan que no nos queremos | They think we are not lovers |
| porque no nos ven bailar; | because they don't see us dance; |
| a tu corazón y al mío | to your heart and to my heart |
| se lo deben preguntar.[3] | the question ought to be asked. |

New Mexican Spanish *coplas* 7 and 8 have identical forms in Aragon and Andalucía.[4]

New Mexican Spanish *copla* 13 has a very similar form in Andalucía:

| | |
|---|---|
| Papelito venturoso, | You fortunate little note, |
| ¡quién fuera dentro de ti, | would that I were inside you |
| para darle mil abrazos | to give a thousand embraces |
| al ángel que te ha de abrir![5] | to the angel that opens you! |

New Mexican Spanish *copla* number 17 has the following form in Argentina:

| | |
|---|---|
| Sólo la cama en que duermo | Only the bed I sleep in |
| se compadece de mí, | takes pity at times on me, |
| porque en ella gimo y lloro | because in it I weep and moan |
| desde que mi bien perdí.[6] | since the time I lost my love. |

New Mexican Spanish *copla* 24 has the following form in Andalucía and Argentina:

| | |
|---|---|
| ¡Qué alta que va la luna | How high the moon now appears |
| y el lucero en su compaña! | with the morning star near by! |
| ¡Qué triste se queda un hombre | How saddened a man becomes |
| cuando la mujer lo engaña![7] | when a woman deceives him! |

New Mexican Spanish *copla* 25 is found in identical form in Andalucía,[8] and in slightly different form in Andalucía and Argentina.[9] The Argentine form is:

| | |
|---|---|
| Cuando se emborracha un pobre, | When a poor man drinks too much |
| todos dicen: —¡Borrachón! | everyone says, "The great drunkard!" |
| Cuando se emborracha un rico; | When a rich man drinks too much: |
| —¡Qué alegrito va el señor! | "Our friend is in a jolly mood!" |

New Mexican Spanish *copla* 27 has the following form in Aragon:

| | |
|---|---|
| El amor y el interés | Love and selfishness decided |
| salieron al campo un día; | to go one day to the country; |
| pudo más el interés | selfishness was more powerful |
| que el amor que tenías.[10] | than the love you had for me. |

New Mexican Spanish *copla* 31 has the same form in Andalucía and Argentina.[11]

New Mexican Spanish *copla* 36 has the following form in Andalucía and La Mancha:

| | |
|---|---|
| ¿Qué tienes con San Antonio, | What's your interest in Saint Anthony, |
| que tanto te acuerdas de él? | you who call on him so often? |
| San Antonio está en la gloria | Saint Anthony is in heaven. |
| ¡Quién estuviera con él![12] | Would that I were there with him! |

New Mexican Spanish *copla* 42 has the following form in Castile:

| | |
|---|---|
| Allí arriba, no sé dónde, | Way up there, I know not where, |
| se encuentra no sé qué santo, | there's a certain saint or other; |
| que le rezan no sé qué | what prayers they say I know not |
| y se gano no sé cuánto.[13] | nor how much is offered him. |

In Argentina it has the following form:

| | |
|---|---|
| En la iglesia no sé dónde | In a church I know not where, |
| se alaba no sé qué santo; | some saint or other is worshiped; |
| rezándole no sé qué | by praying I know not what |
| se gana no sé qué tanto.[14] | I know not how much is earned. |

New Mexican Spanish *copla* 48 has the following form in Andalucía:

| | |
|---|---|
| Un fraile me pidió un beso, | A friar wanted to kiss me, |
| yo no se lo quise dar, | and I, or course, turned him down, |
| que los besos de los frailes | because the kisses of friars |
| saben a huevos sin sal.[15] | taste just like unsalted eggs. |

## The Music of the *Coplas* and Ballads

Let us now consider briefly the music of the New Mexican Spanish ballads and *coplas*.

The question has often been raised whether the ballads of the fourteenth and fifteenth centuries were originally composed in quatrains. For the oldest historical ballads, those that are in reality fragments of the early epics, the quatrain form cannot be seriously considered. For the shorter novelesque ballads of lyric character, which were perhaps often sung and not merely chanted, however, the quatrain form may be very old.[16]

However that may be, the melodies of the Spanish ballads as now sung in Spain and Spanish America, whether it be in Castile, Andalucía, Chile, or New Mexico, have as a rule only four fundamental variations: one for each octosyllabic measure of two verses. This means that whatever original strophic form may have been, the musical scheme has been arranged on the quatrain form. In this repect the ballad melodies are similar to the melodies of the quatrain *coplas*, although these often may have only two variations, one for each two octosyllabic verses.

Since the number of variations is the same for the ballads and the *coplas*, the ballads, even the traditional ones, are frequently sung with the melodies of the *coplas*, especially in cases in which the older ballad melodies have been forgotten, but there still are preserved in Spanish New Mexico a few conspicuous and eloquent examples of traditional Spanish ballad melodies. The ballad melodies published in my New Mexican ballad collections, referred to in the notes, are considered traditional Spanish ballad melodies by competent Spanish musical authorities, among them Eduardo Martínez Torner.[17]

The melodies or *tonadas* of the *coplas* are numerous, and all probably show modern developments and changes. Some have only two fundamental variations, as already indicated, but most of them have four, like the ballads, and when the *copla* is a sixain, the last two verses repeat the third and fourth variations. An example of this type of melody is found in the *copla* from *Los pastores*. Any *copla* may be sung with the first three melodies. These three are characteristic *valse despacio* melodies—that is, the music of the New Mexican Spanish *valse despacio*, which was popular in New Mexico throughout the nineteenth century and the first years of the twentieth century but which is now almost forgotten. It is a type of waltz performed by groups of four holding hands and moving slowly in a circle to the right, while the four regular variations are played by violinists and *guitarristas*; often, the *coplas* are sung, after which the partners break the circle and dance by pairs the same four variations, but now prestissimo, marcato.

Years ago the *cantador*—often the *guitarrista* and the *cantador* were the same person—was a regular institution in New Mexico. During dances he often sang traditional and well-known *coplas* that praised the personal charms of the young ladies who were dancing, or made fun of the young men, but when necessary he invented new ones for the occasion. With malicious intention or to divulge lovers' secrets, the *cantador* would sometimes sing traditional or newly made *coplas* that revealed everything *al buen entendedor*, "to the one who could understand." Of the *coplas* cited above, number 5, for example, would reveal bashful and timid lovers; *copla* 31 would warn the lover that he need not be too sure of victory over all possible rivals; and *copla* 47 would warn the rival who has succeeded for the moment in winning the favor of a young lady that she is really or practically engaged to someone else—the one who owns the *corona*. When the evening is well advanced and the customary refreshments are not forthcoming—wine, chocolate, or coffee, with *bizcochitos* (cookies), *empanadas* (traditional Spanish fruit or meat turnovers or pies, fried in lard), or *buñuelos* (fritters), the *cantador* bluntly sings *copla* 49 or one like it.

## The *Décima*

There is another type of New Mexican Spanish narrative and lyric poetry that deserves special attention as one of the outstanding examples of the persistence of Spanish tradition in New Mexico, namely, the *décimas*, or series of ten-verse strophes, usually in octosyllabic meter and introduced by a quatrain. This special form of poetic composition, with varying rhyme schemes that are also traditional, is also quite old in Spanish literary tradition—often as old as the later ballads—but in general it may be said that it is not as popular and not as genuinely representative of the spirit of the people. The *décimas* are often semilearned and composed by educated people. In subject matter they have practically no limitations, although the narrative, lyric, philosophic, religious, and riddle types are the most popular. The narrative *décimas* are more popular today than the ballads, which are no longer in a creative period.

While some of the *décimas* may be traditional in subject matter as well as in form, comparative studies give very little positive evidence of this because very few collections have been published from modern oral tradition. There are only five large collections of modern popular *décimas*: one from Chile, two from Argentina, a collection of 23 from New Mexico, and a large and important collection of 245 from Puerto Rico.[18] In general, the modern New Mexican, Argentine, Chilean, and Puerto Rican *décimas* are traditional only in form. How such a complicated form as the *décima*—with its specific number of strophes and of verses for each strophe, special and varied rhyme schemes, and introductory verses repeated in a special way—has been preserved in the oral tradition of New Mexico, often in exactly the same form as that used by Lope de Vega and other poets in the seventeenth century, can be understood only when we consider the extraordinary vigor and persistence of Spanish tradition in New Mexico in all aspects of life and culture.

In Spanish literature *décima* strophes of various types, especially the type *abaabcdcdc*, have been used since the fifteenth century. Juan de Mena, Frey Íñigo de Mendoza, and other poets of the court of John II used these poetic forms. A more conventional *décima* strophe was used in Spanish literature by Vicente Martínez Espinel (1550–1624), the author of *Diversas rimas* and of *Marcos de Obregón*. For this reason, the *décima* is often called in Spanish *espinela*. As used by Espinel and the many poets who used it later, the *décima* is a strophe of ten octosyllabic verses, the first rhyming with the fourth and fifth, the second with the third, the sixth with the seventh and tenth, and the eighth with the ninth. This is the traditional structure of the *décima* employed by its creator Espinel and those who followed him, and in general it is the structure of the popular *décima* to the present day. This rhyme arrangement, *abbaaccddc*, seems to be followed also in a very large number of the octosyllabic *décimas* from Puerto Rico, Chile, and New Mexico, but there are many new alterations. The fact that the old traditional literary type is still followed, however, shows clearly the traditional character of the material. Certainly there are no popular schools of poetry in Puerto Rico, New Mexico, or anywhere else where the popular poet may learn to compose *décimas* in a traditional Spanish fashion. In short, there seems to be a fixed type of *décima* found in Spanish tradition, although its old models are not very abundant in literary history, and this special type has suffered little or no change in the oral tradition of the people. Inasmuch as the type just mentioned is the one that seems to have preserved all the earmarks of a well-known and traditional type, the following observations will be limited largely to this type.

The word *décima* may be used in various senses. In the first place, it is the strophe of ten octosyllabic verse-lines in the rhyme arrangement already mentioned, or in other rhyme arrangements developed from it. One such strophe is called a *décima*. By extension, a series of any number of such strophes—that is, a series of any number of *décimas* treating of the same matter—came to be called a *décima* also. Later, when other meters were used, the *décima* was again the single strophe or a series of any number of strophes. In any given composition of the class in question, therefore, the *décima* may be either the entire composition or any one of the strophes which compose it. For this reason the word is rare in the singular. Since a composition of several strophes is composed of various *décimas*, the composition often has the title of *décimas*, in the plural. This is true of the old *décimas* of the sixteenth and seventeenth centuries as well as of the modern ones. The use of the singular for the entire composition, however, is also very common.

If one may properly judge from the published collections of *décimas* of the sixteenth and seventeenth centuries and from the modern published popular collections, it seems that when series of *décimas* were composed on special subjects, the first strophe or *décima* was in the nature of an introduction and the last in that of a conclusion. The number of strophes was not fixed.

In the poetry of the seventeenth century, however, the introductory strophe seems to be developed as a special part of the *décimas*. It was reduced from its regular *décima* form to a strophe of four or five verses; in other words, the introduction to the *décima* was now not a *décima* strophe but a *quintilla* (a five-verse strophe) or a *cuarteta*. Thus there gradually developed a special type, with an introductory strophe followed by a series of *décimas* (of no fixed number) and a final concluding strophe. Among the known literary sources there are many examples of *décimas* with an introductory *cuarteta* and a few with an introductory *quintilla*. The next step in the development of the conventional types seemed to have been the limitation of the number of *décima* strophes of which a *décima* could consist. Various types developed, and we have examples of many of them both in the classic poetry of the seventeenth century and in modern popular tradition.

The most common type of conventional *décima* came to consist of a *cuarteta* or *redondilla* followed by four regular *décima* strophes. This was already a well-developed type in the sixteenth and seventeenth centuries. In the *Romancero y cancionero sagrados* of Justo Sancha, for example, there are many *décimas* of this type from the Spanish literature of these centuries.[19] This is also the most popular type in modern tradition. In New Mexico,

Mexico, Puerto Rico, Argentina, and Chile there are many kinds of *décimas*, but the most popular form is that of the conventional *cuarteta* plus four *décima* strophes.

Although some of the earlier *décimas* of Spanish literature have no special feature aside from the general arrangement just mentioned, there also developed very early a scheme of verse repetition which resulted in a more specialized form of the octosyllabic *décima*. This scheme involved the repetition, in the four regular strophes of the *décima*, of the four verses of the quatrain. The last verse of the first strophe is the same as the first of the quatrain; the last verse of the second strophe is the second verse of the quatrain; the last of the third, the third verse; and the last of the fourth, the fourth. In this way the four verses of the quatrain, which serve as an introduction, stating the subject of the *décima*, are repeated in the *décimas*. This additional characteristic of the *décima* is a special sign of poetic skill, and the repetition adds force and coherence to the *décima* as a whole. The New Mexican *décimas* usually follow this traditional scheme.

This type of *décimas* (with the scheme of repetition described in the preceding paragraph), which appears in literary works of the classic period, became the conventional type of *décimas* of Spanish folk-poetry. *Décimas* of this type are found in the popular Nativity plays and in the *autos sacramentales* and other literary works as well as in independent compositions. As an example of this traditional type, we give below one from *Los pastores de Belén*, by Lope de Vega.[20] With respect to poetic form, it is exactly like the five New Mexican Spanish *décimas* presented in the pages that follow.

| | |
|---|---|
| *A esta aldea bien venida* | *Welcome be to this village* |
| *seáis, niña tierna y fuerte,* | *gentle and virtuous maiden,* |
| *porque habéis de dar la muerte* | *since you come to destroy him* |
| *al que nos quitó la vida.* | *who deprived us of our life.* |
| Eva, primera pastora, | Eve, our very first shepherdess, |
| la vida al mundo quitó, | deprived the world of all life, |
| mas ya, hermosa labradora, | but now, most beautiful maiden, |
| si por ella se perdió, | if through her this came to pass, |
| por vos se restaura agora; | through you life is now restored; |
| la vida entonces perdida | our life lost to us through her |
| venís, naciendo, a traer; | you now have come to restore. |
| pues si nos traéis la vida, | Therefore if you bring us life, |
| ¿quién, como vos, puede ser | whom else can be welcome more, |
| *a esta aldea bien venida?* | *welcome be to this village?* |
| Mató un león animoso, | Samson, going to Tamnata, |
| yendo a Tamnata Sansón, | did kill a ferocious lion, |
| y volviendo cuidadoso, | and approaching with great care |
| halló en el muerto león | he found inside the dead lion |

un panal dulce y sabroso.
  ¿Qué mucho que el hombre
acierte
este enigma celestial,
y que, si a vos se convierte,
como león y panal,
*seáis, niña tierna y fuerte?*
  Pero como del león
salió a Sansón el panal,
ya que tan distintos son,
de vos, panal celestial,
saldrá el cordero a Sion.
Éste dará muerte al fuerte
enemigo, y vos daréis
vida al mundo de tal suerte,
que tierna y fuerte seréis,
*pues habéis de dar la muerte.*
  Apenas pudo tener
de que a una mujer burló
la sierpe antigua placer,
cuando Dios la amenazó
con el pie de otra mujer.
Si vos, reina esclarecida,
la luna habéis de pisar
vos seréis del sol vestida,
la planta que ha de matar
*a quien nos quitó la vida.*

a honeycomb sweet and savory.
What wonder can there be then

that the enigma is solved,
and that we consider you
as both honeycomb and lion,
*gentle and virtuous maiden?*
  And just as from the lion
the sweet honeycomb came forth,
both being entirely different,
from you, celestial honeycomb,
the lamb will come forth to Zion.
For the lamb will then destroy
the common enemy, and you
will restore life to the world,
by being gentle and strong,
*since you come to destroy him.*
  Hardly any satisfaction
did the old serpent receive
when it did deceive a woman,
for God straightway threatened it
with another woman's heel.
If you, most illustrious queen,
shall rest your feet on the moon,
the rays of the sun will clothe you,
for you are to destroy the one
*who deprived us of our life.*

Below, again both in the original Spanish and in English translation, we cite five examples of New Mexican Spanish *décimas*: a narrative *décima*; a lyric *décima* on a love theme; a philosophic *décima* on the eternal problem of poverty versus wealth, somewhat humorous in tone; a beautiful religious *décima* on the Nativity; and a riddle *décima*, the answer being Adam. The last two are perhaps traditional and may have come down from original seventeenth-century versions.

With respect to poetic form, all five of the New Mexican *décimas* represent the traditional Spanish type described above: four ten-verse strophes introduced by a four-verse strophe, with the last verse of each *décima* repeating one of the four verses of the introductory quatrain. The rhyme of the ten-verse strophes is also like that of the *espinela*: *abbaaccddc*. In the third and fifth examples, the *espinela* arrangement is perfect; in the other three there are some irregularities in at least one of the four principal strophes.

The subject matter of the first *décima* deserves special attention. This narrative type has invaded both the field of the traditional ballads and that of the modern *corridos* and other balladlike narratives. It describes the political unrest of the Spanish inhabitants of New Mexico during the first years of the American occupation and mocks the United States for not recognizing the Mexican Empire, apparently the Empire of Maximilian. It was probably composed in New Mexico during the 1860's.

*"Jarirú, Jari, camón,"*
*dice el vulgo americano.*
*Comprende, pero no quiere*
*el imperio mejicano.*

*Nomás* los gobernadores
lo han dado por decomiso;
*ora* no son valedores
porque han dado libre el piso.
Varios han perdido el juicio
por esta mala invención,
que por rajar tablazón
nos han parado la fuente.
Ya *nomás* dice la gente,
*"Jarirú, Jari, camón."*

Todos los indios de Pueblo
se han hecho a la banda de ellos.
Dicen que es nueva conquista
la ley de estos fariseos.
Varios no somos con ellos,
pero hemos jurado en vano.
*Nomás* no digan, "Fulano
no ha prestado su atención;"
porque en cualquiera ocasión
*dice el vulgo americano.*

Todos los días esperamos
las fuerzas que han de venir,
pero al fin ya nos quedamos
como el arcaz del fusil.
En esto no hay que decir,
"Por si se nos ofreciere."
Que se apure quien quisiere
y adiós hasta el otro invierno,
porque el supremo gobierno
*comprende, pero no quiere.*

En fin, si fuerzas esperan
espérenlas por el norte,
pero de esta misma gente
no de la suprema corte.
Cada uno con su consorte
*nomás* no se muestre ufano,
que Dios nos dará la mano.

*"How d'you do, Harry, come on,"*
*that the Americans say.*
*They do not wish to recognize*
*the great Mexican Empire.*

Only the authorities
consider it an invasion;
they are now without respect
having offered no resistance.
Many people have gone mad
on account of this attitude,
for in order to gain profit
they are bringing us to ruin.
All that people say now is,
*"How d'you do, Harry, come on."*

All the Indians from the pueblos
have already joined their ranks.
"It's a new conquest," they say,
"The law of these Pharisees."
Many of us are not with them
but we took the oath in vain.
Lest people go and declare,
"So and so's not patriotic,"
because no matter what happens
*that the Americans say.*

Day after day we await
the forces that are to come
but in the end we remain
with guns and no ammunition.
And there is no use in saying,
"All this may be our defense."
There is no use for us to worry,
and good-bye until next winter,
because the persons in power
*don't wish to recognize.*

In short, if you expect help,
expect it all from the north,
but from these very same people
and not from our supreme court.
Let ur protect our families
and not be overly proud,
for some day God will help us.

Será cuando le convenga;
pero ya no hay quien sostenga
*el imperio mejicano.*[21]

This will be when it's His will,
but now no one will support
*the great Mexican Empire.*


*Te mando este papelito,*
*recíbelo en tus manitas;*
*dame lugar para hablarte*
*unas cuatro palabritas.*
Desde que vi tu hermosura,
procuré con gran desvelo
el emplearme en ese cielo
con amorosa cordura.
Que platiquemos procura,
aunque sea por un ratito.
Este favor solicito
para que no pierdas tu honor,
y para hacerlo mejor
*te mando este papelito.*
Si contestarme te agrada
y de hablarte tengo el gozo,
me contemplaré dichoso
con que seas mi prenda amada.
Sin que nadie sepa nada,
esto ha de ser a solitas;
por eso mi amor lo invitas
como del tuyo lo espero.
Agarra el papal primero,
*recíbelo en tus manitas.*
Mi contesta se reduce
a ser tu afecto amoroso.
Te explico como humoroso
lo que firme te propuse,
haciendo ver que no excuse
vida para idolotrarte.
Y para que pueda darte
prenda de amor en tus manos,
así espero, muy ufano,
*me des lugar para hablarte.*
Me lleno de confusiones
cuando me siento a escribir
y en poner tantas razones
que no puedo discurrir.
Y asi te quiero advertir
por medio de estas letritas
que espero te des lugar
con tus manos exquisitas,

*This little note I send you,*
*pray receive it in your hands;*
*and your permission I seek*
*to address you a few words.*
Ever since I saw your beauty,
with great diligence I've tried
to win for myself that heaven
with discreet and sincere love.
Let us have a conversation,
only a few words, perhaps.
I ask of you this great favor
so that you may not be blamed,
and that is why, my loved one,
*this little note I send you.*
If it's your pleasure to answer
and I'm free to speak to you,
how fortunate I will be
to have you as my beloved.
Without anyone at all,
knowing it all this must be;
accept my love, I beg you,
as I expect it from you.
But first of all take this letter,
*pray, receive it in your hands.*
My reply will simply be
to promise to be your love.
I explain as best I can
the true promise I gave you,
and you must know that forever
I will love and adore you.
And so that I may give you
in person a sign of love
I live with hope, quite content,
*and your permission I seek.*
I am so filled with confusion
when I seat myself to write
and to give so many reasons
that it's hard for me to think.
But I do wish to ask you
by means of these paltry lines
to deign to send me an answer
in your own exquisite hand,

para así poderte hablar,
*unas cuatro palabritas.*[22]

so that I may have the joy
*to address you a few words.*


*Lo mismo es pobre que perro*
*para tratar a uno mal;*
*al pobre lo echan afuera*
*y el perro le dicen, "Sal."*
Del todo me hallo sin juicio
y torpe de la cabeza,
sin más mal que la pobreza
pues de otra no hallo resquicio.
A morir estoy propicio
porque ya vivir es yerro.
Hágase luego mi entierro
en un cóncavo profundo;
porque en este triste mundo
*lo mismo es pobre que perro.*
   ¿Qué pobre hay que tenga gusto
ni aprecio en parte ninguna?
Todo lo que hace importuna
y cuanto pide es injusto.
El rico siempre robusto
y alegre con su caudal;
sólo él es sabio y formal,
político y cortesano,
y ése siempre tiene mano
*para tratar a uno mal.*
   Si es pobre, no es de talento
aunque otro Séneca sea.
Al rico nada le afea.
El rico, aunque sea un jumento,
es hombre de entendimiento.
No piensen que esto es quimera,
y el que lo dude *ondequiera*
observará esta verdad,
y en todas partes verá
*que al pobre lo echan afuera.*
   En fin, me basta razón
para estar tan enfadado,
por lo que he determinando
tener paciencia, y chitón.
Pues les digo en conclusión
que un perro, siendo animal,
puede pasar menos mal,
ofreciéndose intervalos,
porque al pobre le dan palos
*y al perro le dicen, "Sal."*[23]

A *poor man is like a dog*
*when it comes to being abused;*
*the poor man people throw out,*
*to the dog they say, "Get out."*
I've completely gone insane
and certainly lost my mind,
and all my trouble is poverty;
for nothing else disturbs me.
I'm now quite ready to die
for it's foolish to live longer.
Let me be buried at once
in a grave as deep as can be,
for in this sad world of ours
*a poor man is like a dog.*
   What poor man has any pleasures
or is esteemed anywhere?
Whatever he does is vexing,
whatever he seeks unjust.
The rich man is always healthy
and happy with all his money.
He alone is wise and serious,
a courteous and discreet man,
and he always finds a poor man
*when it comes to being abused!*
   The poor man never has talent
though a Seneca he be.
Nothing makes a rich man ugly.
Though he be a perfect ass
he's always a man of judgment.
There is no doubt about this,
and whoever doubts can note
that what I say is the truth,
and everywhere he will see
*that the poor man they throw out.*
   I've many reasons, you see,
for being awfully angry,
but I have made up my mind
to have patience and be silent.
So I'll tell you, to conclude,
that a dog can get along,
though an animal much better,
at least for part of the time,
since the poor man receives beatings;
*to the dog they say, "Get out."*

*En una redoma de oro*
*traigo almendras de cristal,*
*para darle cuando llore,*
*al pájaro cardenal.*

¡Qué lucido resplandor
el de la Virgen María
en aquel dichoso día
en que nació el Redentor!
De aquella divina flor
nació el más fino tesoro,
donde con tanto decoro
su gracia y todo lo criado
se quedó sacramentado
*en una redoma de oro.*

Luego que resplandeció
en el mundo su belleza,
fue tan celestial pureza
que hasta el infierno tembló.
La gloria entera se abrió
de alegría espiritual,
y con amor maternal
la Trinidad en alta voz
dice: "Para el mismo Dios
*traigo almendras de cristal."*

Mil parabienes le daban
las imágenes más bellas;
el sol, la luna y estrellas
para Belén caminaban;
de Jerusalén brotaban
a honrar su santo nombre.
Para que siempre se adore
a María en su misterio,
coge agua del bautismo
*para darle cuando llore.*

Mas mirando el resplandor
del Niño Jesús estaban,
y a su Majestad le daban
gracias las aves del viento.
El gallo en aquel momento
dio su aviso general,
que de vientre virginal
había nacido el Mesías,
a darle los buenos días
*al pájaro cardenal.* [24]

*El día en que yo nací*
*en la hora me bautizaron;*

*In a golden vial I bring*
*some diamonds of almond shape,*
*whenever he starts to weep,*
*to give to the cardinal bird.*

How wonderfully resplendent
the Virgin Mary became
on that most happy of days
when Christ, Our Savior, was born!
From that flower most divine
was born the greatest of treasures,
in which with utmost propriety
His grace as well as His favors
were fixed in the sacraments,
*that is, in a golden vial.*

As soon as her wondrous beauty
shone forth upon all the world,
so heavenly was her purity
that Hell itself became frightened.
The gates of heaven were opened
so great was then the rejoicing,
and with pure maternal love
the Trinity clearly spoke,
saying: "For God himself I bring
*some diamonds of almond shape.*

The fairest things of creation
offered her felicitations;
the sun, the moon, and the stars
to Bethlehem all set out;
from Jerusalem they sallied
to honor her holy name.
That Mary may always be
adored in her great mystery,
take of the baptismal water
*whenever he starts to weep.*

The radiance all admired
of Jesus, the new-born Child,
and even the birds of the air
to His Majesty gave thanks.
The cock at that awesome moment
pronounced publicly the message,
that from the womb of a Virgin
the Messiah had been born,
the kind greetings of the morning
*to give to the cardinal bird.*

*The day on which I was born*
*immediately I was baptized;*

ese *día pedí mujer,*
*y ese día me casaron.*

Mi madre es una criatura
que no tiene entendimiento,
ni vida, ni sentimiento,
ni sabe hablar porque es muda.
Mi padre es imagen pura,
incomprensible, y así
que habiéndome creado a mí
con su poder sin segundo,
me nombro solo en el mundo
*el día en que yo nací.*

Fuí en el nacer admirable
porque no soy engendrado,
ni tampoco bautizado
en la iglesia, nuestra madre.
Y para que más les cuadre
tres y uno solo me crearon.
Por mi nombre me nombraron;
y para más entender
luego que yo tuve el ser,
*en la hora me bautizaron.*

Yo soy padre de mi hermana
y me tuvo por esposo,
pues Dios como poderoso
me la dio por desposada.
Pues ella no fue engendrada,
Dios la creó con su poder.
De mi edad la quiso hacer
con su poder infinito,
y yo por no estar solito
*ese día pedí mujer.*

Confieso que soy criatura
y de la tierra nací;
antes de formar a mí,
formaron mi sepultura.
Me *vide* en tan alta altura
que muchos me respetaron.
Con cuatro letras me hablaron
cuando en el mundo me vi,
y en el día en que nací
*ese día me casaron.* [25]

*on that day I sought a wife,*
*and on that day I was married.*

My mother is a poor creature
possessing no understanding,
without life and with no feelings,
and being deaf, she cannot speak.
My father is a pure spirit,
far beyond our understanding.
And having created me
thanks to his infinite power,
he put me alone on earth
*the day on which I was born.*

My birth was extremely strange
because I was not begotten;
nor did I receive baptism
in our Holy Mother Church.
To please you more I will say
three and one created me.
They bestowed my name on me;
and so that you may know more,
as soon as I was alive
*immediately I was baptized.*

I'm the father of my sister,
and at the same time her husband,
for the all-powerful God
gave her to me as a wife.
She likewise was not begotten,
God also created her.
Of my same age he made her
thanks to His infinite power;
and so not to be alone
*on that day I sought a wife.*

I confess I am a creature
and was born of mother earth;
before I was given form
a grave for me was created.
I enjoyed a place so high
that I was revered by many.
Four letters my name contained
when I existed on earth,
and on that day I was born,
*on that same day I was married.*

# Traditional Spanish Proverbs in New Mexico

The Metrical Structure of Proverbs and Riddles. Traditional Spanish
Riddles in New Mexico. Games of Children and Nursery Rhymes.

In New Mexico, as in all Spanish-speaking countries, proverbs, called
*refranes* or *dichos*—never *proverbios*—constitute like the *coplas* a philosophy
of life. They are much older, however, than the *coplas* and have more
authority with the common people. A proverb is considered by the common folk as the final word on almost any subject and on almost any
occasion. Most of the proverbs known today in Spanish-speaking countries
are traditional and very old. Many are in assonance or rhyme and have
changed little or not at all in their transmission across the ages and from
country to country. They may be considered petrified specimens of popular
philosophy—the philosophy of Western civilization in Spanish garb, living
today in the same form they had in earlier centuries. A few have become so
popular that they exist in several forms: in a single line, in assonanced or
rhymed couplets, or in octosyllabic quatrains.

The proverbs of Spanish tradition number in the thousands. Even a
brief list of those that are traditional and common to all Spanish-speaking
countries would require many pages. Hundreds of those found in Spanish
literature before the end of the seventeenth-century—in the *Corbacho*, in
the *Celestina*, in the picaresque novels, and in *Don Quixote*, for example, and
in such abundant collections as the seventeenth-century *Vocabulario de refranes y frases proverbiales* of Gonzalo de Correas—are preserved in modern
Spanish tradition everywhere.[1] Twenty-two examples of assonanced or
rhymed proverbs and eighteen of those not so arranged are given below.
Both groups have been selected from those that appear to be traditional,
since they have identical or almost identical versions in other parts of
Spanish America and in Spain. Numbers 3, 5, 9, and 12 are found in
exactly the same form in *Don Quixote*. The English translations are literal
and not in the actual form of the original Spanish versions.

[1] Al que no está hecho a bragas  The seams scratch those who
las costuras le hacen llagas.   are not accustomed to pants.

[2] Caras vemos,   We see faces, but we know
corazones no sabemos.   nothing about the heart.

[3] Cada oveja  
con su pareja.

Each sheep associates with  
another sheep (its own kind).

[4] Da más el duro  
que el desnudo.

The miser gives more than  
does the indigent.

[5] De lo dicho a lo hecho  
largo trecho.

There is a great difference  
between saying and doing.

[6] El hombre propone,  
y Dios dispone.

Man proposes, and  
God disposes.

[7] El que da lo que ha menester  
el diablo se ríe de él.

The devil laughs at the person  
who gives away what he needs.

[8] El que mucho habla  
pronto calla.

He who talks too much is  
soon silent.

[9] En casa llena,  
pronto se guisa la cena.

Where there is plenty  
dinner is soon prepared.

[10] Haz bien  
y no acates a quién.

Do good and never  
mind to whom.

[11] La mona,  
aunque se vista de seda,  
mona queda.

The monkey, although she may  
dress in silk, is still  
a monkey.

[12] Los duelos  
con pan son buenos.

Sorrows are not sorrows  
where there is bread (plenty).

[13] Muerte no vengas  
que achaque no tengas.

When death comes, it always has  
some excuse.

[14] Natural y figura  
hasta la sepultura.

Human nature and figure  
never change.

[15] No se ganó Zamora  
es una hora.

Zamora was not captured  
in one hour.

[16] Pan ajeno  
hace al hijo bueno.

Other people's bread makes  
a boy a good son.

[17] Recaudo hace cocina,  
no Catalina.

Plenty of provisions make  
a good meal, not the cook.

[18] Vale más un mal arreglo  
que un buen pleito.

A bad settlement is better  
than a good lawsuit.

[19] Vanidad y pobreza  
todo es de una pieza.

Vanity and poverty are made  
of the same cloth.

[20] Ya sirvió María,  
fuera María.

Mary has done her work,  
so out with her.

[21] A palabras necias, oídos
sordos.

For foolish words, deaf ears.

[22] Con deseos no
se hacen templos.

Temples are not made
with wishes.

[23] Más vale un pájero en la
mano
que cien volando.

A bird in the hand is better

than a hundred flying.

[24] Al que se hace de miel
se lo comen las moscas.

The flies eat those who
are as sweet as honey.

[25] Al que Dios se la tiene
San Pedro se la bendice.

When God favors anyone,
St. Peter adds his blessing.

[26] Con la vara que mides
serás medido.

You will be judged (measured)
as you judge.

[27] Como es la vida
así es la muerte.

As life is,
so is death.

[28] Dime con quién andas
y yo te diré quién eres.

Tell me with whom you associate
and I'll tell you who you are.

[29] De tal palo tal astilla.

The splinter is like the branch
(like father, like son).

[30] El que al cielo escupe
en la cara le cae.

If you spit at heaven
it falls on your face.

[31] El que tiene boca
a Roma va.

Whoever can talk
can get to Rome.

[32] El que ha de ser
real sencillo
aunque ande
entre los doblones.

He who is to be
a simple *real* (five-cent piece),
it matters little that he
associate with doubloons.

[33] En boca cerrada
no entra mosca.

No fly can enter
a closed mouth.

[34] Es como el perro
del hortelano:
ni ladra ni deja ladrar.

He is like the gardener's dog,
neither does he bark
nor does he let others bark.

[35] El rey, con ser rey, ha
menester de sus vasallos.

The king, although a king,
needs his vassals.

[36] Fue por lana
y lo tresquilaron.

He went for wool
and came back shorn.

[37] Lo que el corazón piensa
la boca lo dice.

What the heart thinks
the mouth says.

[38] Le dan el pie                 Give him your foot
     y se toma la mano.            and he takes your hand.

[39] No hay mal que por bien       There is no evil that does
     no venga.                     not bring some good.

[40] Se espantan los muertos       The dead marvel at the sight
     de los degollados.            of the decapitated.

Spanish riddles preserved today, whether in Spain or in Spanish America, are also for the most part traditional. More than half of all the Spanish riddles found today in oral tradition have come down in a fixed metrical form from the sixteenth and seventeenth centuries. This has been amply proved by comparative study.[2]

By far the largest number of Spanish riddles employ as objects of comparison and description anatomical, physiological, physical, and sociological characteristics, peculiarities, and functions that refer both to human beings and to animals. Power of description is necessary for riddle invention. When general descriptions are sufficient, they may often have a very general application. For this reason, similar descriptions are quite frequent in the initial introductory formulae. Round objects are described in essentially the same language; vegetables of similar structure are described in the same way, and so on. These introductory formulae, so similar in many of the riddles, are followed by a more specific description or characterization. Among the commonly repeated introductory formulae are the following: *redondito y redondón*, "round and round"; *capita sobre capita*, "one layer over another layer"; *entre dos paredes blancas*, "between two white walls"; *mi comadre la narizona*, "my long-nosed *comadre*"; *mi cuñada la negrita*, "my little black sister-in-law"; *blanco* (or *negro*) *salí de mi casa*, "I was white (or black) when I left home."

So much for the ordinary, simple type of riddle that is to be guessed from a general description or characterization with respect to color, shape, structure, function, and so on. This type, of course, is by far the most numerous, but there are in Spanish tradition many other kinds of riddles. There are riddles involving mathematical problems; riddles that involve play upon words, puns, jests, and the like; riddles that involve anecdotes or folktales (riddle-tales); and, last, traditional riddles in *décima* form. Examples of all these types are found in New Mexico.[3]

The metrical structure of Spanish riddles is somewhat complicated. A few riddles are in octosyllabic quatrains or quintains, but most of them are in irregular syllabic meters, with well-defined rhythmic groups of four, five, or six syllables, as a rule, and divided into two, three, or four verses by assonances or rhymes. In general, this metrical system of the Spanish riddles is archaic and is similar to the popular rhythmic verse commonly used also in nursery rhymes and in some of the proverbs. It is a popular type of verse structure which was commonly used in Spain in the sixteenth century. Thus, many modern Spanish riddles present in this respect a fixed metrical form unchanged since the sixteenth century or perhaps earlier. Those given below are examples of New Mexican Spanish riddles of the more general types. Most of them have similar or identical versions in other parts of Spanish America and Spain and are further examples of the persistence of Spanish tradition in New Mexico.

[1] Ando de costillas,
 corro de talones,
 topes y topes
 por los rincones.
                    (Escoba)

I walk about on my ribs
and run on my heels,
banging and banging
against the corners.
                    (Broom)

[2] Arca del cielo
 de buen parecer,
 que no hay carpintero
 que la pueda hacer;
 sólo Dios del cielo
 con su gran poder.
                    (Cuerpo humano)

Chest of heaven
of fine appearance,
that no carpenter
can ever construct;
only God of heaven
with His great power.
                    (Human body)

[3] Cajita de Dios bendita,
 que se abre y se cierra
 y no se marchita.
                    (Ojo)

A little box, blessed by God,
that opens and shuts
but never wears out.
                    (Eye)

[4] Cuatro rueditas
 van para Francia,
 camina y camina
 y nunca se alcanzan.
                    (Ruedas del carro)

Four little wheels
are going to France,
always moving, but
they never meet.
                    (Wheels of a wagon)

[5] En alto vive
 y en alto mora,
 y en alto teje
 la tejedora.
                    (Araña)

She lives on high,
she dwells on high,
she weaves on high,
the weaver.
                    (Spider)

[6] Entre dos paredes blancas
 hay una cuenta amarilla.
                    (Huevo)

Between two white walls
there is a yellow bead.
                    (Egg)

[7] Extendido no alcanza
   y doblado hasta sobra.
            (Brazo)

Extended it is too short
and folded it is even too long.
            (Arm)

[8] Fui a la huerta
   y *truje* de ella;
   fui a mi casa
   y lloré con ella.
           (Cebolla)

I went to the garden
and brought some;
then I went home
and wept with it.
            (Onion)

[9] Mi comadre, la narizona,
   se come todo
   lo que hay en la loma.
           (Estufa)

My long-nosed *comadre*
eats up everything there is
in the mountains.
            (Stove)

[10] Mi madre tenía una sábana
   que no la podía doblar;
   mi padre tenía tanto dinero
   que no lo podía contar.
        (Cielo y estrellas)

My mother had a sheet
that she could not fold;
and my father so much money
that he could not count it.
        (Heaven and stars)

[11] Olla de carne,
   carne de hierro
   y hierve sin fuego.
       (Boca de caballo y freno)

A pot made of flesh
and meat made of iron,
and it boils without fire.
       (Mouth of horse and bit)

[12] Por un agujero se empieza
   y por otro se acaba,
   y queda techada.
           (Media)

You begin with one hole
and end with another one,
and the roof is finished.
           (Stocking)

[13] ¿Qué es? ¿Qué es,
   que te lo tragas
   y no lo ves?
           (Aire)

What is it? What is it,
that you swallow,
but cannot see?
           (Air)

[14] Redondito y redondón,
   *sin aujero* y con tapón.
           (Melón)

Round and round,
with a plug, but no hole.
           (Melon)

[15] Rita, Rita,
   que en el monte grita,
   y en su casa calladita.
           (Hacha)

Rita, Rita, she screams
in the mountains, but
at home she is silent.
           (The ax)

[16] Señores, vamos a ver
   una que nació sin brazos.
   *Pa* sacarle el corazón
   la están haciendo pedazos.
           (Sandía)

We are going to see a lady
who was born without arms.
To take out her heart
they are tearing her to pieces.
           (Watermelon)

[17] Una vieja,                An old woman,  
     con un solo diente,        with just one tooth,  
     recoge a toda su gente.    gathers all her people.  
                (Campana)                       (Bell)

[18] Ve el pastor en la montaña     The shepherd sees in the mountains  
     lo que el rey no ve en España,  what the Spanish king cannot see,  
     ni el Pontífice en su silla,    nor the Pontiff in his chair,  
     ni el que gobierna esta villa,   nor the governor of this city,  
     ni Dios con ser Dios lo ve.    nor God Himself can see.  
          (Pastor ve otro pastor,       (Shepherd sees another shepherd,  
          rey no ve otro rey, etc.)    king does not see another king, etc.)

As an example of the extraordinary parallelism that exists among the Spanish versions from New Mexico, Spanish America, and Spain, and to show again what has been emphasized many times already, namely, the persistence of Spanish tradition in New Mexico, an Argentine version and a peninsular Spanish version of the last New Mexican riddle just cited are given below. A similar parallelism exists for the other New Mexican riddles cited.

The version from Argentina is:

El pastor ve en la montaña     The shepherd sees in the mountains  
lo que el rey no ve en España,   what the king in Spain doesn't see,  
ni el Papa en su silla,        nor the Pope in his chair,  
ni Dios con su divino poder    nor God with His Divine power  
pudo ver.[4]                    could ever see.

The version from Spain is:

Un pastor vio en la montaña    A shepherd saw in the mountains  
lo que el rey no vio en España   what the king in Spain didn't see,  
ni el Pontífice en su silla,    nor the Pontiff in his chair,  
ni Dios, sin ser maravilla.[5]   nor God, without a miracle.

## Games of Children and Nursery Rhymes

Spanish tradition in New Mexico is especially strong and rich in children's games and nursery rhymes.[6] Comparative studies have revealed, as in the case of the other New Mexican Spanish folklore materials discussed in previous chapters, that most of the New Mexican Spanish children's games and nursery rhymes are traditional and have similar versions in the peninsular Spanish collections published by Fernando Llorca, Rodríguez Marín, and others. As in the case of the proverbs and riddles, the words of the games and nursery rhymes have fixed metrical forms that have changed very little in their transmission from Spain to America.[7] The majority of these games are played by young children from three or four to twelve years of age. Older children and even adults often play them with children, especially as leaders or to teach the younger ones how to play them. A few of these traditional Spanish games from New Mexico are described below.

| [1] "La Tuturuleca," | "The Tuturuleca," |
|---|---|
| or "La Tuerta Culeca" | or "The Half-Blind Hen" |
| La Tuturuleca | The Tuturuleca |
| pasó por aquí, | passed by here, |
| convidando | inviting |
| a todos sus amos, | all her masters, |
| menos a mí. | excepting me. |
| Cuchara, salero, | Spoon, saltcellar, |
| esconde tu dedo, | hide your finger, |
| que te pica el gallo. | for the cock will peck it. |
| ¡Se lo llevó el gavilán! | The hawk took it away! |

The leader, an older child or an adult, asks the children to place their hands with fingers spread out flat against the floor or a table, in a circle. The leader then recites the above verses until he reaches the word "finger" or "cock," striking gently a finger of the circle successively from left to right at each accented syllable or at each word. When the word "finger" or "cock" is pronounced—either one depending on custom—the leader strikes the finger harder. This finger is then bent under the hand by the child. This procedure is repeated many times until a single finger remains outstretched; this last finger is the victim of the supposed hawk, for when the last verse, "The hawk took it away!" is repeated, the leader pinches the remaining finger and raises it up, as if flying away with it.

In New Mexico there are various versions of this game, which, of course, is a game for very young children. A similar game, with verses not very different from the New Mexican ones, is well known in Spain. The forms and procedure closest to the New Mexican game cited are those from Andalucía[8] and from Valencia.[9]

| [2] "Puño, Puñete" | "Fist, My Fist" |
|---|---|
| —¿Qué tienes *ai*? | "What have you there?" |
| —Puño, Puñete. | "My Fist." |
| —Quítatelo de *ai* | "Take it away and strike |
| y pégate en la frente. | your forehead." |

The children form a column with their fists. The leader speaks first, beginning the verses. The dialogue is repeated with each child, and each strikes himself on the forehead with his fist, as told. When only one fist remains, the dialogue continues between the leader and the one whose fist remains, in the following manner:

| | |
|---|---|
| —¿Qué tienes *ai*? | "What have you there?" |
| —Una cajita. | "A little box." |
| —¿Y adentro de la cajita? | "What is inside of the box?" |
| —Una hormiguita. | "A little ant." |
| —A ver si pica. | "Let us see whether it bites." |

As the one whose hand has remained says "A little ant," he crosses the index and middle finger of his right hand over those of the left hand, forming a very small square aperture, and pinches the finger of any child who sticks a finger into it to "see whether it bites."

Similar versions are found in many parts of Spain.[10]

[3] "Juego de los dedos"      "Counting the Fingers"

Beginning with the little finger, the fingers of a child's right hand are counted in the following manner:

| | |
|---|---|
| Éste se halló un huevito. | This one found a little egg. |
| Éste lo echó a freír. | This one began to fry it. |
| Éste lo meneó. | This one turned it. |
| Éste le echó sal. | This one put salt on it. |
| Y este viejo cuzco | And this old glutton |
| se lo comió. | ate it up. |
| | |
| Éste es el chiquito y bonito. | This one is little and pretty. |
| Éste es el señor de los anillos. | This one is the ring finger. |
| Éste es el largo y vano. | This one is long and vain. |
| Éste es el chupa-cazuelas. | This one licks the pans. |
| Y éste es el mata venados. | This one kills the deer. |

These are two common versions from New Mexico, but there are many more. There are similar American Spanish and peninsular Spanish versions of both. A peninsular Spanish version of the first one is the following:

| | |
|---|---|
| Éste compró un huevo. | This one bought an egg. |
| Este lo puso al fuego. | This one put it to fry. |
| Éste le echó sal. | This one put salt on it. |
| Éste lo probó. | This one tasted it. |
| Y éste pícaro gordo | And this fat rascal |
| se lo comió.[11] | ate it up. |

The following Spanish version is from Santa Barbara, California:

| | |
|---|---|
| Éste mató un pollito. | This one killed a little chick. |
| Éste puso el agua a calentar. | This one put the water to heat. |
| Éste lo peló. | This one plucked it. |

| | |
|---|---|
| Éste lo guisó. | This one cooked it. |
| Y éste se lo comió. | And this one ate it up. |

| | |
|---|---|
| [4] "Los cíbolos" | "Buffalo hunting" |
| Cuando vayas a los cíbolos | When you go hunting for buffalo |
| no me traigas carne | don't get me any meat |
| de aquí, ni de aquí, | from here, nor from here, |
| ni de aquí, sino de aquí. | nor from here, but from here. |

One child strikes another one on the arm, beginning at the wrist, striking first very gently and progressively striking a little harder as he strikes higher and higher up the arm, until he strikes a hard blow at the shoulder as he says *"but from here."* Some peninsular Spanish versions are quite similar. One from Andalucía is the following:

| | |
|---|---|
| Cuando vayas a la carnicería, | When you go to the meat-market |
| que te corten una libra de carne; | have them cut you a pound of meat; |
| pero que no te la corten de aquí, | but not from here, |
| ni de aquí, ni de aquí, | nor from here, nor from here, |
| sino de aquí, sino de aquí.[12] | but from here, from here. |

| | |
|---|---|
| [5] "Las inditas de San Juan" | "Indian girls from San Juan" |
| ¡Rique, rique, riquesón! | Ricka, ricka, rickasaw! |
| Las inditas de San Juan | Indian girls from San Juan |
| piden pan y no les dan. | ask for bread and don't get any. |
| Piden queso | They ask for cheese |
| y les dan un hueso, | and they get a bone, |
| y se sientan a llorar | and they sit down to weep |
| en las trancas del corral. | on the bars of the corral. |
| ¡Tan, tan, tan! | Ding, dong, dong! |

Holding the child's hands, one sways back and forth, reciting or singing the verses. The peninsular Spanish versions are quite similar to the New Mexican, but instead of the line "Indian girls from San Juan," they have "The bells of Saint John" or "The logs of Saint John." Few of these verses make any sense, but the New Mexican versions seem to have more meaning than the Spanish originals.[13]

[6] The game or ceremony of becoming *compadres*, "Valerse al compadre y a la comadre. This game has been described in chapter 5.

[7] "Juego de colores"        "Game of colors"

This is a contest between the *Ángel Bueno*, the Good Angel, and the *Ángel Malo*, the Bad Angel. To start the game, two players are selected as angels, and a color is assigned to each child. As the children march by, the Good Angel chooses children for his side, and then the Bad Angel chooses children for his side, by means of the formulae cited below. After the selection is completed, the children hold hands and pull in opposite directions to see which side wins.

| | |
|---|---|
| —Voy quebrando | "I am crushing |
| bolitas de oro. Tan, tan. | little gold balls. Tan, Tan." |
| —¿Quién es? | "Who is it?" |
| —El Ángel Bueno. | "The good Angel." |
| —¿Qué quiere el Ángel Bueno? | "What does the Good Angel wish?" |
| —Colores. | "Colors." |
| —¿Qué color? | "What color?" |
| —Blanco (o lo que sea). | "White (or whatever it may be)." |
| | |
| —Voy quebrando | "I am crushing |
| bolitas de oro. Tan, tan. | little gold balls. Tan, tan." |
| —¿Quién es? | "Who is it?" |
| —El Ángel Malo. | "The Bad Angel." |
| —¿Qué quiere el Ángel Malo? | "What does the Bad Angel wish?" |
| —Colores. | "Colors." |
| —¿Qué color? | "What color?" |
| —Colorado (o lo que sea). | "Red (or whatever it may be)." |

The game may continue as a game of redeeming forfeits, especially when the Bad Angel wins. The Good Angel brings all the children won by the Bad Angel (the children of both sides) one by one before a judge (sometimes the one who has been the Bad Angel), and each is given a sentence which the child must fulfill before being set free. The Good Angel brings each child before the judge on his back. The following dialogue takes place:

| | |
|---|---|
| —Tan, tan, | "Rap, rap." |
| —¿Quién es? | "Who is it?" |
| —El Ángel Bueno. | "The Good Angel." |
| —¿Qué trae el Ángel Bueno? | "What does the Good Angel bring?" |
| —Un preso. | "A prisoner." |
| —¿Qué delito cometió? | "What crime did he commit?" |
| —Que lo encontré comiendo | "I found him eating cheese |
| queso y no me dio. | and he didn't give me any." |
| —Pues la sentencia que | "The sentence I pronounce |
| le doy es que le den dos | is that he be given |
| buenas nalgadas. | two good spanks." |

The last two verses of the rhymes vary according to the pleasure of the players. The peninsular Spanish versions end with a tug of war. The game of forfeits in the New Mexican version may be a modern addition. Fernando

Llorca, pages 133–34, gives a version very similar to the New Mexican, but it does not end with the game of forfeits.

Games of forfeits are also found in New Mexico. A very interesting one follows:

[8] "El rey y la reina"　　　　　"King and Queen"

The children form a circle, holding hands, and two of them have the following dialogue:

| | |
|---|---|
| —El rey y la reina se fueron por agua. | "The King and queen have gone for water." |
| —¿Qué es del agua? | "Where is the water?" |
| —Se la bebieron los pollitos. | "The chicks drank it." |
| —¿Qué es de los pollitos? | "Where are the chicks?" |
| —Andan comiendo huesitos. | "They are eating little bones." |
| —¿Qué es de los huesitos? | "Where are the little bones?" |
| —Se los llevó el rey. | "The king took them." |
| —¿Qué es del rey? | "Where is the king?" |
| —Se fué a decir misita. | "He went to say Mass." |
| —¿Qué es de la misita? | "Where is the Mass?" |
| —La envolvió en un papelito. | "He wrapped it in a paper." |
| —¿Qué es del papelito? | "Where is the paper?" |
| —Voló al cielo. | "It flew to heaven." |

The children then disperse quickly and run to hide themselves, crying:

| | |
|---|---|
| ¡Guel, guel, guel, que te picó el gallo! Nos vamos a esconder en las lomitas de San Miguel. | Gobble, gobble, gobble, the rooster pecked you! We are going to hide in the little hills of Saint Michael. |

Each child has been given the name of a fruit. A judge is named, and he is asked what fruit he wishes and when he replies, the child with that name comes out to be judged.

| | |
|---|---|
| —¿Qué te gusta? | "What do you like?" |
| —Manzana (o lo que sea). | "Apple (or whatever it may be)." |

The last part of the game is similar to the continuation of game number 7, described above:

| | |
|---|---|
| —Tan, tan. | "Rap, rap." |
| —¿Quién es? | "Who is it?" |
| —El rey. | "The King." |
| —¿Qué trae? | "What does he bring?" |
| —Un preso. | "A prisoner." |
| —¿Qué delito cometió? | "What crime did he commit?" |

—Que lo hallé royendo      "I found him gnawing a bone
un hueso y no me dio.      and he didn't give me any."
—La sentencia que le doy      "I sentence him to growl
es que gruña como perro.[14]      like a dog."

Similar games of forfeits are found in all Spanish-speaking countries. The long introductory dialogue of the king and queen is especially well known in Spanish tradition, often only as a rhyme series, with the game of hiding and redeeming forfeits forgotten.[15]

# New Mexican Spanish Folktales, I

Folktales, Myths, and Legends. The Schools of Folklore. The Origin and
Transmission of Folktales. The Folktales of Spain and Spanish America.

More importance has been attached to the folktale than to any other branch
of folklore. Not only folklorists, but anthropologists, ethnologists, philol-
ogists, historians, psychologists, sociologists, and students of comparative
literature as well have studied the popular narrative known as the folktale
with great profit during the course of their investigations. For this reason
we know more about folktales than about any other branch of folklore, and
it is in this special branch that folklorists have developed a scientific
method and achieved fairly definite conclusions with respect to origins and
diffusion. In fact, the history of the science of folklore has been on the whole
the history of studying the origin, meaning, development, and transmission of folktales.[1]

The term *folktale* is very loosely used by most writers. Any narrative of
popular source and development is often called a folktale, but strictly
speaking this definition is incorrect. A narrative or story that is on the
whole an interpretation of the phenomena of nature, such as primitive man's
narratives to explain the rising and setting of the sun, rain, thunder, and so
on, we call a myth. Narratives concerning the origin and early history of
man that involve supernatural agencies are also called myths. Certain
special types of creation myths which explain the origin of mankind from
animals we call totemic myths or totemic tales. Narratives, tales, or stories
that deal with historical or semihistorical persons, but in which there are
often elements outside the realm of reality, such as the narratives about
Buddha, many of the Greek heroes, and King Arthur, we call legends. The
folktale proper is a traditional, popular narrative that deals with human
beings—ordinary human beings—but in which the heroes and heroines
often receive supernatural help in order to realize the ideals of justice of the
common people. The traditional folktale is never localized and as a rule is
essentially amoral. Moral tales, merry tales, and the *fabliaux* are later,
somewhat literary developments of what in origin were probably traditional folktales.

The earliest popular narratives of primitive peoples were probably

myths and totemic tales. The *Jatakas*, or Buddha birth stories—tales from
India that date from about 500–200 B.C.—are a combination of myths,
legends, and folktales. The earliest folktales originated when life was already quite complicated, perhaps about 4000 B.C., although some of the
elements incorporated in folktales are much older and seem to have their
origin in the earliest activities and ideas of primitive man. Folktales have
been known and recorded since writing began. We have a few folktales from
Babylonia and Assyria and from ancient Egypt and extensive collections
from Old India and Persia. The Greeks and Romans and later peoples also
recorded them. In the Middle Ages, Boccaccio and other story writers took
some of their materials from popular tradition, and in the sixteenth and
seventeenth centuries, Straparola and Basile in Italy, Timoneda in Spain,
Troncoso in Portugal, and Perrault and Madame D'Aulnoy in France collected and published folktales taken from popular tradition.

The modern history of the folktale in Europe begins with the Grimm
collection of the year 1812. When the Grimm folktales were first published, some scholars believed that such folkloristic materials were to be
found only in Germany. Under the leadership of Max Müller, a school of
folklore arose, the so-called mythological school, that attempted to explain
European folktales as the last decaying remnants of primitive Aryan myths.
It was believed that the Germans were the only pure Aryans and thus they
alone had inherited the old Aryan traditions—the folktales. This theory
lost ground when it was discovered that folktales similar to those of the
Grimms were to be found in all parts of the Occident. And it was abandoned completly when it was discovered that there were Oriental parallels
in most cases. The Indian parallels were studied by the German scholar
Theodor Benfey in 1859 in his epoch-making study of the Indian tales of
the *Panchatantra*. The mythological school then gave way to the Oriental
school, under the leadership of Benfey, which originated the theory that
practically all European folktales had come from India within historical
times. After the publication of Edward B. Tylor's *Primitive Culture* in 1870,
the work in which the term *survival* was first popularized, there arose still
another school, the anthropological school, that opposed the theory of the
Orientalists and under the leadership of Andrew Lang attempted to explain
the development of folktales independently in each country, without transmission in most cases. Primitive people thought in the same way, argued
these anthropologists, and therefore they developed independently similar
myths and folktales.

There is, of course, some truth in the theories of both the mythological
and the anthropological schools, but on the whole, modern folklorists find

that the European folktale has the habit of tracing its path back to India. Benfey was wrong, of course, when he believed that almost all European folktales had come from India, and he was also wrong in assuming that they had come in historical times, but he came close to the facts as we now accept them. We now know that a large number, certainly more than one half, of the folktales of Europe have Oriental sources or are definitely of Oriental origin. The specific number and the dates of transmission, however, are problems that as yet have not been definitely settled. Many European folktales, at least in their primitive types, no doubt came from the Orient, or from the original home of the Indo-Europeans, in prehistoric times. That many came later, in historical times—through the Greeks, Romans, Jews, Arabs, Spanish Saracens, Crusaders, and the like—is also quite certain. After a folktale has been traced back to the Orient (to India or Persia), we still cannot say for sure that the folktale originated there. We simply mean that it can be traced that far back. The folktales that come from the Orient may have been transmitted to the Orient from another area. For the present, however, we may assume that most folktales that we can trace to the Orient—and that means most of the European materials—are Oriental in origin.

This does not mean that the folktales that have been thus transmitted have not changed. Some have not changed, some have changed a little, and others have changed considerably to adapt themselves to new conditions of life and culture. The tale of "The Twelve Truths of the World," discussed in chapter 12, for example, has carried with it vestiges of each culture encountered in its transmission from India to Europe.

In general, the folktales of Europe and their cultural descendants in America may be classified under three divisions with respect to their origin:
1. Folktales that have come from Oriental tradition with practically no changes whatever.
2. Folktales that were formed in Europe, but from motifs or incidents already definitely developed in the Orient.
3. Folktales that are completely or almost completely of European creation.

## The Folktales of Spain and Spanish America

The folktales of Spain are part of the folktale materials of all Europe.[2] And the same can be said of almost all the folktales of Spanish America. In all parts of Spanish America where the Indian racial elements are not dominant, the folktales that have been collected are for the most part similar to those found in peninsular Spanish collections. In some parts of Mexico, Chile, and Peru the Indian elements are important, but this is not true in New Mexico. In the Spanish folktales of New Mexico there is almost a complete absence of Indian elements. Of the folktales that have been collected from among the Pueblo Indians, on the other hand, about 10 percent are almost in their entirety, or partly, of Spanish source.[3] The Indians absorbed much of the culture of their Spanish neighbors but gave little in return. It is important to note that native Indian elements, either from Mexico or from New Mexico, have had little influence on the New Mexican materials. In Mexico, however, the Indian influence has been much stronger.[4]

The folktale materials that have been collected in New Mexico are rich and abundant. It must be remembered that this is a special field in which changes are taking place continually and in which elements of foreign cultures may be easily assimilated. In the special types of popular narratives known as anecdotes and local legends, for example, New Mexico has abundant materials that are of local origin and development, and among them there are some that reflect Indian and English influences and sources. But in the case of the folktale proper, most of the New Mexican Spanish materials are traditional and directly of Spanish source.

Language, of course, plays a most important role in cultural history. Ballads, proverbs, riddles, folksongs, folktales, and other types of folk literature are an integral part of the linguistic inheritance of a people and continue in one form or another as long as the language lives. The various types of folkloristic tradition that have come from Spain to the New World since the sixteenth and seventeenth centuries are a living part of the language—fixed forms of Spanish cultural expression that, dignified with the weight of tradition and possessing the eternal power to amuse both young and old, continue in New Mexico, as in other parts of Spanish America, to preserve the ballads, proverbs, folktales, and other traditional materials that our European ancestors of ages past enjoyed.

What types of Spanish folktales are preserved in New Mexican oral tradition? It may be said that all types and classes found in Spain have parallel versions in Spanish America and in New Mexico.[5] There are riddle tales, moral tales, religious tales, human tales of adventure, romantic tales of enchantment and adventure, demon and ogre tales, tales of persecuted women of the general type of Genoveva of Brabante, Cinderella and King Lear types, picaresque tales of all sorts (such as the tales of Pedro de Urdemalas, called Perico Argumales or Juan Bobo in Spain), animal tales, cumulative tales, and others.

New Mexicans going to town on a horse-drawn wagon in the vicinity of Albuquerque, 1902. *Photograph by D. T. Duckwall, Jr., courtesy of the Photograph Collection, Library of Congress.*

For reasons of space, only a few examples of New Mexican folktales may be given here, and these only in English translation. Before giving complete versions, however, let us glance at brief résumés of fifteen New Mexican folktales taken from two published collections;[6] they illustrate various types and classes, and all are of peninsular Spanish origin.

### The Story of the Riddle (*El cuento de la adivinanza*)

A youth of humble origin hears that a princess has been offered in marriage to the one who propounds a riddle that she cannot solve. On his way to the king's palace, the youth invents several riddles based on his own experience. The princess fails to answer correctly, but the king refuses to let her marry him until the hero performs several difficult tasks. The first is to herd a flock of wild rabbits out in the open without losing a single one. With the aid of a witch, he not only does this, but also succeeds in humiliating various members of the royal family in their several attempts to defeat him. The youth is next asked to fill three sacks with abstract things. The last sack must be filled with facts, and he does so by relating the series of events that have taken place since the announcement of the princess's marriage offer. After naming each event, the court agrees that it is a fact, and the youth pretends to put it in the sack. But just as he starts to tell about a shameful experience suffered by the king in his attempts to deprive the youth of one of the rabbits, the king shouts: "Stop! Stop! The sack is full." The king admits the youth's cleverness and allows him to marry his daughter.[7]

## The Three Riddles (*Las tres adivinanzas*)

A youth in the service of a priest wins the latter's admiration by his great cleverness. On one occasion the priest is asked by the king to solve three riddles under pain of death. With his master's consent, the servant appears before the king disguised as the priest. The first question that is put to him is, "How much am I worth?" He answers, "Our Lord was worth thirty coins, but you are worth only twenty-nine." The second question is, "How deep is the ocean?" His answer is, "The distance that a stone cast into it will travel." When the king asks the last question, "Of what am I thinking?" the youth replies: "You think that you are speaking to the priest, but you are speaking to the priest's servant." The priest's life is saved.[8]

## The Story of the Goat (*El cuento del castrao*)

A man tells his wife that he has killed a man and buried him in a certain place, and he has her promise that she will not tell anyone. It is not long, however, before she tells the secret to a dear friend, and the latter to someone else, and so on, until the whole town knows it. The police arrest the betrayed husband, and he leads them to the place where the victim lies buried. They dig and find a goat in place of a man. When asked to explain the meaning of all this, the husband states that he just wanted to find out how far a woman could be trusted.[9]

## Doña Bernarda

A father states that his daughter may marry no man except one with gold front teeth and silver molars. The devil appears in the acceptable form, and the heroine must marry him. As she is preparing to leave for Hell with her husband, a little mare that she owns advises her not to go in first when they come to a certain stream. She follows the advice and, as a consequence, the devil has to enter the stream first. The moment he goes in, everything disappears, and she is left alone in the desert. The heroine succeeds in arriving at the home of her former lover, whom she marries. Her husband has to go off to war, and while he is away, she bears a child. When the husband's father sends the news to his son, the devil intercepts both the father's and the son's messages and puts spurious ones in their places. As a result, the heroine's eyes are plucked out and her arms cut off, and she is cast out in the mountains with her child. The Virgin appears, restores the heroine's health, and provides a home for the outcasts. When the husband returns home several years later, he learns what has happened and sets out in search of his wife. He finally finds her and they live happily ever after. [10]

### Our Lady of the Rosary (*Nuestra Señora del Rosario*)

A prince falls in love with a beautiful but poor girl. He gives her beautiful dresses and a pair of gold slippers. Some jealous friends of the girl poison the slippers so that she loses consciousness the minute she puts them on. Two young girls, mistaking the heroine for a statue, remove the slippers, and the heroine regains consciousness. The prince, who has been watching from a hiding place, comes forth and rewards the girls. He marries the heroine. [11]

### The Mountains of Mogollón (*La Sierra de Mogollón*)

A girl who marries a prince enchanted in the form of a frog loses him when her mother treacherously burns the frog skin while the prince sleeps in his human form. The girl must follow the prince to a remote place called La Sierra de Mogollón. On the way, she encounters three brothers who are quarreling over three magic objects: a stick that brings the dead back to life, a piece of rug that conveys as fast as they wish those who stand on it, and a hat that renders invisible the one who wears it. The heroine gains possession of these objects through trickery. She then visits, in turn, the moon, the morning star, and the sun and tries to find out from them where La Sierra de Mogollón is. They fail to give her the information she wishes, but each of them gives her a present. She next visits the wind's wife and son, and they tell her that the wind is the only one who can give her the necessary information, but he is now dead. The heroine goes to the wind's grave, and after she resuscitates him with her magic stick, the wind not only gives her the information, but takes her to her destination as well. When the heroine arrives, she discovers that her husband is in the power of a witch and that he is about to marry one of her daughters. By means of the gifts and magic objects, the heroine recovers her husband. [12]

### John the Bear (*Juan del Oso*)

A girl, who has been stolen by a bear, has a son by him and names him John the Bear. With the help of her son, who displays remarkable strength, she escapes to her parents' home. John does not find his new environment entirely agreeable and starts out in search of adventures. On his way, he is joined by two strong companions, Mudarríos, River-Mover, whose occupation is to change the course of streams, and Mudacerros, Mountain-Mover, whose work consists of moving mountains. One day, while Mudarríos is alone fixing dinner, a dwarf appears, throws dirt and spits in the food, and then gives Mudarríos a beating. The next day, the same thing happens to Mudacerros when he is left alone. The third day, John stays, and when the dwarf tries the same trick, John gives him a blow with an immense cane he carries and cuts off one of his ears. The dwarf flees and disappears into an underground cave. The three companions secure some rope and decide to go down to explore the cave. Mudarríos and Mudacerros, each in turn, go down first, but they become frightened and return before reaching the bottom. John is then let down, and he rescues, one after the other, three princesses, the first of whom is guarded by a giant, the second by a tiger, and the third by a serpent. When the princesses have been pulled up, the two companions treacherously leave John in the cave. By threatening to eat the dwarf's ear, which he still has in his pocket, John forces the dwarf to take him out and to convey him at once to the king's palace. When he arrives there, he reveals the companions' treachery, proves that he is the real hero, and marries the youngest of the princesses. [13]

### The Three Dogs (*Los tres perros*)

Accompanied by three dogs that have magic powers, a youth sets out in quest of adventures. He comes to a city where a king has wasted his armies fighting a giant. The youth goes to the giant's mansion and gets into the giant's bed. When the giant finds him and is about to kill him, the youth calls on his dogs for help, and they tear the giant to pieces. The youth goes off, then, to another city, where a princess is about to be fed to a serpent. When the princess is taken out to the serpent, the youth stays with her and offers to save her on condition that she will marry him, which she accepts. When the serpent appears, the youth calls on his dogs, and they destroy it immediately. The hero cuts off the seven tongues of the serpent and gives them to one of the dogs to keep for him. Shortly afterwards, a Negro finds the serpent dead and cuts off the seven heads and goes back to the palace to claim the princess as his reward. During the wedding banquet, the dogs come to fetch food for their master. As a consequence, the youth is imprisoned, but the dogs come to his aid. The youth then declares that he is the one who killed the serpent and proves it by producing the serpent's tongues. The Negro is put to death, and the hero marries the princess. [14]

### Peter the Rogue (*Pedro de Ordimalas*)

When his mother dies, Peter leads the parish priest to believe that the priest's dogs caused his mother to fall from an ass and die. As a result, the priest not only pays the funeral expenses but pays damages to Peter. Peter sets out to seek adventures. He comes to a tree on whose branches he places a number of coins; he then pretends that it is a money-bearing tree and sells it for a good sum of money. Farther on, he meets a man who wishes to see some of Peter's famous tricks. He tells the man that he has left them at home but that if he will lend Peter his horse he will fetch them. The man lets him have the horse. As soon as Peter mounts, he shouts: "This is one of my tricks." And he leaves the man in the middle of a plain. Peter next hires himself to a man, and they agree that the one who becomes angry first shall allow the other to cut a strip of flesh from his back. Peter is sent to do several tasks, but everything he does he does wrong. One night Peter overhears his employer and wife planning to drown him. The night that Peter is to be drowned, he moves the wife to his bed while she is asleep and lies down in her place. Peter tells the husband that it is now time to drown the servant, and they toss the wife into the ocean. When the employer discovers Peter's trick, he becomes furious and has to allow the strip of flesh to be cut from his back. Peter then enters the service of a priest on whom he also plays a number of tricks. When Peter dies, he is sent in turn to purgatory, limbo, and hell, but he is not wanted in any of these places. He finally tricks St. Peter into letting him enter heaven, where he must remain in the form of a rock. [15]

### John the Cowherd (*Juan de la Vaca*)

A band of thieves takes by force a cow that is being herded by a youth. When they are slaughtering it, the youth begs them for a strip from the cow's hide, which they grant him. He returns home and tells his mother that he has sold the cow at a good price, but that he must collect the money in three installments. Disguising himself in turn as a girl, as a doctor, and as a priest, the youth visits the thieves on three separate occasions. He cleverly fixes it so that he is left alone with the captain of the band each time; on each occasion he takes out the strip of hide, gives him a whipping, and carries away one third of the thieves' wealth. When the youth learns that the thieves are going to attempt to steal again, he places himself in a hiding place and burns a brand on each of them. The thieves give up stealing and hire themselves to a man, but the youth appears and claims them as his slaves, declaring that they all have his brand. [16]

## The Seven Oxen (*Los siete bueyes*)

Seven brothers and one sister live near the house of a witch. The sister goes to the house of the witch for fire. The witch tries to catch her, but she escapes. The witch causes corn and other vegetables to grow near the children's house. The brothers eat them and become oxen. The girl marries a king after he promises to care for the oxen. She has a child. The king goes to war. The witch sees the reflection of the girl in a well, finds her, and sticks a pin into her head, transforming her into a dove. She takes the girl's place in the palace. When the king returns, the servants tell him about the dove that visits the garden and they catch it; the king, caressing it, takes out the pin, and the dove is transformed into his wife. The witch is made to disenchant the seven oxen and then is burned to death. [17]

## John the Gambler (*Juan Pelotero*)

A boy sells his soul to the devil in settlement of a gambling debt. He falls in love with the devil's daughter. The devil gives him three different tasks, all of which he performs with the aid of the devil's daughter. The daughter plans to elope with John and leaves three spittles on the bed. They begin the flight on the thinnest horse in the stables. When the devil's wife talks to the daughter, the spittles answer. The flight is finally discovered, and first the devil and then his wife set out in pursuit. The elopers escape first through magic transformations: the hero becomes a sacristan; the devil's daughter, a church; the horse, a bell. Then they escape by throwing back a magic comb that becomes a forest with rivers and canyons. A sea is formed, and they become two fishes. The devil and his wife give up the chase, but the devil's wife pronounces a curse upon them: that the hero will forget his bride. The hero visits his mother, and when she embraces him, he forgets his bride. With the aid of three magic doves, which she whips, the hero feeling the blows, the devil's daughter finally makes him remember her and the marriage takes place. [18]

Gold Star (*Estrella de oro*)

A father gives his daughter and his stepdaughter each a cow. The daughter is sent to the river to wash the entrails of her cow. She meets the Virgin Mary, who helps her for being good and caring for the Child and St. Joseph, and she leaves with a star on her forehead. The stepdaughter is sent also, but she does not obey the Virgin and leaves the house of the Virgin with a green horn on her forehead. The Virgin gives the daughter a magic rod that gives her everything she wishes. Dressed beautifully, she goes to church, and a prince falls in love with her. He picks up a slipper she drops on leaving the church hastily, and through it he finds the beautiful daughter and marries her. [19]

Stupid John Nightgown Who Killed Seven at One Push
(*Juan Camisón que mató siete de un arrempujón*)

A stupid boy is sent to fight with the Christians against the Moors. He goes to sleep in the middle of the road. Soldiers find him with his name inscribed on a banner. The king promises to give him his daughter in marriage if he wins the war. With sword in hand he rides the famous horse of a dead hero whom the Moors feared. The Moors believe the dead hero has come to life and flee in dismay. The victory is attributed to the stupid boy, and he marries the princess. [20]

The Cricket and the Lion (*El grillo y el león*)

A cricket challenges a lion to battle for supremacy. The lion brings together all the quadrupeds: lions, tigers, elephants, wolves, and so on. The cricket brings together all the birds and insects. The bees and wasps lead the attack of the cricket's army, sting the quadrupeds, and make them run into the water for safety. The cricket wins. [21]

# New Mexican Spanish Folktales, II

The Three *Manofashicos* (Dunces). The Three Counsels. The Three Brothers. The Enchanted Prince. The Twelve Truths of the World.

The following folktales, given in English translation, are some of the best-known examples found in New Mexico. All five are traditional, of direct Spanish provenience, and notably well preserved in the oral tradition of New Mexico.

## The Three *Manofashicos* (Dunces)

Three *manofashicos* once arrived at a town. They did not know how to speak Spanish. "I am going to learn Spanish," said the first one. And he learned to say the word *nosotros* (we). The second *manofashico* then said, "I am going to learn Spanish also." He learned to say the words *porque sí* (because, for a reason). And then the third one said, "Now I am going to learn Spanish." And he learned to say the words *muy justo es* (that is very just).

While they were in the town a man was killed. While the investigations were being carried on, they found the three *manofashicos*. When asked who killed the man, the first one replied, "*Nosotros*" (We). They took them before the judge and he asked them, "Why did you kill the man?" The first *manofashico* was silent because he knew no more Spanish, and the second one replied, "*Porque sí*" (For a reason). The judge then said to them, "In that case we shall have to hang all three of you." And then the third *manofashico* declared, "*Muy justo es*" (That is very just).[1]

## The Three Counsels

Once there was a poor man who was married and who had a sixteen-year-old son. One day he decided to leave his wife and son and go far away from home to seek his fortune. He finally arrived at a place where he found work with a very good master, who treated him very kindly. He made an agreement to work for seven years for seven bags of money.

When the seven years had elapsed, the man said that he wished to go home to see his wife and son. The master then said to him, "I must now pay you your wages, but I wish you would tell me whether you prefer that I give you three counsels instead of the seven bags of money." The man thought for a while and then he said, "I think it will be better for me to accept the three counsels." "Very well," said the master. "The counsels are these: never leave the main road for a bypath; never ask about things that do not concern you; and don't act on the first impulse."

The man heard the counsels, said good-bye to his good master, and left. Very soon he came to a fork in the road where two men had stopped. One of them said to the poor man, "The main road is too long. If you come with us by the path, we will reach the next place sooner." But the poor man remembered the counsel of the master and refused to go by the path. He continued along the main road.

After walking along for about a league, he heard shouts, and turning his head he saw a man running toward him. When he approached, he saw that the man was wounded, and he soon heard what had happened. As they went along the path, robbers had attacked him and his companion, and killed one of them. He, although wounded, had escaped. The poor man thanked heaven that he had followed the first counsel of his good master, for he had thus escaped death.

Our traveler then arrived at a very large but quiet house. It was nightfall, so he decided to seek shelter there. He knocked at the door, and a very tall and thin man opened the door and asked him to enter. He entered, and the skeletonlike man asked him to sit down in a large and lugubrious room. He went away and left the man there alone for many hours. Everything around him was like a tomb. He did not move in order not to make any noise.

About dinner time, the thin man entered and asked the traveler to go with him into the dining room for dinner. He took him to a long table, where there was food in abundance and all sorts of wines. There were cakes and cookies and fruit in great abundance. The table service was of gold and silver. After they had seated themselves and begun to eat, the wife of the thin man came slowly into the dining room and, without saying a word, sat down. The traveler noticed that she had brought in with her a human skull, and it was in this skull that she had her food served. Then she began to eat out of the skull with her fingers. The traveler wondered why she ate out of the skull and many times was on the point of asking what it meant. But he remembered the second counsel of his good master, that he should not ask about things that did not concern him, and he asked no questions. He had already seen how he had escaped death by following the first advice, so he thought he would also follow the second.

After dinner the owner of the house took the poor man to a room where he told him he could sleep. The room was also very large, and everything around was as quiet as a tomb. There the man slept, but not very soundly, for he was thinking of what he had seen and was wondering what it all meant.

The next morning the thin man appeared at the room of the traveler and asked him to go with him to breakfast. The traveler was glad day had come, and entered the dining room. Again the woman entered and ate out of the skull. The traveler asked no questions. When they finished breakfast and the woman had left, the traveler said he wished to continue his way and thanked the thin man for his hospitality. The latter then said to him, "I am very much surprised that you asked no questions when you saw my wife eat out of the skull. Why didn't you ask about it?" And the traveler answered, "I have been advised not to ask about things that do not concern me." The thin man then spoke thus, "Now that you have not asked any questions, I shall tell you the reason. My wife and I do not belong on earth. During our worldly life we were very rich and miserly. God condemned us to live in this way, my wife eating out of that skull. We were condemned to live here in this inn, giving free lodging to all, and all those who asked why my wife ate out of that skull died. Come and see them."

Then he took the traveler to a deep underground cavern where there were all sorts of dead people, some long dead, others who had died recently. "Now that you have not asked that question, we are free," he said. He then gave him the keys of the whole house, telling him that there was much wealth concealed there, and that all belonged to him now. He had no sooner said this when he and his wife disappeared, and the dead people disappeared also; and there he was in possession of the house and of all the riches it contained. Very happy at the idea that he had not only escaped death twice, but also had become rich by following his master's counsels, he left the house and continued on to his home far away.

He arrived home one day at nightfall. As he approached the house, he looked through the window and saw his wife seated on a bed caressing the head of a young priest. The man became excited, thinking that his wife had a lover, and was about to enter the house to kill the young priest. But he remembered his master's third and last counsel, not to act on the first impulse. He went to the door and knocked. His wife and the young priest opened the door. He asked her who the young priest was. She at once recognized her husband and said, "My dear husband, he is your son, the son you left when you went away!" The traveler then embraced his wife and his son, and all three wept with joy. He related his adventures and how he had escaped death twice and become rich and avoided killing his son by follow-ing the counsels of his good master. And the next day they went to the treasure house that had been given to him.

The good master was God, who wished to make the man rich and happy by means of those three counsels.[2]

The Three Brothers

In a certain kingdom there lived a powerful king who loved his people very much. One of his subjects had three sons, and the king ordered him to send them away so that each one of them could learn a trade. He also ordered that the father should accompany them until they came to a pine tree, and that they should meet at that pine tree before coming home after they had learned their trades. The king also ordered that the one that arrived first at the pine should stick his dagger into it and that if blood should come out, it meant that one of the brothers was dead, and that if nothing happened, all were alive.

The father accompanied his sons until they came to a pine tree, and then he returned to his home. The three brothers went away and each one of them reached a different place. Each learned a trade and then they returned. The oldest brother had learned to be a silversmith, the second had learned to be a carpenter, and the third had learned the trade of thief.

The oldest son returned first to the pine tree. He stuck his dagger into the pine, and no blood came out, so he was certain his brothers were safe and he waited for them. Soon the second son arrived, and he also stuck his dagger into the pine and no blood came out. They waited, and finally the youngest of the sons, the thief, arrived. "I learned the silversmith trade," said the oldest of the brothers. "I can make the most beautiful jewels you can imagine." "And what trade did you learn?" he asked the second brother. "I learned to be a carpenter, and I can make the finest and most beautiful furniture you can imagine," he replied. "And what about you?" the two older brothers asked of the youngest. "I am really ashamed to say what my trade is," he replied. "The trade I learned is not an honest trade, so I am ashamed to tell you." "It doesn't matter," said the brothers. "Go ahead and tell us." Then the youngest of the brothers said, "I am ashamed to tell you, but I learned the trade of thief."

The three brothers then went home to see their father. The father received them with great joy and at once wished to know what trades they had learned. The two older brothers at once told their father the trades they had learned, but the youngest one was ashamed to speak. "Yes, I also have learned a trade," he said, "but I am ashamed to tell you what it is." The father begged him to tell him and finally he told him that he had learned the thief's trade. The father was not pleased, but he had to tell the king the truth. The king said that he would try out the brothers to see whether they had really learned the trades they reported.

The king first called the oldest brother and asked him to make for the queen a set of silver jewelry, more beautiful than any that had ever been made, to consist of rings, earrings, pins, and other jewels. The silversmith did the work immediately, and the king and queen were satisfied with the workmanship. Then the king called the second son and asked him to make the most beautiful set of furniture that anyone had ever seen. This he did to the satisfaction of the king and queen. He was then asked to fix all the doors and windows of the palace, and this he did also to the satisfaction of all.

The king then called the third son and told him that he wished to see if he really had ability as a thief. He sent a servant to the mountains to get a black lamb and told him that a thief was going to try to steal it from him and to be on the watch. Then he told the thief to go and see whether he could steal that lamb. "That is very easy," said the thief, "I will come back with the lamb very soon."

He went to his father's house and asked him to buy him a pair of boots. The father bought the boots and gave them to him. Immediately he set out to look for the servant who was to get the lamb. He went behind him and as soon as he saw the flock of sheep from which the servant was to take a black lamb, he stopped on a narrow path that led through a little canyon and dropped one of the boots in the middle of the path. Then he turned back through the canyon and dropped the other boot a short distance from the other, also in the middle of road. Then he hid himself behind a tree near the second boot and waited.

The servant got the lamb and was coming back with it through the little canyon with great care so that no one would steal it from him. But since he saw no one, he thought he was perfectly safe. Soon he came upon the first boot in the middle of the path, and picking it up he said, "Goodness, what a beautiful boot! But what can I do with just one boot?" So he threw it away and continued on his way with his lamb. But he soon came upon the second boot, picked it up, and greatly surprised said, "Goodness gracious, here is the other boot! How can I get the other one that I threw away a moment ago?" He thought it over carefully, thinking that someone might steal his lamb if he went back alone, but seeing no one around, he finally decided to get off his horse, tie the lamb to a tree, and go back for the other boot.

The thief immediately came out and took the lamb, got on the horse with it and departed. The servant came back with the first boot just in time to see the dust of the departing thief riding his horse with the lamb tied to the saddle. The thief arrived at his father's house with the lamb and said, "It was very easy. Not only did I steal the lamb, but I stole the horse also. Here they are." "How did you do it?" asked the father. "Take them to the king, father, and don't ask me any questions," said the thief. The father then took the lamb and the horse to the king and told him that his son had stolen them from the king's servant. The king was surprised and said, "Go and tell your son that the horse and the lamb are his." Later the servant arrived on foot, very tired, and when he learned how it had all happened, he was so ashamed that he didn't say a word.

The next day the king called his servant again and said to him, "Today you are going to get a white lamb. The thief is going to try to steal it again, so be very careful." The thief then set out to follow the servant, this time on horseback, with the black lamb tied to his saddle. The servant soon arrived at the place where the sheep were, took a white lamb, put it on his horse and started on his way home. The thief, who had followed him all the way, let loose the black lamb that he had stolen the day before as soon as he arrived at the entrance of the canyon. Then he hid behind a rock. The servant came along with the white lamb and suddenly saw the black one. "Well, well," he said, "there is the black lamb that was stolen from me yesterday." So he immediately dismounted and went to catch it. It took him a long time to do so, and when he came back to where he had left his horse and the white lamb, he found nothing. The thief had already come out and stolen both horse and lamb. In the distance he could see the man galloping away and said, "That thief got the best of me again!"

The thief arrived at his father's house and said to his father, "It was very easy. Here is the lamb and also the horse. Take them to the king." The king was greatly surprised and said to the man, "He seems to be able to steal anything. But as a last proof, I wish to know whether he can rob me. Tell your son that tonight I am going to put some money under my pillow and I will leave the door of my room open. If he can steal the money, he will be free forever."

When night came, the king put a bag of money under his pillow, and he and the queen went to bed. He left the door of the room open, but remained awake so the thief would not steal his money. Soon the thief appeared, with a rubber-man, full of water, in front of him. It was dark, but the king and queen heard him enter. "There he comes!" said the king to the queen in a low voice. "I am going to kill him with my knife." The thief came forward until he was near the bed, but pushing in front of him the rubber-man. The king got out of bed quickly, took his knife and cut the rubber-man open with one thrust, so that the water began to run out. In the meantime the thief jumped behind the bed without being seen. "I have killed him! I have killed him!" the king cried out. "We must dig a hole and bury him." "I will get a light," said the queen. "Oh, no," said the king, "we must do it all in the dark so no one will see us." So both of them left the room in the darkness to dig a hole.

While they were outside digging the hole, the thief took the bag of money from under the pillow and disappeared. When the king and queen came back, they lit a candle to find the body and saw that what the king had cut open was a rubber-man. And then the king looked under the pillow, and the money was missing. "That rascal has fooled us again!" he said.

The next morning the thief's father went to the palace to take the stolen money to the king, but before he could say a word, the king said to him, "I know what you are coming for. Do not tell me anything because I know all about it. Please tell your son to keep the money and not to show his face in my presence again." [3]

## The Enchanted Prince

Once there was a woman who had nine daughters. The oldest had nine eyes, the next had eight eyes, the next seven eyes, the next six eyes, the next five, the next four, the next three, the next one eye, and the youngest two eyes.

One day the daughters went out for a walk through a forest, and the youngest one, the one who had two eyes, left the others and met a beautiful green bird, and he asked her to marry him. He told her that he was an enchanted prince and that if she did as he asked, she would some day be a queen. Two Eyes promised to marry him and agreed to do what he asked. Green Bird then flew away.

Two Eyes then went to her sisters and told them all about her meeting with the bird. They immediately began to make fun of her. "What are you going to do with a bird?" they asked her. "He will take you away to a nest somewhere." "It is my wish," she replied. "I am going to marry him even if he is a bird." And from there they went home to tell their mother.

Soon the bird arrived to ask for Two Eyes in marriage. The mother and the sisters objected. But Two Eyes insisted and finally went away with the bird and married him. Green Bird took her to the mountains to a beautiful palace. He gave his bride the keys to all the rooms of the palace. He told her again that he was an enchanted prince, to be very careful, and not say a word about the enchantment. He furthermore told her that the palace had nine windows and that he would be with her only during the night; that he would fly away in the morning and come to sing at each one of the nine windows at nine o'clock and then remain. He then gave her a little bottle of sleeping water and told her to put some on the sheets of the bed so that anyone sleeping on it would go to sleep and would not see him or hear him sing. The bird then flew away for the first time.

The mother of the daughters became envious and called Nine Eyes and said to her, "You must go now to see your sister in order to find out who the bird is. You have nine eyes and you can see more than your sisters." Nine Eyes left immediately.

When she arrived at her sister's beautiful palace, Two Eyes went out to meet her, took her inside, and showed her the nine windows of the palace. "But I don't see your husband, Green Bird, anywhere," she said. Two Eyes did not say anything in reply. Finally Nine Eyes got tired of seeing all the things the palace contained and she said she wished to go to bed. Two Eyes took her to a bed, and secretly she put a few drops of the sleeping water on the sheets. Nine Eyes went to sleep immediately.

Green Bird arrived at nine o'clock as he had promised, sang beautifully before each of the nine windows of the palace, and Nine Eyes didn't see anything or hear anything. Then he entered the palace as a handsome prince. He asked his wife, "Who came?" "My sister, Nine Eyes," replied Two Eyes. "Well and good," said the prince. "If there is no envy, everything is all right, but if there is envy and we get into trouble, I will leave and you will never see me again." Before dawn he left again, but he told his wife to give her sister anything she wished from the things she had in the palace.

In the morning Nine Eyes woke up and went to see her sister. She was surprised that she had seen nothing of the bird. She asked Two Eyes, but Two Eyes said nothing that would satisfy her. She remembered what her husband had told her and did not wish to betray him. Nine Eyes then went home laden with rich gifts, and she told her mother that she had not seen any bird at the palace.

The next night Eight Eyes was sent to the palace of Two Eyes. "Your sister who has nine eyes has not seen the bird," said the mother. "Now let us see whether you can see anything." She arrived at the palace and asked about the bird, but Two Eyes merely took her around and showed her all the palace, the nine windows, and everything else. She fell asleep also after Two Eyes put her to bed with sleeping water on the sheets. At nine o'clock Green Bird appeared again, sang at the nine windows, and again remained with his wife. Eight Eyes did not see or hear anything.

The same thing happened to Seven Eyes, to Six Eyes, to Five Eyes, to Four Eyes, and to Three Eyes. All did as Nine Eyes and Eight Eyes had done. Each one of them went to sleep and saw nothing. And each evening, when they were in the palace asleep, Green Bird arrived at nine o'clock, sang at each one of the nine windows, and remained all night with his wife without being seen by them. "Now we must be more careful than ever," the prince said to his wife. "If there is no envy, I shall soon be disenchanted and we will be king and queen."

One Eye then said to her mother and to her sisters, "I have only one eye, but I am going to show you that I can see more than all of you together."

The next morning, after Green Bird had flown away to the mountains, Two Eyes looked out of one of her windows and saw One Eye coming. "Well, there is my one-eyed sister coming to see me," she said. She awaited her gladly and as soon as she arrived, she went out to meet her. "How are you, sister?" said One Eye. "Very well, indeed," said Two Eyes. "You must let me show you the palace that Green Bird, my husband, gave me." "I am too tired," said One Eye. "I really don't care to see anything. Now that I have seen you, I think I had better go home." "Oh, no," said Two Eyes, "you must stay for dinner!" Finally she stayed. At night she went to bed also, but Two Eyes did not put the sleeping water on the sheets. "My little sister is so small and she is so tired; surely she will not see anything," she said. When One Eye went to bed, she said to Two Eyes, "Cover me up with the sheet." When Two Eyes went away, she made a hole in the sheet to look through.

At nine o'clock Green Bird arrived and sang at the nine windows, and One Eye saw and heard everything. She was covered with the sheet, but through the hole she saw with her one eye. When the bird sang at the last window, he became a handsome prince, as he did every evening, and One Eye saw everything.

"Good Evening, my love," said the prince to Two Eyes. "Who came this evening?" "My sister, my little sister," replied Two Eyes. "Yes, I know all about it," said the prince. "You have been ungrateful and unfaithful to me. Tomorrow you will see me leave in a carriage drawn by a black crow." Then he left, and she remained very said.

"What did you see, little sister?" asked Two Eyes of One Eye late in the morning when she got up. "Nothing, I didn't see anything. Please give me my breakfast so that I can go home." Two Eyes gave her her breakfast, and she left. Then Two Eyes remained alone, abandoned by her sisters and by her husband.

As soon as One Eye reached home, she told her mother and her sisters all she had seen. "My sisters with so many eyes could not see anything, and I with just one eye have seen everything," she said. When the envious mother had heard everything, she said, "This evening I am going myself." And she did as she said. She went secretly and placed pieces of glass in all the windows so the bird would cut himself and die, and she and her daughters would come to possess the beautiful palace. As soon as she had done the mischief, she left.

The bird arrived at nine, as was his custom, and began to sing at the first window. He sang well there, but as he continued to sing at the other windows, his voice became weaker and weaker, because he was all cut up with the broken glass the mother of Two Eyes had placed on the windows. He entered his room very weak and said to Two Eyes, "What an ungrateful thing you have done! Now I must leave, as I told you. You will never see me again." A carriage appeared, drawn by a black crow, the wounded prince entered, and he soon disappeared.

Two Eyes almost died of grief. But she watched the direction the carriage had taken, and taking her royal garments and her little bottle of sleeping water with her, she departed in search of her husband. She traveled and traveled, and finally, almost exhausted, she sat down at the foot of a poplar to rest. Presently she heard some birds in the tree conversing. One bird was saying that the prince was very ill and that there was only one way he could be cured. "How can he be cured?" asked another bird. "By killing us and taking the blood and anointing the wounds of the prince with it. In that way all the glass will come out, and he will get well."

When Two Eyes heard this, she emptied the sleeping water out of her little bottle. The little birds then went to sleep, and she killed them all and put their blood in the bottle. Then she went her way in search of the prince, her husband. She searched and searched, but could not find him.

Finally she went to see the moon. She asked the moon whether she had seen a sick prince anywhere. "I have been at every window of every house in the world, and have not seen such a prince," said the moon. Then she went to see the sun. She asked the sun the same question. "Indeed I have seen him," replied the sun. "He is very ill at his father's house. I cannot take you there, but maybe the wind can take you." Two Eyes then went to see the wind. "Yes, indeed, I know that prince well," said the wind. "The king, his father, has brought doctors from all parts of the world, but none can cure him. If you wish, I can take you to where he is." Two Eyes thanked him and asked him to take her at once. "Get inside of this leather bag and take that knife with you," said the wind. "I will blow you over there, and as soon as you land, cut a hole in the bag and get out."

A great wind arose and took the bag to the house of the prince. When it was grounded, Two Eyes cut a hole through the leather and got out. She went to the door of the palace and asked the servants about the prince. "He is very ill," they said. "The doctors say he will surely die." Then she told them to tell the king that if they would allow her to go into the palace, she could cure the prince. The king said that she could come in. When she entered, the king told her. "If you can really cure the prince, I will support you for the rest of your life." She asked for a sheet and put on it the blood of the birds that she had in the little bottle. Then she ordered that the prince should be wrapped in it so the blood would cover the wounds. This she did three times, and the pieces of glass began to come out from the wounds. And soon all the pieces came out, and the prince was completely cured. The king then built a house for Two Eyes and said he would fulfill his promise.

The prince, however, had forgotten his former bride and was about to be married to a beautiful princess. And Two Eyes knew everything and saw everything. And she had with her her dresses, her rings, and other presents that the prince had given her. When the day of the wedding arrived, the princess came to the palace of the prince because he was much richer. And when the ceremony was about to begin, Two Eyes went to her house and dressed herself in her queenly garments, with her rings and with her crown. When the prince entered the church with his new bride, Two Eyes suddenly appeared at his side also. The prince at once recognized her and said, "Here is my true wife!" And he left the new bride and went out with his wife.

And the envious mother and sisters found no palace at all. All they found was a deserted plain.[4]


The Twelve Truths of the World

Once there was a very poor man who was married and had a very large family. When his wife had another child, he could find no one to be the godfather of the child, and when his wife asked him whom he was going to invite as godfather, the man became very angry and replied, "I am going to invite the devil!"

He then left the house. He wandered away and arrived at a forest, where he met a very fine-looking man, who was the devil himself. The latter came out from behind a tree and asked the poor man, "Where are you going, my friend?" "I am going to look for godparents for a child," he replied. "Would you like me to serve as godfather?" asked the devil. "I am ashamed to accept," said the poor man. "You seem to be very rich, and I am very poor." To this the devil replied, "If you let me be the godfather of your child, you will be very rich. As a *compadre* I promise you that. And it is on one condition only, and that is that you will have to keep my godson for twelve years less one day. You can now go to your house and take away all the crosses and images of saints that you have in your house. Also you must not teach the child to pray. And after the twelve years less one day, I will come to take my godson away." The poor man agreed to everything. He told his wife, and she said nothing.

When the devil arrived, the poor man took him into the house and said to him, "I am sorry to say that all I can give you to drink is some coffee." The devil told him not to worry. He ordered his servants to bring all sorts of food and wines. They arrived with four wagons full of food and wines and cakes, and other good things. The devil also had carpenters come, and in a few hours they built a palace for the poor family.

Soon after that, the devil's wife appeared in a beautiful carriage, and the devil and his wife took the child to have him baptized. When they came back, they said the boy's name was Twelve and Less. The tables were set, and they had a great feast. Then the godparents left, saying that in twelve years less one day they would return for the child.

At the time agreed upon, the devil arrived for his godson. He had ordered that the child should be placed in a room without crucifixes or images of saints. The mother of the child heard the steps of the *compadre* first, and began to pray to God, asking Him to free her child from his clutches. The devil knocked at the door, and when no one opened it, he cried out to his godson, "Open the door, Twelve and Less." There was no answer, and he cried out again, "Open the door, Twelve and Less, for I am your godfather!" But the child was fast asleep. The child's guardian angel then appeared and replied for the child, "I don't want to open the door. I am too sleepy." "It doesn't matter. Open the door!" replied the devil. And the child's guardian angel said, "I am telling you that I will not open the door! Don't bother me!" "If you don't open the door, I'll break it down!" said the devil. "I am in a hurry!" And the fact was that after twelve o'clock he could not do anything. For the third time the devil said, "Open the door!" "I will not do it!" said the guardian angel.

Finally the devil got tired and said, "If you can tell me the Twelve Truths of the World (*las doce verdades del mundo*), I will not break down the door." The child's guardian angel replied, "I agree to that. I can tell them." The devil then said,

"Catholic and faithful Christian, tell me the Twelve Truths of the World. Tell me the One." And the angel replied,

"The One is God, Christ Who came down to bless the Holy House at

Jerusalem, where He lives and where He will reign forever and ever, amen."
The devil gave a jump backwards and cried out,

"Catholic and faithful Christian, tell me the Twelve Truths of the
World. Tell me the Two." And the angel replied,

"The Two, the two Tables of Moses; the One is God, Christ Who came
down to bless the Holy House at Jerusalem, where He lives and where He
will reign forever and ever, amen." The devil gave another jump backwards
and cried out,

"Catholic and faithful Christian, tell me the Twelve Truths of the
World. Tell me the Three." And the Angel replied,

"The Three, the three Persons of the Holy Trinity; the Two, the two
Tables of Moses; the One is God, Christ Who came down to bless the Holy
House at Jerusalem, where He lives and where He will reign forever and
ever, amen." The devil gave another jump and said,

"Catholic and faithful Christian, tell me the Twelve Truths of the
World. Tell me the Four." And the angel replied,

"The Four, the four gospels; the Three, the three Persons of the Holy
Trinity [etc.]" Again the devil gave a jump and said,

"Catholic and faithful Christian, tell me the Twelve Truths of the
World. Tell me the Five." And the angel replied,

"The Five, the five wounds, the Four, the four gospels [etc.]" Again the
devil gave a jump and said,

"Catholic and faithful Christian, tell me the Twelve Truths of the
World. Tell me the Six." And the angel replied,

"The Six, the six candlesticks, the Five, the five wounds [etc.]" Again
the devil gave a jump and said,

"Catholic and faithful Christian, tell me the Twelve Truths of the
World. Tell me the Seven." And the angel replied,

"The Seven, the seven joys, the Six, the six candlesticks [etc.]" Again
the devil gave a jump and said,

"Catholic and faithful Christian, tell me the Twelve Truths of the
World. Tell me the Eight." And the angel replied,

"The Eight, the eight choirs, the Seven, the seven joys [etc.]" And the
devil again gave a jump and said,

"Catholic and faithful Christian, tell me the Twelve Truths of the
World. Tell me the Nine." And the angel replied,

"The Nine, the nine months, the Eight, the eight choirs [etc.]" And
again the devil gave a jump and said,

"Catholic and faithful Christian, tell me the Twelve Truths of the
World. Tell me the Ten." And the angel replied,

"The Ten, the Ten Commandments, the Nine, the nine months [etc.]"
And again the devil gave a jump and said,

"Catholic and faithful Christian, tell me the Twelve Truths of the World. Tell me the Eleven." And the angel replied,

"The Eleven, the eleven thousand virgins, the Ten, the Ten Commandments [etc.]" And still again the devil gave a jump and said,

"Catholic and faithful Christian, tell me the Twelve Truths of the World. Tell me the Twelve." And the angel replied,

"The Twelve, the twelve apostles, the Eleven, the eleven thousand virgins, the Ten, the Ten Commandments, the Nine, the nine months, the Eight, the eight choirs, the Seven, the seven joys, the Six, the six candlesticks, the Five, the five wounds, the Four, the four gospels, the Three, the three Persons of the Holy Trinity, the Two, the two Tables of Moses, the One is God, Christ Who came down to bless the Holy House at Jerusalem, where He lives and where He will reign forever and ever, amen."

Then the devil disappeared amidst a roar of thunder, and the parents kept their child.[5]

This last tale is one of the most extraordinary examples of the persistence of a folkloristic tradition, not only as regards Spanish tradition in New Mexico, but also as an example of the transmission of a religious formula across the ages from Persia to Europe through Jewish and Arabic versions and from Europe to America through Spanish and English versions. This folktale and doctrinal series of numbers called *Las doce verdades del mundo* ("The Twelve Truths of the World") is usually called in peninsular Spanish tradition *Las doce palabras retorneadas* ("The Twelve Reversed Words") and in French and Italian "The Twelve Words of Truth." The last part, the doctrinal series of numbers recited by the guardian angel of the youth promised to the devil, is considered in Hispanic tradition as an elementary doctrinal guide, as a powerful prayer, and sometimes as an exorcism or superstitious prayer. Some have heard it and fear it as a witch prayer. In the sixteenth century a Portuguese woman accused of being a witch, Anna Martins, declared before a Christian tribunal that it was one of her favorite prayers.

The history of this tradition is very old. There are versions from every country in Europe, from Persia, and from Arabia, and the Jews have a version in their Paschal rites. The oldest version is apparently the old Persian tale of Ghôst i Fryâno, from the *Book of Arda Virai*, which contains both the folktale and the doctrinal series of numbers. The actual reply to each one of the questions or numbers of the doctrinal series varies consider-

ably from country to country, in each particular version the replies being
fitted to the culture and religion of the people that preserve it. The Jewish
and Christian versions, however, are very similar.

In Hispanic tradition the doctrinal series is very common, both in Spain
and Spanish America, but the versions that preserve both the folktale and
the doctrinal series of numbers, such as the above New Mexican version and
a known peninsular Spanish version cited above, are very few. In Germanic
tradition only the doctrinal numbers are preserved. In English tradition the
doctrinal series is sung or recited as a Christmas carol. One English version
begins:

I'll sing you one-o.
Green grow the rushes-o.
What is your one-o?
One is One and all alone,
and ever more shall be so.

Thus the song continues until twelve is reached, all the previous numbers in each case being repeated inversely each time.

The other numbers are the following:

Two, two lily-white babes, clothed all in green-o
Three, the three rivals (Trinity).
Four for the Gospel-makers.
Five for the symbols at your door.
Six for the six proud walkers.
Seven for the seven stars in heaven.
Eight for the April rainers.
Nine for the nine bright shiners.
Ten for the Ten Commandments.
Eleven for the eleven who went to heaven.
Twelve for the twelve Apostles.

In mediaeval Latin tradition the typical version is the following:

| | |
|---|---|
| Unus est Deus, | One is God. |
| Duo sunt testamenta. | The two Testaments. |
| Tres sunt Patriarchae. | The three Patriarchs. |
| Quattuor Evangelistae. | The four Evangelists. |
| Quinque libri Moysis. | The five books of Moses. |
| Sex sunt hidriae positae | The six wine-jugs of the |
| in Cana Galileae. | Marriage Feast at Cana. |
| Septem sacramenta. | The seven sacraments. |
| Octo beatitudines. | The eight beatitudes. |
| Novem angelorum chori. | The nine choirs of angels. |

| | |
|---|---|
| Decem mandata Dei. | The Ten Commandménts. |
| Undecim stellae a Josepho visae. | The eleven stars seen by Joseph. |
| Duodecima Apostoli. | The twelve Apostles. |

In mediaeval and modern European tradition there are, to be sure, many other types of number symbolism in regular and fixed series. Some of these, such as the parodies of the Twelve Words of Truth, are obviously based on the traditional doctrinal series of Christian origin. In European folklore we find parodies even of the Lord's Prayer and the Latinisms of the Mass. The well-known European tradition of the soldier who goes to hear Mass with a deck of cards, which constitute the doctrinal series, is also based on the traditional Twelve Words of Truth. There are other types, however, that appear to be of independent origin. Among these the best-known in Europe are the Celtic and Scandinavian versions. Some of these are of pagan origin and perhaps as old as the original tale of Ghôst i Fryâno that seems to be the source of the Christian tradition. The symbolism of numbers is as old as the history of the human race.[6]

# Traditional Spanish Religious Folk Drama
# in New Mexico

*Los pastores. La primera persecución de Jesús. El niño perdido. Auto de la aparición de Nuestra Señora de Guadalupe. Las posadas. Los desposorios de San José y María Santísima.*

The history of New Mexican folk drama is little down. We know a good deal, it is true, of some popular religious representations, such as *Los pastores* and *El niño perdido*, discussed below, but very little of popular secular drama. The New Mexican religious folk drama is for the most part either traditional or based on traditional compositions, but the secular folk drama known to us is of native origin.

First let us take up the religious folk drama. Numerous scenes of the Passion, already discussed, were dramatically staged in New Mexico up to the end of the nineteenth century, and a few of them, such as the descent from the Cross, are still performed in some localities. Most of these dramatic scenes and processions, however, have now disappeared. A shadow of the former dramatic representations is preserved in the practices of the Penitentes, who enact in a way the march to Calvary and recite and chant narratives that relate the complete account of the Passion. In the *moradas* during Holy Week, the Penitentes chant with real dramatic feeling some Passion narratives that have responses in every strophe. Moreover, there are several popular religious compositions known in New Mexico that do not deal directly with the Passion. Cited below are some of the principal ones that are still performed or of which I was able to find manuscripts or recent copies made from manuscripts in northern New Mexico. Each one will be described briefly, and when possible, an account of its sources will be given.

## Los Pastores

I have found manuscript copies of the Nativity play *Los pastores* (The shepherds of Bethlehem) in Santa Fe, Cubero, Taos, and Arroyo Seco, and other copies are known to exist. The manuscript versions from Santa Fe and Cubero are very much alike, and both are very similar to the copies from Taos and Arroyo Seco. The New Mexican version from San Rafael, printed by M. R. Cole in 1907,[1] is also similar to the four mentioned. Space prevents a detailed discussion of the five versions here, but it is quite clear that all five are based on the same original. I have also found a California version of *Los pastores* in Santa Barbara. It is similar to the Texas version published by Cole,[2] but both of these versions are different enough from the five New Mexican versions cited above to warrant the conclusion that they come from a different original.

The Spanish Nativity plays, beginning with the beautiful and inspiring *Los pastores de Belén*, by Lope de Vega, are legion. Most of them deal with similar situations, and it is natural that similarities in plot, incidents, and often even language should be found among them. In the eighteenth and nineteenth centuries Nativity plays were still being written both in Spain and America. In Mexico they were especially popular, and very often the Mexican plays were based on traditional Spanish versions of the sixteenth and seventeenth centuries and imitated some of the scenes and verses, especially the Nativity *coplas*. But even so, no direct source has yet been found in printed form for the New Mexican version of *Los pastores*. The play represented by the five versions cited above may have come from Mexico in the eighteenth century, but it could have come from Spain directly. In the versions now extant there are many indications of its traditional lineage, but there is also some evidence of many years, perhaps more than a century, of New Mexican elaboration. Even if we assume that the New Mexican *Los pastores* versions are derived directly from Mexican eighteenth-century sources, these would still be traditional Spanish sources, for the religious drama of Mexico in that century, whether popular or learned, was part of the popular and learned dramatic literature of Spain.[3]

*Los pastores* is a Nativity play, as the title indicates. In most of the Mexican printed *pastorelas*, as well as in the *Pastores de Belén* of Lope de Vega and in other Spanish Nativity plays of the Golden Age, the play usually begins with the marriage of Joseph and Mary, although it sometimes starts with the Annunciation of the birth to Mary. In the New Mexican play the first scene is that of the Virgin and Saint Joseph seeking shelter at Bethlehem before the birth of the Savior. This incident is also the subject matter of a separate New Mexican Spanish dramatic composition of a very brief character, *Las posadas* (The Inns), discussed below. Some of the parts of *Los pastores* are sung, and others are recited. The choruses by groups of shepherds, and the individual *coplas* of the shepherds when each makes his offering to the Child Jesus, are all sung. The principal characters are a few shepherds, all with traditional Spanish names—Tetuán, Tubal, Bartolo (the glutton and lazy shepherd), Bato, Tebano, Lípido—an angel, Saint

Michael; the archangel, Lucifer; a hermit; and Gilita, a young and beautiful shepherdess. The Virgin, Saint Joseph, and the Child Jesus, usually a small image, are passive characters. The brief outline of the play as given below is based on the version from Cubero.

In the opening scene all the shepherds, except Bartolo, together with the angel and Saint Michael enter singing of how Saint Joseph and the Virgin Mary seek shelter and can only find refuge in a stable in Bethlehem. The opening verses are:

| | |
|---|---|
| Cuando por el oriente sale la aurora | When dawn appears in the East, |
| caminaba la Virgen, Nuestra Señora. | Our Blessed Lady was traveling. |

When at last they find refuge in a stable, where the mule and the ox adore them, an angel appears and informs the shepherds that Christ is born. The shepherd Tetuán goes to see the newborn Child and returns to give his companions the glad tidings. One by one all the shepherds gather and go to see with their own eyes the great miracle. The shepherds present their gifts as they sing:

| | |
|---|---|
| Duérmete, Niño Lindo, | Go to sleep, Pretty Child, |
| en los brazos del amor. | in the embraces of love. |
| Que te arrulle tu madre, | Let your mother lull you |
| cantándote, "Alarrú." | singing to you, "Lullaby." |
| ¡Alarrú, alamé, | Alarru, alame, |
| alarrú, alamé! | Alarru, alame! |
| ¡Alarrú, alamé, alarrú! | Alarru, alame, alarru! |
| No temas a Herodes | Have no fear of Herod, |
| no temas a Herodes, | have no fear of Herod. |
| nada te ha de hacer. | for he cannot harm you. |
| En los brazos de tu madre | When in your mother's arms, |
| nadie te ha de ofender. | no one can harm you. |
| ¡Alarrú, alamé | Alarru, alame |
| alarrú, alamé! | alarru, alame! |
| ¡Alarrú, alamé, alarrú! | Alarru, alame, alarrú! |

Lucifer appears and expresses his wrath at the mystery of the birth of the Savior who is to save mankind. An angel then appears and replies to the words of Lucifer, and a chorus sings the praises of the incarnation and the redemption through the sacrament of the Eucharist. This ends the first part.

The second part of *Los pastores* opens with a procession of a large group of shepherds on their way to Bethlehem. Gilita and the lazy and gluttonous Bartolo are among them. They enter singing:

| | |
|---|---|
| De la real Jerusalén | From Jerusalem, the royal, |
| salió una estrella brillando, | a most brilliant star arose |
| que a los pastores va guiando | that goes on guiding the shepherds |
| para el Portal de Belén. | to the Manger of Bethlehem. |
| Al que con finos amores | To Him Who with purest love |
| y un humilde corazón | and a very humble heart |
| virtió su sangre en la Cruz | shed his blood upon the Cross |
| por la humana redención. | for the redemption of all. |

The shepherds sing *coplas* to express their joy at the birth of the Savior. They encounter snow and hail on the way, and this incident gives occasion to one of the most beautiful choruses in this part; it begins thus:

| | |
|---|---|
| Cielo soberano, | Supreme, sovereign heaven, |
| cielo soberano, | supreme sovereign heaven, |
| ten de nos piedad, | have pity on us, |
| que ya no sufrimos | for we cannot suffer |
| la nieve que cae, | the snow that is falling, |
| que ya no sufrimos | for we cannot suffer |
| la nieve que cae. | the snow that is falling. |
| Las estrellas vuelan, | The stars fly by quickly |
| las estrellas vuelan, | the stars fly by quickly |
| y luego se paran, | and then they stop short |
| y absortas se quedan | absorbed in amazement |
| de ver tal nevada, | at the great snowfall, |
| y absortas se quedan | absorbed in amazement |
| de ver tal nevada. | at the great snowfall. |

The shepherds eat and then retire to sleep for the night. Lucifer appears again and after a long speech wherein he laments the birth of the Savior, he determines to kill all the shepherds while they sleep. An angel appears and, awakening the hermit, warns him against the temptations of sin. Lucifer, however, tempts the hermit, who steals from the shepherds and is about to carry away the young girl, Gilita. The shepherds wake up in time and give the hermit a thrashing. The latter explains that Lucifer had tempted him during his sleep.

An angel appears to the shepherd Tubal and tells him that the newborn Child at Bethlehem has invited the shepherds to go to see him. Tubal in great joy and excitement gives the message to the other shepherds. Some believe him, while others express doubts. Lucifer appears again, and Saint Michael descends from heaven to defend the shepherds. The chorus sings:

| | |
|---|---|
| Del cielo lucido | From the brilliant heavens |
| bajó San Miguel; | Saint Michael came down; |
| aquestos pastores | these very same shepherds |
| vino a defender. | he came to defend. |

There follows a long contest between Saint Michael and Lucifer, first with words and finally with weapons, and Lucifer is defeated. Here the famous verses of Góngora are found:

| | |
|---|---|
| Aprended, flores de mí, | Learn from me, flowers, the difference |
| lo que va de ayer a hoy; | between yesterday and today; |
| que ayer maravilla fui, | yesterday I was a wonder, |
| y hoy sombra de mí no soy. | today not even my shadow. |

(In Góngora's poem the fourth verse reads: "y hoy sombra mía aun no soy.") These verses form the quatrain that introduces a *décima* of the traditional Spanish type so frequent in New Mexico, as described in chapter 9. The *décima* is recited by Lucifer when he is defeated at the hands of Saint Michael. The angel appears again and invites the shepherds to go to Bethlehem to visit the Child Jesus. They set out, each bearing a gift and singing *coplas* individually and in groups. The *coplas* that end the play are among the most beautiful parts of *Los pastores*. The last two quatrains of a long series recited by all the shepherds—the two that close the play—are the following:

| | |
|---|---|
| Adiós, José, adiós, María, | Good-bye Joseph, good-bye Mary, |
| adiós, mi manso cordero, | good-bye, my most gentle lamb, |
| que ya se van los pastores | the shepherds are going away |
| hasta el año venidero. | until they return next year. |
| Échanos tu bendición | Give all of us now your blessing, |
| a todos, y al ermitaño. | to all of us, including the hermit. |
| Préstanos vida y salud | Give us life and give us health |
| para volver al otro año. | that we may return next year. |

### La Primera Persecución de Jesús

The play *La primera persecución de Jesús* (The first persecution of Jesus) is called an *auto sacramental*, or sacramental play, but it is not written especially to honor the Eucharist like the usual type of *auto sacramental*. It has as its principal theme the slaughter of the innocents by King Herod and the flight into Egypt of Mary and Joseph with the Child Jesus. The play is not as well known as *Los pastores*. In fact, I know of only one complete version, a manuscript that has been in my family for four generations. The manuscript came into the possession of our family in Taos during the years 1860–80, and copies of it were apparently made during those years, because a manuscript copy from Taos obtained recently follows the older manuscript almost verbatim, although it omits about one-third of the text. This play has not been popular in New Mexico for several generations, but it is known that it was presented in Taos during the years mentioned.

Since it is very poorly written, the manuscript can hardly be the first copy of a printed play: there are too many errors in it. It is most certainly a second or third copy of a printed play or of an original manuscript. The entire play is in octosyllabic verse and is composed for dramatic recitation, with no parts for singing. The entire character of the play, the vocabulary, and the elevated style reveal a learned, literary source. Its language is not popular speech, and there are numerous orthographic archaisms, such as *Joseph* and *Josef* for *José*. It was certainly not composed in New Mexico, and it is apparently a copy of a Spanish or Mexican-Spanish original manuscript or printed work that came to New Mexico in the early part of the eighteenth century. The characters that take part are the following: the Virgin Mary; Saint Joseph; two angels; three women (Rosaura, Laura, and Anabelita); the three Magi Kings (Balthasar, Melchor, and Gaspar); King Herod; Suetonius, a doctor or learned man; Chapín, an innkeeper; three doctors or learned men; three executioners; one judge; two farmers (*labradores*); and Lucifer. A brief outline of the play follows.

In traditional Spanish fashion, the attention of the audience is requested by an announcer before the play begins:

| | |
|---|---|
| Atención, noble auditorio! | Hear me, noble audience! |
| A vuestra corporación, | I request this guild of yours |
| y a todo este consistorio, | and all this consistory |
| repito, pido atención. | to give us your kind attention. |

The play proper begins with a long scene in which the three Magi Kings speak of the prophecies, the appearance of the mysterious star, and the coming Messiah. They determine to journey to Judea to visit the newborn king. Balthasar speaks first to the other two:

| | |
|---|---|
| —Reyes Gaspar y Melchor | Kings Gaspar and Melchor, |
| de vuestras proezas no ignoro | with respect to your deeds |
| la solicitud que blasona | I am fully aware of their worth, |
| la fama con lenguas de oro. | for golden tongues proclaim them. |

They set out promising to offer the Child Jesus myrrh, incense, and gold.

In the next scene Herod addresses Suetonius on the prophecies, royal power, and so on. Soon the Magi Kings appear and meet Herod. He greets them courteously:

| | |
|---|---|
| Para darle más honor | So as to do greater honor |
| a mi corona y mi cetro, | to my crown and to my sceptre, |
| nobilísimos señores, | at once, my most noble lords; |
| con la salud que os deseo, | with the good health I wish you, |
| seáis bien venidos y en paz. | I welcome you bringing peace. |

The Magi Kings tell Herod about the star that has led them to Bethlehem to see the new Messiah. Herod is not pleased and consults his wise men, especially Suetonius. Herod expresses great indignation when he learns that all the signs point to the birth of the Savior. The Magi Kings leave. Lucifer appears and in a wrathful monologue decides to bring turmoil, hatred, and destruction to the world in order to prevent the redemption of mankind.

The scene then changes to the stable in Bethlehem, where Mary holds in her arms the Divine Child. The Magi Kings approach, remove their crowns, and adore the Child. They offer Him myrrh, incense, and gold. They leave, and then an angel appears and tells Joseph that God ordains that he leave immediately for Egypt with Mary and the Child. They prepare for the journey. When all is ready, the Virgin takes the Child from the crib where He is sleeping and says:

| | |
|---|---|
| Dormido estás, Vida Mía; | You are asleep, My Beloved, |
| pierde el sueño, que postrada | awake; kneeling beside you |
| tu esclava te lo suplica | your slave implores it of You; |
| y la fuerza lo demanda. | necessity demands it. |

When they are already on their way, the Child Jesus cries, and the Virgin consoles Him, saying:

| | |
|---|---|
| No llores, Amado Mío, | Do not weep, my Dearest Love, |
| desterrado de mi alma. | My Beloved Exiled Child. |
| Deja en paz a Palestina, | Leave Palestine now in peace, |
| despídete de tu patria. | take leave of your native country. |
| ¡Adiós, Nasaret, Belén, | Good-bye, Nazareth, Bethlehem, |
| tierra bendita y sagrada! | our blessed and sacred land! |
| ¡Adiós, humildes pastores | Good-bye, all you humble shepherds |
| que habitáis en su comarca! | who inhabit its environs. |

On their way to Egypt, they meet a farmer planting grain. The Virgin asks him what he is planting. He replies in a courteous manner, and the Virgin tells him to go and get his laborers with sickles to reap the grain. Miraculously the grain has grown and ripened at once. They meet another farmer, who replies with great arrogance when the Virgin asks him what he is planting. His crop yields only stones.

In the next scene, the slaughter of the innocents takes place, as Rosaura and Anabelita express their indignation at the cruelties of Herod. Herod seeks the child who has been born a king. Those who seek Joseph and the Virgin Mary come upon the first farmer and ask him about the fugitives. He replies that they passed by when he was sowing his grain—the grain that he is now harvesting. The pursuers turn back, and when they report to Herod, the judge and the learned men decide that the time mentioned in the prophecies has now elapsed and that the persecution must stop.

### El Niño Perdido

*Auto del niño perdido* (The lost child) is another New Mexican religious dramatic work that most certainly is not of native composition. As in the case of *The First Persecution of Jesus*, however, the sources of this play are, beyond all doubt, also traditional. I have copies of two manuscripts, one from Cerro and the other from Taos. The better version is the one from Cerro.[4] Both point to a single original—perhaps a printed seventeenth- or eighteenth-century Spanish or Mexican play. Many of its lines and even a few scenes are based on classic Spanish models. The contents of the play are as follows:

A chorus begins by singing the following quatrain:

| | |
|---|---|
| Vamos a darlo, que es hora, | Let us start it, for it's time, |
| y para que nazca el sol | and so that the sun may rise |
| nos alumbre su farol, | may its luminary shine, |
| la más refulgente aurora. | that most brilliant morning star. |

The sun represents the Child Jesus and the morning star, the Virgin Mary. Lelio then announces in a long speech the opening of the play, and the chorus begs the attention of the public, as in the case of *The First Persecution of Jesus*. In the play of *The Lost Child*, however, the audience is called "Illustrious Senate," as was the custom in the Spanish theatre in the seventeenth century.

| | |
|---|---|
| Atención, Senado Ilustre, | Attention, Illustrious Senate, |
| que ya se comienza el auto | for the play is to begin |
| en que obró el Niño Jesús | in which the Blessed Child Jesus |
| un descuido y con cuidado. | by design made a mistake. |

Carrasco then appears and gives further information about the play that is about to begin:

| | |
|---|---|
| En la tierra está la gloria; | Heaven has been brought to earth; |
| todos venir con presteza, | hasten hither all of you, |
| no a todas horas se llega | for not always are displayed |
| en el mundo esta grandeza. | such grandiose scenes in this world. |
| | |
| Hoy el misterio inefable | Today the ineffable mystery |
| de la superior alteza | of the majesty of Jesus |
| de Jesús, Niño Perdido, | as the Beloved Lost Child, |
| la Santa Iglesia celebra. | our Holy Church celebrates. |

The play proper begins with the following quatrain, in balladlike lines sung by the chorus:

| | |
|---|---|
| María busca a Jesús | The Virgin is seeking Jesus |
| por montes, selvas, collados; | over mountains, forests, hillocks; |
| auxilio pide a los cielos | She begs assistance from heaven |
| para poder encontrarlo. | to be able to find Him. |

The Virgin appears and expresses her grief in eighty-eight octosyllabic *romance* lines in *a-o* assonance. The first four verses are:

| | |
|---|---|
| Decidme, montes y selvas, | Pray, tell me, mountains and forests, |
| sotos, grutas y collados, | thickets, caverns and hillocks, |
| ¿dónde hallaré a mi Jesús? | where am I to find My Jesus? |
| ¿dónde encontraré a mi Amado? | where can I find My Beloved? |

Saint Joseph then appears and expresses his grief. Next, the Child Jesus appears and meditates on His future Passion. (This is one of the most beautiful parts of the play.) An angel appears to comfort the Child, who describes all the scenes of His future Passion, called *palacios*, or palaces, in the play: the house of Annas, the house of Caiphas, the house of Arquelaus, and the house of Pilate.

The Lost Child then arrives at the house of a rich man, who is having a great feast. The chorus sings the praises of the rich and their pleasures. The rich man gives gold chains to his musicians. When the Child asks for something to eat, the rich man is offended and calls him arrogant. The Child Jesus attempts to appease the anger of the rich man with kind and wise words, but the rich man is obstinate and cruel and finally sets his dogs on the Child. The Child leaves, and the rich man continues to eat and drink and enjoy himself. At the house of Rosaura and Gosabel (Josabel in one manuscript), the Child is received courteously and kindly. Given food, He eats and weeps. Gosabel consoles Him, saying:

| | |
|---|---|
| Come, Niño de mi vida, | Please eat, my Beloved Child, |
| come y no derrames perlas, | eat, and do not shed those pearls, |
| yo iré a buscar a tus padres | for I'll go and find Your parents |
| brevemente en la Judea. | very shortly in Judea. |

The Child Jesus replies:

| | |
|---|---|
| ¡Ay, señora, yo aseguro, | Alas, madam, I assure you, |
| lo que mi madre me ama! | that My mother loves me dearly! |
| Han de pasar ya tres días | It must be surely three days |
| que no le veo la cara, | that I haven't seen her face, |
| y esta ternura me saca | and it is due to this love |
| las lágrimas de mis ojos, | that tears appear in My eyes, |
| anudando la garganta. | and I feel lumps in my throat. |

In the next scene the Virgin appears again in great anguish. An angel comes once more to console her. Then Saint Joseph appears and meets the Virgin. The Virgin finally arrives at the house of Gosabel, and when she asks for the Child, Gosabel begs the Virgin to describe Him. The Virgin does so, and Gosabel is then sure that the child who ate at her house is the Child Jesus. She directs the Virgin to the Temple, and there the Child is found conversing with the doctors. Six doctors argue about the prophecies, the coming of the Messiah, and other related subjects, and the Child explains everything. As the Child pronounces His last words, the Virgin enters and finds Him. He explains to her that He is doing the work of His Father. The doctors exclaim:

> Gracias al Niño, que a todos
> nos sacó de conferencia.

> Thanks be given to the Child,
> Who has explained everything.

The Virgin says to the Child:

> ¿Cómo lo habéis hecho así,
> Hijo, que con diligencia,
> vuestro padre y yo os buscamos,
> llenos de dolor y pena?

> Tell me, how have You done this,
> My Child, when with diligence
> Your father and I have sought You,
> filled with deep sorrow and grief?

The Child Jesus replies:

> ¿Pues, para qué me buscáis?
> ¿No sabéis dónde se encuentran
> los negocios de mi Padre?
> Me entrego a mi diligencia.

> Why are you looking for Me?
> Truly, don't you know the place
> where My Father's business is?
> I am merely doing My duty.

### La Aparición de Nuestra Señora de Guadalupe

The popular play *Auto de la aparición de Nuestra Señora de Guadalupe* (The apparition of Our Lady of Guadalupe) is a dramatic composition of Mexican Spanish source. It is written for the most part in the traditional Spanish octosyllabic verse, with many irregular lines. I have three manuscript copies; two of them are complete: one from Chimayó, probably an eighteenth-century manuscript, and the other from Santa Fe, a later, perhaps an early-nineteenth-century, copy. There is much dialectic and "fractured" Spanish in both copies, especially in the part of the Indian Juan Diego. The eighteenth-century copy may be either New Mexican or Mexican; the more recent copy is a New Mexican manuscript.[5]

The play is based on the apparition of the Blessed Virgin to the Mexican Indian Juan Diego which occurred, according to tradition, on the three days of December 9–12 of the year 1531 on the hill of Tepeyac near Mexico

City. It follows the historical and legendary accounts of the apparition very closely. The following is a brief outline of the Chimayó version:

Juan Diego is on his way to Santiago Tluteluco to look for a priest who will hear the confession of his uncle, Juan Bernardino, who is very ill. The first lines are:

| | |
|---|---|
| Parece que se lo pagan | It seems that he does it |
| a este mi tío Juan, tan enfermo, | purposely, this very sick uncle of mine, |
| que antes que lo salga el sol | for before sunrise he wishes |
| quiere un *totachi* trayendo. | me to get a priest for him. |

As he reaches the hill of Tepeyac, the Blessed Virgin appears to him. Juan Diego asks her what she is doing in the mountain so early in the morning. The Virgin replies that she is looking for him to give him an important message. Juan Diego explains the purpose of his own trip and asks the Virgin to state her message quickly. The Virgin tells him that she is the mother of God and begs him to go to the archiepiscopal palace and tell the archbishop that she desires a temple in her honor at Tepeyac, where she wishes to be with the Indians, her children. Juan Diego hesitates, saying that no one will believe him and that he will be whipped and called a witch. Urged by the Virgin, however, he goes to the palace. The priest who receives him at the door hears his story, calls him a liar and a witch, and sends him away. But when the archbishop hears what has happened, he asks that Juan Diego be found and brought to him.

In the meantime Juan Diego decides to continue on his way in search of a priest for his uncle. The Blessed Virgin appears to him a second time. Juan Diego explains what has happened to him:

| | |
|---|---|
| Lo mismo que lo pensé. | Just exactly as I thought. |
| Me lo dijeron *chicero*, | They said it to me a witch, |
| y no me dejaron ver | and they did not allow me |
| al *sulustrísimo* señor | to see His Excellency, |
| porque no me lo creyeron. | for they did not believe me. |
| Mira, Señora, es mejor | Look, it is better, dear Lady, |
| que lo hagas tu mensajero | that you make your messenger |
| un gachupín, que no yo. | a Spaniard, rather than me. |
| O anda tú, porque con eso | Or you go, because that way |
| verán lo bonito que eres, | they'll see how pretty you are, |
| y así te lo van creyendo. | and then they will believe you. |

The Blessed Virgin convinces Juan Diego that he alone must go again to the archiepiscopal palace to deliver her message. He does so, and this time he is received courteously. The archbishop asks him to request some miraculous sign from the Blessed Virgin. He returns to the hill of Tepeyac, and for the third time the Virgin appears to him. When he asks for a miraculous sign, the Virgin asks him to gather flowers from the top of the mountain. Instead of the usual ice and stones, Juan Diego finds there beautiful roses.

The Virgin asks him to take the roses to the archbishop in his *tilma* (blanket). He does so, and when the archbishop and all those present kneel down to acknowledge the miracle of the roses, they behold the image of the Blessed Virgin beautifully stamped on the *tilma* just as Juan Diego has described her.

## Las Posadas

*Las posadas* (The inns) is a brief dramatic composition. As already stated, some forms of this episode are actually a part of *Los pastores*. It is often found, however, in separate manuscripts, and it is frequently performed independently or as a curtain raiser before *Los pastores* begins. The independent forms are hardly more than a few brief scenes representing Saint Joseph and the Virgin Mary as they wander through the streets of Bethlehem seeking shelter on the eve of the birth of the Savior. They are rejected at various houses or *posadas* (inns) and finally find refuge in a stable, where the ox and the mule with their breath warm the Infant Jesus. The manuscripts of this dramatic incident are numerous; some are popular, and others are apparently of recent literary source. The older forms are traditional; the more recent ones perhaps have a direct literary source.

One of the best and longest versions, which is from Santa Fe, is called *Las nueve posadas de la Virgen* (The nine *posadas* of the Virgin) and contains some 240 octosyllabic verses. The characters are Saint Joseph, the Virgin Mary, and those who reply from within (*Adentro*, or *Los de adentro*) when refusing shelter to the wanderers. The first lines of this version begin thus:

| San José: | Saint Joseph: |
|---|---|
| "Ya, gracias a Dios, estamos | "Thanks be to God that at last |
| en la ciudad de Belén. | we've arrived at Bethlehem. |
| Si os parece, amado bien, | If it pleases you, my love, |
| por sus calles discurramos, | let's walk up and down its streets, |
| por ver si allá encontramos | to see whether we can find |
| algún pariente o amigo | some relative or some friend |
| que nos proporcione abrigo | who will deign to give us shelter |
| en tan crítica ocasión." | at this most critical time." |

This version was apparently given separately before the beginning of *Los pastores*, because at the end, in the most beautiful verses of the composition, the Virgin Mary thanks the shepherds for their visit to the Infant Jesus. The first six lines of the concluding series are as follows:

| | |
|---|---|
| Yo os agradezco, pastores, | I am grateful to you, shepherds, |
| el obsequio que a mi Hijo | for the honor done My Son; |
| habéis hecho; conoced | you must know that you have been |
| que entre todos habéis sido | among all mortals the first |
| los primeros que humando | to have seen Him here on earth— |
| en este mundo lo han visto. | in inspiring human form. |

## Los Desposorios de San José y María Santísima

*Los desposorios de San José y María Santísima* (The marriage of Saint Joseph and the Blessed Virgin) is not properly a play, but rather a dramatic narrative, recited to the audience, sometimes before the performance of *Las posadas*, all in the third person and in a long series of octosyllabic quatrains. The best and longest of several known manuscript versions has seventy-seven such quatrains or *coplas*. The subject matter is the gospel narrative of the marriage of Saint Joseph and the Virgin Mary, the Annunciation, the sorrow of Saint Joseph, the visit of the Archangel Gabriel to Saint Joseph in a dream, and other related themes. The first and last quatrains are given below:

| | |
|---|---|
| A unos desposorios santos | To a very holy marriage |
| convida la iglesia, amigos. | the church invites us, my friends. |
| Los desposorios son santos; | Very holy is this marriage; |
| vamos a ver tal prodigio. | we are going to see this wonder. |
| | |
| Pidamos a esta Señora | Let us ask this Blessed Lady |
| y a su esposo, que benignos, | and Saint Joseph to help us |
| nos alcancen muerte en gracia, | to die in a state of grace |
| para ir a alabar a su Hijo. | to join in praising her Son. |

It is evident that the popularity of traditional Spanish religious folk plays in New Mexico has been extraordinary. It should also be noted that the New Mexican descendants of the Spanish *conquistadores* have always performed these religious plays with great reverence and respect. They have been produced not only to amuse the people, but also—and above all—as real professions of faith, to instruct. At least two of those discussed above, *La primera persecución de Jesús* and *El niño perdido*, are undoubtedly derived from copies of seventeenth-century Spanish originals. They compare favorably with any compositions of the Golden Age of Spanish literature, with the exception, of course, of those by dramatists of the rank of Lope de Vega or Calderón, who produced masterpieces of their type.[6]

# Spanish Secular Folk Drama in New Mexico

*Juegos de moros y cristianos. Los comanches. Los Tejanos,* A Nineteenth-Century
Play. Spanish and Indian Elements. The Dance of *Los matachines.* The
*Corridas de gallos.*

Secular plays dating back to Spain's Golden Age in all likelihood were
performed in Santa Fe and other New Mexican communities as late as the
nineteenth century. The fact that manuscript copies of religious plays
probably first printed in the seventeenth century, such as *La primera persecu-*
*ción de Jesús* and *El niño perdido,* are still to be found in New Mexico, and that
these plays were given in some communities up to the end of the nineteenth
century and even in the early years of the present century tends to
strengthen this belief. But we have no record of them. We do know,
however, that the traditional dramatic representations of jousts or battles
between Moors and Christians, called *autos entradas* or *juegos de moros y*
*cristianos,* were well known in New Mexico, just as they were in all parts of
Spain and Spanish America during the past three centuries. Villagrá, in
Canto XVI of his *Historia de la Nueva México,* tells us that when Oñate took
possession of New Mexico at San Juan de los Caballeros in 1598, a comedy
especially composed for the occasion and also the dramatic *juegos de moros y*
*cristianos* were performed by the Spanish soldiers. According to trustworthy
testimony, these *juegos* were performed every year during the last half of the
nineteenth century in the town of Santa Cruz, New Mexico.

## *Juegos de Moros y Cristianos*

In Spain the *juegos de moros y cristianos* have been popular for several centuries. Professor Ángel González Palencia, of the University of Madrid, has
written that he often witnessed these representations when a boy in the
village of Tovar, Cuenca, in the early years of this century. He describes
them as follows: There were, of course, two opposing groups, Moors and
Christians, and dressed as such. The Moors appeared first on the scene to
attack a defenseless Christian village. The leader of the Moors would give a
long harangue expressing his hatred for the Christians and his intention to
destroy Christianity. In the attack against the village the Moors would often

carry away a statue of the Blessed Virgin that the Christians were carrying in a procession. As they were withdrawing with the statue, the Christian army appeared, a battle or battles would take place, and the Christians, often helped by boys dressed as angels, would be victorious. The statue of the Virgin was then returned to its church amid the rejoicing and shouts of the people.

We have two manuscript copies of this dramatic composition, obtained from Cuenca, Spain, where one of them was produced in 1934. One of the two versions, which are very similar, is briefly described below. It is a manuscript entitled *Entrada de moros y cristianos* and is dated June 3, 1889. It consists of 788 octosyllabic verses, or 273 more than the New Mexican *Los comanches*, which will be described later. The characters that take part in the play are four Christian warriors; four Moorish warriors; Coscolín, a Christian follower; the Moor Tragasantos (Swallower or Devourer of Saints); and two angels.

The *Entrada* begins with a festival procession in a Christian village, the people carrying a statue of the Blessed Virgin with great pomp and ceremony. The leader of the Christian warriors sings the praises of the Virgin and exhorts his followers to protect the statue against the enemies of Christianity:

| | |
|---|---|
| ¡Bien venida, hermosa imagen! | Welcome, most beautiful statue! |
| ¡Luz brillante, bien venida! | Welcome, most resplendent light! |
| Salid pronto y alegrad | Come forth quickly and bring joy |
| con tu vista peregrina | with your very wondrous presence |
| las casas, calles y plazas | to the houses, streets and plazas |
| de aquesta devota villa, | of this your devoted village, |
| que sin igual te venera | that now to you renders homage, |
| y a tus pies se halla rendida. | and humbly asks your assistance. |
| . . . . . . . . . . . . . . . . . . . . | . . . . . . . . . . . . . . . . . . . . |
| Y yo, como fiel cristiano | And I, as a faithful Christian |
| y caudillo de esta tropa, | and the captain of this troop, |
| verteré toda mi sangre | shall willingly shed my blood |
| si con arrogancia loca, | if with arrogance those heathens, |
| presumiendo de valientes, | boasting of their bravery, |
| a tu imagen bella tocan. | your lovely statue dare touch. |

The encounters with the Moors follow. There are two principal battles. In each case the Moors are about to win the victory and take possession of the statue of the Virgin when an angel appears and admonishes the Moors to abjure Mohammedanism and to become Christians. The long speeches of the Christian leader and of the angels, with constant references to the

Blessed Virgin and her Divine Son, the images of whom are before them, remind one of the speeches of General Diego de Vargas to the Indians during the reconquest of New Mexico in the 1690s.[1] Finally the Christians are victorious, the procession is resumed, and the statue of the Blessed Virgin is taken back to its chapel amid the rejoicing of the people. The last speech is by one of the angels, who announces not only the victory of the Christians but also the conversion of the Moors to Christianity; it closes with verses that relate briefly the fundamental Christian dogmas on the creation of man, the birth and Passion of Christ, and the redemption.[2]

New Mexico has contributed to the drama of the modern Hispanic world at least two original, native, secular dramatic productions, both of a historical character. Spain is the only European nation that has had a national drama, that is, a drama based on its national legends and history. Lope de Vega and Guillén de Castro in the seventeenth century, José Zorrilla in the nineteenth century, and Eduardo Marquina and José Pemán in our day developed in Spain a national drama based on the national legends and history of Spain. Although thousands of miles away from Spain, New Mexico has made its contribution to this Spanish national drama by continuing to exalt the deeds of Hispanic heroes. The two plays that continue this tradition are the historical plays *Los comanches* (The Comanches), and *Los tejanos* (The Texans).

### Los Comanches

*Los comanches* was composed in New Mexico when the territory was still a part of the old Spanish Empire in America. During the eighteenth century the Comanche Indians were the most ferocious enemies of the Spanish colonists in New Mexico. After several punitive expeditions had been sent against them by the Spanish governors of New Mexico between the years 1747 and 1762, their power was weakened, but they still continued their violent attacks and depredations on the Spanish colonists.[3] As one contemporary described them: "Their only idols are freedom and war; and in their frequent trade with the Spaniards, unwisely permitted, they have come to lose whatever respect was instilled in them by the first conquerors, whom they looked upon as an immortal people. They are not intimidated by firearms, because they use and handle them with greater skill than the Spaniards who taught them; and the great success which they achieve through their insults, raids and depredations has made them unconquerable."[4]

In 1774, a formidable expedition led by the brave old Indian fighter Captain Don Carlos Fernández set out to destroy the Comanches. Under their great Comanche leader Cuerno Verde (Green Horn), they were met at the Staked Plains, east of the present Antón Chico, New Mexico, where a bloody battle took place, the outcome of which was acclaimed by the Spaniards as a great victory. But Cuerno Verde himself and some of his bravest warriors escaped, and the Comanches continued their attacks. In 1777 they made one of their most merciless attacks on the Spanish settlements. In a raid on the town of Tomé, south of Albuquerque, over a score of the inhabitants were taken by surprise and massacred. When Juan Bautista de Anza assumed the governorship of New Mexico in 1778, one of his first tasks was to bring Cuerno Verde to terms and put an end to the Comanche peril. In 1779, Anza, after careful planning, led a well-organized expedition in pursuit of the enemy, and Cuerno Verde and his warriors were decisively defeated. Cuerno Verde was left dead on the field with hundreds of his companions in arms. Captain Carlos Fernández, who had attained fame for his part in the important 1774 expedition against the Comanches, also participated in the decisive 1779 victory.[5]

The play Los comanches appears to be based largely on the 1774 expedition, but since it ends with the death of Cuerno Verde, which occurred in 1779, the author obviously borrowed from Anza's 1779 expedition as well. Therefore, the first manuscript of the play was written sometime after 1779. Be this as it may, the composition has a truly historical basis, confirmed by official documents of the period. The play has always been popular in New Mexico, and many New Mexicans of the past generation could repeat a great number of its lines from memory. For many years, up until quite recently, the play was enacted with local talent in many New Mexican villages on festive occasions. The following description of the play is based on a manuscript copy that belonged to Don Amado Chaves of Santa Fe, now deceased, which I copied and published in 1907. The manuscript is a copy made in the middle of the nineteenth century and is probably not a first copy of the original. This version of the play is composed of 515 octosyllabic verses.[6]

The characters of the play are the following: Don Carlos Fernández, the Spanish general and leader of the New Mexican forces; Don Toribio Ortiz, a Spanish general; Don José de la Peña and Don Salvador Rivera, two Spanish captains; an unnamed Spanish lieutenant; Barriga Dulce (Sweet Belly), a Spanish camp follower; Cuerno Verde (Green Horn), the chief of the Comanches; and Oso Pardo (Gray Bear), Cabeza Negra (Black Head), Lobo Blanco (White Wolf), and Zapato Cuento (Beaded Moccasin), Comanche chieftains.

The play opens with the arrival of Cuerno Verde, the chief of the

Comanches, who in eighty-two assonanced verses recites his heroic deeds
and boasts that he will turn into ashes the Spanish fortress that he sees
before him:

| | |
|---|---|
| Desde el oriente al poniente, | From the sunrise to the sunset, |
| desde el sur al norte frío | from the South to the cold North |
| suena el brillante clarín | shines the glitter of my arms |
| y brilla el acero mío. | and my trumpet blares go forth. |
| Entre todas las naciones | And boldly among all nations, |
| campeo, osado, atrevido, | fearless, I excel in battle, |
| que es tanta la valentía | for such is the matchless valor |
| que reina en el pecho mío. | that prevails within my breast. |

When Cuerno Verde has drawn very near to the Spanish fortress and
camp, he challenges the Spanish general, Don Carlos Fernández, to battle.
Don Carlos accepts the challenge:

| | |
|---|---|
| ¡Aguarda, infiel, impío, | Bide your time, oh bloody heathen! |
| que vengo sin que me llames! | I come forth without your call. |
| No es menester carteles, | Your vile challenge is not needed; |
| que tus valentías he oído. | I have heard your boasts and all. |

Cuerno Verde replies with more boasts and insults. Don Carlos tells him
that all nations tremble at the mention of the word "Spaniard" and that he
will crush his insolent pride:

| | |
|---|---|
| porque mentando españoles | when the name Spaniard is heard |
| todas las naciones tiemblan. | all nations tremble with fear. |
| Tú no has topado un rigor, | You have never met such valor, |
| ni sabes lo que es fiereza | nor do you know the great fierceness |
| de las católicas armas. | Catholic arms display in battle. |
| Por eso tanto braveas. | That is why you boast so much. |

The two leaders then separate to assemble their forces for the battle.

Don Carlos calls his men to arms. He consults with his captains, and all
of them offer their enthusiastic support and loyalty. Cuerno Verde addresses
his chieftains, heaping insults on the Spaniards, whom he despises. The
Comanche chieftains Oso Pardo, Lobo Blanco, and the others appear and
express their eagerness to start the battle. Don Toribio Ortiz, the leader of
the Spanish militia, appears and challenges the Comanches.

Don Carlos orders the attack in traditional Spanish fashion:

| | |
|---|---|
| Y así, esforzados leones, | And so, my courageous lions, |
| todos al arma, guerreros. | to arms, to arms, all my warriors. |
| ¡Suénese tambor y guerra | Let the trumpets of war sound |
| en el nombre de Santiago | in the name of good Saint James |
| y de la Virgen María! | and in the name of the Virgin! |

When Cuerno Verde hears the sound of the Spanish trumpets, he leads his men into battle. The Spaniards are victorious, and the Comanche rout is described, in sixty-seven octosyllabic assonanced verses, by Barriga Dulce, a Spanish camp follower. Cuerno Verde has been killed. With the speech of Barriga Dulce the play ends.

This New Mexican dramatic composition is in reality a local development or continuation of the traditional *juegos de moros y cristianos*, or jousts between Moors and Christians. Representing the battle between the New Mexican Spaniards and the Comanches, it was performed of course in an open field like the *juegos*. The spectators watched and applauded from the sidelines and followed the warriors as they moved about or charged at full speed on their horses. As a spectacle it was extraordinary. Those who took the parts of the Spaniards were attired after the manner of the *conquistadores*, and were mounted on beautiful and richly caparisoned horses, while those who took the Comanche parts were attired as such, with buckskin pants, gorgeous beads and feathers, and faces daubed with paint.

## Los Tejanos

We know of only one manuscript of the New Mexican historical play *Los tejanos* (The Texans)—one that I obtained in 1931 from Doña Bonifacia Ortega of Chimayó, New Mexico, a small town some twenty-five miles northeast of Santa Fe. Written in assonanced octosyllabic verse, as in the case of *Los comanches*, it contains 497 lines, eighteen fewer than *Los comanches*. The script shows evidence of considerable handling, sufficient to warrant the conclusion that the play was presented more than once. The manuscript text, as may be judged from the script, belongs to the years 1850–80. The language of the play contains numerous New Mexicanisms, and the orthography and punctuation are very defective. The Spanish spoken by the Indian from Pecos, who takes an important part in the play, is of paramount interest and importance: some of the Pueblo Indians of New Mexico use the same type of Spanish even today. In view of the numerous dialectic forms that indicate popular New Mexican Spanish pronunciation, and the metrical errors, showing omission of words, and lines that are too long, the present manuscript is clearly not the original. It is probably a second or third copy of the original and apparently was taken down from dictation. Just when the original play was composed it is not easy to say, although one may guess that it was written soon after the Texan expeditionary force which provides the theme of the play was captured in 1841, and certainly before 1846, when Armijo was no longer popular. The exact title of the play, which for convenience I have called *Los tejanos*, or *The Texans*, is not known, since the title page is missing. Although the name Menclaude, or McLeod, appears after the last lines at the bottom of the last page, indicating the possibility that the manuscript is incomplete, the actual ending in the manuscript is a logical ending of the play.[7]

The play deals with the capture of General Hugh McLeod, the leader of the Texan–Santa Fe Expedition of 1841, and his forces by the soldiers of General Armijo of New Mexico. In general, the play follows the historical accounts very closely.[8] A brief outline of the play follows:

After a group of soldiers of General McLeod's vanguard is captured by the New Mexicans and three of them have been executed in Santa Fe, an Indian from Pecos is captured by the Texans. The Indian had been sent ahead by the New Mexicans to be captured by the Texans and then to betray the New Mexican Don Jorge Ramírez to the Texans as part of a ruse to capture General McLeod. The Indian and Don Jorge succeed in leading McLeod into an ambush, and he is captured by the soldiers of General Armijo. How the rest of the army surrenders we are not told in the play. Perhaps that part was narrated in the missing folio, if the manuscript is not complete.

The play opens in the Texan camp. General McLeod is asking his trusted Texan lieutenant, Navarro, to question the newly captured Pecos Indian about recent events in Santa Fe:

| | |
|---|---|
| —Acabo de tener parte | "The report has just reached me |
| se ha agarrado un natural | that an Indian has been captured |
| de Pecos, pueblo muy grande, | from the great pueblo of Pecos, |
| que nos soltó el general | who has been released to us |
| de los nuevomejicanos. | by the New Mexican general." |
| | |
| —Como mi segundo harás | "As my second in command, |
| que este indio se me presente | have this Indian brought to me |
| y me diga la verdad | so that he may state to me |
| de todo lo sucedido. | the truth of all that has happened." |

Navarro talks with the Indian and questions him. The Indian asks for food and clothes, and after receiving them, he tells his story. The various speeches of the Indian, purposely written in grotesque Spanish, furnish some of the most interesting and amusing lines of the play. A few lines from his first long speech follow:

| | |
|---|---|
| —¡Agora sí, muh contento! | "Now indeed I'm very happy! |
| ¿No ves ya yo engalaná? | See how well dressed I am now? |
| Quizás agora fiscal, | My pueblo will now elect me |
| quizás gobernadorcillo, | maybe public prosecutor |
| quizás capitán de guerra | or the governor perhaps, |
| mi pueblo me eligirá. | or maybe even war-captain." |

. . . . . . . . . . . . . . . . . .　　. . . . . . . . . . . . . . . . . .

| | |
|---|---|
| —Quince días yo pasá | "Two weeks ago I was passing |
| por esa la capital, | through that capital of theirs, |
| y allá staba uno taliano | and I heard that an Italian |
| que isque dijo la verdá | was there who told everything |
| a su Excelencia, el gobierno. | to his Excellency, the government. |
| Cuando muncho platicá | After talking a good deal |
| dijo que tú y tu gente | said he that you and your people |
| ya viene para robá. | were on your way here to steal." |

The Indian states that General Armijo has captured the Texan vanguard and that he had had three of the prisoners shot—those who had been caught stealing corn. He says that Armijo is powerful and has fine soldiers. Navarro is alarmed, but McLeod wishes to continue on his way to Santa Fe. He orders that the Indian be shot, but after the latter promises to lead the Texans to where a New Mexican spy, Ramírez, is concealed, McLeod revokes his order. The Indian fulfills his promise, and the Texans capture Ramírez. McLeod tells him that unless his story is similar to that of the Indian he will be shot. Ramírez confesses that he is a spy, but that being an Andalusian, he will betray Armijo. McLeod believes the words of Ramírez, who intends to deliver the Texans to General Armijo, and says:

| | |
|---|---|
| —El caso es que usted proponga | "Now all that remains is that |
| el modo que se ha de dar | you explain to me the plan |
| de entregarme a Don Manuel | whereby to me is delivered |
| Armijo, su general. | General Manuel Armijo." |

Ramírez then leads McLeod, Navarro, and the others to where Armijo's army lies in ambush, and the Texans are captured. When the Texans appear, a New Mexican officer exclaims:

| | |
|---|---|
| —Ah, tejanos atrevidos! | "Oh, insolent, greedy Texans! |
| ¿Se atreven a profanar | How dare you profane the land |
| las tierras del mejicano? | of the proud Mexican people? |
| Ahora su temeridad | Now your rash foolhardiness |
| le pondrá freno a su orgullo, | will put a stop to your pride. |
| ¡y a todos he de acabar! | This will be the end of you!" |

When McLeod becomes aware of the ambush, he exclaims:

| | |
|---|---|
| —¡Traición, Don Jorge me has hecho! | "You have betrayed me, Don Jorge! |
| Ahora vengo a calcular | Now I start to realize |
| como el indito de Pecos | that the little Pecos Indian |
| me decía la verdad. | was indeed telling the truth." |

The question of the historical authenticity of the details of this folk play, composed perhaps a year or two after the events narrated, is yet to be solved. Although the events are for the most part well known, there are some discrepancies between the play and the accounts of the Texans who took part in the expedition. Only two of the Texan leaders mentioned in the play can be clearly identified: McLeod, who appears as Menclaude, and Navarro. Another, named Guillermo, who has charge of the artillery in the play, may be Captain William P. Lewis, McLeod's captain of artillery. The others mentioned—Bonifás, Bill, Guillermo, and Seliman—are not easily identified. There were at least two Williams among the leaders, William G. Cooke and William P. Lewis, but both of them had been captured before the capture of McLeod and could not have been present in the incidents in question. Lewis, in fact, was the traitor of the expedition. The Guillermo and Bill included, therefore, must be other Williams or else errors.[9]

As for the New Mexican leaders and *dramatis personae*, several can be identified. The New Mexican leader Armijo is, of course, the well-known general, Manuel Armijo. The *oficial de la guardia* who captures Menclaude at the end of the play is unnamed. He is probably Lieutenant-Colonel Juan Andrés Archuleta, to whom McLeod finally surrendered at Laguna Colorado on October 5.[10] Although mentioned many times, Armijo does not appear in the play. The Indian mentions Chuleta (Archuleta) as the one who captured the band of one hundred Texans—the party led by Cooke—at Tonchico (Antón Chico). He has either confused Archuleta with Salazar, the New Mexican leader who was with Armijo at the surrender of the group of Texans, or with a Captain Pantaleón Archuleta, one of Armijo's most trusted lieutenants, to whom two persons who had deserted from the Texan forces revealed the movements of the Texans, according to Zamacois;[11] or, possibly, the reference to Archuleta might have been part of the Pecos Indian's game of confusing the Texan leaders. One of the Texan deserters was an Italian, and this was the Italian mentioned by the Indian in the play: "y allá staba uno taliano."[12] The Indian also states that Chuleta (Archuleta) not only captured but tied up the party of one hundred Texans at Tonchico (Antón Chico). Since this episode involved Salazar and not Archuleta in, actual fact, the play version, then, may be attributed to one of two causes: either there was uncertainty concerning the facts on the part of the author of the play, or the mention of Juan Andrés Archuleta by the Pecos Indian was intended to throw fear into the Texans and thus eventually induce McLeod to surrender without bloodshed. Don Antonio Sandoval, mentioned in the play by McLeod as one of the wealthy citizens of New Mexico, was one of Armijo's trusted officials; as regards the references to members of the Chávez family, also referred to by McLeod as wealthy New Mexicans, Kendall makes special mention of Francisco Chávez as "a wealthy haciendero [*sic*]"; Mariano Chávez and Manuel Chávez are mentioned among Armijo's military leaders; and José Antonio Chávez was engaged in the Santa Fe trade.[13]

In contrast with the contemporary Texan accounts, the New Mexican play gives evidence of the greatest respect and loyalty to Armijo on the part of the New Mexicans, but the play may represent only the opinion of Armijo's supporters. The behavior of Armijo during the American occupation under Kearny leads us to believe that the play was composed and first represented in New Mexico before the occupation—perhaps at some time during the years 1841–45. The general tone of the play does not substantiate Binkley's statement that "there is no conclusive evidence to the effect that the people expressed in any way their opposition to the Texans."[14] In fact, many of the statements in the play are definite evidence to the contrary. Furthermore, a growing antipathy toward Texans in general on the part of many New Mexicans dates from that time, and this traditional viewpoint has not yet entirely disappeared among some of the older Spanish-speaking residents.

As we have seen, the important discrepancy between the contemporary Texan accounts and the New Mexican play has to do with the details surrounding McLeod's surrender; otherwise, the events presented in the play are in general substantiated by contemporary accounts, both Texan and Mexican. With regard to the final capture of McLeod, however, the traditionally accepted accounts state that he surrendered to the soldiers of General Armijo without resistance, whereas, according to the play, McLeod was captured by means of a ruse carried out by Armijo's lieutenants. The dearth of information concerning the details of the surrender of McLeod is difficult to explain; hence the play version cannot be dismissed without definite evidence to the contrary. Were the play version true, the silence of the Texans could be easily understood; they speak of Armijo as an unpopular leader and of his army as worthless, and yet they gave in to him without resistance. Indeed, the manner in which Cooke's party was induced to surrender at Antón Chico would tend to place the play version of McLeod's capture well within the realm of possibility.[15]

A play is literature rather than history, and a popular play, even when it is supposed to be historical, draws frequently from folklore, from hearsay, or from the imagination of the author. Undoubtedly there are some elements of such origin in the play under discussion. It may be that the Pecos Indian is a purely fictitious character, although he appears as a dramatic character worthy of a master playwright. His character is so well defined, and the story he tells is on the whole so true, however, that we cannot dismiss him from the historical scene without further inquiries. It is he who reports the capture of the three Texans who were shot at Santa Fe—obviously Baker and Howland, as mentioned in Kendall, and Rosenbury, who was killed when recaptured at San Miguel and not at Santa Fe. The Indian states correctly that the three captured men had escaped, were recaptured, and then were killed. [16]

Since the play should be interpreted primarily as a dramatic effort, it seems fair to state that the author was attempting to present, in a patriotic folk play, a composite picture of the New Mexican victory over the Texans—depicted as foreign invaders—with no strict adherence to chronology, and combining in a single dramatic scene the most interesting and representative details of the piecemeal surrender of the Texans.

As we have seen, two known New Mexican Spanish folk plays of a historical character exist, *Los comanches* and *Los tejanos*; there may be others that await discovery.

### Los Matachines

In a discussion of the New Mexican folk drama, a few words should be said about the important folk dance of dramatic character called *Los matachines*. Although much has been written about this dance, American Indianists long failed to record the fact that a somewhat similar dance, with exactly the same name, was very popular in Spain in the seventeenth century. The Spanish dance of the *matachines* of the seventeenth century, however, is a mock-battle dance, similar to the old *Danza de la espada*, or sword dance, and in some respects similar to the traditional and well-known *juegos de moros y cristianos*.

In *Folklore y costumbres de España* the following description of the Spanish dance of the *matachines* is given:

> The dance of the *matachines* has always been a sort of mock-battle, with musical accompaniment. In the 17th century it was performed by men dressed in a ridiculous manner, with multicolored masks and garments closely fitted from head to foot. They usually formed a group, and with the accompaniment of pleasing music they made burlesque gestures and would strike one another

with wooden swords or bladders filled with air. It was generally danced during the Carnival season.

In 1637 the King's guards performed the *matachines* on horseback with different liveries and ridiculously attired. "Six men, representing lackeys, rode along one after the other dancing the *matachines*; two old men played military drums, and they wore beards that reached to their waists, two inflated wine gourds being used for the purpose. They reached the place where the King was seated, rode by in pairs and veered their horses very well; afterwards the groups came together, three groups of them being *matachines*; and this they did before His Majesty wonderfully well." [17]

From the above descriptions it is clear that there were variations in the manner of executing the Spanish *matachines*. In general it was a mock battle, but the accompanying features seem to have been numerous and varied. In this respect also it is similar to the Spanish-Indian *matachines*, in which, as a matter of fact, two distinct elements are executed simultaneously: the *matachines* dance proper, and the mock fight between the *abuelo*, or grandfather, and the bull.

Although these mock-battle dances are well known in Europe, and the Spanish *matachines* dance is apparently but one of them, it is not certain that one can establish a direct relationship between the Spanish *matachines* and the Spanish-Indian *matachines*. The *matachines* of New Mexico, as executed by the Pueblo Indians of the Rio Grande Valley and some New Mexican Spanish communities, seems to be a variant of the Spanish dance, with Indian elements incorporated into it. Surely the name of the dance is Spanish; the leading figure, the *monarca*, a king, which the Indians pronounce as a rule *monanca*, and *La Malinche*, a derivative of *María*, pronounced *Malía* by the Indians, are Spanish; and, what is equally important, the mock battle between the bull and the *abuelo* may be an imitation of a Spanish bullfight.

Whatever may be the Indian element involved, the essential purpose of the dance is the celebration of the birth of Christ on the twenty-fifth of December. The Franciscan missionaries probably introduced and developed the *matachines* dance in the New Mexican pueblos, largely with traditional Spanish elements. They introduced Indian features for obvious reasons, but the fact remains that the dance of the *matachines* is but one part of the festivities that commemorate the birth of Christ. Montezuma and Spanish conquest legends are brought in quite naturally. The church festivities and processions, both before and after the dance in the Rio Grande pueblos, are a mixture of Spanish and Indian elements—including the processions of the saints, the *abuelos*, the *luminarias*, and so on.

At San Juan and other pueblos, the *matachines* dance—but without the bull and *abuelo* fight—was performed inside the church up to recent years. The *abuelo*, or *abuelos* when there were two of them, would enter the church, but never with the bull. The bull and *abuelo* fight began when the dance was performed outside the church. At Isleta, a dance performed before the image of the Child Jesus is similar to the *matachines*, but it is an Indian dance and is not called the *matachines*, although the number of dancers is the same: there are six men and six women instead of the ten men and *monarca* and Malinche of the *matachines*. The dancers sing praises to the Virgin Mary and the Child Jesus. The *matachines* of San Juan and the other pueblos was obviously a dance executed primarily for the same religious purpose.

The music of the *matachines* is not Indian. Musical critics agree that it is definitely European and quite unlike any of the Pueblo Indian patterns. Spanish authorities who have heard the music of the *matachines* qualify it as Spanish martial music. The rhythmic movements and steps are even compared to those of the Austrian *danza prima*. What then are the Indian elements of the *matachines*? The details of the accompanying jests and the fight between the *abuelo* and the bull have certainly been added by the Indians, although the bullfight itself is of Spanish origin. This element, with the details of the slaughter of the bull and the scattering of the parts among the women, was added by the Indians perhaps to ridicule the religious character of the dance. The costumes worn—including masks, rods, crowns, mitres, and so on—are of course a mixture of Spanish and Indian elements. The ultimate Spanish origin of the dance can also be seen in the fact that in the pueblos of San Juan and San Ildefonso, and perhaps in other pueblos, the performers are not all Indians. The role of *La Malinche*, for example, is often played by a New Mexican Spanish girl, and the musicians, violinist and *guitarrista*, are always New Mexicans.

## Corridas de Gallos

The *Corridas de gallos* (Games, or running, of the roosters) are dramatic games of violence. Instead of bullfights, which do not seem to have ever been popular in New Mexico, the usual sport for men throughout the nineteenth century was the game of *el gallo* or *gallos*, generally called *corridas de gallos*, games or running of the roosters. The game was played as a rule on the festival of Santiago, the twenty-fifth of July, but it was also played on other festivals, such as St. John's Day. Today the game is still played, even by the Indians,[18] but it is no longer popular.

The New Mexican form of the game is brutal and dangerous. A rooster is buried alive in the ground with only its head showing. Men and boys on horseback, in turn, ride by the rooster at full speed and attempt to seize the rooster by the head. The one who succeeds in pulling the rooster out of the ground in this manner rushes off with his prey, and the other players start out in pursuit in order to try to take the cock away from him. Being hit violently in the face with the rooster and tearing the rooster to pieces are some of the milder occurrences of these brutal games. The one who seizes the rooster, either from the ground or from another horseman, immediately becomes the object of attack by the others, and the coveted possession of the cock is rarely enjoyed for more than a few minutes. Falls from horses, with serious consequences, are quite common.

The *corridas de gallos* are undoubtedly of Spanish origin. In many villages of Castile there is a cock festival, *la fiesta del gallo*, celebrated usually on Candlemas, February 2, immediately after Mass. In most of these villages the young men and women have *reinados*, or assemblies of their representatives, to take care of such festivities—that is, the secular parts of the religious festivals that are of interest to the young people. There are *reinados* of young men and *reinados* of young women. The ceremony of the *fiesta del gallo* conducted by these *reinados* after Mass on Candlemas has been described as follows:

The young women of the *reinado*, dressed in white, leave the church in a body, headed by their *reina* or queen, and go to the plaza, where the *alcalde* of the village awaits their coming. They bring with them a live rooster. The queen salutes the *alcalde* and asks permission to kill the rooster in the middle of the plaza. After the permission is granted, the ceremony begins. The young men of the *reinado* now appear in a body, and after receiving the rooster from the young women, they hang it by the legs with a long cord from a beam or especially constructed scaffold. They also tie cords to the rooster from different directions to be able to move the rooster in any direction at will. The *reina* or queen then attacks the rooster with a sword, trying to cut off its head. As she swings the sword, the young men move the rooster out of her reach by pulling on the cords. In the end the *reina* succeeds in killing the rooster, usually after several bloody strokes, and the ceremony ends with a supper attended by the young men and women and a *baile* in the plaza. Inasmuch as the rooster sacrificed at the fiesta is not sufficient for the supper, the *reina* who has killed it marches through the village, followed by the two *reinados*, with the head of the dead rooster at the point of her sword, to demand food for the rooster; in this way they collect food for the supper. Various parts of the ceremony are accompanied by verses that accuse the rooster of treachery and deceit and explain the necessary sacrifice.

Instead of hanging the rooster from a beam, in some villages the rooster is buried in the ground in the same way as in the New Mexican game. The person who attacks the rooster with a sword is again the queen of the *reinado* at first, but the attacker is blindfolded and has only a certain fixed time for the blows. If she fails to kill the rooster, others try their skill, until the rooster is killed. The ceremony takes place in the presence of the civil and ecclesiastical authorities, and ends as in the case of the first ceremony described above. This last ceremony is the one that most closely resembles the New Mexican *corridas de gallos*, which appear to be a further development of the Castilian *fiesta del gallo*.

The *fiesta del gallo* of Castile may be a survival in modern form of certain ceremonies of the Roman Lupercalia. If the New Mexican *corridas de gallos* are directly related to the Castilian ceremonies of the *fiesta del gallo*, especially to those in which the rooster is buried in the ground, the New Mexican game would be not only a Castilian traditional sport or ceremony, but also a survival, in part at least, of an old Roman tradition.[19]

APPENDICES

# Two Essays

by

Aurelio M. Espinosa

# The Spanish Language of Northern New Mexico and Southern Colorado

During the first centuries of the reconquest of Spain by the Christian Spaniards, the important languages or dialects of the peninsula derived from Vulgar Latin were Leonese, Castilian, Portuguese-Galician, Navarro-Aragonese, the Catalonian dialects, and Mozarabic, a dialect spoken in central and southern Spain in the regions occupied by the Saracen invaders. During the tenth century Leonese was the most important of the languages of the peninsula, principally for political reasons. The armies of the kings of León were slowly advancing into the territories occupied by the invaders. At that time Castile was but a small territory ruled by its famous counts and subject to the kings of León.

In the next century, however, Castile began her great role in history. Fernando I, the first of the rulers of Castile to be called a king, inherited the kingdom of León in the year 1037. This union of Castile and León was the beginning of the ascendancy of Castile. After the death of Fernando I, the Castilians found in Alfonso VI and in the Cid Ruy Díaz the first leaders of a united Spain in the struggle against the Saracens. The Cid is not only the greatest of Spanish heroes; he is also the great protagonist of Castilian hegemony. By the end of the eleventh century the powerful Moorish kingdom of Toledo had fallen into the hands of Alfonso VI and his Castilian and Leonese warriors, and the Cid with his exiled Castilian knights had captured Valencia. During the twelfth and thirteenth centuries the victories of the Castilians continued, and Zaragoza, Córdoba, and Sevilla were captured. All the territories occupied by the Saracens, with the exception of Granada, were added to those of the powerful and triumphant kings of Castile. Castilian, the language of the reconquerors, soon became the dominant language of all Spain. Towards the end of the thirteenth century, Alfonso the Learned (1252–84) proclaimed Castilian as the official language of all his kingdom.

By the time of the discovery of America and the capture of Granada in 1492, Castilian had come of age. In that same year the great humanist Nebrija published his Spanish *Grammar*, the first grammar of a modern language to be published anywhere in Europe. At that time great Spanish

231

poets such as the Marqués de Santillana, Juan de Mena, and Jorge Manrique; historians such as Pérez de Guzmán, Hernando del Pulgar, and Enríquez del Castillo; the dramatist Juan del Encina; and novelists such as Diego de San Pedro and the author of *La Celestina* employed Castilian for their literary masterpieces.

After the first half-century of Spanish discoveries and conquests on the American continent, the real work of colony building and the transmission of culture were begun in earnest. That work took place in the last half of the sixteenth century and throughout the seventeenth century, the Golden Age of Spanish culture, when the Castilian language reached its full development and became the vehicle of a great body of literature that has been a source of admiration and inspiration for all ages. Some of the world's greatest spirits lived in Spain at that time and employed Castilian in some of the finest literary productions of human genius: the lyric poets Fray Luis de León, San Juan de la Cruz, and Góngora; the dramatists Lope de Vega, Tirso de Molina, and Calderón de la Barca; the great mystic and lover of souls Santa Teresa de Jesús; the humanist Juan de Valdés; the historian Juan de Mariana; the philosopher Baltasar Gracián; and lastly, the greatest of them all, the immortal author of *Don Quijote*, Miguel de Cervantes.

The Castilian language of the Golden Age, enriched and embellished with elements taken from the other languages and dialects of Spain, even from some of the Indian languages of the New World, and by now called Spanish instead of Castilian, was the language of the Spaniards who came to America in the sixteenth and seventeenth centuries. Not all the *conquistadores*, missionaries, and colonists spoke and wrote Castilian as did the literary masters, but many did. The language of the letters of Cortés; of some of the missionaries; of the historians of the Indies, such as Gonzalo Fernández de Oviedo and Bartolomé de las Casas; and of a host of other *conquistadores*, missionaries, and historians of the Indies is the same as the language used by Cervantes and Lope de Vega. The majority of the soldiers and colonizers, and some of the *conquistadores* and missionaries also, spoke popular Spanish, it is true, but the differences between popular and learned or literary speech were not very pronounced. Spanish is a very conservative language, and those differences are not pronounced even today. In the great writers of the sixteenth century—such as Santa Teresa, Fray Luis de León, and Cervantes—in the picaresque novel, and in the genial dramatic productions of Lope de Vega in the seventeenth century we find not only the conciseness, dignity, and realism of popular speech, but also much of the vocabulary, idiomatic expressions, and subtle niceties of popular speech itself. Santa Teresa used in her writings the ordinary speech of the people of her native Ávila.

All languages are always in a continuous process of evolution. But in Spanish America linguistic change has been very slow. From New Mexico to Chile and Argentina the uniformity of development is extraordinary. If we examine the Spanish American dialectic dictionaries and works on dialectology, we discover that the so-called dialectic peculiarities of each region are as a matter of fact common, almost in their entirety, to all parts of the Spanish-speaking world, including Spain. These facts speak eloquently for the uniformity of the Castilian language of the sixteenth and seventeenth centuries when it came to Spanish America, and for the uniformity of Spanish linguistic development. The problem of the uniformity of phonetic developments throughout Spanish America cannot be definitely solved yet because we do not have sufficient materials at our disposal. However, there is ample evidence to show the extraordinary uniformity of Spanish phonetic developments in Spain and Spanish America.[1] And what is more, the majority of the phonetic developments in question are found in the popular and even in the learned literature of the Golden Age.

Since certain features of American Spanish are also found in southern Spain, some scholars have concluded that American Spanish has been strongly influenced by Andalusian speech habits. Other scholars, however, have cast doubts on such a conclusion. Today it is felt that many of the traits of American Spanish and their counterparts in Andalusian Spanish probably developed independently on both sides of the Atlantic.

After traveling extensively in the various regions of Spain, including Old and New Castile and Andalucía, my own observations do not lead me to believe that American Spanish, except perhaps in the Antilles and La Plata, is more Andalusian than Castilian.

With the exception of the confusion of Castilian *s* and *z*, the outstanding characteristics of Andalusian Spanish, such as the frequent fall of final consonants, *so* for *sol*, *ve* for *vez*, *papé* for *papel*, *andá* for *andar*, etc.; the frequent change of *l* to *r* before a consonant, *argo* for *algo*, *arguno* for *alguno*, *arto* for *alto*, *gorvé* for *volver*, *er deo* for *el dedo*, etc.; the frequency of the opposite change in *sel* for *ser*, *venil* for *venir*, *selmón* for *sermón*, *dolmil* for *dormir*, etc.; the special forms *miste* or *misté* for *mire usted*, *vi a* for *voy a*, the tendency of medial *d* to fall in all positions, not only *comprao* for *comprado* and *toa* for *toda*, which occur everywhere, but also *abrigaíco* for *abrigadito*, *salío* for *salido*, *toíco* and even *tuico* for *todico*, *deo* for *dedo*, *mieo* for *miedo*, *menúo* for *menudo*, etc., are practically unknown in the Spanish of America outside of the Antilles and some regions of La Plata.

The language of Castile which we now call Spanish is spoken today in Spain, in a score of American republics, in some parts of the Balkan peninsula and northern Africa by Spanish Jews, in the Philippines, in New

Mexico and other regions of our Southwest, and in other parts of the United States, such as the New York area, Florida, and Puerto Rico. In spite of dialectic peculiarities, it is still the dignified, sonorous language of Santa Teresa, Cervantes, and Lope de Vega, easily understood everywhere in the Spanish-speaking world. The most ignorant tillers of the soil from Castile, Cuba, New Mexico, and Chile easily understand one another. Among the educated, the linguistic differences are, of course, less significant than among the illiterate. The fundamental differences are in pronunciation. All Hispanists agree that in American Spanish, from New Mexico and California to Chile and Argentina, and in the Spanish of Spain, grammar, syntax and idioms, and most of the vocabulary are essentially identical. If Cervantes were to return to the Spanish world and speak with natives from Castile, Andalucía, or New Mexico, he would observe practically the same words, idioms, grammar, and syntax today that he himself used in the sixteenth century, but his pronunciation would be different from that of all of the above regions.

In this connection it is not without significance to point out that although the greatest literary historian and critic that the Spanish world has produced in modern times was a Castilian, Marcelino Menéndez y Pelayo; the greatest poet of the modern Spanish world, Rubén Darío, was a Nicaraguan; the best Spanish grammar we possess is by a Chilean and a Venezuelan, Andrés Bello and Rufino José Cuervo; and the last great example of a picaresque novel is by a Mexican, *El periquillo sarniento* by Fernández de Lizardi.

The Spanish colonizers who entered New Mexico with Oñate in 1598, and the Spanish and Mexican Spanish colonizers who entered in the seventeenth and eighteenth centuries, lived a more independent and isolated existence than any other group of colonists of the old Spanish Empire in America. The language they spoke was the current popular Spanish, with certain modifications common to all regions of Spanish America at that time. Many dialectic peculiarities have developed in the area which are archaic and somewhat impoverished, it is true, but the language is still very much like the spoken Spanish of other regions of Spanish America and Spain.

The phonology and morphology of American Spanish as it is spoken today in New Mexico, southern Colorado, and some parts of Texas and Arizona, as well as the English elements in its vocabulary, constitute an interesting study, but a detailed discussion of this topic is not needed here. I shall call attention in this study only to some of the outstanding characteristics.

First of all, there are general and fundamental differences in pronunciation between American Spanish, including of course New Mexican, and Castilian Spanish. These have to do with the pronunciation of three orthographic symbols. The consonant *z*, or *c* when before *e* or *i*, is pronounced in Old and New Castile as a voiceless interdental continuant, similar to English *th* in *thin*. In American Spanish generally, including New Mexico, the pronunciation of *z*, or *c* when before *e* or *i*, is the same as that of American Spanish *s*, a voiceless dental continuant, similar to English *s* in *stop*. In Spain outside of the Castiles the dental *s* pronunciation, as in American Spanish, prevails. The pronunciation of *z* and *c* as English *th* before *e* or *i* is considered pedantic by Spanish Americans. Andalusians confuse the interdental and dental sounds, *usté* and *uzté*, *así* and *azí*, and so on. Next in importance is the pronunciation of *ll*. The pronunciation of this letter as a voiced palatal lateral, considered by Spaniards and by phoneticians generally as the Standard Spanish or Castilian sound, occurs only in Old Castile. In New Castile, including Madrid, and other Spanish regions, *ll* is usually pronounced as a *y* sound. This *y* sound is also general in Spanish America. But in Andalucía, Argentina, and sporadically also in Mexico, New Mexico, and other regions, the *ll* in the medial position may develop either to a sound similar to English *j* in *joy* or to a sound similar to French *j* in *jour*. And lastly there is the problem of the pronunciation of the *s*. In the Castilian of Old and New Castile generally, and sporadically also in other parts of Spain, *s* is ordinarily pronounced as a voiceless alveolar continuant. The tip of the tongue touches the alveoles of the upper front teeth, but not the teeth. In American Spanish, *s* is ordinarily pronounced as a dental continuant, as in English and French, and very often it is weakened to a mere English *h* sound.[2]

Any discussion of the outstanding characteristics of New Mexican Spanish may very properly begin with the problem of the development of *ll*. In northern New Mexico and southern Colorado *ll*, while often pronounced as a *y*, tends to disappear entirely in the groups *alli*, *elli*, *olli*, *illu*, *ulli*, *illa*, *ille*, *illo*, *ella*, *ello*, whether before or after the accent. The rule seems to be as follows: medial *ll* in New Mexican Spanish is pronounced as a *y*, or may fall completely in the groups *ello*, *ella*, or when before or after *i*. Examples: *gallina* > *gayina*, *gaína*; *ella* > *eya*, *ea*; *estrella* > *estreya*, *estrea*; *apellido* > *apeyido*, *apeído*; *sellos* > *seyos*, *seos*; *semillas* > *semiyas*, *semías*; *trillar* > *triyar*, *triar*; *silleta* > *siyeta*, *sieta*; *chillido* > *chiyido*, *chiído*; *cuchillo* > *cuchiyo*, *cuchío*; *pollito* > *poyito*, *poíto*.[3] This fall of *y* from medial *ll*, although not so common as in New Mexico, occurs also in northern Mexico, Nicaragua, some regions of Ecuador and Guatemala, and in Jewish Spanish.

Medial *d* presents in New Mexican Spanish a special problem. In careless and rapid pronunciation, it tends to fall generally, but it may as frequently maintain itself as a voiced interdental continuant similar to English *th* in *other*. The loss of medial *d* in almost all positions and also in the group *dr*, so common in Spanish America and almost universal in Andalucía (*nada* > *naa*, *na*; *miedo* > *mieo*; *pedazo* > *peazo*; *vida* > *vía*), occurs in New Mexico, but only sporadically. The Andalusian development in which *d* falls in the groups *adi*, *udo*, *ido*, *ida*, and some others (*agarradito* > *agarraíto*; *menudo* > *menúo*; *marido* > *marío*; *subida* > *subía*, and so on) is unknown in New Mexican Spanish.

In the end *ado*, however, New Mexican Spanish not only drops the *d* generally, but *ao* has sometimes become *au*, as in Spanish *causa*. Examples: *comprado* > *comprao*, *comprau*; *estados* > *estaos*, *estaus*; *lado* > *lao*, *lau*.[4] This extreme development to *au* occurs also in the rustic speech of Castile and other parts of Spain.

In the vocalization of the consonants *b*, *c*, and *p* in the groups *abs*, *acc*, *act*, *ecc*, *ect*, *apt*, *epc*, *ept*, New Mexican Spanish offers a few special developments. The group *abs* becomes *aus*, sometimes merely *as* with silent *b*: *absoluto* > *ausoluto*, *asoluto*; *absolución* > *ausolución*. The groups *acc*, *act* become *ais*, *aus*, and *ait*, *aut*, respectively: *acción* > *aisión*, *ausión*; *facción* > *faisión*, *fausión*; *carácter* > *caráiter*, *caráuter*; *intacto* > *intaito*, *intauto*, also *intuato* by metathesis. The groups *ecc*, *ect*, *ept* develop to *es*, *eis*, *eus*, and *et*, *eit*, *eut*, respectively: *lección* > *lesión*, *leisión*; *corrección* > *corresión*, *correisión*, *correusión*; *sección* > *sesión*, *seisión*, *seusión*; *correcto* > *correto*, *correito*, *correuto*; *respecto* > *respeto*, *respeito*, *respeuto*; *excepto* > *eseto*, *eseito*, *eseuto*. The group *apt* usually becomes *aut*, often *at*: *adaptar* > *adatar*, *adautar*. The group *epc* before *ci* becomes *es*, *eis*, *eus*, and in Santa Fe and vicinity it also becomes *aus*, perhaps by analogy to the groups that begin with *a* instead of *e*: *excepción* > *esesión*, *eseisión*, *eseusión*, *esausión*; *concepción* > *concesión*, *conseisión*, *conseusión*, *consausión*. Most of these developments occur in dialectic Spanish everywhere. The development of *epc* to *aus*, however, is exclusively New Mexican.[5]

In the groups *ae*, *ee*, with the accent on the first vowel of the group, and also when after *ch*, *ll*, or *y* in final syllables, the vowel *e* becomes *i* in New Mexican Spanish: *cae* > *cai*; *traen* > *train*; *creen* > *crein*; *lee* > *lei*; *leche* > *lechi*; *coche* > *cochi*; *calle* > *cayi*, *cai*; *oye* > *oyi*, *oi*. Sometimes this change takes place also after *ñ* and the *sh* sound: *sueñe* > *sueñi*; *punshe* (tobacco) > *punshi*.[6]

In the case of juxtaposed vowels some special developments have taken place also. Hiatus is rare in New Mexican Spanish. Like vowels usually contract into one: *creer* > *crer*; *todo* > *too, to*. In the groups *ea, eo, eu*, and *oa, oe, oi*, when in normal Spanish these groups are disyllabic, whether within a word or between words, the initial *e* become consonantal *i*, English *y*, and the initial *o* becomes consonantal *u*, English *w*. These changes occur in other Spanish regions, but not commonly. In New Mexican Spanish the developments are general. Examples within a word, syneresis: real > rial; *desear* > *desiar*; *peor* > *pior*; *reunir* > *riunir*; *toalla* > *tuaya*; *poeta* > *pueta*; *mohino* > *muino*; *oír* > *uir*. Examples between words, synalepha: *me han* > *mian*; *me oyó* > *mioyó*; *de un lado* > *diun lau*; *no hay* > *nuay*; *lo ha dicho* > *lua dicho*; *todo es así* > *todués así*; *quiero irme* > *quiéruirme*.[7]

In a few special cases, however, hiatus is destroyed by the introduction of a *y* or even a *g* sound: *cree* > *creyi*; *creo* > *creyo*; *vea* > *veya*; *idea* > *ideya*; *caer* > *cayer*; *yo o tú* > *yo go tú*; *yo o él* > *yo u él, yo güel*.[8]

Numerous phonetic phenomena in the Spanish language of northern New Mexico and southern Colorado are found in the popular Spanish of many parts of Spain and Spanish America. Some of these are the following: *aguja* > *abuja*; *abuelo* > *agüelo*; *hueso* > *güeso*; *buenó* > *güeno*; *ciruela* > *cirgüela*; *volar* > *golar*; *volver* > *golver*; *advertir* > *alvertir*; *adversión* > *alversión*; *alquilar* > *arquilar*; *nadie* > *nadien*; *jaula* > *jabla*; *querrá* > *quedrá*; *Antonio* > *Antoño*; *ahorcar* > *orcar*; *Europa* > *Uropa*; *reír* > *rir*; *veía* > *vía*; *diez y ocho* > *diciocho*; *seguro* > *siguro*; *señor* > *siñor*; *aunque* > *anque, onque*; *mentira* > *mintira*; *principal* > *prencipal*; *para* > *pa*; *mucho* > *muncho*; *instrumento* > *estrumento*; *instituto* > *estituto*; *había* > *habiá*; *fuerte* > *juerte*; *fuimos* > *juimos*. The numerous cases of New Mexican Spanish *j* for Castilian silent *h*, such as *jiede, jayar, jondo, juir*, and so on, for *hiede, hallar, hondo, huir*, and so on, are cases where Old Spanish aspirated *h*, English *h* sound, is still retained and confused with *j*, as in many other Spanish dialects, whereas in Castilian the aspiration was finally lost.[9]

A few very rare and special features of New Mexican Spanish, such as the development of nasal vowels and of syllabic consonants need not be discussed here.

In morphology some of the special characteristics of the Spanish language of New Mexico are the following: the analogical shift of accent to the first syllable and change of *m* to *n* in the first person plural of the present subjunctive tense: *hablemos* > *háblenos*, *tengamos* > *ténganos*, *vayamos* > *váyanos*, *digamos* > *díganos*; the ending *-tes* instead of *-ste* in the second person singular of the preterit indicative tense: *hablates* for *hablaste*, *dijites* for *dijiste*, *comites* for *comiste*; the use of the forms *losotros, los*, both rare, for the forms *nostros, nos*; the special verb forms *meramente, meramenten, mente, menten, ente, enten*, with the meanings *parece, parecen*, created from the adverb *meramente*, exactly, exactly like, for reasons of verbal analogy and semantics; and the almost universal use of the form *¿quese?*, Old Spanish *¿qué es de?*, meaning *¿dónde está?*, *¿dónde están?*.[10]

There are of course numerous archaisms in the Spanish of New Mexico—words and expressions preserved from the sixteenth and seventeenth centuries that are no longer used in modern Castilian or that have changed their form somewhat. In the following brief list the modern Spanish forms are included within parentheses: *agora* (*ahora*), *anque* (*aunque*), *ansí, ansina* (*así*), *arredo vaya* (*arredro vaya*), *arismética* (*aritmética*), *cuasi* (*casi*), *demoño* (*demonio*), *dende* (*desde*), *dijieron* (*dijeron*), *emprestar* (*prestar*), *escrebir* (*escribir*), *escuro* (*obscuro*), *Ingalatierra* (*Inglaterra*), *lamber* (*lamer*), *mahucar* (*machacar*), *mesmo* (*mismo* and *mesmo* both used in Spanish until the end of the sixteenth century, now only *mismo* in literary speech), *mijor* (*mejor*), *muncho* (*mucho*), *quese* (discussed above), *tresquilar* (*trasquilar*), *trujo* (*trajo*), *vide, vido* (*vi, vio*), *vía* (*veía*).

Another syntactical feature of New Mexican Spanish, which is also found in some parts of Spain and Spanish America, is the use of *ustedes* and the third person plural of verbs in place of *vosotros, vosotras*, and the second person plural of the verb, as in Standard Spanish: *ustedes vienen* instead of *vosotros, -as, venís*, you (*plural*) come. In poetic compositions printed in the newspapers, in printed and traditional prayers, hymns, religious ballads, and other poetic compositions, the second person plural is still used, but not generally. In some of the manuscript materials it is often confused with the third person plural.[11]

The English elements are also very important in the Spanish of New Mexico. To this frontier land of the old Spanish Empire in America, English has come as the language of a permanent invader, the language of a materially superior culture. Since the middle of the nineteenth century the Spanish language in New Mexico has been under the constant and inevitable influence of the English language through the media of the schools, commerce, industry, political life, radio, and television. The meeting of the two language groups, English and Spanish, in the Spanish Southwest has influenced the language and vocabulary of each. There are hundreds of English words regularly Hispanicized and currently used in New Mexican Spanish.[12]

Speech mixture is not rare, and a Spanish-speaking New Mexican on one occasion may say *Echó um buen espichi*, "He made a good speech," with a regularly Hispanicized form *espichi*, and on another occasion he may be conscious of the English word and say *Echó um buen speech*, pronouncing the word in question in normal English. Real speech mixture of this last sort is practiced of course only by those who speak English as well as their native Spanish.

Many New Mexican Spanish words of English source are of wide usage, especially those that have to do with phenomena of common use in commerce, industry, and political life. Among these are the following: *belís* from valise, *bogue* from buggy, *breca* from brake, *craque* from cracker, *cute* (overcoat) from coat, *dipo* from depot, *escrepa* from scraper, *espichi* from speech, *esteble* from stable, *esteque* from steak, *estraique* from strike, *fon* from fun, *greve* from gravy, *güincheste* from winchester, *juisque* from whiskey, *jolón* (insult, reprimand) from hold on, *lonchi* from lunch, *otemil* from oatmeal, *panqueque* from pancake, *porchi* from porch, *pulman* from pullman, *queque* from cake, *sinque* from sink (kitchen drain), *suichi* from switch, *trampe* from tramp, *troca* from truck (wagon), *broquis* from broke, *cranque* from cranky, *jaitún* from high-toned (proud, well-dressed).[13]

The regularly Hispanicized verbs derived from English are conjugated throughout all the moods and tenses. All belong to the first conjugation and add the infinitive termination *-iar*, or *-ar* when the consonantal *i* is absorbed by a preceding *ch* or *sh* sound. The conjugation of all these verbs is based, however, on the Spanish conjugation in *-ear*, reduced in New Mexican Spanish to *-iar*. Among the most common New Mexican Spanish verbs derived from English are the following: *baquiar* from back + *iar*, *cambasiar* from canvas + *iar*, *chachar* from charge + *(i)ar*, *chequiar* from check + *iar*, *chitiar* from cheat + *iar*, *lonchar* from lunch + *(i)ar*, *roseliar* from rustle (to be an eager laborer and money-earner) + *iar*, *trampiar* from tramp + *iar* (to behave like a tramp, to steal). As examples of conjugation, the present and preterite indicative of *chitiar*, to cheat, are as follows: *chiteo*, I cheat, *chiteas*, you cheat, *chitea*, he cheats, *chitiamos*, we cheat, *chitean*, you or they cheat. *Chitié*, I cheated, *chitiates*, you cheated, *chitió*, he cheated, *chitiamos*, we cheated, *chitiaron*, you or they cheated.[14]

The English language, at the same time, has adopted hundreds of Spanish words, and often the manners, customs, or institutions that these words represent, as in the case of acequia, arroyo, bronco, burro, calaboose from *calabozo*, cañon, caporal, corral, fandango, lariat, mesa, paisano, patio, peon, pinto, pronto, rancho, rodeo, tortilla, and vamos or vamoose. These are but a few of the Spanish words that have become a part of the spoken and written vocabulary of the western United States.[15]

# Spanish Tradition Among the Pueblo Indians

The influence of Spanish culture on the Pueblo Indians of New Mexico is a fascinating subject on which much further study remains to be done.[1] The following pages call attention to a few of the most important manifestations of this influence.

Let us consider first the linguistic influence: Spanish culture has been carried to many parts of the world through the medium of its language. Until very recently, practically all the Pueblo Indians of the upper Rio Grande Valley spoke Spanish. The older Indians, in fact, still speak Spanish very well. In the more distant pueblos of the Keres family—Acoma, Laguna, and nearby Paguate—little Spanish is spoken today, but there is evidence that Spanish was spoken in them until the end of the nineteenth century. Most of the pueblos employ Spanish as a *lingua franca* or inter-pueblo language.[2] I have seen letters written by an Isleta Indian to a Taos Indian in Spanish; since the Indians of these pueblos speak different dialects of the Tiwa language, they communicated with each other in Spanish. When the former president of Stanford University Dr. Ray Lyman Wilbur was awarded an honorary degree by the University of New Mexico in 1928, the Pueblo Indians made him an honorary member of their clans, and in doing so the Indian governor of Taos addressed him in Spanish. Many similar cases of use of Spanish by the Pueblo Indians could be cited.[3]

Hundreds of Spanish words are commonly employed by the Pueblo Indians in the everyday use of their native languages. Some are used with little or no change—perhaps with consciousness of their Spanish source. But many more have been completely assimilated into the native languages, often with so many phonetic changes that they can hardly be recognized as Spanish in origin. In collecting folktales and other folklore materials, especially among those who speak Spanish, I have recorded hundreds of words that are obviously of Spanish source.

The following lists of Tiwa, Tewa, and Keres words of Spanish origin, in some cases already assimilated into the native linguistic forms, are indicative of the types of Spanish words that first entered into Pueblo culture. In general, they are also indicative of the type of acculturation that the Indians of the pueblos have received during their contacts of several centuries with their Spanish neighbors. I transcribe the words in the Spanish alphabet, but use three symbols with English phonetic values: $\hat{g}$ for English g in gem, sh for English sh in cash, and w for English w in we. The examples are from the pueblos of Isleta, San Juan, and Laguna, respectively.

| SPANISH | TIWA | TEWA | KERES |
|---|---|---|---|
| | (Isleta) | (San Juan) | (Laguna) |
| aceite | aceite | aceite | aceit |
| altar | artar | altar | ———— |
| caballo | cani de | cabayo | cabayo |
| potrillo | ———— | cabayo a | cabayo washti |
| carne de cochino | cuchi túa | ———— | cuĝino ischañe |
| carne de vaca | vaca túa | wacu peve | waca ischañe |
| comadre | comaire | comadre | comale |
| compadre | compairi | compadre | compale |
| durazno | durásumu | ———— | lulás |
| iglesia | misa tu | misa te | misa ĝía |
| jabón | jabún | jabón | ———— |
| listón | na listón | detón | listoni |
| misa | misa | misa | misa |
| oro | oro, uro | oro | ulo |
| paño | na payu | pano | ———— |
| pimienta | pimienta | pimienta | ———— |
| santo | santun | santo | santo |
| tápalo | tápalo | tápalo | tápalo |
| toro | turu de | toro | toro, doro |
| rosario | rusayu | ———— | rosario |
| vaca | vaca de | wasi e | waca |
| madrina | in madrina waí | madrina | ———— |
| padrino | in padrinu waí | padrino | ———— |

As the examples cited above show, native prefixes and suffixes have been added to many Spanish words. The words *madrina* and *padrino* in the Tiwa language of Isleta are *in madrina waí* and *in padrinu waí*, respectively. In the Keres language, *washti* or *washtri* means the young of an animal. For Spanish *potrillo*, colt, therefore, the words "young horse" are used: *cabayo washti* in Laguna, *cabayo washtri* in Cochití. In the Tiwa of Taos, the term for colt is *cau (caballo) una*, and in San Juan *cabayo a*. In Tiwa only the syllable *ca* of *caballo* remains, the terms being in Isleta *cani de*, and in Taos *cagueno*. In Tiwa the word for meat or flesh of an animal is *túa* or *túane*; in Keres, it is *ischañe* or *isañe*. These words are combined with the Spanish words for the various animals involved to form the words for pork and beef, respectively: *carne de cochino*, Isleta *cuchi túa*, Taos *cuchi túane*, Laguna *cuĝino ishañe*, Cochití *pisochi isañe*; *carne de vaca*, Isleta *vaca túa*, Taos *casi* (from *wacasi*) *túane*, Laguna *waca ischañe*, Cochití *vacais isañe*. In Tewa meat is *peve*; hence, beef is *waca peve*. The number of Spanish words concealed in such formations must be very numerous.

In a few cases Spanish terms had no exact equivalents in the Pueblo Indian culture. Examples of these are the months of the year, the days of the week, names of poltical officers imposed on the pueblos, ecclesiastical terms, and of course, baptismal names. The months of the year and the days of the week are usually indicated by their Spanish names among the Tiwas and Tewas, although the forms are often so much changed phonetically that they are hardly recognizable. The Taos Indians who speak Spanish use the regular Spanish forms for the days of the week when speaking Spanish with their Spanish-speaking neighbors; but when they speak their native Tiwa language among themselves and refer to the days of the week, they employ Indianized forms of Spanish words. I give below the two lists, furnished to me by the same informant.

| *When speaking Spanish* | *When Speaking Tiwa* |
| --- | --- |
| domingo | tumígug |
| lunes | lúnesi |
| martes | máltesi |
| miércoles | miálculesi, miélculesi |
| jueves | juávasiqui, juévesiqui |
| viernes | viálnasiqui, viélnesiqui |
| sábado | sábalu |

The ecclesiastical terms of Spanish origin employed by the Pueblo Indians are numerous. In the sixteenth century and later in the seventeenth century, many Spanish words from the Christian prayers and hymns translated into their native languages by the Franciscan missionaries must have been learned by the Indians. Today the Indians who are nominally Catholics pray in Spanish or English. A few old Spanish prayers and ejaculations, such as making the sign of the cross, still survive, in Indian-Spanish and in apparently Spanish forms, but in some cases my informants did not know the exact meaning of the words. In San Juan, for example, an octogenarian Indian who spoke Spanish well recited the following version in blessing himself, with the usual signs with the right hand:

| | |
|---|---|
| Nansi pawe, | En el nombre del Padre |
| nansi cónguere, | y del Hijo, |
| sanjuen, wiwi. | y del Espíritu Santo |
| En Jesú. | Amén Jesús. |

*Nansi* is apparently all that remains of *En el nombre del*. *Pawe* is clearly the Spanish word *padre*. The final words *En Jesú* are obviously for *Amén Jesús*.[4]

The Spanish formula for making the sign of the cross found by Dr. Elsie Clews Parsons in Zuñi is preserved word by word:

| | |
|---|---|
| Pola senyá | Por la señal |
| ela santu kulusi | de la Santa Cruz |
| le mishta inimicu | de nuestros enemigos |
| liplan, siniola Yos. | líbranos, Señor Dios. |
| Imimi pale, | En el nombre del Padre |
| elelejo, | y del Hijo, |
| el eshpintu santo, | y del Espíritu Santo, |
| Amí Kiasusi. | Amén Jesús.[5] |

A special case of the survival of a Spanish word among the Pueblo Indians is the word *Castilla*. They learned this word in the sixteenth century, with the special meaning of "Castilian" or "Spanish," both as a noun and as an adjective. The Keres of New Mexico and the Hopis of Arizona use the word with that meaning to this day in numerous variant forms. In the epic poem of Gaspar de Villagrá, *Historia de la Nueva México*, printed at Alcalá de Henares in 1610,[6] the Keres from Acoma always address the Spanish *conquistadores* as *Castillas*, obviously because the *conquistadores* always told them they were from *Castilla*, that they had come in the name of the king of *Castilla*, and so on. Two examples follow:

| | |
|---|---|
| Allí Zutapacán me preguntaba | And then Zutapacán asked me |
| si atrás otros Castillas me seguían. | whether other Spaniards followed me. |
| (Canto XIX) | |
| No soy de parescer que a los Castillas | I do not believe that we should show |
| enemistad ninguna se les muestre. | any hostility to the Spaniards. |
| (Canto XXI) | |

I will cite here a few of the many variants I recorded in one Hopi and four Keres pueblos: Oraibi (Hopi), Castila, Cástila; Santo Domingo (Keres), Castila, Castira, Castela, Castera; Cochití (Keres), Castera, Cástera; Acoma (Keres), Caschira, Caschera; Laguna (Keres), Cashtira, Caschira, Cashchira, Cachila.[7]

The Christianization of the Indians was, of course, an important task of the Spaniards. The Franciscan missionaries, to whom the Cochití Indians still refer with great reverence, calling them *totachi cástera*, or Castilian fathers, worked diligently to accomplish that task. In the early 1630s the Franciscan provincial of New Mexico, Fray Alonso de Benavides, documented the success of the missionaries in the following words:

> This land, where formerly there was nothing but *estufas* of idolatry, today is entirely covered with very sumptuous and beautiful churches which the friars have erected. . . . They bring the Indians here . . . and teach them the entire Christian doctrine and good habits. They also teach the children reading, writing, and singing; and one is moved to praise God when he sees so many choirs, with organ accompaniment, established within such a short time. So, too, they instruct them in all trades and useful occupations.[8]
>
> Once the Indians have received holy baptism, they become so domestic that they live with great propriety. . . . Before Mass, they pray together as a group, with all devotion, the entire Christian doctrine in their own tongue. They attend Mass and hear the sermon with great reverence. . . . During Lent they all come with much humility to the processions, which are held on Monday, Wednesday, and Friday. On these days of meeting with the friars, they perform penances in the churches. During Holy Week they flagellate themselves in most solemn processions.[9]

As is well known, the Christianization of the Indians was not accomplished. In the eighteenth and nineteenth centuries, the work of the Catholic missionaries suffered many relapses, and today the number of Pueblo Indians who are Christians is relatively small. Nevertheless, the Spanish Catholic influence on Indian culture is highly significant. Through the Catholic Church the Indians have received much that is often difficult to appraise, but it is obvious that, through its influence, their manners, customs, and way of life are today more in harmony with those of modern Christian peoples than they were in the sixteenth and seventeenth centuries.

Their native religious traditions persist, but in some cases tempered and even modified more or less by Christian traditions. In some pueblos, such as Isleta, Cochití, San Ildefonso, and San Juan, Indian and Spanish-speaking New Mexicans, who have been neighbors for centuries, attend the same churches for their devotions and religious festivals. For all the important religious festivals, the Indians also have their own native dances and ceremonies, which they perform outside the churches. At Isleta, the Indians dance inside the church on Christmas Eve, singing praises to the newborn Child and to the Virgin Mary in their own Tiwa language. This is an old tradition at Isleta. In most of the pueblos of the Rio Grande Valley many of the Indians, who are practicing Catholics in name only, take part in all the religious feasts, attend Sunday Masses, and baptize their children. Catholic marriages are common in some of the pueblos, but in certain pueblos, notably in Jémez and Santo Domingo, Catholic marriages take place once a year, on the feast of the patron saint of the pueblo, and in groups—including all those already married according to Pueblo custom. Death and burial rites usually follow Indian religious custom. A priest is seldom called to administer the sacraments to a dying person. He is merely asked to bless the grave after the burial.[10]

The Pueblo Indians do practice, however, many Catholic devotions and ceremonies. They take part in the fiestas and attend Sunday Masses as already stated. They also offer prayers and novenas to the Virgin Mary, to the Child Jesus, and to the saints, and they have their Catholic processions and *velorios de santos*. These are exactly like those of their Spanish neighbors, and even when attended only by Indians, the prayers and hymns are all in Spanish.

In July, 1932, I attended a Tiwa *velorio de santos* at Chical, near Isleta, accompanied by my son José Manuel. A group of some twenty men, women, and children transported in a procession, singing hymns, the statue of Our Lady of Guadalupe from the Pueblo church at Isleta to Chical, four miles away, stopping three times on the way to rest and engage in conversation. At the home of one Francisco Lucero, of Chical, the statue of the Virgin was placed on a small table covered with a white cloth, with a candle on each side, at one end of a room from which all furniture had been removed except a few chairs at the opposite end. The procession took place in the afternoon. The *velorio* proper began at eight o'clock in the evening. Prayers and hymns alternated, as in the case of all Spanish *velorios*. There were, of course, the usual intermissions—three or four during the evening—for conversation and smoking outside the *velorio* room or in an adjoining room. In the adjoining room most of the men were engaged in conversation almost all of the time. (This happens also in the regular New Mexican Spanish *velorios*.) Aside from the two invited guests, only two men were in the *velorio* room: Juan Rey Lucero, the leader of the prayers and the singing of hymns, and a young boy who accompanied him. All the others, about fifteen in number, were women. Most of them sat on the floor as they prayed and sang. Only the two leaders and a few women knelt for prayer. The most important intermission, at about eleven o'clock, was for the "eats." These consisted of Spanish *buñuelos*, *chile con carne*, and Indian cakes and breads, served buffet style on a long wooden table set up for the occasion, and also coffee and soft drinks. The prayers and hymns were of the type current among New Mexican Spaniards. The two most popular hymns, each sung twice during the *velorio*, were *Jesús es mi amor* and *Virgen Guadalupe, reina de las Indias*, both of which are well known in the Spanish folk literature of New Mexico.

In regard to their beliefs, superstitions, and general folkloristic behavior, the Pueblo Indians have also received much from their Spanish-speaking neighbors. The Spanish influence on their folktales is well known. Boas and Parsons have published nine folktales of Spanish origin from Laguna and Zuñi, and nineteen from Acoma, Laguna, and Zuñi that have important elements of Spanish provenience.[11] A San Juan Indian, José Ramos Archuleta, recited for me in Spanish a complete version of the well-known European Spanish tale of "The Language of Animals." Dr. Parsons and I found similar versions in Taos, San Juan, Isleta, Laguna, and Paguate. The Pueblo Indian versions are very similar to the typical Spanish American versions from New Mexico, Mexico, and other regions. A Taos Indian, Onésimo Romero, recited in Spanish a version of the European tale of "The Riddle of the Shepherd." An Indian from Isleta, Juan Rey Lucero, recited, also in Spanish, a version of the European tale of "The Various Children of Eve."[12] The "Tar Baby" story, a folktale that, originating in India, traveled to Europe and Africa and from Europe and Africa to America, is also well known among the Pueblo Indians. The Pueblo Indian versions have added one apparently native element: the coming to life of the killed and cooked rabbit when a portion is dropped on the ground while it is being eaten.[13]

Many of the beliefs, practices, and folktales that concern witchcraft are deeply tinged in European Spanish tradition. Some of the witch tales with animal transformations which I collected in San Juan, San Ildefonso, and Cochití are Spanish versions in new dress. The following tale from San Juan is a version of a Spanish witch tale that is well known in Spanish America; it very likely has a peninsular Spanish source.

A certain Indian woman from San Juan became ill, bewitched by a Santa Clara woman who was suspected of being a witch. One evening a little black dog entered the room of the sick woman. The relatives became frightened and beat the dog to death. They went out to collect wood in order to burn the dead dog, but when they returned, the dog had disappeared. The next day they heard moans and cries coming from the house of Juana, the witch woman. Entering her house, they found her badly beaten and covered with blood. She asked for mercy, and then died from her wounds.[14]

Spanish influence appears even in the nursery rhymes. The following lullaby from San Juan is apparently an imitation, almost a translation, of a Spanish lullaby which has almost identical versions in Spain and Spanish America:

| | |
|---|---|
| Arrerú, arrerú, oyó jaiwabe. | Lullaby, baby, go to sleep. |
| Wewo juwí, itó tsabio, tsabio sendó. | The bugaboo, the old bugaboo, will take you. |
| Si piribó, oyó cumbe, nabi añu keyé. | Keep still and go to sleep, my dear child. |

I give below two very similar Spanish versions, the first one from Spain, and the second from California:

| | |
|---|---|
| Duérmete, niño chiquito que viene el coco, y se lleva a los niños que duermen poco. | Go to sleep little baby, for the bugaboo is coming, to carry away the children who do not sleep enough. |
| Duérmete, niño duérmete ya, que allí viene el viejo y te comerá. | Go to sleep, baby, go to sleep now, for the old man is coming and he will eat you up.[15] |

The Spanish pagan custom of throwing a tooth at the sun or to the roof of a house and asking the sun or the roof for a new tooth is well known and practiced in the pueblos of Taos and San Juan. In Castile a child who has just lost a tooth takes it in his hand, throws it over the roof of the house, and cries:

| | |
|---|---|
| Tejadito nuevo, toma este diente viejo y dame otro nuevo. | My new little roof, take this old tooth and give me a new one. |

In Spanish New Mexico the child throws the tooth toward the sun and cries:

| | |
|---|---|
| Sol, sol, toma este diente y dame otro mejor. | Sun, sun, take this tooth and give me a better one. |

The Pueblo Indian versions from Taos and San Juan, obviously of Spanish origin, are the following:

| | |
|---|---|
| Kitamena tulena, mamu wíe wiaya shoy chémay. | Father sun, take this tooth and give me a better one. |
| "Tan sendó, tan sendó, weeng weeng sambi dimen. | Old man sun, old man sun, take this tooth and give me a new one.[16] |

An unusual custom of the Spanish-speaking people of New Mexico, once very popular but now forgotten, is that of the *agüelos,* which was also observed in some of the Indian pueblos. The *agüelo* (*abuelo,* or grandfather) represented the "bogeyman" or "bugaboo" (called *el coco* in Spain), who, according to tradition, visited the homes in which there were small children on Christmas Eve, or a day or so earlier, to punish those who had been bad or who had not said their prayers during the year. The children were led to believe that the *agüelo* was a supernatural being; he appeared dressed in black, or in animal skins, with an ugly mask and buffalo horns and carried a whip to frighten the children. The arrival of the *agüelo* in the evening inspired great fear in the smaller children, but was a festive occason for the older ones. The *agüelo* snapped his whip and made the children dance and sing and promise that they would learn their prayers. In the case of the Pueblo Indians, the *agüelo* came at Christmas time to punish "bad and disobedient children." The custom appears to be an old Spanish one, but it is quite possible that its unique development in New Mexico was influenced by a custom already in existence among the Pueblo Indians, for there is no evidence that it existed in other parts of Latin America. The *agüelo* also appears in the dance known as *Los matachines* [described in chapter 14, above], of Spanish transmission performed by some of the Pueblo Indians at Christmastime in the pueblos of San Juan, Santa Clara, Cochití, and others, and also in New Mexican Spanish towns in the vicinity of San Juan Pueblo, where I observed the dance.[17]

One of the most extraordinary survivals of Spanish culture among the Pueblo Indians is that of the traditional Spanish ballads. Together with many prayers and hymns, the Pueblo Indians learned some religious ballads from the Franciscan missionaries and the Spaniards, and even today they recite and sing a few versions. Among the one hundred and some versions of traditional Spanish ballads which I have collected in New Mexico,[18] there are nine versions from the Pueblo Indians of Isleta, Santa Clara, and San Juan. The best is one of several Indian versions of the religious ballad *Por el rastro de la sangre* (The bloody way of the Cross), from San Juan, recited by José Benito Abeyta; it consists of sixteen regular ballad lines, plus eight octosyllabic verses that convert the ballad into a prayer.[19] I reproduce the first four lines of this version below:

Por el rastro de la Cruz—que Jesucristo llevaba,
camina la Virgen Pura—en una fresca mañana.
De tan de mañana era—a la hora que caminaba,
las campanas de Belén—solas se tocan el alba.

Following the way of the Cross, that Jesus carried,
the Virgin, one cool morning, walked sadly on ahead.
So early it was in the morning, when she traveled on her way,
that Bethlehem's bells alone rang out the dawning of the day.

An equally fascinating subject is the Spanish influence on the native religious ceremonies and practices of the Indians, particularly those that involve prayers for rain, vows, petitions, and, also, their masked dances. The Catholic and Spanish influence seems to be stronger in the eastern pueblos, where Spanish influences have been observed even in the Kachina dances.[20] In the western pueblos, such as Acoma and Zuñi, Spanish influences were often assimilated into the native ceremonies and practices, whereas in the eastern pueblos—Taos, San Juan, San Ildefonso, Santa Clara, Cochití, Isleta, and others—the continuous presence of the Catholic missions and more regular religious services at the pueblo churches have maintained Catholic tradition as such and more definitely separated from the pagan ceremonials of the Indians.

An obvious assimilation of the Catholic concept of God is the reference to "God, our Father" instead of "sun, our father" in some of the Indian ceremonies, in Taos and San Juan. In letters written by a Taos Indian to a New Mexican member of his Taos clan, not an Indian, I found the following illuminating phrases. The letters are written in Tiwa, with the use of Spanish and English orthography.

| | |
|---|---|
| Yeane kitomena wayama, ti melemei nowan guvi cona chuyai. | That is what we ask God our Father, that you remain in good health. |
| Kitomena wayama waju qui masu muya wiwa, an puy jumwai. | Hoping that God our Father willing, we will see each other again, dear friend. |

In the above examples the words *kitomena wayama* correspond to the Spanish phrase, "God, our Father." In Tiwa *tomena* means "father" and *wayama* is the word for "God." In the Indian invocations and prayers that I have collected, however, the Tiwas of Taos always use the words *kitomena tulena* for "our father the sun," "God," or "the supreme being." According to their beliefs, the sun, *tulena* or *thulena*, is the supreme being and the creator of all things. They also use purely Christian invocations, such as the following one from Taos:

| | |
|---|---|
| Kitomena wayama enkana Mílhina mamdamá. | May God our Father and the Virgin Mother help us. |

Spanish influence on Pueblo culture is also important in their administrative and political institutions. In part at least, the government and administration of the pueblos are those that were established for them by the *conquistadores* in the seventeenth century, similar to those established by Spain in all parts of the Hispanic world. The Pueblo Indians have two governments: the Spanish system of government imposed upon them, consisting of a *gobernador*, *teniente gobernador*, *alguaciles*, *fiscales*, and so on, that governs in general their economic and civil life, especially in their relations with the foreigner, formerly the Spaniard, now the American, and the somewhat secret religious system of government that seems to be the real power that dominates the life of the Indians in all matters of spiritual importance, such as their secret religious and ceremonial life and their native traditions, beliefs, and practices. The religious leader, or chief, of their primitive form of government, called the *cacique*,[21] is apparently more powerful than the *gobernador*.

The names of the officers of the "secular" or Spanish type of government are still for the most part Spanish, although with many changes. The word *gobernador* is used only when the Indians are speaking Spanish. When they speak their native languages, various Indian words are used instead of the Spanish term: *tapup* in Zuñi, *tabupu* in Laguna, *tabuna* in Taos, *tabude* in Isleta, *toyo* or *tunhun* among the Tewas. Indian words are used often in combination with Spanish words: in Taos, *tinienti wamo* is used for lieutenant governor, or *teniente gobernador*, and *picali dun wamo* for *fiscal mayor*. *Fiscal* is *picali* in Taos, and *picá* in San Juan. *Alguacil* is *awasí* in San Juan, and *cuela* in Taos. In Santa Clara the ex-governor is called *kenerá*, apparently derived from the Spanish word *general*. The Spanish word *principales*, *prencipales*, is a term used by the Pueblo Indians to designate in a general manner the older leaders who have held "secular offices," but sometimes it is used to designate the ceremonial chiefs.[22]

Among the Spanish influences on the Pueblo Indians, it is significant that six of the nineteen inhabited Indian pueblos in New Mexico bear the names of the patron saints designated for them in the early days by the Spanish Franciscan missionaries, names which will probably remain as long as the pueblos exist: Santa Ana, Santa Clara, San Felipe, San Ildefonso, San Juan, and Santo Domingo. The other pueblos bear their traditional Indian names or Spanish place-names. Each of the nineteen pueblos has its Catholic mission church, each church with its patron saint designated in Spanish.

# Notes

## Abbreviations Used in the Notes

AME—Aurelio M. Espinosa
AME Jr.—Aurelio M. Espinosa, Jr.
JME—J. Manuel Espinosa

### Chapter 1. Espinosa's New Mexican Background and Professional Career

1. Family records, files of Gilberto Espinosa, Albuquerque, New Mexico.
2. *Ibid.*
3. *Ibid.*
4. *Ibid.*
5. *Ibid.*
6. The bibliography on studies of the Tierra Amarilla grant is extensive and need not be discussed here.
7. Files of Gilberto Espinosa.
8. Family records, files of JME, Glen Echo, Maryland.
9. Files of Gilberto Espinosa. At least two of Julián Espinosa's brothers, Donaciano and Francisco, also born in El Rito, New Mexico, settled in the El Carnero area with their families. Following the outbreak of the Civil War, on July 4, 1861, Donaciano enlisted in the Union Army at Fort Union, New Mexico. He served as a sergeant in Captain Julián Espinosa's company of New Mexico Volunteers during the years 1861–62. After his discharge from the army, he settled in La Garita, about ten miles east of El Carnero. In the 1880 census of Saguache County, his occupation is given as cattle farming. (Family records of Anita Espinosa, a descendant of Donaciano Espinosa, Parker, Colorado.)
10. AME, "Autobiographical Sketch," manuscript, 1938, in the files of JME. Aurelio was the second oldest of the children. His older brother, Tobías, also graduated from the University of Colorado and obtained his M.D. at the medical school there in 1902. He started practice in Del Norte, then moved to Chama, New Mexico, where he was physician and surgeon for the Denver and Rio Grande Railroad Company. He later moved to Albuquerque. In 1929 he took up residence in Española, where he became well known in the region as a country doctor for a wide area, including some of the neighboring Indian pueblos. He practiced there for nearly half a century, served as mayor of Española, and continued to be active in community affairs. Another brother, Ramón, was a government official in the U.S. Securities and Exchange Commission. Two other brothers, Gilberto and Juan Celso, became lawyers. Gilberto became a prominent attorney and civic leader in Albuquerque. A fifth brother, José Edmundo, was head of the Spanish Department at the University of Detroit. Aurelio's two other brothers entered private business and government

service. One of his sisters, Carmen Gertrudis, taught Spanish at several universities. Another sister, Imelda, married the first Hispanic U.S. Senator from New Mexico, Dennis Chávez. Gilberto, José Edmundo, and Carmen published books and articles on New Mexican history, folklore, and folk art.

11. AME, "Autobiographical Sketch," 1938.

12. *Ibid.*

13. *Ibid.* Margarita Espinosa's grandmother, on her mother's side, was Francisca Sánchez of Santa Fe, the wife of Judge Samuel Ellison, a Kentuckian who served as a captain in the Mexican War and settled in New Mexico in 1848, where he spent the rest of his life. Judge Ellison was a prominent civic leader and government official in Santa Fe. In the course of his career he served on the governor's staff; as territorial librarian; as speaker of the House in the New Mexico legislature; as acting governor of the Territory for a brief period, while the governor was absent from the capital during the Confederate invasion of New Mexico; and as U.S. Commissioner. (See JME, "Memoir of a Kentuckian in New Mexico, 1848–1884," *New Mexico Historical Review*, 13 (1938): 1–12.)

Aurelio and Margarita Espinosa had five children: Margarita, Aurelio M. (Jr.), José Manuel, Josefita, and Francisco Ramón. Four of them became educators. The three sons, among their other pursuits, collected and published important Hispanic folklore materials.

14. AME, "Autobiographical Sketch," 1938.

15. *Ibid.*; *Annual Register, and Announcements, Summer Quarter*, University of Chicago, 1907–1908, 1908–1909, 1909–10.

16. AME, "Autobiographical Sketch," 1938; *Stanford Alumni Review*, 47 (1946), 5–6. Espinosa was visiting professor during summer sessions at the University of Chicago (1914), the University of California, Berkeley (1912, 1915, 1922, 1925), and the University of Southern California (1926) and during the autumn semester at Wellesley College (1928). He delivered a series of lectures on Spanish folklore at the University of Havana in January, 1929, at the invitation of Dr. José María Chacón y Calvo, president of the Institución Hispano-Cubana de Cultura. Later he lectured during summer sessions at the University of British Columbia and the University of Guadalajara (Mexico). For two years after his retirement at Stanford he taught at the San Francisco College for Women, where he had helped plan the curriculum for the Spanish department.

In 1918–19, during World War I, he was on leave from Stanford, engaged in U.S. government service in Washington, D.C.

17. For example, his comments in *The Spanish Language in New Mexico and Southern Colorado*, Historical Society of New Mexico Publication No. 16, (1911), 2, 28, 29; *Circular Letter* to colleagues in California, 1917; "Spanish Folk-Lore in New Mexico," *New Mexico Historical Review*, 1 (1926): 135–38.

18. AME, "Autobiographical Sketch," 1938; T. M. Pearce, "The New Mexico Folklore Society," *New Mexico Folklore Record*, 15 (1980–81): 5.

19. The first decade of this century was the pioneering period of modern research studies on the Spanish Southwest by scholars in the United States in many fields. Anthropologists contributed significant specialized studies on the Indian civilization of the region. The precursor was Adolph F. Bandelier (whose publications relating to the Pueblo Indians began in 1879), followed by Frank H. Cushing, John W. Powell, Frederick Webb Hodge, Edgar L. Hewitt, and others. The first to focus broad, comparative attention on the folklore of the native Indian cultures of the region were Franz Boas and Elsie Clews Parsons. As Aurelio M. Espinosa's studies on New Mexican Spanish folklore appeared, Boas and Parsons became especially interested in his findings relating to Spanish influences on the folklore of the Pueblo Indians, and they gained new insights from his research. In historical studies, the pioneer professionally trained scholar was Herbert E. Bolton, whose publications on the Spanish borderlands began in the first decade of the century. He cataloged and studied

extensive unexplored archival materials in Mexico and Spain, opening the way for modern research on the history of the Spanish Southwest.

20. A complete bibliography of his publications on this subject is included below.

21. The only earlier publications touching on aspects of this subject are a forty-two-page article by E. C. Hills, "New Mexican Spanish," in *Publications of the Modern Language Association of America* (Boston, 1906), and a six-page discussion of American Spanish pronunciation, including a listing of borrowed Spanish words used by English-speaking residents of the Spanish Southwest, published by Frank W. Blackmar in 1891 in an article in *Modern Language Notes* and republished in his book *Spanish Institutions of the Southwest*, 271—77.

22. In 1930, Espinosa stated that he was completing a separate study, *Diccionario de nuevomejicanismos*, which he had begun prior to World War I. During the war the *Revue de Dialectologie Romane*, in which his "Studies" were published (1909—14), and in which he had planned to publish his additional study, found it necessary to stop publication. He continued to revise the study, but it was not completed for publication (AME, "Apuntaciones para un diccionario de nuevomejicanismos: Algunas formas verbales raras y curiosas," in *Estudios Eruditos in Memoriam de Adolfo Bonilla y San Martín* [Madrid: 1930], 2).

23. "Speech Mixture in New Mexico," in *The Pacific Ocean in History*, ed. Herbert E. Bolton and Henry Morse Stevens (1917), 408—28.

24. Letter from H. L. Mencken to Alfred A. Knopf, June, 1934. Copy in the files of J. Manuel Espinosa, courtesy of Mr. Knopf.

25. The only earlier publications worthy of mention relating to the folk literature of the region are those of Rallière, Bourke, and Lummis. In 1877, Father J. J. B. Rallière, S.J., pastor of the Catholic church at Tomé, New Mexico, from 1858 to 1913, published *Colección de cánticos espirituales*, a hymn book which contained some hymns that were popular among the people and that were perhaps collected from them.

Captain John J. Bourke published several articles on the Spanish folk customs of the region in the *Journal of American Folk-Lore* in 1893, 1894, and 1896. One of those articles dealt with the religious folk play *Los pastores*. Charles F. Lummis, in his book entitled *The Land of Poco Tiempo* and in several articles in *Cosmopolitan* and in his magazine *Land of Sunshine*, later named *Out West*, which appeared between 1892 and 1901, published examples of New Mexican Spanish folksongs collected by him. In his chapter in *The Land of Poco Tiempo* entitled "New Mexican Folk-songs," he states that he collected, largely from shepherds in northern New Mexico, "several thousand of these quaint ditties . . . preserved by oral transmission." The chapter includes a dozen popular songs and seven short verses in Spanish and in English translation. The selection contains a fragment of one traditional seventeenth-century ballad which he entitled *El pastor tonto* and which he refers to as "a very different ballad, equally of folk-song rank, but much more clever in motive and treatment." He was unaware of the fact that this was a fragment of a longer traditional Spanish ballad, or *romance tradicional*, many of which were collected later by Aurelio M. Espinosa. Lummis was in error when he wrote, "Of anything like ballads, the New Mexicans have very few specimens."

26. In 1916, Espinosa published thirteen versions of traditional Spanish ballads which he had collected in California from recent immigrants from southern Spain. In 1924 he published nineteen versions and nine fragmentary versions of six traditional Spanish ballads collected from Californians who represented the Mexican-Spanish tradition of the late eighteenth century. In 1930 he published an interesting miscellany of popular poetic compositions collected by him from Mexican-Spanish residents who preserved the oral tradition introduced into California from Mexico in the late eighteenth century. Some of the poems contain lines derived from older traditional Spanish ballads of the type he had found in northern New Mexico and southern Colorado. He collection contains an unusual twenty-

two-line fragment of a modern ballad entitled *La batalla de los Tulares*, collected by Espinosa from oral tradition in southern California in 1920. The verses describe historical events which took place in 1824. According to the account, in May of that year the Indians of Santa Barbara, California, rebelled and escaped to the vicinity of Los Tulares (a place which was then and is still known by this name); they were overtaken by the soldiers of the Presidio, and a battle raged there for several days. Documents in the Bancroft Library, University of California, confirm that the events actually took place and that the soldiers named in the ballad were known persons of that period.

27. Franz Boas, "Romance Folklore among American Indians," *Romanic Review*, 16 (1925): 199–207; reprinted in Boas, *Race, Language and Culture*, 518, 519.

28. Herbert E. Bolton, "Defensive Spanish Expansion and the Significance of the Borderlands," in *The Trans-Mississippi West*, ed. James F. Willard and Colin B. Goodykoontz (Boulder: University of Colorado, 1930), 39; reprinted in Bolton, *Wider Horizons of American History*, 102.

## Chapter 2. Major Stages in the Development of Espinosa's Folklore Studies

1. Complete references to Aurelio M. Espinosa's specific publications referred to in this chapter may be found in the bibliography of his publications on folklore and dialectology included at the end of this volume.

2. The first of these two listings is included in AME, *The Spanish Language in New Mexico and Southern Colorado* (1911), 29–37. Both lists, in combination, identify the specific items of folk literature, customs, and related materials that he had collected up to that time. A few examples of folk literature had been referred to or were included in his "Studies," published in 1909; others were in the process of being published in separate studies. The first of the two lists published in 1911 also includes examples of the texts of some of the types of folk literature he had found up to that time. Listed are the following:
Traditional ballads:
   1. *La dama y el pastor*, four versions with music.
   2. *La esposa infiel*, six versions.
   3. *La delgadina*, six versions, with music.
   4. *Gerineldo*, four versions, with music.
   5. *El pastor desgraciado*, one version, with music.
   6. *La aparición*, three versions, with music.
   7. *Las señas del marido*, one version.
Modern ballads or *corridos*, from about three score collected.
   1. *Macario Romero*, four versions, with music. He describes it as "A very spirited and charming ballad, not inferior to the best of the old ballads." Espinosa includes the text of this modern ballad, a forty-line version, as recited to him by Juanita Lucero, of Juan Tafoya, New Mexico, eighteen years of age.
   2. *Isabel Aranda*.
   3. *Luis Rodarte*.
   4. *Jesús Leal*.
   5. *Luisita*.
   6. *Las mañanas de Belén*.
   7. *Reyes Ruiz*, with music.
   8. *Pachuca*.
   9. *Apolonia*.
   10. *Chaparrita*, with music.
   11. *Rumaldo*.
   12. *Ignacio Parras*.

13. *David.*
14. *Cruz Cháves.*
15. *Don Fernando.*
16. *Monteros.*
17. *Faustín Sánchez.*
Vulgar ballads. Very numerous, such as *La cabra*, *El chapulín*, and *El renganchi* (train-gang).
*Décimas.* Ten versions without music.
*Inditas*, *cuandos*, series of *quintillas*, and so on. Some two score, with the music for six. Some with refrain, and sung when danced. Riddles and riddle questions. Some 150. Traditional. The texts of 4 are given as examples.
Proverbs (*refranes* or *dichos*). A little over six hundred, mostly of a traditional character. Six are presented as examples.
Games and diversions of adults. Men's games: *la barra*, *la pelota*, *las iglesias*, *el cañute*, *el piojo y la liendre*, and so on. Diversions and popular amusements of men: *el gallo*, *carreras de caballo*, *peleas de gallo*, and so on. Diversions for both sexes: dances, with music.
Children's games and nursery rhymes, mostly traditional: twenty-five children's games, with words and music; some fifty nursery rhymes, with the music of a large part of them. The texts of several are given as examples.
Popular folktales. Some twenty long tales, nearly all traditional and very old. Espinosa notes that similar tales, both long and short, are very abundant in New Mexico. He cites versions of *Pedro de Urdemalas*, *Mano Fashico*, and *La Zorra* as examples.
*Cancionero popular nuevomejicano.* Over one thousand *coplas* or *versos*. The texts of eight are given as examples. Most of them are of New Mexican origin; perhaps one-fifth of them are traditional.
Religious plays (item 24): *Aparición de Nuestra Señora de Guadalupe*, one complete and one incomplete version. *Las posadas*, dealing with the life of Christ, one manuscript. *Primera persecución de Jesús*, one very old manuscript.
3. *Journal of American Folk-Lore*, 23 (1910): 395.
4. *Ibid.*
5. *Ibid.*
6. See the discussion on this subject in AME, "Los romances tradicionales en California," in *Homenaje a Menéndez Pidal* (1924), 1: 299–300. See also Ramón Menéndez Pidal, "Los romances tradicionales en América," *Cultura española*, 1 (1906): 72–111, reprinted in Ramón Menéndez Pidal, *Los romances de América, y otros estudios*.
In July, 1909, Menéndez Pidal wrote to AME, "I hope that you will send me a small collection of ballads from New Mexico, which, from so distant and isolated a region, would be a pearl in my collection. As for their existence, I do not have the slightest doubt that they are to be found in New Mexico, for it is my firm belief that the ballad exists wherever Spanish is spoken; a belief well confirmed by interesting surprises from countries where everyone affirmed that the tradition did not exist" (editor's translation). AME, "Romancero nuevomejicano," *Revue Hispanique*, 33 (1915): 454.
7. *Journal of American Folk-Lore*, 27 (1914): 211. AME is referring here to his earlier statements in the *Journal*, 24 (1911): 398, 423: "I hold it as a dogma . . . that practically all the New-Mexican Spanish folk-lore material is traditional; i.e., its sources are to be found in the Spain of the fifteenth to the seventeenth century. . . . This, I believe, is true of the folk-tales, as it is true of the ballads, proverbs, riddles, nursery rhymes, *coplas*, myths, superstitions, and other folk-lore material." In this same article Espinosa adds: "The fact that the folk-lore material from New Mexico is practically all traditional makes its study of great importance, as it helps to interpret better general Spanish folk-lore, and is also a key to the interpretation of the problem of the progress and change of the old

material as it has been preserved in the oral tradition of the New Mexicans for some three hundred years." After his folklore expedition to Spain in 1920, Espinosa stated: "I, personally, at least, have seen my old theories with respect to the origin of the folklore of New Mexico, and of some of the other regions of Spanish America, fully confirmed." AME, *Cuentos populares españoles, recogidos de la tradición oral de España* (1946–47), 1: xxxiv.

8. Stanley L. Robe, ed., *Hispanic Folktales from New Mexico: Narratives from the R. D. Jameson Collection*, Folkore Studies, 30: 7–9.

### Chapter 3. Espinosa's Folklore Fieldwork

1. AME, *The Spanish Language in New Mexico and Southern Colorado* (1911), 29, 31, 34.
2. AME, "Romancero nuevomejicano" (1915), 451–54.
3. AME, *Romancero de Nuevo Méjico* (1953), 279–87.
4. *Ibid.*, 17.
5. Between 1916 and 1931, Espinosa also visited all of the Indian pueblos of northern New Mexico and northeastern Arizona, where he found Spanish influences in the Indians' vocabulary, folklore, and customs. His findings and experiences among the Pueblo Indians are summarized in Appendix B.

During the period between 1911 and 1919 he also collected traditional Spanish ballads, folktales, miscellaneous verses, and riddles in California. The materials were collected from Mexican-Spanish residents in localities along the old Camino Real between Santa Barbara and San Francisco. In publishing the ballads and folktales, he gave the names and ages of the narrators and the localities where the versions were recited to him. As in all of his published texts, these materials were written down by him in the Spanish dialect spoken by the informant. He states that the materials were "collected from descendants of the old Mexican and Spanish colonizers of California."

6. This account of AME's folklore expedition to Spain is based on his own published reports: "A Folk-Lore Expedition to Spain," *Journal of American Folk-Lore*, 34 (1921): 127–42; "Viajes por España," in ten parts, *Hispania*, 4 (1921): 15–17, 56–60, 223–26; 5 (1922): 25–28, 83–86, 149–56, 365–68; 7 (1924): 187–90; 9 (1926): 345–49; and his *Cuentos* (1946–47), 1: xxxi–xxxiii.
7. AME, *Cuentos* (1946–47), 1: xxxiii–xxxiv, xxxiv–xxxvii.
8. *Ibid.*, 1: xxxiii; AME, "A Folk-Lore Expedition to Spain" (1921), 138–40. In the course of his visit to Spain, Espinosa also collected about two hundred versions of forty different ballads; he donated the entire collection to Ramón Menéndez Pidal, as a contribution to Menéndez Pidal's ballad research, in his own name and in the name of the American Folklore Society.
9. AME, *Cuentos* (1946–47), 1: xxxiii.

### Chapter 4. Espinosa's Folklore Concepts and Research Methodology

1. AME, "Folklore in European Literature" (1935), 3–4. This is the syllabus he prepared and printed for his course on folklore at Stanford.
2. *Ibid.*, 5–7.
3. *Ibid.*, 7.
4. AME, "Romances de Puerto Rico," *Revue Hispanique*, 43 (1918), 309–64.
5. Stith Thompson, "Historic-geographic method," in *Funk & Wagnalls Standard Dictionary of Folklore, Mythology, and Legend*, 1: 498.

6. AME, *Cuentos* (1946—47), 1: xxii—xxiii; 2: 14.

7. *Ibid.*, 1: xxiv.

8. *Ibid.*, 1: xxiv—xxvi. See also his "Spanish Folklore," *Funk & Wagnalls Standard Dictionary of Folklore* (1949—50), 2: 1067—68.

9. AME, *Cuentos* (1946—47), 1: xxiii.

10. "Bolte, Johannes," *Funk & Wagnalls Standard Dictionary of Folklore*, 1: 154.

11. AME, "The Classification of Folktales" (1935; manuscript in the files of JME), 2, 4. AME considered that the principal defect in Ralph S. Boggs, *Index of Spanish Folktales*, Folklore Fellows Communications No. 90, was the fact that the author did not separate Hispanic types from those indicated in Aarne-Thompson (AME, "La clasificación de los cuentos populares," *Boletín de la Academia Española*, 21 [1934]: 226).

12. This discussion is based on AME's "The Classification of Folktales" (1935), his "La clasificación de los cuentos populares" (1934), and his *Cuentos* (1946—47).

13. AME, "The Classification of Folktales" (1935), 3—4.

14. This is stated frequently in his references to the preparation of his *Cuentos* (1946—47). See the introduction to that work, vol. 1: 14—15.

15. AME, "La clasificación de los cuentos populares" (1934), 176.

16. *Ibid.*, 176—77.

17. AME, "The Classification of Folktales" (1935), 5—6; AME, *Cuentos* (1946—47), 2: 165. His comparative study of the "Tar Baby" story is contained in pages 163—227 of the latter.

18. AME, "La clasificación de los cuentos populares" (1934), 177.

19. *Ibid.*, 177—78.

20. *Ibid.*, 178.

21. *Ibid.*, 202.

22. *Ibid.*, 203—204.

23. AME, "The Classification of Folktales" (1935), 7.

24. AME, *Cuentos* (1946—47), 2—3: *passim.*

25. Quoted from Stanley L. Robe in his introduction to his *Hispanic Folktales from New Mexico*, Folklore Studies, 30: 7, 9, 10.

26. In preparing his *Cuentos* (1946—47), AME studied approximately 1,000 versions of Spanish folktales; in addition to the 302 he himself collected in Spain from oral tradition, and approximately 140 collected previously by others, he had at his disposal 511 versions from Old Castile and from the two Leonese provinces of León and Zamora collected by his son AME Jr., in 1936. See AME Jr., "More Spanish Folktales," *Hispania*, 22 (1939): 103—14; seventy-two of the tales were published by the latter in his *Cuentos populares de Castilla*.

27. AME, "Spanish and Spanish-American Folktales," *Journal of American Folklore*, 64 (1951): 151—62.

28. *Ibid.*, 152.

29. *Ibid.*, 155.

30. *Ibid.*, 157. See also George M. Foster, "Mexican and Central American Indian Folklore," *Funk & Wagnalls Standard Dictionary of Folklore*, 2: 711—16. Foster, a distinguished North American anthropologist, states that "the folklore of Mexico and Central America [and] Middle America . . . represents the product of 400 years of fusion of two basic strains, that of the indigenous cultures of the New World, and that of Old World cultures, principally Spanish. To a greater extent than is perhaps the case in North and South America, the Indian cultures of this region have blended with those of Europe to such a degree that the term 'Indian' must be used advisedly. Anthropologists are beginning to suspect that some groups, at least, are as nearly 16th century Spanish in terms of the content of their cultures as they are Indian" (711, 716).

31. AME, "Spanish and Spanish-American Folktales" (1951), 155.

Chapter 5. Spanish Tradition in America

1. See AME, "La ciencia del folklore," *Archivos del folklore cubano* (Habana), 3, no. 5 (1929): 1–16.

2. AME, "Studies in New Mexican Spanish, Part II: Morphology" (1912), 101–103; AME, *Cuentos* (1946–47), 1: 600–601, no. 258; 3: 400–10; AME, "Spanish Folk-Lore in New Mexico" (1926), 143–46; and Theodor Benfey, *Panchatantra*, 1: 609–10.

3. See AME, "A Folklore Expedition to Spain" (1921), 127–42.

4. AME, "New Mexican Spanish Folklore: Part V, Popular Comparisons," *Journal of American Folk-Lore*, 26 (1913): 114, no. 624.

5. AME, "New Mexican Spanish Folklore: Part XI, Nursery Rhymes," *Journal of American Folk-Lore*, 29 (1916): 513.

6. See Antonio Machado y Alvarez, ed., *Biblioteca de las tradiciones populares españolas*, 1: 277; 8: 242; and Julio Vicuña Cifuentes, *Mitos y supersticiones recogidos de la tradición oral chilena*, 183–84.

7. Machado y Alvarez, *Biblioteca de las tradiciones populares españolas*, 1: 253–55; 8: 243–46; and Vicuña Cifuentes, *Mitos y supersticiones*, 177–80.

8. See Machado y Alvarez, *Biblioteca de las tradiciones populares españolas*, 8: 257–64; AME, "New Mexican Spanish Folklore: Part I, Myths, Part II, Superstitions and Beliefs," *Journal of American Folk-Lore*, 23 (1910): 395–418; Vicuña Cifuentes, *Mitos y supersticiones*, 83–107; and Rafael Salillas, *La fascinación en España*.

Chapter 6. Traditional Spanish Ballads

1. John Gibson Lockhart, *Ancient Spanish Ballads: Historical and Romantic*, 48–50. For the Spanish version, see Fernando José Wolf and Don Conrado Hofmann, eds., *Primavera y flor de romances*, No. 29.

2. See Ramón Menéndez Pidal, *Romancero hispánico (hispano-portugués, americano, y sefardí): Teoría e historia*; Ramón Menéndez Pidal, *Obras Completas de R. Menéndez Pidal*, vol. 9, *Estudios sobre el romancero*; Ramón Menéndez Pidal, *Los Romances de América, y otros estudios*; and Marcelino Menéndez y Pelayo, *Antología de Poetas Líricos Castellanos*, vols. 11–12, *Tratado de los romances viejos*. For a brief introduction to the history of Spanish balladry, see AME, *El romancero español* (1931), and Menéndez Pidal, *El romancero español*.

3. The most important published ballad collections from Spanish America are listed in the Bibliography.

4. *The Land of Poco Tiempo*, 242–47.

5. AME, "Romancero nuevomejicano" (1915), 446–560.

6. AME, *Romancero de Nuevo Méjico* (1953). See also AME, "Traditional Spanish Ballads in New Mexico," *Hispania*, 15 (1932): 89–102.

7. See AME, *Romancero de Nuevo Méjico* (1953), 271, no. 244.

8. Eleven versions in *ibid.*, 38–47, nos. 26–36.

9. Seven versions in *ibid.*, 49–57, nos. 37–43.

10. In Ramón Menéndez Pidal, ed., *Flor nueva de romances viejos*, 281–84.

11. Seven versions in AME, *Romancero de Nuevo Méjico* (1953), 32–36, nos. 19–25.

12. Six versions in *ibid.*, 58–61, nos. 44–49.

13. Eleven versions in *ibid.*, 23–27, nos. 1–11.

14. Seven versions in *ibid.*, 28–31, nos. 12–18.

15. Four versions in *ibid.*, 85–86, nos. 76–79.

16. AME, "Traditional Spanish Ballads in New Mexico" (1932), 96–97.

17. *Ibid.*, 97–98.

18. *Ibid.*, 98.

19. AME, *Romancero de Nuevo Méjico* (1953), 170–77, 179–80, nos. 153–63, 167–69, includes New Mexican versions. More than twenty New Mexican versions of this ballad have been published. AME also published two versions from California in "Los romances tradicionales en California," *Homenaje a Menéndez Pidal* (1924), 1: 311–12.

For versions from Spain, Portugal, Mexico, Chile, Cuba, and Argentina, see AME, *Romancero de Nuevo Méjico* (1953), 181 n; AME, "Romancero nuevomejicano, Addenda," *Revue Hispanique*, 40 (1917): 218–23; Juan B. Rael, *The New Mexican Alabado*, 27–29. For peninsular Spanish versions collected in Cuba from recent Spanish immigrants, see Carolina Poncet, "El romance en Cuba," *Revista de la facultad de letras y ciencias* (Havana), 18 (1914): 299–300; and Carolina Poncet, "Romancerillo de Entrepeñas y Villar de los Pisones," *Revue Hispanique*, 57 (1923): 31–33. For versions recently collected in Colombia, mostly from old local tradition, see Gisela Beutler, *Studien zum spanischen Romancero in Kolumbien in seiner schriftlichen und mündlichen Überlieferung von den Zeit der Eroberung bis zur Gegenwart*, 218–25. For versions from Nicaragua and Venezuela, see Luis Santulliano, *La poesía del pueblo: Romances y canciones de España y América*, 335–36, 338.

The oldest known Spanish version is the one beginning with the words, "Por el rastro de la sangre—que Iesu Christo dexaua," published by Juan López de Ubeda in his *Cancionero general de la doctrina christiana* and in his *Vergel de flores divinas*. Subsequent editions of the *Cancionero* were published in 1585 and 1586 after Ubeda's death. For a thorough bibliographical study of these works, see Antonio R. Rodríguez-Moñino, *Juan López de Ubeda, poeta del siglo XVI*. Justo de Sancha, *Romancero y cancionero sagrados*, 91, no. 250, contains Ubeda's version of the ballad, with minor changes in punctuation, giving as his source "Ubeda, *Cancionero*."

20. Sixteen versions in AME, *Romancero de Nuevo Méjico* (1953), 159–69, nos. 137–52. See also, AME, "Traditional Spanish Ballads in New Mexico" (1932), 99.

21. Three versions in AME, *Romancero de Nuevo Méjico* (1953), 218–20, nos. 204–206.

22. Barbara Freire Marreco and AME, "New-Mexican Spanish Folklore," *Journal of American Folk-Lore*, 29 (1916): 543–44; AME, "Romancero nuevomejicano, Addenda" (1917), 224–27; nine New Mexican versions are published in AME, *Romancero de Nuevo Méjico* (1953), 182–86, nos. 170–79.

23. Two versions in AME, *Romancero de Nuevo Méjico* (1953), 198–99, nos. 189–90.

24. *Ibid.*, 173–74, no. 158.

25. *Ibid.*, 159, no. 137.

26. *Ibid.*, 220, no. 206.

27. Two other versions in *ibid.*, 198–99, nos. 189–90.

28. AME, "Traditional Spanish Ballads in New Mexico" (1932), 101; four versions in AME, *Romancero de Nuevo Méjico* (1953), 82–84, nos. 72–75, and related versions, 85–86, nos. 76–79.

29. Six versions in AME, *Romancero de Nuevo Méjico* (1953), 87–91, nos. 80–85.

30. Five versions in *ibid.*, 129–30, nos. 123–26.

31. *Ibid.*, 82–83, no. 73.

32. Georg Wilhelm Friedrich Hegel, *Asthetik*, ed. Georg Lukács (Berlin: Aufbau-Verlag, 1955), 991; F. P. B. Osmaston, trans. and ed., *The Philosophy of Fine Art by G. W. F. Hegel*, 4 vols. (New York: Hacker Art Books, 1975), 4: 182–83.

## Chapter 7. Hymns, Prayers, and Other Religious Verses

1. From as early as the 1840s visitors to New Mexico from the United States have been fascinated by the Roman Catholic religious ceremonies of the Penitentes, and a great number of newspaper and magazine accounts, most of them unreliable, have appeared in

the second half of the nineteenth century and in the present century, usually by Protestants who found the Penitente religious ceremonies, especially the practice of self-flagellation as penance for their sins, abhorrent.

The best general survey of the history of the Penitentes is Marta Weigle's *Brothers of Light, Brothers of Blood: The Penitentes of the Southwest*. Weigle has also published an annotated bibliography, which lists virtually every publication on the subject worth mentioning, entitled *A Penitente Bibliography*. Brief accounts of the origin, history, and religious ceremonies of the Penitentes, and their cultural contributions, may be found in Rael, *New Mexican Alabado*, "Introduction," 9–19; Warren A. Beck, "The Cultural Contributions of the Penitentes," reprinted in Richard N. Ellis, *New Mexico Past and Present: A Historical Reader*, 171–83; and AME, "Penitentes, Los Hermanos," *Catholic Encyclopedia*, 11: 635–36. See also Carlos E. Cortés, ed., *The Penitentes of New Mexico*, which reprints A. M. Darley's *The Passionists of the Southwest* (1893), A. C. Henderson's *Brothers of Light* (1937), and Dorothy Woodward's *The Penitentes of New Mexico* (1935). Darley's book was published privately in Pueblo, Colo., and reprinted by Rio Grande Press, Glorieta, N. Mex., 1968; Henderson's book was first published by Harcourt, Brace and Company, New York; the study by Woodward was her doctoral dissertation at Yale University, published for the first time in the volume edited by Cortés.

2. The matter-of-fact manner in which Fray Alonso de Benavides, writing in the early 1630s, refers to self-flagellation as practiced by penitent Spaniards during Holy Week helps to explain why later Franciscan friars saw no special reason to mention the practice in their accounts—it was nothing unusual among the faithful, both among the friars and the laity. Father Benavides mentions self-flagellation by Christian Pueblo Indians as penance, as an example of their successful conversion to Christianity. He writes that on an occasion when he was preaching to a large group of Indians an old sorcerer shouted, "You Christians are crazy." He said: "I asked him in what respect we were crazy. He had been, no doubt, in some Christian pueblo during Holy Week when they were flagellating themselves in procession, and thus he answered me: 'How are you crazy? You go through the streets, in groups, flagellating yourselves, and it is not well that the people of this pueblo should commit such madness as spilling their own blood by scourging themselves.'" In another place, Benavides, referring to the Indians, writes: "During Lent they all come with much humility to the processions, which are held on Monday, Wednesday and Friday. On these days of meetings with the friars, they perform penance in the churches. During Holy Week they flagellate themselves in most solemn processions." (Frederick W. Hodge, George P. Hammond, and Agapito Rey, eds. and trans., *Fray Alonso de Benavides' Revised Memorial of 1634*, 66, 100; and Fray Alonso de Benavides, O.F.M., *Benavides' Memorial of 1630*, trans. Peter P. Forrestal, ed. Cyprian G. Lynch, 21–22.)

3. The increase in the membership and in the activity of the Penitentes in New Mexico in the late eighteenth and early nineteenth centuries was in large part a reaction to the neglect of the Catholic Church in the area by the ecclesiastical authorities in Mexico, the secularization of the Franciscan missions, the anticlerical actions of the government of the Republic of Mexico, and the consequent absence of any Catholic Church leadership in upper New Mexico to maintain the normal religious services for the faithful. In 1797 the parish churches at Santa Fe, Santa Cruz, and Albuquerque were secularized. In 1833 the Congress of Mexico enacted laws curtailing appropriations for the support of the churches and the clergy. In 1834 the complete secularization of the New Mexico missions was effected, against the protest of the friars. By 1840 there were no longer any Franciscan friars working in New Mexico. Even during the golden age of the Franciscan missions in New Mexico, in the early seventeenth century, there were never enough priests to minister to the faithful. Outside the several principal Spanish *villas* or towns, and the major Indian pueblos, the Spanish settlements were visited by the clergy and Mass was performed only on scheduled visits spread throughout the year. In some of the outlying settlements local lay

religious brotherhoods, or *cofradías*, built and maintained a local chapel and kept it in readiness for the periodic visit by a priest, which occurred anywhere from once a month to once every several months. In the interim the faithful, led by the local church sodalities, held religious prayers on Sundays and conducted other religious functions and ceremonies that were within the power of civilians.

Thus, during the virtual abandonment of the Catholic Church in upper New Mexico in the first half of the nineteenth century, the most devout took into their own hands the responsibility to keep the faith alive. Among them the Penitentes were especially prominent. In many small communities along the upper Rio Grande north of Tomé and Albuquerque, and especially between Santa Fe and the southern border of what is now the state of Colorado, the chapels built by the Penitentes, their *moradas* or meeting places, were among the first local churches for the community. In the nineteenth century the early missionary work of the Franciscan friars was abandoned by the authorities in the Republic of Mexico and harassed to a degree during the early years after the Catholic hierarchy in the United States took jurisdiction over the Catholic Church in New Mexico in 1851.

4. AME, "New Mexican Spanish Folklore: Part XI, Nursery Rhymes" (1916), 522; Ciro Bayo, *Romancerillo del Plata*, 86; Francisco Rodríguez Marín, *Cantos populares españoles*, 1: 61, no. 124.

5. William Henry Husk, *Songs of the Nativity*, "Introduction," 2.

6. Salvador Fernández Ramírez, ed., *Los pastores de Belén*, 2: 36–37.

7. AME, *Romancero de Nuevo Méjico* (1953), 193–94, no. 184.

8. See also Sancha, *Romancero y cancionero sagrados*, 214, no. 551.

9. Ramón A. Laval, "Oraciones, ensalmos i conjuros del pueblo chilenos," *Revista de la sociedad del folklore chileno*, 1 (1910), 75–132, no. 84.

10. Another New Mexican Spanish version is given in J. J. B. Rallière, *Coleccion de cánticos espirituales*, 175–76. For other versions from Spain and Spanish America, see Laval, "Oraciones," 84–97; Rodríguez Marín, *Cantos*, 1: 424, no. 984; and Fernán Caballero, *Cuentos, oraciones, adivinas y refranes populares e infantiles*, 313.

11. This traditional bachelor's prayer in verse has several New Mexican changes and developments, as one might expect, among them the use of the English words *no* and *yes* and the Hispanicized New Mexican Spanish word of English source *tustepe*, from two-step. See AME, "Romancero nuevomejicano" (1915), 446–560, no. 46.

## Chapter 8. Modern Local Ballads (*Corridos*)

1. Agustín Durán, ed., *Romancero general: O colección de romances castellanos anteriores al siglo XVIII*.

2. *Ibid.*, 2: 289–90, no. 1285.

3. *Ibid.*, 2: 386–87, no. 1342.

4. The above four New Mexican Spanish ballads were published in AME, "Romancero nuevomejicano" (1915), 488–97, nos. 38, 39, 40, 41; and in AME, *Romancero de Nuevo Méjico* (1953), 132–49, nos. 127–33.

5. Julio Vicuña Cifuentes, *Romances populares y vulgares*, 147–50, 150–53nn, nos. 68–70.

6. AME, "Romancero nuevomejicano" (1915), 485, no. 31; and AME, *Romancero de Nuevo Méjico* (1953), 122, no. 116.

7. The New Mexicans, in general, looked with disdain on the foreigners from the United States who came to govern them in 1846. This disdain has continued, especially in the smaller villages where the Spanish language has not yet been supplanted by English. They have referred to the American settlers from the United States as *mericanos*, *miricachos*, *mericaches*, *gringos*, *yanques* or *yanquis*, *bolios*, *paiquespiques* (from General Zebulon Pike,

who gave the name Pike's Peak to a mountain in Colorado), *güeros*, *dochis* (from the English word Dutchman), and by a number of other names, some more disparaging than others. AME, "Romancero nuevomejicano" (1915), 509 and n.

8. *Ibid.*, 509-10, no. 52; AME, *Romancero de Nuevo Méjico* (1953), 248-50, no. 227.

9. AME, "Romancero nuevomejicano" (1915), 537-41, no. 78; AME, *Romancero de Nuevo Méjico* (1953), 251-54, no. 228.

10. A composite version of this ballad, or *alabado*, based on variants with stanzas missing, collected in northern New Mexico and southern Colorado, is published in Rael, *New Mexican Alabado*, 62-65, no. 29.


## Chapter 9. The Spanish *Coplas Populares*

1. These *coplas* were previously published in AME, "New Mexican Spanish *Coplas Populares*," *Hispania*, 18 (1935): 135-50. See also, AME, "Folklore de California," in *Miscelánea filológica dedicada a D. Antonio M. Alcover*, (1930), 111-31.

2. Rodríguez Marín, *Cantos*, 3: 142-43, no. 4165.

3. Juan José Jiménez de Aragon, ed., *Cancionero aragonés*, 109, no. 48.

4. *Ibid.*, 143, no. 3; 146, no. 35; and Rodríguez Marín, *Cantos*, 2: 74, no. 1501; 152, no. 1808.

5. Rodríguez Marín, *Cantos*, 2: 31-32, no. 3565.

6. Juan Alfonso Carrizo, *Antiguos cantos populares argentinos*, 191, no. 843.

7. Rodríguez Marín, *Cantos*, 4: 91, no. 6240; Carrizo, *Antiguos cantos*, 182, no. 700.

8. Rodríguez Marín, *Cantos*, 4: 204, no. 6659; Eusebio Vasco, *Treinta mil cantares populares*, 2: 287, no. 2885.

9. Machado y Alvarez, *Biblioteca*, 5: 78; Carrizo, *Antiguos cantos*, 154, no. 252.

10. Jiménez de Aragón, *Cancionero*, 394, no. 404. There is a similar version from La Mancha; See Vasco, *Treinta mil cantares populares*, 2: 396, no. 3506.

11. Rodríguez Marín, *Cantos*, 4: 236, no. 6830; Fernán Caballero, *Cuentos y poesías populares andaluces*, 123; Carrizo, *Antiguos cantos*, 210, no. 1140.

12. Rodríguez Marín, *Cantos*, 4: 153, no. 6436; Vasco, 367, *Treinta mil cantares populares*, 1: no. 1131.

13. Gabriel María Vergara, *Cantares populares de Castilla la vieja*, 19.

14. Carrizo, *Antiguos cantos*, 218, no. 1279.

15. Rodríguez Marín, *Cantos*, 4: 337-38, no. 7274.

16. See S. Griswold Morley, "Are the Spanish Romances Written in Quatrains?—and Other Questions," *Romanic Review*, 7 (1916): 42-82; and Eduardo Martínez Torner in *Romances que deben buscarse en la tradición oral* ed. María Goyri de Menéndez Pidal, 27-33.

17. AME, "Romancero nuevomejicano" (1915), 553-59, and his *Romancero de Nuevo Méjico* (1953), 291-302. Additional melodies are included in Rael, *New Mexican Alabado*, 139-52, and several other works. John Donald Robb, *Hispanic Folk Music of New Mexico and the Southwest*, is the most extensive recent collection of Hispanic ballad melodies of the area.

18. The Chilean *décimas* were published by Rudolfo Lenz in Adolph Tobler, *Abhandlungen*, 141-43. The two Argentine collections were Juan Alfonso Carrizo's *Antiguos cantos* and his *Cancionero popular de Salta*. The Puerto Rican *décimas* were published in J. Alden Mason and AME, "Porto-Rican Folklore: Décimas, Christmas Carols, Nursery Rhymes and Other Songs," *Journal of American Folk-Lore*, 31 (1918): 289-425. The New Mexican collection was AME's "Romancero nuevomejicano" (1915).

19. Sancha, *Romancero y cancionero sagrados*.

20. Fernández Ramírez, ed., *Los pastores de Belén*, 1: 90-91.

21. AME, "Romancero nuevomejicano" (1915), 524-25, no. 67.

22. *Ibid.*, 530, no. 70.

23. *Ibid.*, 521, no. 64.
24. *Ibid.*, 516–17, no. 59.
25. *Ibid.*, 514, no. 56.

Chapter 10. Traditional Spanish Proverbs in New Mexico

1. A collection of 632 New Mexican Spanish proverbs, 167 in assonance or rhymed couplets and 31 in octosyllabic quatrains, may be found in AME, "New Mexican Spanish Folklore: Part IV, Proverbs," *Journal of American Folk-Lore*, 26 (1913): 97–114. See also Rubén Cobos, *Southwestern Spanish Proverbs: Refranes españoles del sudoeste.*

2. In the great Argentine collection of Robert Lehmann-Nitsche, *Folklore argentino*, vol. 1, *Adivinanzas rioplatenses*, a little over one thousand in number, one-third have parallels in the Spanish collections of Rodríguez Marín, *Cantos*, and others. In the collection from New Mexico published in AME, "New Mexican Spanish Folklore: Part IX, Riddles," *Journal of American Folk-Lore*, 28 (1915): 219–352, a total of 165 in number, 40 percent have identical or practically identical versions in the riddle collections of Spain, Argentina, and Chile. See also AME, "California Spanish Folklore: Riddles," *California Folklore Quarterly*, 3 (1944): 293–98.

3. An example of a riddle *décima* was given in chapter 9.

4. Lehmann-Nitsche, *Folklore argentino*, 1: no. 721a.

5. Rodríguez Marín, *Cantos*, 1: 305, no. 917; Antonio Machado y Alvarez [Demófilo], *Colección de enigmas y adivinanzas en forma de diccionario*, 258–59, no. 915.

6. An abundant collection of both was published in AME, "New Mexican Spanish Folklore: Part X, Children's Games: Part XI, Nursery Rhymes and Children's Songs," *Journal of American Folk-Lore*, 29 (1916): 505–35; and AME, "Folklore infantil de Nuevo Méjico," *Revista de dialectología y tradiciones populares* (Madrid), 10 (1954): 1–49.

7. AME, "Folklore infantil de Nuevo Méjico."

8. Rodríguez Marín, *Cantos*, 1: 44, no. 49.

9. Fernando Llorca, *Lo que cantan los niños*, 114.

10. See especially *ibid.*, 115; Machado y Alvarez, *Biblioteca*, 2: 149–51; Carreras y Candi, ed., *Folklore y costumbres de España*, 2: 558; and Rodríguez Marín, *Cantos*, 1: 45, no. 52. For a similar English nursery game, see William Wells Newell, *Games and Songs of American Children*, 175.

11. See AME, "New Mexican Spanish Folklore: Part X" (1916), 510–11; Machado y Alvarez, *Biblioteca*, 2: 126; Rodríguez Marín, *Cantos*, 1: 43–44, no. 46, and 158, no. 110; and Llorca, *Lo que cantan los niños*, 12.

12. Machado y Alvarez, *Biblioteca*, 2: 130–31; *El folklore andaluz* (Sevilla), 1 (1882–83): 168; Carreras y Candi, *Folklore y costumbres de España*, 2: 543, and Llorca, *Lo que cantan los niños*, 15.

13. The New Mexican Spanish version is longer than any of the peninsular versions and may represent an older form. The version most similar to the New Mexican is in Rodríguez Marín, *Cantos*, 1: 51, no. 82; see also 50–52, nos. 81, 83. Also Machado y Alvarez, *Biblioteca*, 2: 124, and Llorca, *Lo que cantan los niños*, 14.

14. *Journal of American Folk-Lore*, 29 (1916): 516–17. For the peninsular Spanish versions, see Machado y Alvarez, *Biblioteca*, 2: 137; Aurelio de Llano Roza de Ampudia, *Cuentos asturianos*, 279, no. 185; and *Revista Lusitana* (Porto-Lisboa), 4 (1890): 380. Spanish American versions are the following: *Archivos del folklore* (Habana), 3 (1928): 265; *Journal of American Folk-Lore*, 4 (1891): 35–38; and Carrizo, *Cancionero popular de Salta*, 1: 17, no. 15.

15. One of the best of such independent dialogues from Spain, and one very similar to the New Mexican, is no. 280 of AME, *Cuentos* (1946–47), 1: 631.

Chapter 11. New Mexican Spanish Folktales, I

1. See Stith Thompson, *The Folktale*; AME, "La transmisión de los cuentos populares," *Archivos del folklore cubano* (Habana), 4 (1929): 39−52; and AME, *Cuentos* (1946−47), Introduction, xxi−xxxviii.

2. In general the 280 folktales in AME, *Cuentos* (1946−47), the largest single collection of popular tales taken from oral tradition in Spain, represent the same types of folktales and the same motifs and ideas of the Grimm tales collected a century and ten years before.

3. The important publications of Franz Boas, Elsie Clews Parsons, and others in the general field of Indian anthropology and folklore, and folktales in particular, number more than a score of large volumes and over two hundred shorter articles and monographs. They are published for the most part in the publications of the Bureau of American Ethnology, of the American Anthropological Association, and of the American Folklore Society.

4. AME was the first to collect and study traditional Spanish folktales from New Mexico. See especially his "New Mexican Spanish Folklore, Part III: Folktales," *Journal of American Folk-Lore*, 24 (1911): 397−444, and "New Mexican Spanish Folklore, Part VII: More Folktales," *Journal of American Folklore*, 27 (1914): 119−47, which contain some 50 New Mexican Spanish folktales. Two larger collections, however, are those of JME, *Spanish Folk Tales from New Mexico*, Memoirs of the American Folklore Society, 30, and Juan B. Rael, *Cuentos españoles de Colorado y de Nuevo Méjico* (*Spanish Tales from Colorado and New Mexico*). The former contains 114 versions of some 60 different folktales. Rael's collection is perhaps the largest and best from anywhere in Spanish America. For about six years he explored southern Colorado and New Mexico during summer vacations, and his collection consists of over 510 versions of about 150 different folktales. These two collections are from the northernmost region of the Old Spanish Empire in America, for Santa Fe, Santa Cruz, Taos, and the towns of New Mexico north of Taos and in southern Colorado are the extreme northern points of Spanish conquest and colonization in the New World. The two collections complement each other, with no overlap in informants and practically no overlap in the localities from which the stories were collected. JME's tales were collected in the early 1930's from forty-two informants in twenty-five localities, nearly all from along the Rio Grande Valley between Albuquerque and Taos; Rael's tales were collected in the 1930s and 1940s from ninety-eight informants in twenty-one localities, nearly all from the region north of Taos, including the Spanish-speaking communities of southern Colorado.

In the above two collections of folktales from northern New Mexico and southern Colorado we have over 600 versions of a little over 200 different folktales, enough folktale materials to reach fairly definite conclusions about their origins. In JME's collection there are 5 of the 114 that may be of American Indian origin. There are 3 that show definite traces of such a source—less than 3 percent. The curious fact remains that 104, or over 90 percent of the entire collection, are definitely of direct peninsular Spanish origin or have developed from incidents and motifs of the same origin. Rael's collection contains more anecdotal material than does JME's, and these materials are often of a local character. Nevertheless, a provisional tabulation of sources shows that over 80 percent of the entire number of versions are of European Spanish source. On their way to northern New Mexico these folktales passed through New Spain (Mexico), of course, but they have remained essentially Spanish. See AME, "Spanish and Spanish-American Folktales" (1951), 151−62; also, AME, "Spanish Folktales from California," *Hispania*, 23 (1940): 121−44.

See also the interesting collection of Spanish folktales, published in English translation, collected for the late R. D. Jameson by his students at New Mexico Highlands University in the 1950s, largely from the Las Vegas area (Robe, ed., *Hispanic Folktales from New Mexico*).

In the Mexican folktales from Oaxaca collected by Paul Radin, *El folk-lore de Oaxaca*, the native Mexican Indian elements are quite pronounced. Much depends on the region of Mexico which is studied. Another folklore student, Mr. Howard T. Wheeler, collected about two hundred folktales from Jalisco in 1930; they were published in his *Tales from Jalisco Mexico*. In these the European Spanish sources are almost as dominant as in the New Mexico and Colorado collections. See also Américo Paredes, *Folktales of Mexico*, and Stanley L. Robe, *Index of Mexican Folktales, Including Narrative Texts from Mexico, Central America, and the Hispanic United States*.

5. So true is this that JME and Rael classified their collections following closely the classification of AME, *Cuentos* (1946−47).

6. That is, JME and Rael collections.

7. This folktale is a version of the European tales cataloged in Antti Aarne and Stith Thompson, *The Types of the Folktale: A Classification and Bibliography*, Folklore Fellows Communications [FFC] No. 74, 2d ed., 851 and 570 [hereafter cited as Aarne-Thompson]; and AME, *Cuentos* (1946−47), 1: 15−24, nos. 5−7; 2: 79−88.

8. This is a version of a well-known European tale, Aarne-Thompson, 922, and AME, *Cuentos* (1946−47), 1: 39−40, no. 13; 2: 101−11.

9. This is a version of a well-known European tale, Aarne-Thompson, 893, and AME, *Cuentos* (1946−47), 1: 127−28, no. 69; 2: 287−93.

10. This is a version of the European tale of the persecuted wife, Aarne-Thompson, 706, and AME, *Cuentos* (1946−47), 1: 179−201, nos. 99−104; and 2: 376−96.

11. This tale is a version of Aarne-Thompson, 709, and AME, *Cuentos* (1946−47), 1: 240−46, nos. 115−16; 2: 431−41.

12. This tale is a version of Aarne-Thompson, 425, and AME, *Cuentos* (1946−47), 1: 283−99, nos. 127−30; 2: 483−97.

13. This tale is a version of Aarne-Thompson, 301, and AME, *Cuentos* (1946−47), 1: 303−14, nos. 133−35, 2: 498−504.

14. This tale is a version of Aarne-Thompson, 300, and AME, *Cuentos* (1946−47), 1: 391−97, no. 157, 3: 110.

15. This tale is a version of Aarne-Thompson, 1000 and 1011, and AME, *Cuentos* (1946−47), 1: 407−26, nos. 163−67; 3: 130−50.

16. This is a version of a well-known European and Hispanic tale, Aarne-Thompson, 1538, and AME, *Cuentos* (1946−47), 1: 490−93, no. 192, and 3: 207−12.

17. This is a version of the well-known European tales 327 and 408 of Aarne-Thompson, and AME, *Cuentos* (1946−47), 1: 235−40, no. 114; 252−55, no. 120; and 255−57, no. 121; 2: 427−31, 460−69.

18. This is a version of the well-known European tale of the magic flight, Aarne-Thompson, 313, and AME, *Cuentos* (1946−47), 1: 258−78, nos. 122−25; 2: 470−82.

19. This tale is a version of the Cinderella story, Aarne-Thompson, 510, 511, and AME, *Cuentos* (1946−47), 1: 221−31, nos. 111, 112; 2: 414−421.

20. This is a version of the European tale 1640 of Aarne-Thompson, and AME, *Cuentos* (1946−47), 1: 496−500, no. 194; 3: 222−28.

21. This is a version of the well-known European tale of animal supremacy, Aarne-Thompson, 222, and AME, *Cuentos* (1946−47), 1: 569−72, nos. 247, 248; 3: 356−63.


Chapter 12. **New Mexican Spanish Folktales, II**

1. JME, *Spanish Folk Tales from New Mexico*, 165, no. 75. This is an extraordinarily well preserved version of a well-known European tale, Aarne-Thompson, 360, 1697, and AME, *Cuentos* (1946−47), 1: 95−96, no. 52; 2: 254−57. There are versions from most European countries, and the peninsular Spanish versions are quite similar to the New Mexican, except in the title, *manofashico*, a popular development of (*her*)*mano Francisco*. In the Spanish versions the characters are usually *tres gallegos*, three Galicians.

2. This is a very fine version of a well-known European folktale, Aarne-Thompson, 910B, and AME, *Cuentos* (1946–47), 1: 113–22, nos. 63–66; 2: 271–80. In European tradition there are two general types, a Celtic type and a Romance type. This New Mexican version is a well-preserved version of the Romance type, practically the same as AME, *Cuentos* (1946–47), 1: 116–19, no. 64.

3. This New Mexican folktale is a version of a special Hispanic form of the European tale of the clever thief. It is similar to the general European tale of Aarne-Thompson, 1525D. For other New Mexican versions, see JME, *Spanish Folk Tales from New Mexico*, 130–34, nos. 56 and 57.

4. *Ibid.*, 90–93, no. 36. This New Mexican Spanish tale is a beautiful version of the well-known European tale of the prince enchanted as a bird, Aarne-Thompson, 432, but adds the motif of the envious sisters that have nine, eight, seven, six, five, four, and three eyes and one eye.

5. JME, *Spanish Folk Tales from New Mexico*, 116–18, no. 50. This New Mexican version, which preserves both the folktale and the doctrinal series of numbers, is very similar to the peninsular Spanish version in AME, *Cuentos* (1946–47), 1: 40–43, no. 14; 2: 111–43.

6. For a special study of this Oriental and European tradition, see AME, "Origen oriental y desarrollo histórico del cuento de las doce palabras retorneadas," *Revista de filología española* (Madrid), 17 (1930): 390–413.

## Chapter 13. Traditional Spanish Religious Folk Drama in New Mexico

1. M. R. Cole, trans. and ed., *Los pastores, A Mexican Play of the Nativity*, Memoirs of the American Folk-Lore Society, 9. The text of the version from San Rafael published by Cole is based on the manuscript obtained by Honora de Busk (*ibid.*, xii, and Appendix III, 211–34). It was the first text of a version of *Los pastores* from New Mexico to be published (Juan B. Rael, *The Sources and Diffusion of the Mexican Shepherds' Plays*, 144).

2. This version of *Los pastores*, published by Cole, was witnessed in Rio Grande City, Texas, in 1891, by Captain John G. Bourke, who had the text copied for him by the play director (*ibid.*, ix). See John G. Bourke, "The Miracle Play of the Rio Grande," *Journal of American Folk-Lore*, 6 (1893): 88–95.

3. More than twenty versions of *pastorela* manuscripts that depict the traditional theme of the Nativity and childhood of Jesus have been collected in northern New Mexico and southern Colorado, some more complete than others (Rael, *Shepherds' Plays*, 45–55). Arthur L. Campa concluded that they represent at least eight independent plays dealing with the Nativity known throughout New Mexico (Arthur L. Campa, *Spanish Religious Folktheatre in the Southwest* [*Second Cycle*], The University of New Mexico Bulletin, Language Series, 5, No. 2: 5). Campa's study, pp. 11–154, contains the texts of the following four versions of popular Nativity plays from New Mexico: *Coloquio de San José, Coloquio de los pastores, Auto de los reyes magos*, and *El Niño perdido*. Aurora Lucero-White Lea, in *Literary Folklore of the Hispanic Southwest*, has published the texts of four versions collected by her entitled: *Coloquios de los pastores, La aurora del nuevo día, Los tres reyes*, and *Auto del santo Niño*. See also her *Coloquios de los pastores*. See also items in the Lorin W. Brown manuscripts listed in Lorin W. Brown, Charles L. Briggs, and Marta Weigle, *Hispano Folklife in New Mexico*, 261, 263.

Rael's extensive study cited in note 1 of this chapter, above, throws new light on the origins and development of the Nativity folk drama in Spain, on the origins and diffusion of the Mexican shepherds' plays, and on the comparative study of the existing Nativity folk plays in Mexico and the southwestern section of the United States.

On the music of the *pastorelas* or shepherds' plays, see especially Richard B. Starke, assisted by T. M. Pearce and Rubén Cobos, *Music of the Spanish Folk Plays in New Mexico*; and Rael, *Mexican Shepherds' Plays*, 558–80. See also J. D. Robb, "The Music of Los Pastores," *Western Folklore*, 16 (1957): 263–80.

The literature on the religious folk drama in New Mexico is fairly extensive. Other books and articles on the subject are cited in the bibliography at the end of this volume.

4. This version was copied by Juan B. Rael. The texts of two versions of this play are published in Campa, *Spanish Religious Folktheatre (Second Cycle)*, 121–54, and Lea, *Literary Folklore*, 75–85.

5. Both are similar to the one published from old manuscripts by L. Anchondo and R. Samaniego in *La Revista Católica* in 1933. The text of a version of this play is published in Lea, *Literary Folklore*, 86–106, based on a manuscript in her possession (*ibid.*, p. 17).

6. Of the various Spanish manuscripts of religious folk plays collected in New Mexico, there are two plays dealing with the Old Testament which have not been discussed in this chapter: *Adán y Eva* and *Caín y Abel*. The former, enacted in Mexico City in 1532, was one of those popular in Europe that was adapted by the missionaries as a means of encouraging the conversion of the Mexican Indians. When these religious folk plays were introduced into New Mexico from Mexico is unknown. The Spanish text of a version of *Adán y Eva* was published by Arthur L. Campa in his *Spanish Religious Folktheatre in the Spanish Southwest (First Cycle)*, The University of New Mexico Bulletin, Language Series, 5, No. 1: 19–48. That version is from a manuscript dated 1893 which he obtained from Próspero Baca of Bernalillo, New Mexico. The Spanish text of another version was published by Lea in *Literary Folklore*, 52–65, as obtained by Lea from a local resident in Las Vegas, New Mexico (*ibid.*, 10). A version of the Spanish text of *Caín y Abel* was published by Campa in his *Spanish Religious Folktheatre in the Spanish Southwest (First Cycle)*, 49–69.

## Chapter 14. Spanish Secular Folk Drama in New Mexico

1. A good example is Governor Vargas's speech to the Indians of the Hopi pueblos in 1692, eloquently described by the famous contemporary Mexican scholar Sigüenza y Góngora. As Vargas approached the pueblos, accompanied by fewer than one hundred men, he was met by a force of about eight hundred heavily armed warriors, who, having vowed to annihilate the Spaniards, attempted to provoke a battle. But Vargas turned imminent disaster into victory by boldly addressing the natives in the following manner:

'Ah Indians, ah you dogs of the worst breed that the sun warms! Do you think that my tolerance is owing to fear of your numbers? Pity is what I have had for you in not killing you, for by a single threat on my part, you would all perish! . . . [How is it that] you do not humbly cast yourselves upon the ground and revere the true Mother of Your God and mine, who, in the image which ennobles this banner, comes with forgiveness to offer you salvation! Kneel, kneel at once before I consume you all with the fire of my indignation!'

Continuing the description of the incident, Sigüenza writes: "The crash of a thunderbolt would have left them less awe-struck than these words and, having no answer to give, they laid down their arms and knelt on the ground to worship the Most Holy Mary in her image, striking their breasts many times." (Irving A. Leonard, ed., *The Mercurio Volante of Don Carlos de Sigüenza y Góngora: An Account of the First Expedition of Don Diego de Vargas into New Mexico in 1692* [Los Angeles: Quivira Society, III, 1932], 82. See also, JME, *First Expedition of Vargas into New Mexico, 1692*, 212–14.)

2. The *juegos de moros y cristianos* of various types are still performed not only in Spain, but also in many parts of Spanish America. The literature on the subject is very extensive.

See Carreras y Candi, *Folklore y costumbres de España*, 2: 389–94. The text of a New Mexican version of the play obtained by Lea is published in her *Literary Folklore*, 107–12. In this version a wooden cross instead of a statue of the Blessed Virgin is recovered from the Moors. Several incomplete manuscript versions have been found in New Mexico in the first half of the century.

3. Alfred Barnaby Thomas, ed. and trans., *Forgotten Frontiers: A Study of the Spanish Indian Policy of Don Juan Bautista de Anza, Governor of New Mexico, 1777–1787*, 57–63. Thomas's documents clarify various tentative historical conclusions contained in AME's *Los Comanches, A New-Mexican Spanish Heroic Play*, University of New Mexico Bulletin, Language Series, 1.

4. Anonymous Report, Santa Rosa, September 3, 1776, printed in *Historia de la Nueva México por el Capitán Gaspar de Villagrá*, 2, Appendix III, 90.

5. Thomas, *Forgotten Frontiers*, 66–71; 119–36.

6. AME, *Los Comanches*. An English translation of this copy of the play was made by Gilberto Espinosa and published in the *New Mexico Quarterly*, 1 (1931): 133–46, and subsequently as a chapter in his *Heroes, Hexes and Haunted Halls*, 27–42. Another version of the play was published more recently by Arthur L. Campa, *Los Comanches: A New Mexican Folk Drama*, University of New Mexico Bulletin, Language Series, 7, No. 1. The Campa version contains 715 verses. In the 1930s Campa found several other incomplete versions (*ibid.*, 15). Both of the published versions contain critical historical and linguistic notes and quote examples of popular New Mexican *versos* (popular poetic compositions on various subjects, usually of four or six lines) concerning the Comanches.

Campa, in his work just cited, pages 12–14, describes a peculiar religious drama known as *Los Comanches* and consisting entirely of singing and dancing. It has been presented at San Rafael, New Mexico, and occasionally in the vicinity of Albuquerque. The central story of the composition is as follows: the local residents of a New Mexican village have made preparations for a Nativity play, when the Comanches attack them by surprise and take the Christ Child as a hostage; the entire community sets out in pursuit, the Comanche chief is outwitted, and the hostage is recovered. The composition consists of a series of detached *coplas*, of which only a few refer to the subject matter of the play. For other folklore items on the Comanches, see also the Lorin W. Brown manuscripts cited in Brown, Briggs, and Weigle, *Hispanic Folklife in New Mexico*, 261; and Rubén Darío Sálaz, *Cosmic: The La Raza Sketch-Book*, 77–82.

7. See AME and JME, "The Texans—A New Mexican Spanish Folk Play of the Middle Nineteenth Century," *New Mexico Quarterly Review*, (Autumn, 1943: 299–308; and AME and JME, "Los Tejanos," *Hispania*, 27 (1944): 291–314. The former is an English translation of the play, with historical notes; the latter is a critical edition of the original Spanish text with extensive linguistic notes, including reference to the purposely grotesque Spanish used in the speech of the Pecos Indian.

8. On the events connected with the ill-fated Texan–Santa Fe Expedition of 1841, see especially *Letters and Notes on the Texan Santa Fe Expedition, 1841–1842*, by Thomas Falconer, one of the members of the expedition, edited with a bibliography and notes by F. W. Hodge (New York: Dunbar and Pine Bookshops Inc., 1930); George W. Kendall (another member of the expedition), *Narrative of an Expedition Across the Great Southwestern Prairies from Texas to Santa Fe*, 2 vols. (New York: Harper and Brothers, 1844); H. H. Bancroft, *History of Arizona and New Mexico* (San Francisco: The History Company, 1888), 320–26; George P. Garrison, ed., *Diplomatic Correspondence of the Republic of Texas* (Washington, D.C.: American Historical Association, Annual Report, 1907–1908), Part 2: 777–83; and W. C. Binkley, "New Mexico and the Texan–Santa Fe Expedition," *Southwestern Historical Quarterly*, 27 (1923): 85–107.

9. A list of those who composed the Texan expedition when it left Austin may be found in Charles J. Folsom, *Mexico in 1842* (New York, 1842), 249–50.

10. Bancroft, *History of Arizona and New Mexico*, 323. There is some doubt as to the exact day of McLeod's surrender.

11. Niceto de Zamacois, *Historia de Méjico*, 22 vols. in 25 (Barcelona and Mexico City: J. F. Párres y Compañía, 1878–1902), 12: 246–47. The reference here seems clearly to be to Lieutenant Colonel Juan Andrés de Archuleta.

12. Evidently this is the Italian Brignoli, one of the deserters. The other deserter was a Mexican guide named Carlos, who may be the Jorge Ramírez of the play, the Andalusian. Falconer, *Letters and Notes*, 38, 51, 130; Garrison, *Diplomatic Correspondence*, 778; Binkley, "Expedition," 103, note 68; Bancroft, *Arizona and New Mexico*, 322.

13. Kendall, *Narrative*, 1: 347; Binkley, "Expedition," 102; Garrison, *Diplomatic Correspondence*, 780; Bancroft, *Arizona and New Mexico*, 327.

14. Binkley, "Expedition," 107.

15. At Antón Chico the Texans were "duped" into surrendering through fear of the size and quality of the New Mexican army, based on the false reports of the Texan traitor Captain W. P. Lewis, and thus fell into an ignoble trap through the "falsehood" and "treachery" of the New Mexicans. The words in quotes are taken from Cooke's own account, which may be found in Garrison, *Diplomatic Correspondence*, 778–82.

16. Bancroft, *Arizona and New Mexico*, 322, note 22.

17. Carreras y Candi, *Folklore y costumbres de España*, 2: 413.

18. Josiah Gregg, *Commerce of the Prairies*, 2: 241–42, describes a rooster contest as performed on St. John's Day by New Mexican Spanish ranchers in the early nineteenth century. Charles F. Lummis presents a colorful description of the sport as performed by the Indians at Acoma pueblo on St. John's Day in *A New Mexican David, and Other Stories and Sketches about the Southwest*, 148–56.

19. On the Castilian *fiesta del gallo*, see AME, "Fiesta del Gallo in Barbadillo," *Modern Philology* (Chicago), 20 (1923): 425–34; and AME, "Spanish Folklore," in *Funk & Wagnalls Standard Dictionary of Folklore, Mythology and Legend*, 2: 1062.

## Appendix A. The Spanish Language of Northern New Mexico and Southern Colorado

1. The paragraphs that follow summarize briefly the basic regional characteristics of the Spanish language as spoken in northern New Mexico and southern Colorado. For a more detailed study of the subject, see the following works by AME: "Studies in New-Mexican Spanish, Part I: Phonology," *Revue de Dialectologie Romane*, 1, no. 2 (April–June, 1909): 157–239, 269–300; "Part II, Morphology," *ibid.*, 3, nos. 3–4 (July–December, 1911): 251 86; 4, no. 1 (January–April, 1912): 241–56, and 5, nos. 1–2 (January–June, 1913): 142–72; and "Part III, The English Elements," *ibid.*, 6, nos. 3–4 (1914): 241–317. Part I was published separately as *Studies in New-Mexican Spanish, Part I: Phonology* (Chicago: University of Chicago Press, 1909), and in the University of New Mexico Bulletin, Language Series, 1, No. 2. Parts I and II were completely revised and published in Spanish as follows: *Estudios sobre el español de Nuevo Méjico*, vol. 1, *Fonética*, ed. Amado Alonso and Angel Rosenblat, and an accompanying essay by Alonso: *Estudios sobre el español de Nuevo Méjico*, vol. 2, *Morfología*, ed. Angel Rosenblat. See also AME, "Speech Mixture in New Mexico: The Influence of the English Language on New Mexican Spanish," in *The Pacific Ocean in History*, ed. H. Morse Stephens and Herbert E. Bolton, 408–28.

See also AME Jr., "Observaciones sobre el léxico nuevomejicano," *Boletín de la Academia Norteamericana de la Lengua Española* (New York), Nos. 2–3 (1977–78): 9–19; Arthur L. Campa, "The Spanish Language in the Southwest," in *Humanidad: Essays in Honor of George I. Sánchez*, ed. Américo Paredes, Chicano Studies Center Publications, Monograph No. 6 (Los Angeles: University of California in Los Angeles, 1977), 19–40; and Anita C. Post,

*Southern Arizona Spanish Phonology*, University of Arizona, Humanities Bulletin, No. 1 (Tucson: 1934).

2. See AME, *Studies in New Mexican Spanish, Part I*, University of New Mexico Bulletin, Language Series, 1 (1909): 102–104, 119–23; Tomás Navarro Tomás and AME, *A Primer of Spanish Pronunciation* (New York: Benj. H. Sanborn & Co., 1927), 86; and Tomás Navarro Tomás, *Manual de pronunciación española*, 4th ed. (Madrid: Publicaciones de la Revista de Filología Española, 1932), 92, 106, 123–24.

3. AME, *Studies in New Mexican Spanish, Part I* (University of New Mexico edition, 1909), 121–23.

4. *Ibid.*, 87–130.

5. *Ibid.*, 127–28.

6. *Ibid.*, 80, 85–86, 88.

7. *Ibid.*, 90–94.

8. *Ibid.*, 96.

9. *Ibid.*, 72, 78–81, 85–87, 90, 106–107, 107–108, 109, 111–12, 113–14, 115, 116, 138, 140.

10. AME, "Studies in New Mexican Spanish, Part II," *Revue de Dialectologie Romane*, 3: 261; 4: 243–45; 5: 168–69.

11. *Ibid.*, 4: 241–42.

12. In AME, "Studies in New Mexican Spanish, Part III," *Revue de Dialectologie Romane*, 6: 362, such words are listed: nouns, 203; adjectives, 22; adverbs not used also as adjectives, 3; verbs, 38; exclamations, 28; personal and place names, 68. These lists certainly do not include all those used. There are probably as many as 500 regularly Hispanicized words of English source used in New Mexican Spanish.

13. AME, "Studies In New Mexican Spanish, Part III," *Revue de Dialectologie Romane*, 6: 245–55, 257–58, 261–63, 265–71, 275–77, 280, 285, 287–88, 289, 291, 293.

14. *Ibid.*, 295–300.

15. See Harold W. Bentley, *A Dictionary of Spanish Terms in English, with Special Reference to the Spanish Southwest*; AME, "Palabras españolas e inglesas," *Hispania*, 5 (October, 1922): 219–28, especially 221; and Frank W. Blackmar, *Spanish Institutions of the Southwest*, 271–77.


Appendix B. **Spanish Tradition Among the Pueblo Indians**

1. This essay, written in the late 1930s, is on linguistic, religious, and folklore influences. Some of the same material was used in an article by AME under the same title in *Estudios Hispánicos: Homenaje a Archer M. Huntington*, 131–41. Recent social anthropologists, notably Alfonso Ortiz, Edward P. Dozier, and Frank Eggan, have greatly increased our knowledge of Pueblo Indian thought and society.

2. Colonial records for the late seventeenth century contain letters written in Spanish to local Spanish authorities by Pueblo Indian leaders. JME, *Crusaders of the Rio Grande*, 182–83, 245; and JME, *First Expedition of Vargas into New Mexico, 1692*, 218.

3. In 1960, the editor (JME), witnessed an address, in traditional New Mexican Spanish, by the elderly Indian governor of San Ildefonso, an eloquent speaker, before a group of Latin American educators who visited the pueblo.

4. See AME, "Miscellaneous Materials from the Pueblo Indians of New Mexico," *Philological Quarterly*, 21 (1942): 125.

5. Elsie Clews Parsons, "All Souls Day at Zuñi, Acoma, and Laguna," *Journal of American Folk-Lore*, 30 (1917): 495–96; comment by AME, *ibid.*, 31 (1918): 550–52.

6. Other examples appear in seventeenth-century New Mexican documents.

7. For a complete study of all the forms recorded from five Keres and one Hopi

pueblo, see AME, "El desarrollo de la palabra 'Castilla' en la lengua de los indios Queres de Nuevo Méjico," *Revista de filología española*, 19 (1932): 261—77; AME, "La palabra *Castilla* en la lengua de los indios hopis de Arizona," *Revista de filología española*, 22 (1935): 298—300.

8. Benavides, *Benavides' Memorial of 1630*, 65—66.

9. Hodge, Hammond, and Rey, *Fray Alonso de Benavides' Revised Memorial of 1634*, 99—100.

10. On a number of occasions the Pueblo Indians have followed the same Catholic religious ceremonies and practices as their New Mexican Spanish neighbors for marriages, wakes or *velorios*, burial rites, and the like—in some cases following them with a separate Indian religious ritual. See Alfonso Ortiz, *The Tewa World: Space, Time, Being and Becoming in a Pueblo Society*, 45—47, 50—56, with specific reference to the Tewa pueblo of San Juan.

11. Elsie Clews Parsons, "Pueblo Indian Folk-Tales, probably of Spanish Provenience," *Journal of American Folk-Lore*, 31 (1918): 216—25; Elsie Clews Parsons and Franz Boas, "Spanish Tales from Laguna and Zuñi, New Mexico," *ibid.*, 33 (1920): 47—72; Franz Boas, "Tales of Spanish Provenience from Zuñi," *ibid.*, 34 (1922): 62—98; Franz Boas, "Romance Folklore among American Indians," *Romanic Review*, 16 (1925): 199—207, reprinted in Franz Boas, *Race, Language, and Culture*, 518—19, 524. See also Elsie Clews Parsons, *Pueblo Indian Religion*, 2: 1110—12, and AME, "Pueblo Indian Folktales," *Journal of American Folk-Lore*, 49 (1936): 69—133.

12. See AME, "Pueblo Indian Folk Tales" (1936), 103—106, 119, 127—29.

13. See AME, "Notes on the Origins and History of the Tar Baby Story," *Journal of American Folk-Lore*, 43 (1930), 129—209; AME, "New Mexican Versions of the Tar Baby Story," *New Mexico Quarterly*, 1 (1931): 85—104, AME, "Another New Mexican Version of the Tar Baby Story," 3 (1933): 31—36; and AME, *Cuentos* (1946—47), 2: 223.

14. Among Spanish New Mexicans there are many similar stories. See also the articles by Elsie Clews Parsons, "Witchcraft among the Pueblos: Indian or Spanish?" *Man* (London), 27, Nos. 70 and 80 (1927); Elsie Clews Parsons, *Tewa Tales*, Memoirs of the American Folklore Society, 19, Introduction, 1—8; and Marc Simmons, *Witchcraft in the Southwest: Spanish and Indian Supernaturalism on the Rio Grande*.

15. The Indian version was published in AME, "Miscellaneous Materials from the Pueblo Indians of New Mexico" (1942), 124. The Spanish version here cited is given by Francisco Rodríguez Marín, *Cantos populares españoles*, 1, 8, No. 38. The California version was published by AME in "Folklore de California," *Miscelánea Filológica Dedicada a D. Antonio M. Alcover*, 118, No. 18.

16. For the peninsular Spanish version see Machado y Alvarez, *Biblioteca de las tradiciones populares españolas*, 10: 85. The Pueblo Indian versions were published by AME, "Miscellaneous Materials from the Pueblo Indians of New Mexico" (1942), 124; No. 12 was from San Juan and No. 13 from Taos.

17. AME, "Los 'Agüelos' de Nuevo Méjico," *Boletín de la Biblioteca Menéndez y Pelayo*, 21 (1945): 71—78. See also Ortiz, *The Tewa World*, 142, 143, 158, 161—62.

18. See AME, "Romancero nuevomejicano" (1915), 446—560; AME, "Traditional Spanish Ballads in New Mexico," *Hispania*, 15 (1932): 89—102; AME, *Romancero de Nuevo Méjico* (1953).

19. These nine versions from the Pueblo Indians are the following: four versions of the Passion ballad *Por el rastro de la sangre*, of which one of the many New Mexican Spanish versions was given, with English translation, in chapter 6; two versions of *En el Monte de Santa Lucía* (see chapter 6, number 5); one brief version of *Jesucristo se ha perdido*; and one novelesque ballad, a version of the popular *Delgadina*. See AME, "Romances españoles tradicionales que cantan y relatan los indios de los pueblos de Nuevo Méjico," *Boletín de la Biblioteca Menéndez y Pelayo*, 14 (1932): 98—109; Barbara Freire Marreco and AME, "New Mexican Spanish Folk-Lore," *Journal of American Folk-Lore*, 29 (1916): 536—46.

20. See Elsie Clews Parsons, "Spanish Elements in the Kachina Cult of the Pueblos," in *Proceedings of the Twenty-Third International Congress of Americanists*, New York, 1928, 582–603, and Parsons, *Pueblo Indian Religion*, 2: 1068–80.

21. The word *cacique*, of Caribbean origin, is of common use in Spanish and is often used, in the same form, even in some of the pueblos. In Taos the term used is *caciqui ina*. In most of the pueblos, however, native Indian words are used.

22. Parsons, *Pueblo Indian Religion*, 1: 146, last note. See also, Elsie Clews Parsons, *The Social Organization of the Tewa of New Mexico*, Memoirs of the American Anthropological Association, No. 36, 278–83. Ortiz, *The Tewa World* (see especially 61–77, 156–58), discusses the political organization of the Tewa pueblos north of Santa Fe, using San Juan pueblo as his model. He states that "Spanish and Tewa political institutions and concepts are now merged to such a degree that no one has yet been able to disentangle them in any analytically satisfactory way."

# Bibliography

## The Writings of Aurelio M. Espinosa on Spanish and Spanish-American Folklore and Dialectology

### 1907

*Los Comanches, A New-Mexican Spanish Heroic Play*, University of New Mexico Bulletin, Language Series, 1. Albuquerque, 1907.

### 1909–14

"Studies in New-Mexican Spanish, Part I: Phonology," *Revue de Dialectologie Romane*, 1 (1909): 157–239, 269–300. Also published by the University of Chicago Press, 1909; and University of New Mexico Bulletin, Language Series, 1 (1909). See listings under 1930 for later edition.

"Studies in New-Mexican Spanish, Part II: Morphology," *Revue de Dialectologie Romane*, 3 (1911): 251–86; 4 (1912): 241–56; 5 (1913): 142–72. See listings under 1946 for later edition.

"Studies in New-Mexican Spanish, Part III: The English Elements," *Revue de Dialectologie Romane*, 6 (1914): 241–317.

### 1910

Review of Rodolfo Lenz, *Los elementos indios del castellano de Chile* (Santiago, 1904–10), in *Revue de Dialectologie Romane*, 2 (1910): 420–24.

### 1910–16

"New Mexican Spanish Folklore: Part I, Myths; Part II, Superstitions and Beliefs," *Journal of American Folk-lore*, 23 (1910): 395–418.

"New Mexican Spanish Folklore: Part III, Folktales," *ibid.*, 24 (1911): 397–444.

"New Mexican Spanish Folklore: Part IV, Proverbs; Part V, Popular Comparisons," *ibid.*, 26 (1913): 97–122.

"New Mexican Spanish Folklore: Part VI, Los Trovos del Viejo Vilmas; Part VII, More Folk-Tales; Part VIII, Short Folk-Tales and Anecdotes," *ibid.*, 27 (1914): 105–47.

"New Mexican Spanish Folklore: Part VI, Addenda," *ibid.*, 28 (1915): 204–206.

"New Mexican Spanish Folklore: Part IX, Riddles," *ibid.*, 28 (1915): 319–52.

"New Mexican Spanish Folklore: Part X, Children's Games; Part XI, Nursery Rhymes and Children's Songs," *ibid.*, 29 (1916): 505–35.

273

## 1911

The Spanish Language in New Mexico and Southern Colorado. Historical Society of New Mexico Publication No. 16. Santa Fe: New Mexican Printing Company, 1911.

"New Mexican Spanish Folklore," American Philological Association, Transactions and Proceedings, 40 (1911): lxiii–lxv.

"La poesía popular de Nuevo Méjico," Revista Positiva (Mexico City), 2, no. 134 (1911): 350–52.

"Penitentes, Los Hermanos (The Penitent Brothers)." In The Catholic Encyclopedia 11: 635–36. New York: The Encyclopedia Press, 1911.

## 1912

"Cuentitos populares nuevo-mejicanos y su transcripción fonética," Bulletin de Dialectologie Romane, 4 (1912): 97–115.

## 1913

"Nombres de bautismo nuevomejicanos: Algunas observaciones sobre su desarrollo fonético," Revue de Dialectologie Romane, 5 (1913): 356–73.

Review of Julio Vicuña Cifuentes, Romances populares y vulgares recogidos de la tradición oral chilena (Santiago, 1912), Bulletin de Dialectologie Romane, 5 (1913): 49–55.

## 1914

Editor of J. Alden Mason, "Folktales of the Tepecanos," Journal of American Folk-Lore, 27 (1914): 148–210.

"Comparative Notes on New Mexican and Mexican Spanish Folktales," Journal of American Folk-Lore, 27 (1914): 211–31.

## 1915

"Romancero nuevomejicano," Revue Hispanique, 33 (1915): 446–560.

Paul Radin and Aurelio M. Espinosa, "Folk-Tales from Oaxaca," Journal of American Folk-Lore, 28 (1915): 390–408.

## 1916

J. Alden Mason and Aurelio M. Espinosa, "Porto Rican Folklore, Riddles," Journal of American Folk-Lore, 29 (1916): 423–504.

"Notes on Barbara Freire Marreco, 'New Mexican Spanish Folk-Lore,'" Journal of American Folk-Lore, 29 (1916): 536–46.

"Traditional Ballads from Andalucía." In Flügel Memorial Volume, pp. 92–107. Stanford, Calif.: Stanford University Press, 1916.

## 1917

"Speech Mixture in New Mexico." In The Pacific Ocean in History, pp. 408–28. Ed.

H. Morse Stephens and Herbert E. Bolton. New York: Macmillan, 1917.

"Romancero nuevomejicano, Addenda," *Revue Hispanique*, 40 (1917): 215–27.

"Nota adicional al Romancero nuevomejicano," *Revue Hispanique*, 41 (1917): 678–80.

Paul Radin and Aurelio M. Espinosa, *El Folk-Lore de Oaxaca*. New York: Escuela Internacional de Arqueología y Etnología Americana and the Hispanic Society of America, G. E. Stechert, 1917.


### 1918

J. Alden Mason and Aurelio M. Espinosa, "Porto-Rican Folklore: Décimas, Christmas Carols, Nursery Rhymes and Other Songs," *Journal of American Folk-Lore*, 31 (1918): 289–450.

"All Souls' Day at Zuñi, Acoma and Laguna," *Journal of American Folk-Lore*, 31 (1918): 550–52.

"Romances de Puerto Rico," *Revue Hispanique*, 42 (1918): 309–64.

"California Spanish Folklore: Circular Letter," Stanford University, May, 1918.


### 1921

"A Folklore Expedition to Spain," *Journal of American Folk-Lore*, 34 (1921): 127–42.

"Sobre la Leyenda de los Infantes de Lara," *Romanic Review*, 12 (1921): 135–45.


### 1921–26

"Viajes por España," published in ten parts in *Hispania*, 4 (1921): 15–17, 56–60, 165–67, 223–26; 5 (1922): 25–28, 83–86, 149–56, 365–68; 7 (1924): 187–90; 9 (1926): 345–49.


### 1922

"Palabras españolas e inglesas," *Hispania*, 5 (1922): 219–28.


### 1922–27

J. Alden Mason and Aurelio M. Espinosa, "Porto-Rican Folklore: Folktales, Part I," *Journal of American Folk-Lore*, 35 (1922): 1–61; Part I, continued, 37 (1924): 247–344; Part II, 38 (1925): 507–618; Part III, 39 (1926): 225–304; Part IV, 39 (1926): 304–69; Part IV, continued, 40 (1927): 313–414.


### 1923

"Los cuentos populares de España," *Boletín de la Biblioteca Meńndez y Pelayo*, 5 (1923): 39–61.

"Folklore from Spain," *Modern Philology*, 20 (1923): 425–34.

"Fiesta de Gallo in Barbadillo," *Modern Philology*, 20 (1923): 425–34.

1923–26

*Cuentos populares españoles*, 3 vols. Stanford, Calif.: Stanford University Press, 1923–26.

1924

"Los romances tradicionales en California." In *Homenaje a Menéndez Pidal*, 1: 299–313. 3 vols. Madrid: Imprenta de los Sucesores de Hernando, 1924.

1925

"Spanish Folk-Lore in the United States," *Modern Language Bulletin*, 10 (1925): 24–25.

"Syllabic Consonants in New Mexican Spanish," *Language*, 1 (1925): 109–18.

*Cuentos, Romances, y Cantares*. Boston: Allyn and Bacon, 1925.

1926

"Spanish Folk-Lore in New Mexico," *New Mexico Historical Review*, 1 (1926): 135–55.

Review of Fritz Krüger, *Die Gegenstandskultur Sanabrias und seiner Nachbargebiete* (Hamburg, 1925), *Hispania*, 9 (1926): 68.

1927

Review of James H. English, *The Alternation of H and F in Spanish* (New York: Instituto de las Españas, 1926), *Hispania*, 10 (1927): 208.

Review of R. Grossmann, *Das auslandliche Sprachgut im Spanischen des Rio de la Plata* (Hamburg, 1926), *Language*, 3 (1927): 20–25.

1927–28

"The Language of the cuentos populares españoles," *Language*, 3 (1927): 188–98; 4 (1928): 18–27, 111–19.

1928

"La ciencia del folklore," *Archivos del folklore cubano*, 3 (1928); reprint, Cultural S.A. Habana, 1929, 1–16.

1929

"El Romancero," *Hispania*, 12 (1929): 1–32.

"El folklore español en América," *La Prensa*, New York, February, 1929.

"La transmisión de los cuentos populares," *Archivos del folklore cubano*, 4 (1929): 39–52; reprint, Cultural S.A. Habana, 1929, 1–16.

"European Versions of the Tar-Baby Stories, *Folk-Lore*, 40 (1929): 217–27.

"Una version española del romance *Las glorias de Teresa*," *Archivos del folklore cubano*, 4 (1929): 153–56.

## 1930

"Folklore de California." In *Miscelánea filológica dedicada a D. Antonio M. Alcover*, pp. 111–31. Palma, Mallorca: Círculo de Estudios Palma, Mallorca, 1930.

"Apuntaciones para un diccionario de nuevomejicanismos: Algunas formas verbales raras, curiosas." In *Estudios Eruditos in Memoriam de Adolfo Bonilla y San Martín*, 2: 615–25. Madrid, 1930.

"Notes on the Origin and History of the Tar-Baby Story," *Journal of American Folk-Lore*, 43 (1930): 129–209.

"A Third European Version of the Tar-Baby Story," *Journal of American Folk-Lore*, 43 (1930): 329–31.

"El folklore en España," *Revista bimestre cubana* (Havana), 25 (1930): 449–62.

"Use of the Conditional for the Subjunctive in Castilian Popular Speech," *Modern Philology*, 27 (1930): 445–49.

*Estudios sobre el español de Nuevo Méjico*, vol. 1, *Fonética*, ed. Amado Alonso and Angel Rosenblat. Buenos Aires: Biblioteca de Dialectología Hispanoamericana, Instituto de Filología, Universidad de Buenos Aires, 1930.

"Origen oriental y desarrollo histórico del cuento de las doce palabras retorneadas," *Revista de filología española* (Madrid), 17 (1930): 390–413.

"El tema de Roncesvalles y de Bernardo del Carpio en la poesía de Cuba," *Archivos del folklore cubano*, 5 (1930): 193–98.

## 1931

"Sobre los orígenes del cuento del muñeco de brea," *Boletín de la Biblioteca Menéndez y Pelayo*, Número extraordinario en homenaje a don Miguel Artigas, 1 (1931): 296–318.

*El romancero español*. Biblioteca Española de Divulgación Científica, 9. Madrid, 1931. Originally published in *Hispania* in 1929; see above.

"New Mexican Versions of the Tar-Baby Story," *New Mexico Quarterly*, 1 (1931): 85–104.

## 1932

"Traditional Spanish Ballads in New Mexico," *Hispania*, 15 (1932): 89–102.

"Romances españoles tradicionales que cantan y relatan los indios de los pueblos de Nuevo Méjico," *Boletín de la Biblioteca Menéndez y Pelayo*, 14 (1932): 98–109.

"El desarrollo de la palabra 'Castilla' en la lengua de los indios Queres de Nuevo Méjico," *Revista de filología española*, 19 (1932): 261–77.

Review of E. F. Tiscornia, *La lengua de "Martin Fierro"* (Buenos Aires, 1930), *Language*, 8 (1932): 57–59.

## 1933

"Another New Mexico Version of the Tar-Baby Story," *New Mexico Quarterly*, 3 (1933): 31–36.

"European Versions of the Tar-Baby Story," *Journal of American Folk-Lore*, 46 (1933): 91–92.

"La leyenda de Don Juan y las Doce palabras retorneadas," *Boletín de la Biblioteca Menéndez y Pelayo*, 13 (1933): 216–19.

## 1934

"Spanish Tradition in New Mexico," *University of New Mexico Bulletin*, 47 (1934): 26–39.

"El desarrollo fonético de la palabra 'todo' en la frase 'con todo y + substantivo' en el español de Nuevo Méjico," *Investigaciones lingüísticas* (Mexico), 2 (1934): 195–99.

"La clasificación de los cuentos populares, Un capítulo de metodología folklórica," *Boletín de la Academia Española*, 21 (1934): 175–208.

"Las fuentes orientales del cuento de la Matrona de Efeso," *Boletín de la Biblioteca Menéndez y Pelayo*, 16 (1934): 489–502.

## 1935

"New Mexican Spanish *Coplas Populares*," *Hispania*, 18 (1935): 135–50.

"La palabra Castilla en la lengua de los indios hopis de Arizona," *Revista de filología española*, 22 (1935): 298–300.

"Folklore in European Literature, A Syllabus for Course E180 in the Department of Romanic Languages, Stanford University." Stanford University, 1935.

## 1936

"Pueblo Indian Folk Tales," *Journal of American Folk-Lore*, 49 (1936): 69–133.

"Hispanic Versions of the Tale of the Corpse Many Times 'Killed,'" *Journal of American Folk-Lore*, 49 (1936): 181–93.

"El tema de la Princesa Orgullosa en la tradición hispánica," *Homenatge a Antoni Rubió i Lluch* (Barcelona, 1936), 3: 621–29.

## 1937

*España en Nuevo Méjico—Lecturas Elementales Sobre la Historia de Nuevo Méjico y su Tradición Española*. New York: Allyn and Bacon, 1937.

## 1938

"Otro romance español tradicional," *Revista Bimestral de la Universidad de los Andes* (Mérida, Venezuela), 2 (1938): 121–27.

"More Notes on the Origin and History of the Tar-Baby Story," *Folk-Lore*, 49 (1938): 168–81.

*Conchita Argüello: Historia y Novela Californiana*. New York: The Macmillan Company, 1938.

Review of Alice Corbin Henderson, *Brothers of Light: The Penitentes of the Southwest*

(New York: Harcourt, Brace and Co., 1927), *Journal of American Folk-Lore*, 51 (1938): 445–49.

### 1940
"Spanish Folktales from California," *Hispania*, 23 (1940): 121–44.

### 1941
"An Extraordinary Example of Spanish Ballad Tradition in New Mexico." In *Stanford Studies in Language and Literature*, pp. 28–34. Stanford, Calif.: Stanford University Press, 1941.
"Sobre la importancia del romancero," *Revista cubana*, 15 (1941): 214–19.

### 1942
"Miscellaneous Materials from the Pueblo Indians of New Mexico," *Philological Quarterly*, 21 (1942): 121–27.

### 1943
"A New Classification of the Fundamental Elements of the Tar-Baby Story on the Basis of Two Hundred and Sixty-Seven Versions," *Journal of American Folklore*, 56 (1943): 31–37.
With J. Manuel Espinosa: "The Texans—A New Mexican Spanish Folk Play of the Middle Nineteenth Century," *New Mexico Quarterly Review*, Autumn, 1943: 299–308.

### 1944
"Peninsular Spanish Versions of the Tar-Baby Story," *Journal of American Folklore*, 57 (1944): 210–11.
With J. Manuel Espinosa, "Los Tejanos," *Hispania*, 27 (1944): 291–314.
"California Spanish Folklore: Riddles," *California Folklore Quarterly*, 3 (1944): 293–98.
Review of *Anuario de la Sociedad Folklórica de México*, Vols. 1–3 (1936–42), in *California Folklore Quarterly*, 3 (1944): 337–38.

### 1945
"Los 'Agüelos' de Nuevo Méjico," *Boletín de la Biblioteca Menéndez y Pelayo*, 21 (1945): 71–78.

### 1946
*Estudios sobre el español de Nuevo Méjico*, vol. 2, *Morfología*. Ed. Angel Rosenblat. Buenos Aires: Biblioteca de Dialectología Hispanoamericana, Instituto de Filología, Universidad de Buenos Aires, 1946.
*Cuentos populares de España*. Buenos Aires and Mexico City: Espasa-Calpe Argentina, 1946.

1946–47
*Cuentos populares españoles, recogidos de la tradición oral de España.* 3 vols. Madrid: Consejo Superior de Investigaciones Científicas, 1946–47.

1949–50
"Spanish Ballad." In *Funk & Wagnalls Standard Dictionary of Folklore, Mythology, and Legend*, pp. 1058–61. New York: Funk & Wagnalls, 1949, 1950.
"Spanish Folklore," *ibid.*, pp. 1061–73.

1951
"Spanish and Spanish-American Folk Tales," *Journal of American Folklore*, 64 (1951): 151–62.
"Las versiones hispánicas peninsulares del cuento del Muñeco de Brea." In *Estudios dedicados a Menéndez Pidal*, 2: 357–81. Madrid: Consejo Superior de Investigaciones Científicas, 1951.

1952
"Spanish Tradition Among the Pueblo Indians." In *Estudios Hispánicos: Homenaje a Archer M. Huntington*, pp. 131–41. Wellesley, Mass., 1952.
"Western Hemisphere Versions of Aarne-Thompson 301," *Journal of American Folklore*, 65 (1952): 187.

1953
*Romancero de Nuevo Méjico.* Madrid: Revista de Filología Española–Anejo LVIII, 1953.

1954
"Folklore infantil de Nuevo Méjico," *Revista de dialectología y tradiciones populares*, 10 (1954): 1–49.

1955
"El endecasílabo de arte mayor en la poesía popular de Nuevo Méjico," *Revista de dialectología y tradiciones populares*, 11 (1955): 442–49.

## Selective Bibliography of Other Works Relating to the Study of Hispanic and Hispanic-American Folk Literature

Aarne, Antti. *Verzeichnis der Märchentypen.* Folklore Fellows Communications [FFC] No. 3. Helsingfors, 1910.

————, and Stith Thompson. *The Types of the Folktale: A Classification and Bibliography.* Trans. and enlarged by Stith Thompson. FFC No. 74. Helsinki, 1928; 2d rev. FFC No. 184. Helsinki: Suomalainen Tiedeakatemia, 1961.

Adams, Eleanor B. "Two Colonial New Mexico Libraries, 1704, 1776," *New Mexico Historical Review,* 20 (1944), 135–67.

————, and France V. Scholes. "Books in New Mexico, 1598–1680," *New Mexico Historical Review,* 18 (1942): 1–45, reprint.

Alcover, Antonio María. *Aplec de rondaies mallorquines.* 14 vols. Palma de Mallorca: Imprenta "Mossèn Alcover," 1936.

Almeida Garrett, João Baptista de. *Romanceiro.* Lisbon: Imprenta Nacional, 1851.

Alonso Cortés, Narciso. *Romances populares de Castilla.* Valladolid: Estab. Tip. de E. Sáenz, 1906.

————. "Romances tradicionales," *Revue Hispanique,* 50 (1920): 190–268.

*Anales de la Universidad de Chile.* Santiago, 1843– .

Anderson, Walter. *Der Schwank vom alten Hildebrand, eine vergleichinde studie.* Dorpat: K. Mattiesens buchdruckerei, 1930.

————. *Kaiser und abt, die geschichte einer schwanks.* FFC No. 42. Helsinki, 1923.

Andrade, Manuel J. *Folklore from the Dominican Republic.* Memoirs of the American Folklore Society, 23. New York: The American Folklore Society, G. E. Stechert and Co., 1930.

*Antología folklórica argentina.* Buenos Aires, 1940.

*Anuario de la Sociedad Folklórica de México.* Mexico City, 1936– .

*Archivo per lo studio delle tradizioni popolari.* 24 vols. Palermo-Torino, 1893–1909.

*Archivos del folklore cubano.* Havana, 1924–30.

Austin, Mary. "A Drama Played on Horseback," *The Mentor,* 16 (1928): 38–39.

————. "Folk Plays of the Southwest," *Theatre Arts Monthly,* 17 (1933): 599–610.

————. "Native Drama in Our Southwest," *The Nation,* 124 (1927): 437–40.

————. "New Mexico Folk Poetry," *El Palacio,* 7 (1919): 146–50.

————. "*Rimas infantiles* of New Mexico," *Southwest Review,* 16 (1930): 60–64.

————. "Sources of Poetic Influence in the Southwest," *Poetry,* 43 (1933): 152–63.

————. "Spanish Manuscripts in the Southwest," *Southwest Review*, 19 (1934): 402–409.

————, Adelina Otero-Warren, and Aurora Lucero. "New Mexico Folk Song," *El Palacio*, 7 (1919): 152–53, 156–59.

Azevedo, Alvaro Rodrígues de. *Romanceiro do archipelago da Madeira*. Funchal: Voz do Povo, 1880.

Bancroft, Hubert Howe. *History of Arizona and New Mexico, 1530–1888*. San Francisco: The History Company, Publishers, 1889.

Barbeau, C. Marius. "The Field of European Folk-Lore in America," *Journal of American Folk-Lore*, 32 (1919): 185–97.

Barker, Mrs. Ruth Laughlin, "New Mexico Witch Tales." In *Tone the Bell Easy*, pp. 62–70. Ed. J. Frank Dobie. Austin: Texas Folklore Society Publications, 1932.

Bayo, Ciro. *Romancerillo del Plata*. Madrid: V. Suárez, 1913.

Beck, Warren A. "The Cultural Contributions of the Penitentes." Paper read at the Western History Association, October, 1968. Reprinted in Richard N. Ellis, *New Mexico Past and Present: A Historical Reader*, pp. 171–83. Albuquerque: University of New Mexico Press, 1971.

[Benavides, O.F.M., Fray Alonso de]. *Benavides' Memorial of 1630*. Trans. Peter P. Forrestal, C.S.C.; ed. Cyprian C. Lynch, O.F.M. Washington, D.C.: Academy of American Franciscan History, 1954.

Benedict, Ruth. *Tales of the Cochiti Indians*. Bulletin of the Bureau of American Ethnology, 98. New York, 1931.

Benfey, Theodor. *Panchatantra*. 2 vols. Leipzig: F. A. Brockhaus, 1859.

Bénichou, Paul. *Romanceiro judeo-español de Marruecos*. Madrid: Editorial Castalia, 1968.

Bentley, Harold W. *A Dictionary of Spanish Terms in English, with Special Reference to the American Southwest*. New York: Columbia University Press, 1932; reprint, Octagon Books, 1973.

Beutler, Gisela. *Studien zum spanischen Romancero in Kolombien in seiner schriftlichen und mündlichen Überlieferung von der Zeit der Eroberung bis zur Gegenwart*. Heidelberg: Carl Winter Universitatsverlag, 1969. Spanish edition, *Estudios sobre el romancero español en Colombia*. Publicaciones del Instituto Caro y Cuervo, No. 43. Bogota, 1977.

*Biblioteca de autores españoles*. 71 vols. Madrid, 1846–80.

Blackmar, Frank W. *Spanish Institutions of the Southwest*. Baltimore: Johns Hopkins University Press, 1891.

Boas, Franz. "Notes on Mexican Folk-Lore," *Journal of American Folk-Lore*, 25 (1912): 204–60.

————. "Romance Folklore among American Indians." *Romanic Review*, 16 (1925): 199–207. Reprinted in *Race, Language, and Culture*. New York: The Free Press, 1940.

————. "Tales of Spanish Provenience from Zuñi," *Journal of American Folk-Lore*, 35 (1922): 62–98.

Boggs, Edna (Garrido). *Versiones dominicanas de romances españoles*. Ciudad Trujillo: Pol Hermanos, 1946.

Boggs, Ralph Steele. *Bibliografía del folklore mexicano*. Mexico City: Instituto Pan Americano de Geografía e Historia, 1939.

―――. *Bibliography of Latin American Folklore*. New York: H. W. Wilson Company, 1940; reprint, Detroit: B. Ethridge-Brooks, 1971.

―――. *Index of Spanish Folktales*. FFC No. 90. Helsinki, 1930.

―――. "Spanish Folklore from Tampa, Florida: I. Background; II. Riddles," *Southern Folklore Quarterly*, 1 (1937): 1–12; "V. Folktales," 2 (1938): 87–106.

―――. "Spanish Folklore in America," *University of Miami Hispanic American Studies*, 1 (1939): 121–65.

*Boletín de la Real Academia Española*. Madrid, 1914– .

Bolte, Johannes, and George Polívka. *Anmerkungen zu den Kinder- und Hausmärchen der Brüder Grimm*. 5 vols. Leipzig: Dietrich'sche Verlagsbuchhandlung, 1913–32.

Bolton, Herbert E. "Defensive Spanish Expansion and the Significance of the Borderlands." In *Wider Horizons of American History*. New York: D. Appleton-Century Company, 1939.

Bourke, John G. "Notes on the Language and Folk-Usage of the Rio Grande Valley (With Especial Regard to Survivals of Arabic Custom)," *Journal of American Folk-Lore*, 9 (1896): 81–116.

―――. "Popular Medicine, Customs, and Superstitions of the Rio Grande," *Journal of American Folk-Lore*, 7 (1894): 119–46.

―――. "The Miracle Play of the Rio Grande," *Journal of American Folk-Lore*, 6 (1893): 88–95.

Boyd, Elizabeth. *Popular Arts of Spanish New Mexico*. Albuquerque: University of New Mexico Press, 1974.

Braga, Theophilo. *Contos tradicionaes do povo portuguez*. 1st ed. Lisbon, 1883; 2d ed. Lisbon: J. Rodriguez & Cía., 1914.

―――. *Romanceiro geral portuguez*. 3 vols. 2d ed. Ed. Manuel Gómez, Lisbon: J. A. Rodriguez & Cía., 1906–1909.

Briz, Francisco Pelayo. *Cansons de la terra: Cantos populars catalans*. 5 vols. Barcelona: E. Ferrando Roca, 1866–77.

Brown, Lorin W.; Charles L. Briggs; and Marta Weigle. *Hispano Folklife of New Mexico*. Albuquerque: University of New Mexico Press, 1978.

*Bulletin de Dialectologie Romane*. 6 vols. Brussels and Hamburg, 1909–14.

Cabal, Constantino. *Contribución al diccionario folklórico de Asturias*. Oviedo: Instituto de Estudios Asturianos, Gráficos Summa, 1951– .

―――. *Del folk-lore de Asturias*. Madrid: Voluntad, 1923.

―――. *Los cuentos tradicionales asturianos*. Madrid: Voluntad, 1924.

Caballero, Fernán. *Cuentos, oraciones, adivinas y refranes populares e infantiles*. Leipzig: F. A. Brockhaus, 1878; 2d ed., Madrid: A. Jubera, 1880.

―――. *Cuentos y poesías populares andaluces*. Leipzig: F. A. Brockhaus, 1861, 1874.

Cadilla de Martínez, María. *Juegos y canciones infantiles de Puerto Rico*. San Juan: Baldrich, 1940.

————. *La poesía popular en Puerto Rico*. Madrid: Universidad de Madrid, 1933.

————. *Raíces de la Tierra: Colección de cuentos populares y tradiciones*. Arecibo: Tipografía Hernández, 1941.

Campa, Arthur L. *A Bibliography of Spanish Folk-Lore in New Mexico*, University of New Mexico Bulletin, Modern Language Series, 2. Albuquerque: University of New Mexico Press, 1930.

————. "El origen y la naturaleza del drama folklórico," *Folklore Americas*, 20 (1960): 13–48.

————. *Hispanic Culture in the Southwest*. Norman: University of Oklahoma Press, 1979.

————. *Los Comanches: A New Mexican Folk Drama*. University of New Mexico Bulletin, Language Series, 7, No. 1. Albuquerque: University of New Mexico Press, 1942.

————. "Religious Spanish Folk Drama in New Mexico," *New Mexico Quarterly*, 2 (1932): 3–13.

————. *Sayings and Riddles in New Mexico*. University of New Mexico Bulletin, Language Series, 6, No. 2. Albuquerque: University of New Mexico Press, 1937.

————. *Spanish Folk-Poetry in New Mexico*. Albuquerque: University of New Mexico Press, 1946.

————. *Spanish Religious Folk Theatre in the Southwest (First Cycle)*. University of New Mexico Bulletin, Language Series, 5, No. 1. Albuquerque: University of New Mexico Press, 1934.

————. *Spanish Religious Folk Theatre in the Southwest (Second Cycle)*. University of New Mexico Bulletin, Language Series, 5, No. 2. Albuquerque: University of New Mexico Press, 1934.

————. "Spanish Traditional Tales in the Southwest," *Western Folklore*, 6 (1947): 322–34.

————. "The New Mexican Spanish Folktheater," *Southern Folklore Quarterly*, 5 (1941): 127–31.

————. *The Spanish Folksong in the Southwest*. University of New Mexico Bulletin, Language Series, 4, No. 1. Albuquerque: University of New Mexico Press, 1933.

Campos, Rubén M. *El folklore literario de Méjico*. Mexico City: Publicaciones de la Secretaría de Educación Pública, Talleres Gráficos de la Nación, 1929.

Carreras y Candi, Francisco, ed. *Folklore y costumbres de España*. 3 vols. Barcelona: A. Martín, 1931–44.

Carrizo, Jesús María. *Folklore argentino: Refranes, frases, y modismos; creencias y supersticiones de la region N.O.* Buenos Aires: Ediciones Theoria, 1971.

Carrizo, Juan Alfonso. *Antiguos cantos populares argentinos*. Buenos Aires: Impresores Silla Hermanos, 1926.

————. *Cancionero popular de Jujuy.* Tucumán: M. Violetto, 1934.

————. *Cancionero popular de la Rioja.* Buenos Aires: A. Baiocco y Cía., 1942.

————. *Cancionero popular de Salta.* Buenos Aires: A. Baiocco y Cía., 1933.

————. *Cancionero popular de Tucumán.* 2 vols. Buenos Aires: A. Baiocco y Cía., 1937, 1939.

————. *Historia del folklore argentino.* Buenos Aires: Ministerio de Educación, 1953.

Carvajal, María Isabel [Carmen Lyra]. *Cuentos de mi tía Panchita.* San José, Costa Rica: Imprenta Española, Soley y Valverde, 1936.

Carvalho-Neto, Paulo de. *History of Iberoamerican Folklore.* Oesterhout N.B., The Netherlands: Anthropological Publications, 1969.

Cascudo, Luis da Camara. *Contos tradicionais do Brasil.* Rio de Janeiro: Americ-Edit, 1946.

————. *Geografía dos mitos tradicionais Brasileiros.* Rio de Janeiro and São Paulo: Livraria José Olympio, 1947.

————. *Os melhores contos populares de Portugal.* Rio de Janeiro: Edição Dois Mundos, 1945.

Castellanos, Carlos A. "El tema de Delgadina en el folklore de Santiago de Cuba," *Journal of American Folk-Lore,* 33 (1920): 43–46.

Castro Leal, Antonio. "Dos romances tradicionales," *Cuba contemporánea* (Havana), 6 (1914): 237–44.

Chacón y Calvo, José María. *Ensayos de literatura cubana.* Madrid: Editorial "Saturnino Calleja," 1922.

————. "Los orígenes de la poesía en Cuba," *Cuba contemporánea* (Havana), 3 (1913): 67–88.

————. "Nuevos romances en Cuba," *Revista bimestre cubana* (Havana), 9 (1914): 199–210.

————. "Romances tradicionales en Cuba," *Revista de la facultad de letras y ciencias* (Havana), 18 (1914): 45–121.

Childers, James W. *Motif-Index of the Cuentos of Juan de Timoneda.* Indiana University Folklore Series, No. 5. Bloomington: Indiana University Press, 1948.

Cirac Estopañán, Sebastian. *Los procesos de hechicerías de Castilla la Nueva.* Madrid: "Diana," Artes Gráficas, 1942.

Claudel, Calvin. "Spanish Folktales from Delacroix, Louisiana," *Journal of American Folklore,* 58 (1945): 209–24.

Cobos, Rubén, ed. *Southwestern Spanish Proverbs—Refranes españoles del sudoeste.* Cerrillos, N.M.: San Marcos Press, 1974.

————, and Bendito Cordova, comps. *Guide to the Rubén Cobos Collection of New Mexican Indo-Hispanic Folklore.* Vol. 1. Colorado Springs: Colorado College, 1974.

Coelho, Francisco Adolpho. *Contos populares portuguezes.* Lisbon: P. Plantier, 1879.

Cole, Mabel Cook. *Philippine Folk-Tales.* Chicago: A. C. McClurg & Co., 1916.

Cole, M. R., trans. and ed. *Los pastores, a Mexican Play of the Nativity.* Memoirs of the American Folk-Lore Society, 9. Boston and New York: Houghton Mifflin Co., 1907.

Consiglieri Pedroso, Zophimo. *Portuguese Folk-Tales*. London: Folklore Society Publications, 1882; reprint, New York: Benjamin Blom, Inc., 1969.

Cortés, Carlos E., ed. *The Penitentes of New Mexico*. New York: Arno Press, 1974. Includes reprints of A. M. Darley, *The Passionists of the Southwest* (1893); A. C. Henderson, *Brothers of Light* (1937); and Dorothy Woodward, *The Penitentes of New Mexico* (1935).

Cossío, José María de, and Tomás Maza Solano. *Romancero popular de la montaña*. Santander: Talleres Tipográficos de la Librería Moderna, 1933–34.

Curiel Merchan, Marciano. *Cuentos extremeños*. Madrid: Biblioteca de tradiciones populares, 1944.

Davis, W. W. H. *El Gringo, or New Mexico and Her People*. New York: Harper, 1857.

Dobie, J. Frank, ed. *Puro Mexicano*. Texas Folklore Society Publications, No. 12. Austin: 1935; facsimile ed., Dallas: Southern Methodist University Press, 1975.

Dorson, Richard M., ed. *Folktales of the World*. 11 vols. Chicago: University of Chicago Press, 1963–67.

———, ed. *Folktales Told Round the World*. Chicago: University of Chicago Press, 1975.

Draghi Lucero, Juan. *Cancionero popular cuyano*. Mendoza: Best Hermanos, 1938.

———. *Cancionero popular de Santiago del Estero*. Buenos Aires: A. Baiocco y Cía., 1940.

Duque y Merino, D. *Contando cuentos y asando castaños*. Madrid, 1897.

Durán, Agustín, ed. *Romancero general: O colección de romances castellanos anteriores al siglo XVIII*. 2 vols. Madrid: Hernando, 1828–32; 2d ed., 1849–1851; later ed., 1930.

Echevarría, Evelio, and José Otero. *Hispanic Colorado, Four Centuries: History and Heritage*. Fort Collins, Colo.: Centennial Publications, 1976.

*El folklore andaluz*. Vol. 1 (1882–83). Ed. A. Machado y Alvarez. Seville: F. Alvarez y Cía.

*El Palacio: History, Archaeology, Ethnology*. Santa Fe: Archaeological Society of New Mexico, 1913– .

Englekirk, John E. "Notes on the Repertoire of the New Mexican Spanish Folktheater," *Southern Folklore Quarterly*, 4 (1940): 227–37.

———. "The Sources and Dating of New Mexican Folk Plays," *Western Folklore*, 16 (1957): 232–55.

Epplen MacKay, Dorothy. *The Double Invitation in the Legend of Don Juan*. Stanford, Calif.: Stanford University Press, 1943.

Espinosa, Jr., Aurelio M. "Cuentos de Castilla." Manuscript, 1936.

———. *Cuentos populares de Castilla*. Buenos Aires and Mexico City: Espasa-Calpe Argentina, 1946.

———. "More Spanish Folk-Tales," *Hispania*, 22 (1939): 103–14.

————. "Spanish-American Folklore," section in "Folklore Research in North America," *Journal of American Folklore*, 60 (1947): 373–77.

————. "The Field of Spanish Folklore in America," *Southern Folklore Quarterly*, 5 (1941): 29–35.

Espinosa, Francisco Ramón. "Folklore español de la Isla de Guam," *Revista de dialectología y tradiciones populares* (Madrid), 9 (1953): 95–125.

Espinosa, Gilberto. *Heroes, Hexes and Haunted Halls*. Albuquerque: Calvin Horn Publisher, 1972.

————. *History of New Mexico by Gaspar Pérez de Villagrá, Alcalá, 1610*. Trans., notes by Frederick W. Hodge. Los Angeles: The Quivira Society, 1933.

————. "Los Comanches," *New Mexico Quarterly*, 1 (1931): 133–46.

Espinosa, J. Manuel. "Additional Hispanic Versions of the Spanish Religious Ballad 'Por el rastro de la sangre,'" *New Mexico Historical Review*, 56 (1981): 349–67.

————. *Crusaders of the Rio Grande: The Story of Don Diego de Vargas and the Reconquest and Refounding of New Mexico*. Chicago: Institute of Jesuit History, Loyola University Press, 1942.

————. *First Expedition of Vargas into New Mexico, 1692*. Albuquerque: University of New Mexico Press, 1940.

————. *Spanish Folk Tales from New Mexico*. Memoirs of the American Folklore Society, 30. New York: G. E. Stechert and Co., 1937; reprint, Millwood, N.Y.: Kraus Reprint Co., 1976.

————. "Spanish Folklore in the Southwest: The Pioneer Studies of Aurelio M. Espinosa," *The Americas*, 35 (1978): 219–37.

————. "The Legend of Sierra Azul," *New Mexico Historical Review*, 9 (1934): 113–58.

————. "The Virgin of the Reconquest of New Mexico," *Mid-America*, n.s. 7 (1936): 79–87.

————. Two articles in collaboration with Aurelio M. Espinosa in 1943 and 1944, listed above in bibliography of the writings of Aurelio M. Espinosa.

Fansler, Dean S. *Filipino Popular Tales*. Memoirs of the American Folklore Society, 12. Lancaster, Pa., and New York: The American Folklore Society, 1921.

————. "Metrical Romances in the Philippines," *Journal of American Folk-Lore*, 29 (1916): 203–34.

Fansler, Harriet Ely, and Isidoro Panlasiguí. *Philippine National Literature*. New York: The Macmillan Co., 1925.

Federal Writers Project, Works Progress Administration. Manuscripts in folklore files, History Library, Museum of New Mexico, Governor's Palace, Santa Fe, New Mexico.

Feijóo, Samuel. *Cuentos populares cubanos*. 2 vols. Havana: Ucar, García, 1960–62.

Fernández Ramírez, Salvador, ed. *Los pastores de Belén*, 2 vols. Madrid and Buenos Aires: Renacimiento, 1930; Madrid and Buenos Aires, Compañía Ibero-Americana de Publicaciones, n.d.

Ferrer-Ginart, Andrés. *Rondaies de Menorca*. Ciutadella, 1914.

Flores, Eliodoro. "Adivinanzas corrientes en Chile," *Revista del folklore chileno*, 2 (1911).

*Folk-Lore*. London, 1890– .

Folklore Fellows Communications [FFC]. Helsingfors and Hamina, 1910– .

Foster, George M. "The Current Status of Mexican Indian Folklore Studies," *Journal of American Folklore*, 61 (1948): 368–82.

———. "Mexican and Central American Indian Folklore." *Funk & Wagnalls Standard Dictionary of Folklore*, 2: 711–16.

———. "Some Characteristics of Mexican Indian Folklore," *Journal of American Folklore*, 58 (1945): 225–35.

Freire Marreco, Barbara. "New Mexican Spanish Folklore," ed. with notes by Aurelio M. Espinosa. *Journal of American Folk-Lore*, 29 (1916): 536–46.

*Funk & Wagnalls Standard Dictionary of Folklore, Mythology, and Legend*. 2 vols. New York: Funk & Wagnalls Company, 1949–50.

Gil, Rodolpho. *Romancero Judeo-Español*. Madrid: Impr. Alemana, 1911.

Goodwyn, Frank. "Another Mexican Version of the 'Bear's Son' Folktale," *Journal of American Folklore*, 66 (1953): 143–54.

Gordon, Dudley. "Charles F. Lummis: Pioneer American Folklorist," *Western Folklore*, 28 (1969): 175–81.

Goyri de Menéndez Pidal, María, ed. *Romances que deben buscarse en la tradición oral*. Madrid: Molina, Impresor, 1930.

Granada, Daniel. *Reseña histórico-descriptiva de antiguas y modernas supersticiones del Rio de la Plata*. Montevideo: A. Barreiro y Ramos, 1896.

Gregg, Josiah. *Commerce of the Prairies*. Ed. Max L. Moorhead. Norman: University of Oklahoma Press, 1954.

Griego y Maestas, José, and Rudolfo A. Anaya. *Cuentos: Tales from the Hispanic Southwest*. Santa Fe: Museum of New Mexican Press, 1980.

Hague, Eleanor. *Spanish-American Folk-Songs*. Memoirs of the American Folklore Society, 10. New York, 1917.

Hammond, George P., and Agapito Rey. *Don Juan de Oñate, Colonizer of New Mexico, 1595–1628*. 2 vols. Albuquerque: University of New Mexico Press, 1953.

Hansen, Terrence Leslie. *The Types of the Folktale in Cuba, Puerto Rico, the Dominican Republic, and Spanish South America*. Folklore Studies, 8. Berkeley: University of California Press, 1957.

Hauptmann, O. H. "Spanish Folklore from Tampa, Florida: Superstitions," *Southern Folklore Quarterly*, 2 (1938): 11–30.

Henríquez-Ureña, Pedro. "Romances de América," *Cuba contemporánea* (Havana), 3 (1913): 347–66.

———, and B. D. Wolfe. "Romances tradicionales de Méjico." In *Homenaje ofrecido a Menéndez Pidal*, 2: 375–90. Madrid, 1925.

Hergueta y Martín, Domingo. *Folklore burgalés*. Burgos: Diputación Provincial, 1934.

*Hispania: Journal of the American Association of Teachers of Spanish and Portuguese.* 1918– .

*Hispanic Folklore Studies of Arthur L. Campa.* Intro. by Carlos E. Cortés. New York: Arno Press, 1976.

*Hispanic Influences in the United States.* New York: The Spanish Institute Inc., 1975.

Hodge, Frederick W.; George P. Hammond; and Agapito Rey, eds. *Fray Alonso de Benavides' Revised Memorial of 1634.* Albuquerque: University of New Mexico Press, 1945.

Huning, Dolores, and Irene Fisher. "Folk Tales from the Spanish," *New Mexico Quarterly*, 7 (1937): 121–30.

———. "Three Spanish Folk Tales," *New Mexico Quarterly*, 6 (1936): 39–49.

Hurtado y Jiménez de la Serna, Juan, and Angel González Palencia. *Historia de la literatura española.* 4th ed. Madrid: Tipografía de Archivos, 1940.

Husk, William Henry. *Songs of the Nativity.* London: J. C. Hotten, [1884?].

Jijena Sánchez, Rafael. *Hilo de oro, hilo de plata.* Buenos Aires: Ediciones Buenos Aires, 1940.

———. *La luna y el sol.* Buenos Aires: Ediciones Buenos Aires, 1940.

Jiménez Borja, Arturo. *Cuentos peruanos.* Lima: Editorial Lumen, 1937.

Jiménez de Aragón, Juan José, ed. *Cancionero aragonés.* Zaragoza: Tipografía "La Académica," 1925.

Joseph Marie, I.H.M., Sister. *The Role of the Church and the Folk in the Development of the Early Drama in New Mexico.* Philadelphia: University of Pennsylvania, 1948.

*Journal of American Folklore.* Boston and New York, 1888– .

Keller, John Esten. *Motif-Index of Mediaeval Spanish Exempla.* Knoxville: University of Tennessee Press, 1949.

Kercheville, F. M. *"A Preliminary Glossary of New Mexican Spanish,"* together with *"Some Semantic and Philological Facts of the Spanish Spoken in Chilili, New Mexico,"* by George E. McSpadden. University of New Mexico Bulletin, Language Series, 5, No. 3. Albuquerque: University of New Mexico Press, 1934.

Krappe, Alexander Haggerty. *The Science of Folklore.* New York: Dial Press, 1930.

Krohn, Kaarle. *Folklore Methodology.* Trans. Roger L. Welsch. Austin: University of Texas Press and American Folklore Society, 1971. Originally published in German as *Die folkloristische Arbeitsmethode.* Oslo: The Institute for Comparative Research in Human Culture, 1926.

Lafuente y Zamalloa, Modesto. *La brujería en Barcelona.* N.p., n.d.

*La Revista Católica.* Las Vegas, N.M., 1875– .

Laval, Ramón A. *Contribución al folklore de Carahue (Chile).* 2 vols. Madrid: Librería General de Victoriano Suárez, 1916; Santiago, 1921.

———. *Cuentos de Pedro de Urdemalas.* Santiago: Imprenta Cervantes, 1925.

———. *Cuentos populares en Chile.* Santiago: Imprenta Cervantes, 1923.

———. "Oraciones, ensalmos i conjuros del pueblo chilenos," *Revista del folklore chileno*, 1 (1910): 75–132.

Lea, Aurora Lucero-White. *Coloquios de los pastores*. Santa Fe: Santa Fe Press, 1940.
———. *Folk-Dances of the Spanish-Colonials of New Mexico*. Santa Fe: Examiner Publishing, 1940.
———. *Literary Folklore of the Hispanic Southwest*. San Antonio, Texas: The Naylor Company, 1953.
Lehmann-Nitsche, Robert. *Folklore argentino*, vol. I, *Adivinanzas rioplatenses*. Buenos Aires: Imprenta de Coni Hermanos, 1911.
———. "Folklore argentino, I, resúmen, adivinanzas rioplatenses," *Boletín de la Academia Nacional de Ciencias, en Córdoba* (Buenos Aires), 20 (1915): 362–68.
Leite de Vasconcellos, José. *Contos populares y lendas*. Vol. 2. Ed. Alda and Paulo Soremenho. Coimbra: Por ordem da universidade, 1969.
———. *Tradições populares de Portugal*. Porto: Livraria Portuense de Clavel & Cía., 1882.
Lenz, Rodolfo. "Cuentos de adivinanzas corrientes en Chile," *Revista de folklore chileno*, 2 (1912): 337–83.
———. "Cuentos de adivinanzas corrientes en Chile, Notas comparativas," *Revista de folklore chileno*, 3 (1914): 267–313.
———. *Estudios araucanos*. Santiago: Imprenta Cervantes, 1895–97.
———. *Un grupo de consejas chilenas*. Santiago: Imprenta Cervantes, 1912.
Leonard, Irving A. *Books of the Brave: Being an Account of Books and of Men in the Spanish Conquest and Settlement of the Sixteenth Century New World*. Cambridge: Harvard University Press, 1949.
Llano Roza de Ampudia, Aurelio de. *Cuentos asturianos*. Madrid: Impr. de R. Caro Raggio, 1925.
———. *De folklore asturiano*. Madrid: Talleres de Voluntad, 1922.
Llorca, Fernando. *Lo que cantan los niños*. Valencia: Prometeo, [1920–?].
Lockhart, John Gibson. *Ancient Spanish Ballads: Historical and Romantic*. Edinburgh and London: W. Blackwood and Sons, 1823; London: J. Murray, 1842; New York: Wiley and Putnam, 1942; other subsequent editions.
Lullo, Orestes de. *El folklore de Santiago del Estero*. Tucumán: Universidad Nacional de Tucumán, 1943.
Lummis, Charles F. *A New Mexico David, and Other Stories and Sketches about the Southwest*. New York: C. Scribner's Sons, 1891.
———. "A New Mexico Folk Song: El Carbonero," *Land of Sunshine*, 10 (1899): 192–93.
———. *Flowers of Our Lost Romance*. Boston and New York: Houghton Mifflin Company, 1929.
———. "New Mexican Folk-Songs," *Cosmopolitan*, 13 (1892): 720–29.
———. *Pueblo Indian Folk-Stories*. New York: The Century Co., 1910.
———. *The Land of Poco Tiempo*. New York: C. Scribner's Sons, 1893.
MacCurdy, Raymond R., Jr. "Spanish Folklore from St. Bernard Parish, Louisiana, Part I, Background; Part II, Jokes and Anecdotes of Quevedo," *Southern*

*Folklore Quarterly*, 13 (1949): 180–91; "Part III, Folktales," 16 (1952): 227–50.

Machado y Alvarez, Antonio, ed. *Biblioteca de las tradiciones populares españolas*. 11 vols. Seville: F. Alvarez y Cía., 1883–86.

———— [Demófilo]. *Colección de enigmas y adivinanzas en forma de diccionario*. Seville: Imp. de R. Baldaraque, 1880.

Magalhães, Basilio. *O Folklore no Brasil*. Rio de Janeiro: Imprensa Nacional, 1939.

Major, Mabel; Rebecca Smith; and T. M. Pearce. *Southwest Heritage: A Literary History with Bibliography*. Albuquerque: University of New Mexico Press, 1935, 1948, 1972.

Mason, J. Alden, and Aurelio M. Espinosa. "Folktales of the Tepecanos," *Journal of American Folk-Lore*, 27 (1914): 148–210.

————. "Porto-Rican Folklore: Décimas, Christmas Carols, Nursery Rhymes and Other Songs," *Journal of American Folk-Lore*, 31 (1918): 289–450.

————. "Porto-Rican Folklore: Folktales, Part I," *Journal of American Folk-Lore*, 25 (1922): 1–61; Part I, continued, 37 (1924): 247–344; Part II, 38 (1925): 507–618; Part III, 39 (1926): 225–304; Part IV, 39 (1926): 304–69; Part IV, continued, 40 (1927): 313–414.

————. "Puerto-Rican Folklore: Riddles," *Journal of American Folk-Lore*, 29 (1916): 423–504.

Maspóns y Labrós, Francisco. *Contes populars catalans*. Barcelona, 1885; rev. ed., Editorial Barcino, 1952.

————. *Lo rondollaire*. 3 vols. Barcelona: Editorial Barcino, 1930.

Mechling, William Hubbs. "Stories and Songs from the Southern Atlantic Coastal Region of Mexico," *Journal of American Folk-Lore*, 29 (1916): 547–58.

Mejía Sánchez, Ernesto. *Romances y corridos nicaragüenses*. Mexico City: Imprenta Universitaria, 1946.

Meline, James F. *Two Thousand Miles on Horseback: A Summer Tour to the Plains, The Rocky Mountains, and New Mexico*. 4th ed. New York: Catholic Publication Society, 1873.

*Memoirs of the American Folklore Society*. New York and Boston, 1894–  .

Mencken, H. L. *The American Language*. 4th ed. New York: Alfred A. Knopf, 1970.

Mendoza, Vicente T. *El romance español y el corrido mexicano*. Mexico City: Imprenta Universitaria, 1939.

Mendoza, Vicente T., and Virginia Rodríguez Rivera de Mendoza. *Folklore de San Pedro Piedra Gorda, Zacatecas*. Mexico: Instituto de Bellas Artes, Secretaría de Educación Pública, 1952.

Menéndez Pidal, Juan. *Poesía popular*. Madrid: Imprenta y Fund. de los Hijos de J. A. García, 1885.

Menéndez Pidal, Ramón. *El romancero español*. New York: Hispanic Society of America, 1910.

————. *Obras completas de R. Menéndez Pidal*, vol. 11, *Estudios sobre el romancero*. Madrid: Espasa-Calpe, 1973.

————. *Flor nueva de romances viejos*. Madrid: Tip. de la *Revista de archivos, bibliotecas, y museos*, 1928.

————. *La leyenda de los Infantes de Lara*. Madrid: Imp. de Librería y Casa Editorial Hernando, 1934; 3rd ed., rev., Madrid: Espasa-Calpe, 1971.

————. *Los romances de América, y otros estudios*. 7th ed. Madrid: Espasa-Calpe, 1972.

————. *Romancero hispánico (hispano-portugués, americano, sefardí): Teoría e historia*. 2 vols. Madrid: Espasa-Calpe, 1953.

————. *Romancero tradicional de las lenguas hispánicas (español, portugués, catalán, sefardí)*. Ed. with notes by María Goyri and Ramón Menéndez Pidal. 11 vols. Madrid: Gredos, 1957–78.

Menéndez Pidal, Ramón; Diego Catalán; and Alvaro Galmés, *Como vive un romance*. Madrid: Revista de Filología Española—Anejo LX, 1954.

Menéndez y Pelayo, Marcelino. *Orígenes de la novela*. 4 vols. Madrid: Nueva Biblioteca de Autores Españoles, Bailly-Ballière e Hijos, 1905–15.

————. *Antología de Poetas Líricos Castellanos*, vol. 10, *Romances populares recojidos de la tradición oral*. Madrid: Librería de Hernando y Cía., 1900.

————. *Antología de Poetas Líricos Castellanos*, vols. 11–12, *Tratado de romances viejos*. Madrid: Librería de Perlado, Páez y Cía., sucesores de Hernando, 1903–1906.

*Mexican Folkways*. Mexico City, 1925–37.

Michaëlis de Vasconcellos, Carolina. *Estudos sobre o Romanceiro peninsular; Romances velhos em Portugal*. Madrid: Imprenta Ibérica, 1909; 2d ed., Coimbra: Imprensa da Universidade, 1934.

Milá y Fontanals, Manuel. *Obras completas*. 8 vols. Barcelona: A. Verdaguer, 1888–96.

————. *Obras completas*, vol. 8, *Romancerillo catalan*. Published as part of the author's *Observaciones sobre la poesía popular*. Barcelona: Imprenta de N. Ramírez, 1853.

Miller, Elaine K., ed. *Mexican Folk Narrative from the Los Angeles Area*. Memoirs of the American Folklore Society, 56. Austin: University of Texas Press for the American Folklore Society, 1973.

Moesser, Alba Irene. "La literatura mejicoamericana del suroeste de los Estados Unidos." Ph.D. diss., University of Southern California, 1971.

Morley, S. Griswold. "Are the Spanish Romances Written in Quatrains?—and Other Questions," *Romanic Review*, 7 (1916): 42–82.

Moya, Ismael. *Romancero*. 2 vols. Buenos Aires: Instituto de Literatura Argentina, Imprenta de la Universidad, 1941.

Murray, Margaret Alice. *The Witch Cult in Western Europe*. Oxford: Clarendon Press, 1921.

Newell, William Wells. *Games and Songs of American Children*. New York: Harper & Brothers, 1883.

*New Mexico Folklore Record*. Albuquerque, N.M.: New Mexico Folklore Society, 1946– .

*New Mexico Quarterly*. Albuquerque, N. Mex.: 1931– .

Noguera, María de. *Cuentos viejos*. 3rd ed. San José, Costa Rica: Imprenta Lehmann y Cía., 1952.

Nuñez Q., José María. *Cuentos*. 2d ed. Panama: Estrella de Panama, 1956.

Olivares Figueroa, Rafael. *Folklore venezolano*. 2 vols. Caracas: Ministerio de Educación Nacional, 1948–54.

Olmedo, Federico. *Cancionero popular de Burgos*. Seville, 1903.

Orduna, Germán. *Selección de romances viejos de España y América*. Buenos Aires: Editorial Kapelusz, 1975.

Ortiz, Alfonso. *New Perspectives on the Pueblos*. Albuquerque: University of New Mexico Press, 1972.

———. *The Tewa World. Space, Time, Being, and Becoming in a Pueblo Society*. Chicago: University of Chicago Press, 1969.

Ortiz, Fernando. *Hampa afro-cubana: Los negros brujos*. Madrid: Editorial-América, 1917.

Otero-Warren, Nina. *Old Spain in Our Southwest*. New York: Harcourt, Brace & Co., 1936.

Pardo, Isaac J. *Viejos romances españoles en la tradición popular venezolana*. Caracas: Universidad Central de Venezuela, 196?

Paredes, Américo, ed. and trans. *Folktales of Mexico*. Chicago: University of Chicago Press, 1970.

———. *Folktales of Mexico*. Chicago: University of Chicago Press, 1969.

———. *"With His Pistol in His Hand": A Border Ballad and its Hero*. Austin: University of Texas Press, 1958.

Parsons, Elsie Clews. "Der Spanische Einfluss auf die Märchen der Pueblo-Indianer," *Zeitschrift für Ethnologie*, 58 (1926): 16–28.

———. *Folklore from the Cape Verde Islands*. Memoirs of the American Folklore Society, 15. 2 vols. Cambridge, Mass., and New York: G. E. Stechert & Co., 1923.

———. *Isleta, New Mexico*. 47th Annual Report of the Bureau of American Ethnology, 1929–30. Washington, D.C.: Smithsonian Institution, 1932.

———. "Navaho Folk Tales," *Journal of American Folk-Lore*, 36 (1923): 368–75.

———. "Pueblo Indian Folk-Tales, probably of Spanish Provenience," *Journal of American Folk-Lore*, 21 (1918): 216–55.

———. *Pueblo Indian Religion*. 2 vols. Chicago: University of Chicago Press, 1939.

———. "Spanish Elements in the Kachina Cult of the Pueblos." In *Proceedings of the Twenty-Third International Congress of Americanists*. New York, 1928.

———. *Taos Pueblo*. Menasha, Wis.: George Banta Publishing Co., 1936; Memoirs of the American Folklore Society, 34. New York: J. J. Augustin, 1940.

———. *Taos Tales*. Memoirs of the American Folklore Society, 24. New York: J. J. Augustin, 1940.

———. *Tewa Tales*. Memoirs of the American Folklore Society, 19. New York: G. E. Stechert & Co., 1926.

———. *The Social Organization of the Tewa of New Mexico*. Memoirs of the American Anthropological Association, No. 36. Lancaster, Pa., 1929.

———. "Witchcraft among the Pueblos: Indian or Spanish?" *Man* (London), 27, nos. 70 and 80 (1927).

———, and Franz Boas. "Spanish Tales from Laguna and Zuñi, New Mexico," *Journal of American Folk-Lore*, 33 (1920): 47–72.

Pearce, T. M. "Southwestern Culture, An Artificial or Natural Growth?" *New Mexico Quarterly*, 1 (1931): 175–209.

Peña Hernández, Enrique. *Folklore de Nicaragua*. Masaya, Nicaragua, 1968.

Pereda Valdés, J. *Cancionero popular uruguayo*. Montevideo, 1947.

Pino Saavedra, Yolando. *Cuentos folklóricos de Chile*. 3 vols. Santiago: Instituto de Investigaciones Folklóricos "Ramón A. Laval," Editorial Universitaria, 1960–63.

———. *Folktales of Chile*. Ed. and trans. Rockwell Gray. Chicago: University of Chicago Press, 1967.

Place, Edwin B. "A Group of Mystery Plays Found in a Spanish-speaking Region of Southern Colorado," University of Colorado Studies, 18. Boulder: University of Colorado, 1930.

Poncet, Carolina. "El romance en Cuba," *Revista de la facultad de letras y ciencias* (Havana), 18 (1914): 180–260, 278–321.

———. "Romancerillo de Entrepeñas y Villar de los Pisones," *Revue Hispanique*, 57, 1–33.

———. "Romances de Pasión," *Archivo de folklore cubano* (Havana), 5 (1930): 5–29.

Pooler, Lolita Huning. "A Fish, a Turtle, a Camel, and a Horse," *New Mexico Folklore Record*, 3 (1948–49): 21–25.

———. "Three Spanish Folk Tales," *New Mexico Folklore Record*, 4 (1949–50): 20–22.

———. "Spanish Folk Tales," *Western Folklore*, 15 (1956): 102–105.

Portell Vilá, Herminio. "Cuentos populares cubanos." Manuscript, Hispanic Foundation, New York.

Radin, Paul, and Aurelio M. Espinosa, eds., *El Folklore de Oaxaca*. New York: Escuela Internacional de Arqueología y Etnología Americana and The Hispanic Society of America, G. E. Stechert, 1917.

———. "Folk-Tales from Oaxaca," *Journal of American Folk-Lore*, 28 (1915): 390–408.

Rael, Juan B. *Cuentos españoles de Colorado y de Nuevo Méjico* (*Spanish Tales from Colorado and New Mexico*). 2 vols. Stanford, Calif.: Stanford University Press, [1957]; rev. ed., Santa Fe: Museum of New Mexico Press, 1977.

————. "New Mexican Spanish Feasts," *California Folklore Quarterly*, 1 (1942): 83–90.

————. "New Mexican Wedding Songs," *Southern Folklore Quarterly*, 4 (1940): 55–72.

————. *The New Mexican Alabado*. Stanford, Calif.: Stanford University Press, 1951.

————. *The Sources and Diffusion of the Mexican Shepherds' Plays*. Guadalajara, Mexico: Librería La Joyita, 1965.

————. "The Theme of the Theft of Food by Playing Godfather in New Mexican Folklore," *Hispania*, 20 (1937): 231–34.

————. "Un Cantar hallado en Tucumán," *Revista Ibero-americana*, 9 (1945): 73–77.

Rallière, Rev. J. J. B. *Colección de cánticos espirituales*. 1st ed. Las Vegas, N.M.: Imprenta de la Revista Católica, 1877; 9th ed., 1933.

Ramírez de Arellano, Rafael. *Folklore portorriqueño*. Madrid: Archivo de tradiciones populares, Avila, Tip., 1926.

Ranke, Kurt. *Die zwei Brüder*. FFC, No. 114. Helsinki, 1934.

Recinos, Adrián. "Algunas observaciones sobre el folk-lore de Guatemala," *Journal of American Folk-Lore*, 29 (1916): 559–66.

————. "Cuentos populares de Guatemala," *Journal of American Folk-Lore*, 31 (1918): 472–87.

Reid, John T. "Seven Folktales from Mexico," *Journal of American Folk-Lore*, 48 (1935): 109–24.

*Revista de dialectología y tradiciones populares españolas*. Madrid, 1944– .

*Revista de filología española*. Madrid, 1914– .

*Revue des Traditions Populaires*. 34 vols. Paris, 1886–1919.

*Revue Hispanique*. Paris, 1894–1920.

Robb, John Donald. *Hispanic Folk Music of New Mexico and the Southwest*. Norman: University of Oklahoma Press, 1980.

————. *Hispanic Folk Songs of New Mexico*. Albuquerque: University of New Mexico Press, 1979.

————. "The Music of Los Pastores," *Western Folklore*, 16 (1957): 263–80.

Robe, Stanley L. *Amapa Storytellers*. Folklore Studies, 24. Berkeley: University of California Press, 1972.

————. *Coloquios de Pastores from Jalisco, Mexico*, Folklore Studies, 4. Berkeley: University of California Press, 1954.

————. *Hispanic Riddles from Panama, Collected from Oral Tradition*. Folklore Studies, 14. Berkeley: University of California Press, 1963.

————. *Index of Mexican Folktales, Including Narrative Texts from Mexico, Central*

*America, and the Hispanic United States.* Folklore Studies, 26. Berkeley: University of California Press, 1973.

―――――. *Mexican Tales and Legends from Los Altos.* Folklore Studies, 20. Berkeley: University of California Press, 1970.

―――――. *Mexican Tales and Legends from Vera Cruz.* Folklore Studies, 23. Berkeley: University of California Press, 1971.

―――――, ed. *Hispanic Folktales from New Mexico: Narratives from the R. D. Jameson Collection.* Folklore Studies, 30. Berkeley: University of California Press, 1977.

―――――, ed. *Hispanic Legends from New Mexico: Narratives from the R. D. Jameson Collection.* Folklore Studies, 31. Berkeley: University of California Press, 1980.

Robinson, Cecil. *With the Ears of Strangers: The Mexican in American Literature.* Tucson: University of Arizona Press, 1963.

Rodríguez Demorizi, Emilio. *Poesía popular dominicana.* Ciudad Trujillo: Editorial La Nación, 1938.

Rodríguez Marín, Francisco. *Cantos populares españoles.* 5 vols. Seville: F. Alvarez y Cía., 1882–83.

―――――. *Más de 21,000 refranes castellanos, no contenidos en la copiosa coleccion del maestro Gonzalo Correas.* Madrid: Tip. de la *Revista de archivos, bibliotecas y museos,* 1926.

―――――. *12,600 refranes más no contenidos en la colección del Maestro Gonzalo Correas ni en "Más de 21,000 refranes castellanos."* Madrid: Tip. de la *Revista de archivos, bibliotecas y museos,* 1930.

―――――. *Los 6,666 refranes de mi última rebusca, que con "Más de 21,000" y "12,600 refranes más."* Madrid: C. Bermejo, Impresor, 1934.

―――――. *Todavía 10,700 refranes más, no registrados por el Maestro Correas, ni en mis colecciones tituladas Más de 21,000 refranes más (1930) y Los 6,666 refranes de mi última rebusca (1934).* Madrid: Imprenta *Prensa española,* 1941.

Rodríguez-Moñino, Antonio R. *Juan López de Ubeda, poeta del siglo XVI.* Madrid: Imprenta y Editorial Maestre, 1962.

Romero, Emilia. *El romance tradicional en el Perú.* Mexico City: El Colegio de México, 1952.

Romero, Sylvio. *Contos populares do Brasil.* Rio de Janeiro: F. Alves & Cía., 1911.

Rubio, Darío. *Refranes, proverbios, y dichos y dicharachos mexicanos.* Mexico City: Editorial A. P. Márquez, 1940.

Sálaz, Rubén Darío. *Cosmic: The La Raza Sketch Book.* Santa Fe, N.M.: Blue Feather Press, 1975.

Salillas, Rafael. *La fascinación en España.* Madrid, 1905.

Salpointe, Most Rev. J. B. *Soldiers of the Cross: Notes on the Ecclesiastical History of New Mexico, Arizona and Colorado.* Banning, Calif.: St. Boniface's Industrial School, 1898.

Sancha, Justo de. *Romancero y cancionero sagrados.* Biblioteca de autores españoles, 25. Madrid: M. Rivadeneyra, 1855.

Sánchez Pérez, José A. *Cien cuentos populares*. Madrid: Editorial SAETA, 1942.

Santulliano, Luis. *La poesía del pueblo: Romances y canciones de España y América*. Buenos Aires: Hachette, 1955.

Saunders, Lyle. *A Guide to Materials Bearing on Cultural Relations in New Mexico*. Albuquerque: University of New Mexico Press, 1944.

————. *A Guide to the Literature of the Southwest*. Albuquerque: University of New Mexico Press, 1942.

Schindler, Kurt. *Folk Music and Poetry of Spain and Portugal*. New York: Hispanic Institute in the United States, 1941.

Sevilla, Alberto. *Cancionero popular murciano*. Murcia: Imp. Sucesores de Nogués, 1921.

Simmons, Marc. *Witchcraft in the Southwest: Spanish and Indian Supernaturalism on the Rio Grande*. Flagstaff: Northland Press, 1974.

Simmons, Merle E. *A Bibliography of the Romance and Related Forms in Spanish America*. Bloomington: Indiana University Press, 1963.

————. "Folklore," in *Handbook of Latin American Studies, Humanities, No. 42, 1980*. Austin: University of Texas Press, 1983.

————. *The Mexican Corrido as a Source for Interpretive Study of Modern Mexico, 1870–1950*. Bloomington: Indiana University Press, 1957.

Sonnichsen, Philip. "Hispanic American Music," *La Luz* (Denver), 7 (September, 1978): 46–50.

Spicer, Edward H. *Cycles of Conquest: The Impact of Spain, Mexico, and the United States on the Indians of the Southwest, 1533–1960*. Tucson: University of Arizona Press, 1962, 1970.

Starke, Richard B.; T. M. Pearce; and Rubén Cobos. *Music of the Spanish Folk Plays in New Mexico*. Santa Fe: Museum of New Mexico Press, 1969.

Steele, Thomas J., S.J. "The Spanish Passion Play in New Mexico and Colorado," *New Mexico Historical Review*, 53 (1978): 239–59.

Suddeth, Ruth Elgin, and Constance Gay Morenus. *Tales of the Western World: Folktales of the Americas*. Austin: The Steck Company, 1953.

Swadesh, Frances Leon. *Los Primeros Pobladores: Hispanic Americans of the Ute Frontier*. Notre Dame: University of Notre Dame Press, 1974.

Tawney, C. H., and N. M. Penzer. *The Ocean of Story*. 10 vols. London: C. J. Sawyer, 1924–28.

Taylor, Archer. "A Classification of Formula Tales," *Journal of American Folk-Lore*, 46 (1933): 77–88.

————. *English Riddles from Oral Tradition*. Berkeley: University of California Press, 1951.

————. Review of *Cuentos populares españoles*, 1–3, by Aurelio M. Espinosa, *Journal of American Folklore*, 61 (1948): 218–20.

————. *Selected Writings on Proverbs*, ed. Wolfgang Mieder. FFC No. 216. Helsinki: Suomalainen Tiedeakatemia, 1975.

Texas Folklore Society Publications. Austin, 1916–  .

Thompson, Stith. *European Tales among the North American Indians*. Colorado College Publications, No. 2. Colorado Springs, 1919.

―――. *Motif-Index of Folk-Literature*. 6 vols. Bloomington: Indiana University Press, 1955–58.

―――. *Narrative Motif-Analysis as a Folklore Method*. FFC No. 161. Helsinki: 1955.

―――. *Tales of North American Indians*. Cambridge, Mass.: Harvard University Press, 1929.

―――. *The Folktale*. Rev. ed. Berkeley: University of California Press, 1977.

―――, and Jonas Balys. *The Oral Tales of India*. Indiana University Folklore Series, No. 10. Bloomington: Indiana University Press, 1958.

Thoms, William John. *Lays and Legends of Various Nations*. 4 vols. in 2. London: G. Cowie, 1834.

*The Thousand and One Nights, commonly called The Arabian Nights' Entertainments*. Trans. Edward William Lane. 8 vols. New York–Philadelphia: F. S. Holby, 1913.

Tobler, Adolph. *Abhandlungen*. Halle, 1895.

Toor, Frances. *A Treasury of Mexican Folkways*. New York: Crown Publishers, 1947.

Trueba, Antonio de. *Cuentos populares*. Leipzig: F. A. Brockhaus, 1885.

Tully, Marjorie F., and Juan B. Rael. *An Annotated Bibliography of Spanish Folklore in New Mexico and Southern Colorado*. University of New Mexico Publications in Language and Literature, No. 3. Albuquerque: University of New Mexico Press, 1950.

Ubeda, Juan López de. *Cancionero general de la doctrina christiana*. Alcalá de Henares: Juan Iñiguez de Lequerica, 1579.

―――. *Vergel de flores divinas*. Alcalá de Henares: Juan Iñiguez de Lequerica, 1582.

Valdés, Ignacio de J., Jr. *Cuentos panameños de la ciudad y del campo*. Panama: Editorial Gráfica, 1928.

Van Stone, Mary R. *Los Pastores*. Cleveland: Gates Press, 1933.

―――. *Spanish Folksongs of New Mexico*. Chicago: R. F. Seymore, 1938.

―――, and E. R. Sims, eds. "Canto del niño perdido." In *Spur-of-the-Cock*, pp. 48–49. Ed. by J. Frank Dobie. Austin: Texas Folklore Society Publications, 1933; facsimile edition, Dallas: Southern Methodist University Press, 1965.

Vasco, Eusebio. *Treinta mil cantares populares*. 2 vols. Valdepeña: Impr. de Mendoza, 1929–30.

Vega Carpio, Lope Félix de. *Pastores de Belén*. Madrid: Melchor Sánchez, Impressor de Libros, 1675.

Vergara, Gabriel María. *Cantares populares de Castilla la vieja*. Madrid: Hernando, 1912.

Vicuña Cifuentes, Julio. *Mitos y supersticiones recogidos de la tradición oral chilena*. Santiago: Imprenta Universitaria, 1915.

————. *Romances populares y vulgares, recogidos de la tradición oral de Chile*. Santiago: Impr. Barcelona, 1912.

[Villagrá, Gaspar de]. *Historia de la Nueva México, por el Capitán Gaspar de Villagrá*. Reimpresa por el Museo Nacional de México, vol. 1. Mexico City: Imprenta del Museo Nacional, 1900.

Wagner, Max L. "Algunas apuntaciones sobre el folklore mexicano," *Journal of American Folk-Lore*, 40 (1927): 105–43.

Weigle, Marta. *A Penitente Bibliography*. Albuquerque: University of New Mexico Press, 1976.

————. *Brothers of Ligh, Brothers of Blood: The Penitentes of the Southwest*. Albuquerque: University of New Mexico Press, 1976.

————. "Ghostly Flagellants and Doña Sebastiana: Two Legends of the Penitente Brotherhood," *Western Folklore*, 36 (1977): 135–47.

————, ed. *Hispanic Villages of Northern New Mexico*. Santa Fe: The Lightning Tree—Jane Lyon Publisher, 1975.

*Western Folklore*. Berkeley, University of California Press, 1947– . Formerly *California Folklore Quarterly*, California Folklore Society, 1942–46.

Wheeler, Howard T. *Tales from Jalisco Mexico*. Memoirs of the American Folklore Society, 25. Philadelphia: American Folklore Society, 1943.

White, Leslie A. "The Pueblo of Santa Ana, New Mexico," *American Anthropologist*, n.s. 44, no. 4, part 2 (1942).

Wolf, Fernando José, and Don Conrado Hofmann, eds. *Primavera y flor de romances*. 1st ed. 2 vols. Berlin: A. Asher y Comp., 1856; 2d ed. in *Antología de Poetas Líricos Castellanos*, 8–9. Ed. Marcelino Menéndez y Pelayo. Madrid: Librería de Hernando y Compañía, 1899.

Zunser, Helen. "A New Mexican Village," *Journal of American Folk-Lore*, 47 (1935): 125–78.

# Index